CHILD and ADOLESCENT DEVELOPMENT

a **south african** socio-cultural perspective

Edited by Joanne Hardman

JENNY JANSEN • MOKGADI MOLETSANE • DAVID NEVES
CRAIN SOUDIEN • LOUISE STROUD • SHARLENE SWARTZ • LAUREN WILD

OXFORD
UNIVERSITY PRESS

SOUTHERN AFRICA

OXFORD
UNIVERSITY PRESS
SOUTHERN AFRICA

Oxford University Press Southern Africa (Pty) Ltd

Vasco Boulevard, Goodwood, Cape Town, Republic of South Africa
P O Box 12119, N1 City, 7463, Cape Town, Republic of South Africa

Oxford University Press Southern Africa (Pty) Ltd is a subsidiary of
Oxford University Press, Great Clarendon Street, Oxford OX2 6DP.

The Press, a department of the University of Oxford, furthers the University's objective of
excellence in research, scholarship, and education by publishing worldwide in

Oxford New York

Auckland Cape Town Dar es Salaam Hong Kong Karachi
Kuala Lumpur Madrid Melbourne Mexico City Nairobi
New Delhi Shanghai Taipei Toronto

With offices in

Argentina Austria Brazil Chile Czech Republic France Greece
Guatemala Hungary Italy Japan Poland Portugal Singapore South Korea
Switzerland Turkey Ukraine Vietnam

Oxford is a registered trade mark of Oxford University Press
in the UK and in certain other countries

Published in South Africa
by Oxford University Press Southern Africa (Pty) Ltd, Cape Town

Child and adolescent development
ISBN 978 0 19 599979 2

© Oxford University Press Southern Africa (Pty) Ltd 2012

Publishing Manager: Alida Terblanche
Publisher: Marisa Montemarano
Project manager: Sarah Floor
Editor: Patricia Myers Smith
Designer: Chris Davis
Indexer: Ethne Clarke
Cover photo: The Bigger Picture
Illustrator: Wayne Jones

Set in Adobe Garamond Pro 11 pt on 13 pt by diacriTech (P) Ltd, Chennai, India

Printed and bound by ABC Press, Cape Town
118255

Acknowledgements
The authors and publisher gratefully acknowledge permission to reproduce copyright material
in this book. Every effort has been made to trace copyright holders, but if any copyright
infringements have been made, the publisher would be grateful for information that would enable
any omissions or errors to be corrected in subsequent impressions.

Abridged contents

Contents

About the authors

Joanne Hardman is a senior lecturer in educational psychology at the School of Education (UCT). A Commonwealth Scholar, she obtained her PhD in education at UCT. She has published numerous articles, reports and book chapters in her field of research interest, developmental psychology and cultural historical activity theory. She is an NRF-rated scientist and Fellow of Bath University (UK). While she is a member of numerous local and international societies, it is her membership of the Cultural–Historical Approaches to Children's Development and Childhood Society that currently informs much of her research. She is currently involved in a collaborative EU-funded project in the School of Education (UCT) that seeks to understand differential attainment in underprivileged schools. Her research on this project focuses specifically on understanding how young children differentially acquire concepts in the Foundation Phase of school.

Giulietta Harrison has worked for 27 years in early childhood development, as an educator, manager and researcher. She obtained her MEd in 2011, specialising in the emotional and social development of pre-schoolers with particular emphasis on the role of the teacher as a mediator to promote self-regulation. She is currently working on her PhD and is engaged in research on early reading competencies in South African grade-1 classrooms.

Peter Hepper undertook a BSc (Hons) in psychology at the University of Exeter before completing a PhD on 'Kin recognition in the rat' at Durham University under the supervision of Professor M.J. Morgan. Peter then moved to Queen's University, Belfast, and was appointed as professor in 1993. He is a chartered psychologist and Fellow of the British Psychological Society. In 2007 he was awarded the Thomas R. Verny Award for Outstanding Contributions to Prenatal and Perinatal Psychology and Health by the American Association of Pre- and Perinatal Psychology and Health. His research concentrates around three main themes: behavioural development and health; animal behaviour; and psychosocial outcomes of facial disfigurement.

Jenny Jansen is deputy chief education specialist at the Education Support Clinic in Port Elizabeth. She obtained her PhD from the University of Port Elizabeth, specialising in stress patterns in families with physically disabled children. Jenny is also a co-author of *Assessment of children in the South African context*. She is a practising psychologist and her research interests lie in development and neurodevelopmental child psychology in the South African context, coping, and educating children with physical and intellectual barriers to learning.

Mary McMahon is a senior lecturer in the School of Education at the University of Queensland, Australia, where she teaches career development and career counselling at postgraduate and undergraduate levels. She researches and publishes in child and adolescent career development, narrative career counselling, and qualitative career assessment, and is particularly interested in developing practical applications of systemic and narrative approaches for use by adolescents, parents and practitioners.

Mokgadi (neé Kekae) Moletsane is an associate professor in the Department of Educational Psychology at the University of the Western Cape. She is a registered educational psychologist. Mokgadi obtained her PhD in educational psychology from the University of Pretoria. She is a HERS–USA Brawn Mawr College alumna. Mokgadi supervises honours, master's and PhD research students, and teaches at both undergraduate and postgraduate levels. Her research interests include child development, learning and behavioural difficulties, inclusive education, psychological assessments and intervention, indigenous knowledge in psychology, and inclusive psychology.

David Neves obtained a master's degree in research psychology from Rhodes University, and holds a research post at the Institute for Poverty, Land and Agrarian Studies (PLAAS), at the University of the Western Cape (www.plaas.org.za). He brings an interest in human development and the micro-dynamics of social change to research that has examined aspects of structural poverty and unemployment in both rural and urban contexts. Previously the country manager for the UK Department for International Development-funded Chronic Poverty Research Centre, much of his research has focused on the dynamics of informal-sector self-employment, social networks and human capital, social protection (specifically state cash transfers), and social policy. He has contributed to a number of edited titles, including *Inter-group relations: South African perspectives*; *Self, community and psychology*; and *Critical psychology* and *Psychology: An introduction*. David's interest in human development also finds expression in his home life, where he is a single father to a toddler.

Crain Soudien was formerly the director of the School of Education at the University of Cape Town and is currently a deputy vice-chancellor. He has published over 140 articles, reviews, reports, and book chapters in the areas of social difference, culture, education policy, comparative education, educational change, public history and popular culture. He is also the co-editor of three books on District Six, Cape Town and another on comparative education, the author of *The making of youth identity in contemporary South Africa: Race, culture and schooling*, and *Realising the dream: Unlearning the logic of race in the South African school*, and the co-author of *Inclusion and exclusion in South African and Indian schools*. He was educated at the University of Cape Town and also holds a PhD from the State University of New York at Buffalo. He is involved in a number of local, national and international social and cultural organisations and was formerly chairperson of the District Six Museum Foundation and immediate past president of World Council of Corporative Education Societies. He is currently the chair of Ministerial Committee on Transformation in Higher Education. He is a fellow of a number of local and international universities and academies.

Louise Stroud is Head of the Department of Psychology at Nelson Mandela Metropolitan University in Port Elizabeth. She is a Clinical Psychologist and collaborates closely with the UK-based Association for Research in Infant and Child Development (ARICD). Her research interests lie in the Griffiths Development Scales, neuropsychology, child development, psychobiographies, and developmental psychology.

Sharlene Swartz is a research director in the Human and Social Development research programme of the Human Sciences Research Council and an adjunct associate professor of sociology at the University of Cape Town. She has a master's degree from Harvard University and a PhD from the University of Cambridge. Her research interests lie in addressing youth marginalisation, moral values and social inequalities. She is the author of *Teenage Tata: Voices of young fathers in South Africa* (with A. Bhana); *Ikasi: The moral ecology of South African's township youth*; *Moral education in sub-Saharan Africa: Culture, economics, conflict and AIDS* (co-edited with M. Taylor); and *Old enough to know: Consulting children about sex education in Africa* (with C. McLaughlin et al.).

Mark Watson is a professor in the Psychology Department of the Nelson Mandela Metropolitan University. He specialises, researches and practises in career, school, and adolescent psychology. Mark has published extensively in international journals, has contributed chapters to international career texts, and is on the editorial advisory board of several international career journals.

Lauren Wild is a senior lecturer in the Department of Psychology at the University of Cape Town. She holds an MA in research psychology from UCT, and a PhD from the University of Cambridge. Her research focuses on family stress, caregiving and child adjustment, and on risk-taking behaviour in adolescence.

Acknowledgements

This book has been a collaborative effort between various authors and its strength lies in the various different perspectives provided by experts in their specific fields. It has been a privilege to work with colleagues and to extend my own knowledge while doing so.

I would like to acknowledge the tireless input from the Oxford University Press team, most notably Marisa Montemarano and Sarah Floor, the editors, whose guidance has made this a more readable text. Marisa, in particular, worked hard to set up the book while heavily pregnant with her first child – I'd like to welcome Chiara to the world and hope that this text will serve Marisa and Johan in some small way as they watch Chiara negotiate her journey to adulthood.

The input from our critical reader Kate Cockcroft is gratefully acknowledged. Her insightful comments have greatly shaped this book. The meticulous editing from Patricia Myers Smith has added coherence across the chapters.

Finally, I must acknowledge the input my own toddler, Isabella, has had on my engagement with the academic study of development. Watching her negotiate developmental hurdles has strengthened my interest in developmental psychology enormously and her delight in even mundane tasks has rubbed off sufficiently on me for me to sit still through long hours of editing!

JOANNE HARDMAN
CAPE TOWN
2012

Preface

Liam and Thandi, three years of age, are sitting in their pre-school class drawing a picture of a horse. Liam says to Thandi, 'I'm going to draw a horse. I'm going to make him brown. Brown horse. Drawing a horse. Brown.' Thandi responds, 'A horse. I am gonna draw, gonna draw this horse. With a tail. Tail. Look. A tail.' This is a fairly standard pre-school interaction, but it tells us quite a lot about Liam and Thandi's developmental stage and points to a number of cognitive achievements that happen at this stage – for example the use of speech to guide one's behaviour. It is also interesting to note that, although Liam and Thandi appear to be talking to each other, they are not in fact engaged in the sort of talk characteristic of a dialogue. Certain questions arise from this interaction:

- How do children think at this age?
- Is there a qualitative difference between the thinking of a pre-schooler and a high-schooler? Or is the difference merely quantitative?
- What cognitive shifts occur throughout development?
- How can the emotional, cognitive and social shifts that occur across development be described?
- How much of development can be ascribed to genetics and how much to the environment?

This book seeks to address these questions. It introduces readers to the field of developmental psychology and its particular importance in South Africa.

Developmental psychology is a scientific field of study occupied with understanding the qualitative shifts that occur across the lifespan of the developing person. The book adopts a socio-cultural perspective to understanding development. This perspective seeks to situate developmental trajectories in the social, cultural and historical milieu in which they are constituted. Understanding the developmental impact of the socio-cultural context and history is of particular importance in a multicultural country such as South Africa, which has a relatively short history of democracy coloured by a long history of inequality.

Foreword

Developmental psychology has come of age in South Africa. The discipline has had considerable growth, and is gaining significant influence in the social sciences. It has also had immense influence in applied fields such as education, health, social and community development. It is therefore appropriate for the authors to contribute to the dissemination of knowledge of developmental psychology, and indeed, they have done this in ways that are accessible to the majority of students in South Africa.

Child and adolescent development begins by providing a theoretically informed outline of 'development-in-context', thus marrying theory and instances of practise within contexts that clarify the nature of the problems that developmental psychology addresses. Such an approach is appropriate for enabling our students to understand how theory could contribute to self-understanding, and an understanding of own social situation.

The book covers the extent of human development from prenatal development, infancy, early childhood, middle childhood and adolescent stages; at each instance providing a theoretical perspective on how these critical periods can be understood and how such understanding can inform appropriate intervention strategies.

Major theoretical traditions in developmental psychology are employed to explore ways of looking into situations and understanding human development. These include Piaget, Vygotsky, Freud, Erikson and Kohlberg. However, students are also encouraged to look beyond these theories to get a fuller understanding of the specific socio-cultural context of human development; thereby extending theories to have relevance to practice.

The last chapters on career development, poverty and adversity, and children and violence re-contextualize the theoretically driven accounts of human development in socio-cultural settings in appropriate ways that encourage students to reflect deeply on the complexities and challenges facing their society, as well as the potential that contemporary, rapidly changing, post-apartheid South African society has.

I therefore think that this book with make a crucial contribution to students' learning and knowledge development, and that students will find it enormously helpful and interesting.

AZWIHANGWISI E MUTHIVHI
SCHOOL OF EDUCATION
UNIVERSITY OF CAPE TOWN

How to use this book

Overview of content

Child and adolescent development introduces readers to developmental psychology, illustrating the qualitative shifts children undergo as they develop into adults. The book is structured in relation to a socio-cultural approach to development, which sees development as a product of the interaction between the individual and his or her socio-cultural and historical context. This approach is of special relevance in South Africa today, given the country's history and multicultural society. Wherever possible, the authors have drawn on South African research to illustrate the developmental concepts covered in each chapter.

Developmental concepts, as with all concepts, can appear decontextualised; in order to make concepts relevant to the reader, case studies open and close each chapter to show how a concept can be used to explain an empirical problem and to illustrate what will be covered in the chapter. These case studies also aim to encourage readers to think about how developmental concepts have real-life applicability. To aid readers in grasping the important concepts in each chapter, 'Check your progress' features and end-of-chapter questions get readers to engage critically with concepts covered.

Child and adolescent development contains 12 chapters and is divided into three parts: Part I introduces readers to theoretical approaches to studying development, Part II discusses the stages of development and Part III contextualises development in South Africa. What follows is a brief outline of each chapter.

Part I: Theoretical approaches
Chapter 1: An introduction to developmental psychology
Chapter 1 introduces readers to developmental psychology by highlighting the history of ideas upon which developmental psychology is based. The chapter also introduces readers to central debates in this field, such as the nature versus nurture debate. The chapter closes by illustrating how a researcher can study development scientifically.

Chapter 2: Theories of development

Chapter 2 introduces readers to the core developmental theories of the twentieth and twenty-first centuries. Readers are introduced to four main paradigms that have dominated developmental psychology: the psycho-dynamic approach; the biological approach; the behaviourist approach and the cognitive development and socio-cultural approach.

Part II: Stages of development

Chapter 3: Prenatal

While chapters 1 and 2 provide very broad overviews of understanding development across the human lifespan, chapters 3 to 7 focus specifically on different stages of development. Chapter 3 discusses the beginnings of human development by focusing on prenatal development to birth.

Chapter 4: Infancy

This chapter introduces readers to development during infancy by focus-ing on various aspects of development, such as physical maturation, cognitive development, psychosocial development and the beginnings of language. A central theory discussed here is the work of Bowlby on attachment. How an infant attaches to his or her primary carer has been shown to impact on the development of prosocial behaviour in adoles-cence. This chapter illustrates, then, how important an understanding of infancy is in understanding later behaviour.

Chapter 5: Early childhood

This chapter is concerned with understanding the development of child-ren from two to eight years of age – that is, the pre-schooler and the child who has just started school. Profound developmental changes happen during this period, with children moving cognitively from pre-operational thinking to concrete operational thinking. The chapter introduces for discussion the notion of moral development.

Chapter 6: Middle childhood

This chapter focuses on development in middle childhood in terms of physical, cognitive and psychosocial development. The chapter illustrates a key developmental shift that occurs during this period, from dependence on the family to a move towards depending on peers for social acceptance.

Chapter 7: Adolescence

For those who work with children, adolescence is a very challenging space indeed. Children who were delightfully sweet appear to change overnight into long-faced, surly children – perhaps this is why this period has become known as the 'terrible teens'! This chapter provides insight into the physical, cognitive and psychosocial changes teens face as they negotiate this period.

Part III: Contextualising contemporary themes in childhood development

Chapter 8: Children and childhood in South Africa

This chapter introduces readers to what childhood means in South Africa. Of particular interest in this chapter is the focus on risk and resilience during childhood.

Chapter 9: Career development of children

Those interested in becoming educational psychologists will find this chapter extremely important as it introduces the notion of career development.

Chapter 10: Poverty, adversity and resilience

South Africa faces enormous challenges in relation to poverty and these impact on children's development. This chapter explains poverty in South Africa and outlines the impact that poverty has on developing children.

Chapter 11: Children and violence in South Africa

Violence, unfortunately, is endemic to development in South Africa. This chapter begins to address the developmental impact of violence by focusing on notions of masculinity as this is understood by participants in a study carried out in the Western Cape Province of South Africa. Bronfenbrenner's ecosystemic theory is used to complement Vygotsky's sociocultural work in a bid to understand the systemic impact of violence and, hence, the need for systemic solutions to violence.

Chapter 12: Health barriers that impede childhood development

This chapter focuses on understanding physical, cognitive and psychosocial development in terms of health-related issues.

How this book progresses through the content

Figure 1 below is divided into three parts to illustrate how the chapters fit together and to provide a quick overview of the logical sequence of the book.
- In Part I: Theoretical approach (chapters 1 and 2), you are introduced to developmental psychology by way of highlighting the various debates in the field and the different theoretical perspectives used to study human development.

- Chapters 3 to 7 outline the various stages of development from pre-natal to adolescent development.
- The final section of this book, Part III, contextualises development in South Africa by highlighting problems children face in our context. Chapter 8 looks at children and childhood in South Africa while chapter 9 focuses attention on a crucial developmental area: career development. Chapters 10 and 11 focus on poverty and violence and the developmental impact of these social problems. Finally, chapter 12 situates development within an understanding of how issues related to health impact on the developing person.

While these different sections may look unrelated, remember that the different chapters provide the basis for understanding the various sections and that Parts II and III should be read as providing elaborated empirical examples of the theories introduced in Part I.

Figure 1 Mindmap of how this book progresses through the content

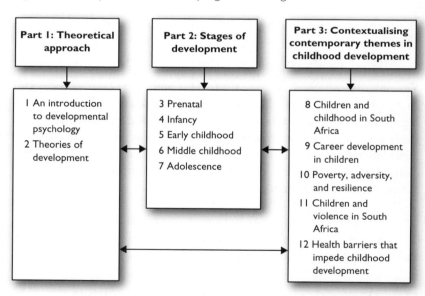

PART I

THEORETICAL APPROACH

CHAPTER ONE

AN INTRODUCTION TO DEVELOPMENTAL PSYCHOLOGY

Joanne Hardman

CASE STUDY

Report portrays 'a tragic picture' of education system

By the age of eight, children from the poorest 80% of households in South Africa are already far behind the school performance of the richest 20%.

'This disadvantage remains throughout their years of education and stays with them when they enter the labour market,' say the University of Stellenbosch researchers who released their findings on Monday.

This startling finding is one of several that 12 researchers in Stellenbosch's economics department use to reach the conclusion that, 17 years into democracy, South Africa's education system still 'generally fails to produce outcomes to help eradicate inequalities'...

'Reinforcing current patterns of poverty and privilege'

... Drawing on datasets including household surveys and internationally comparative studies of literacy and numeracy levels at schools, the report draws stark links between poverty and under-achievement.

For instance, South Africa ranks 10th out of the 15 sub-Saharan African countries tested for reading among grade six learners and eighth out of 15 for maths performance in the same grade. This is despite South Africa's relatively higher state expenditure on education and better teacher/learner ratios across the region.

'Largely ineffective'

That data is to be found in the so-called 'SAQMEQ III' — the project conducted in 2007 by the Southern and Eastern Africa Consortium for Monitoring Educational Quality. The same study showed that the average reading test score for the richest 20% of learners in grade six was much higher than the score for the poorest 20% of learners. A similar discrepancy was found in maths scores. 'South Africa's rural children did far worse than rural children in most other countries in this African sample,' the report says, 'as did the poorest quarter of South African students in comparison with the other countries in the sample' (Macfarlane, 'Report portrays,' 2011).

Schooling as a cultural practice

Interested in investigating the impact culture has on children's ability to engage with school concepts, Muthivhi carried out an experiment in classes in Venda (Muthivhi 2008; Muthivhi & Broom 2009). Traditionally, class teaching in Venda has been dominated by rote-based transmission, with children given very little opportunity to engage critically with the content presented. Venda schooling evolved out of missionary traditions which viewed the text as an authority not to be questioned. The Venda culture is, in fact, quite hierarchical, and the questioning of senior members of the community is not encouraged.

Using an experimental task to test students' understanding of possibility, Muthivhi (2008) found that the grade-seven students he tested produced thinking that would be expected at a grade-five level. That is, developmentally, 12-year-olds are expected to be able to think in abstract ways; what Muthivhi found, however, was that this group of children did not think abstractly but, rather, thought in concrete ways.

ACTIVITY

What do you think? Discuss the following:
1   Why did the children in this study not think in abstract ways?
2   Do you think these children are developmentally 'slow'? Or is there another reason why they do not perform as expected?

LEARNING OBJECTIVES

By the end of this chapter you should be able to:
*   Describe the debates in developmental psychology
*   Decide which methods to use to research developmental questions
*   Understand the history of the ideas that inform developmental psychology
*   Become familiar with the South African context of development.

Introduction

Why a South African text if development is universal?

This book will introduce you to developmental psychology. This is a field of study that focuses on understanding how a child grows into an adult, and on understanding what qualitative processes this transformation involves.

This chapter will initially discuss the field of developmental psycho-logy. It will give you an idea of the research questions developmental psychologists ask. It will also introduce the methods they use to carry out research on developmental questions. It is crucial that you understand research methods in developmental psychology, because it is research that provides us as psychologists with answers to the various questions we ask in this field.

This first chapter starts by introducing the socio-cultural focus of this book, and the South African context of developmental psychology. The chapter then proceeds to discuss the history of the ideas of developmental psychology.

It is important that you know the source of the ideas that inform current debates about development. These ideas are grounded in ancient Greek philosophy. This might seem rather historically remote from the twenty-first century. However, in order to understand modern thinking, you need to understand how this thinking has developed over time.

The chapter will also introduce you to core international debates in developmental psychology. The chapter will then focus on the research methods psychologists use to address these debates. As developmental psychology studies children, the chapter will also address the **ethical** study of children. An ethical study is one in which the researcher aims to do no harm to the participants or to distort the participants' reality in any way.

Ethical
a term that derives from philosophy, where ethics is concerned with understanding and systematising notions of right and wrong

Orientation of the book: A socio-cultural focus of development-in-context

South Africa has seen enormous social and political changes in the past 18 years. It has 11 nationally recognised languages and a variety of cul-tural groups.

The use of racial terminology in this book
The use of racial terminology and the invocation of apartheid-era racial groups are potentially problematic. However, these terms are still popularly salient and analytically useful, and they are therefore retained in several chapters of this book.

In the case study at the start of this chapter, the extract from the article 'Report portrays "a tragic picture" of education system', which appeared in the *Mail & Guardian* newspaper, points at the challenges in South Africa's schooling system. Muthivhi's research (Muthivhi 2008; Muthivhi & Broom, 2009) goes further than the newspaper article to unpack why school performance is so poor in South Africa. While the newspaper article indicates that poverty influences schooling adversely, it also points out that South African students perform worse than children from poorer nations. You might well ask why this is so. Muthivhi provides a potential answer to this question: people's cultural backgrounds influence how they approach the world (Muthivhi 2008; Muthivhi & Broom, 2009). That is, although **maturation** is crucial to explain development, it is insufficient to explain differences in developmental milestones across different cultures.

Development, as the authors of this book perceive it, relies on an interaction between biological, social, and psychological processes that interact with each other in human culture. We understand **culture** as formative of the child's developing consciousness. This does not mean, however, that we ignore the importance of a biological focus. People are, after all, biological beings, and much development would be impossible without maturation.

Previously, these two sides of the debate were referred to as '**nature versus nurture**'. This chapter will investigate this debate. However, in this book, the authors do not take this dualistic stance, because we understand that mind is necessarily social. That is, the brain develops in a social context. This notion of mind as social overcomes the traditional **dualism** that views *either* nature *or* nurture as impacting primarily on the developing child; in contrast to this dualistic view, we understand both nature *and* nurture to be responsible for people's psychology. The stance that the authors take in this book is drawn from the work of the Russian psychologist Lev Vygotsky. His theory, socio-cultural theory, understands mind as being socially situated (Vygotsky, 1978). For Vygotsky, then, people develop their uniquely human ways of thinking by interaction within a socio-cultural milieu.

Maturation
the biological processes underlying development

Culture
a person's knowledge, beliefs and behaviours shaped through symbolic interaction with members of their group through social means

Nature versus nurture debate
debate about whether environment or inborn mental structures impact primarily on a developing child

Dualism
something in two parts

Case study: Victor of Aveyron

Have you ever read the story of Mowgli, the fictional boy in Rudyard Kipling's 1894 tale *The Jungle Book*, who is brought up by wolves after being separated from his family in an Indian jungle? This story grips the imagination because it forces the reader to ponder the 'what ifs' of development. What if a baby is left in a jungle? Will it be adopted by animals? Will it become animal-like? In fact, far from being fantastical imaginary scenarios, such stories of wild, or feral, children do not occur only in fiction, as this case study illustrates.

On a cold winter's day in 1800 a dishevelled, naked child, of about 12 years of age, walked into the French village of Aveyron. He appeared to the villagers to be completely wild. He could not talk or make himself

Figure 1.1 Victor of Aveyron

understood in any way other than to grunt and gesture. He did not show interest in eating cooked food but, rather, ate raw food given to him. This boy, who was given the name Victor, became known as the 'wild boy' of Aveyron. His fame spread throughout France as scholars tried to determine who he was and from where he had come. At this time in history, the Enlightenment, referred to as the Age of Reason, was coming to an end. Philosophers and scientists were seriously re-examining notions of human nature, and they were debating the extent to which outside factors contributed to development. These questions were being asked: What is 'man'? Is 'man' made in God's image, or is 'man' an animal? How does 'man' differ from other animals?

The case of Victor, then, was one of interest to Enlightenment thinkers such as Jean-Marc-Gaspard Itard, a young medical student who took Victor in and attempted to study him and to socialise him. Even though Victor lived with Itard and was taught by him, he never did acquire spoken language. Scientists were never able to establish whether he had been born mentally handicapped or had become cognitively underdeveloped through isolation. Victor died in care, leaving the big question about the environmental impact on human development very much open.

What is developmental psychology?

The case study of Victor of Aveyron highlights some of the questions that psychologists have debated for the past century: How do humans develop? What impact do the environment and genes have on a human child's development? Developmental psychology is a **scientific** field of study that uses scientific methods to investigate psychological, emotional and perceptual changes that occur throughout a human's lifespan. Developmental psychology investigates whether development occurs through the gradual accumulation of knowledge or through stages. Developmental psychologists are also interested in studying the extent to which development depends on experience and innate mental structures. The latter interest arises out of a historical debate about whether a child may be thought of as a blank slate on which the environment writes (nurture), or is born with the mental structures needed to engage with the world (nature). The nature versus nurture debate is centuries old, and can be traced back to ancient Greece and the work of the philosophers Plato and Aristotle.

Scientific
differing from common sense, as data is rigorously collected using agreed-upon, tested methods

Why do psychologists study development?

Investigating how a child develops psychologically helps us to provide that child with appropriate learning experiences. This helps us to interact with children and to make decisions about their environments and activities. Moreover, understanding how a child develops helps us to understand adults more effectively.

Imagine that, in therapy sessions, you have adult clients who disclose that their childhood was painful because their parents got divorced when the clients were children. These disclosures will tell you something about the patterns these clients enact in adult life. So developmental psychology helps us to understand normal development (which informs our understanding of 'unusual' development).

Studying development also helps us to improve self-understanding. An understanding of normal development guides our responses to actual behaviour, and it informs appropriate expectations about children's and adolescents' behaviour. While developmental psychologists do study abnormal development, the primary focus of this book is on understanding normal development. In fact, unless psychologists are able to establish what normal development 'looks like', they are not in a position to say how behaviour potentially deviates from the norm.

Central issues of developmental psychology

The following issues are central to developmental psychology:
- Continuity or discontinuity in development
- Plasticity
- Nature and nurture as sources of development.

Continuity or discontinuity in development

Two questions inform a debate that exists regarding continuity in developmental psychology:
- To what extent is there developmental continuity between humans and animals?
- Is individual development continuous, with small quantitative changes occurring gradually over time, or is development discontinuous, marked by abrupt major qualitative changes over a child's lifespan?

This debate is characterised by two theoretical positions:
- On the one hand, some researchers propose that development is continuous and gradual – as time passes, a child develops through the accumulation of quantitative changes.
- On the other hand, stage theorists indicate that development passes through stages, and at each stage a child negotiates major qualitative changes that alter him or her fundamentally.

ACTIVITY

Find out from people who knew you as a child if they remember when you started to talk. What were your first words? How old were you? Now think about this: do you think you would have learnt to talk if you had not had people around you? If you had somehow been marooned on a deserted island as a baby, for example, would you have learned to talk without human contact?

Plasticity

Plasticity in development refers to the degree to which, and the conditions under which, a child is open to changes. Sensitive periods in development are those periods in which a child is more open to specific changes than at other times. So, for example, children appear more sensitive to language acquisition at an early age than when they are older. This is not to suggest that older children cannot learn language; they can. However, it does seem that children are more sensitive to acquiring language earlier in life.

Plasticity
capacity of the brain to change in response to positive and negative influences from the environment

Case study: Genie and language development

Discovered in 1970 by authorities, Genie (not her real name) had spent most of the 13 years of her life in extreme social isolation, strapped to a potty chair in her bedroom. Genie's parents had four children, two of whom died. Genie was their fourth child. By all accounts, Genie's father was extremely strict and, while he did not apparently abuse her older brother, he

Figure 1.2 Genie

kept Genie locked in her bedroom and restricted her movements by tying her to a potty chair. He would hit her with a stick whenever she vocalised. Genie had a vocabulary of only about 20 words, most of which were negative such as 'no more' or 'stop it'; she made strange 'bunny' like movements when she walked, and she spat and clawed.

Genie was discovered when her mother left her father and attempted to obtain social benefits from the welfare department. When a social worker met Genie, she estimated that the child was six or seven years old. On learning that Genie was 13 years old, she reported the case to her supervisors. Genie's case caused immense interest in developmental circles because of her ability to shed light on the notion of critical or sensitive periods in linguistic development. The hypothesis put forward by researchers was that language development relies on a critical period. If a child has not learnt language by puberty, that child may be able to learn some language skills but will never develop linguistic mastery.

Taken out of her captivity and placed into the home of a researcher, Genie was exposed to a variety of social stimuli previously absent from her life. And indeed, Genie did develop some new behaviours. Specifically, Genie's ability to communicate non-verbally was recognised by researchers. However, Genie never did develop the mastery of grammar that her foster family hoped she would. Although she did increase her repertoire of words, she was only able to form sentences like 'Applesauce store buy'. Sadly, when funding and interest in her case declined due to lack of scientific data, Genie was returned to her mother, who wanted to care for her. Her mother was, however, unable to care for Genie, and she was sent to a variety of foster homes, in some of which she suffered further abuse.

Nature *and* nurture as sources of development

In the twentieth century many developmental psychologists focused on trying to unpack the relative effects of the environment and of innate capacities on developmental paths. The debate referred to as the nature versus nurture debate (mentioned earlier in this chapter) was part of this focus.

Where does development come from? Are people born with innate capacities, or does the environment determine who people will become? In the twenty-first century, few developmental psychologists would argue for a focus on nature *or* nurture as two opposite poles. Rather, today we tend to view development as an interplay between genetic factors and environmental influences.

The field of **evolutionary developmental psychology** studies the interaction between genes and the environment in a child's development. Drawing on the nineteenth-century scholar Darwin's theory of evolution through **natural selection**, evolutionary developmental psychology helps us to understand how genes and the environment interact. **Evolution** refers to gradual changes in the physical structure of an organism over generations (Chiarelli, 1973). Darwin travelled the world aboard HMS *Beagle* as the ship's naturalist.

During his travels, Darwin visited the Galapagos Islands off the South American coast. These islands had been isolated from the mainland, and even from each other, for thousands of years. Darwin noticed that the finches on one island had different beaks to the finches on another island. This prompted him to develop a theory to explain the biological changes that he observed. He wrote in his book *On the origin of species by means of natural selection*:

> As many more individuals of each species are born than can possibly survive, and as consequently there is a frequently occurring struggle for survival, it follows that any being, if it vary however slightly in a

Evolutionary developmental psychology
field that studies the interaction between genes and the environment in a child's development

Natural selection
the evolutionary process whereby organisms better adapted to their environment tend to survive and produce more offspring

Evolution
gradual changes in the physical structure of an organism over generations

manner profitable to itself ... will have a better chance of surviving, and thus being naturally selected ... this preservation of favourable individual differences and variations, and the destruction of those which are injurious, I have called natural selection, or the survival of the fittest (Darwin, 1882, p. 50).

When Darwin mentions 'survival of the fittest', he is not referring to someone who is physically fit because of going to the gym; what he is referring to here is the individual's 'fit' to their environment. Take a giraffe's neck, for example: millennia ago, giraffes did not have particularly long necks. However, a random variation in the species saw to it that some giraffes had longer necks than others. This conferred on them an advantage because they were able to obtain food from high branches that other animals could not reach. Gradually, through the generations, this successful variation was passed on in the giraffe's genes.

Those characteristics, then, that enable people to fit successfully into their geographical context will be naturally selected and passed on in their genes to their children. Less desirable genes will gradually fade from the species.

According to Darwin, three conditions must hold for evolutionary change to occur:

- **Variation:** There must be some random variation in the population that affords that animal some advantage. So there can be short-, medium- and long-necked giraffes.
- **Competition:** When resources are scarce, the giraffe with the longer neck will have an advantage over the shorter-necked giraffes because its long neck will enable it to forage for food higher up. The long neck, then, enables the giraffe to compete successfully for food which is out of reach of giraffes with shorter necks. Having access to food is obviously necessary for reproduction. The successful 'long-necked' gene will then be 'selected' and passed on to the next generation, through inheritance.
- **Inheritance:** A successful random variation will be naturally selected and passed on in the giraffe's genes. The next generation will then have longer necks, and so on down the generations, until there are no longer giraffes without long necks (Henzi, 1996; Ridley, 1993).

The box below expands on this information.

The evolution of the peppered moth

Evolution is defined by Dobzhansky (1937) as 'a change in the frequency of an allele within a gene pool'. These changes generally take place over extremely long periods of time and cannot, normally, be seen as they occur.

However, an extremely interesting case of evolutionary change occurring quickly, and being tracked by scientists, is the case of the peppered moth.

As we have discussed in the chapter, for evolutionary change to occur, variation must exist in a species. Contextual factors, such as drastic environmental change, will determine whether or not this variation will prove successful. Prior to the industrial revolution in the nineteenth century, the peppered moth was generally a light-grey colour with dark speckles (see Figure 1.3). This light colouring enabled these moths to blend well into the light-coloured tree bark in England. Those moths that had random darker colouring (see Figure 1.4) would attract the attention of birds and, consequently, get eaten.

Figure 1.3 Light peppered moth

Figure 1.4 Dark peppered moth

However, due to the Industrial Revolution, the light-coloured trees around the larger industrialised towns in England began to grow darker because the soot from the new coal-burning factories coated them. As a result of the darkening of the trees, the light-coloured moths began to become more visible to predators, and the darker moths became less so (see Figure 1.5). Although light-coloured moths continued to be produced, it was the darker moths that began to flourish. That is, the allele frequency gradually shifted as more dark moths survived and reproduced.

Figure 1.5 Dark and light peppered moths on a tree

Interestingly, in modern times, due to more awareness of pollution, and moves to protect the environment from pollutants, the lighter-coloured moth is beginning to dominate once again (Dobzhansky, 1937).

CHECK YOUR PROGRESS

- To what does 'survival of the fittest' refer?
- What conditions need to hold for evolutionary change to occur?
- Why is developmental psychology referred to as a 'science'?
- What do developmental psychologists study?
- What are the central debates in developmental psychology?

The history of developmental psychology

Empiricism and rationalism: The history of developmental ideas

Plato and Aristotle

An ardent follower of Socrates, Plato (428–347 BCE) believed that knowledge was not **empirical**, nor available through the senses, nor the product of learning, observation or study, but that it was innate. For him, then, children were born with innate knowledge, and they did not need to be taught. Rather, they needed guidance to access the knowledge they already had (Irwin, 2010). Platonism denies the reality of the material world through arguing that objects and events that our senses 'see' are only 'shadows' of their perfect forms (Kahn, 2004). In modern developmental debates, Plato's position would be referred to as pointing to the nativist (or nature) end of the nature versus nurture debate.

> **Empirical**
> information collected using the senses

Aristotle, one of Plato's students, took a completely different view to his teacher. For him, a newborn baby's mind was a blank slate (***tabula rasa***) on which the environment and experience 'wrote'. For Aristotle, then, empirical reality, what a child knows through his or her senses, is paramount in developing the child's psyche (Barnes, 1995). It is here in ancient Greek philosophy that we find the basis for the modern debates about nature and nurture.

> **Tabula rasa**
> a blank slate

Figure 1.6 Plato

Figure 1.7 Aristotle

Locke, Descartes and Rousseau

During the Enlightenment, intellectuals were fascinated with questions about human knowledge acquisition. René Descartes (1596–1650), a French philosopher, set out to establish what he could know and how he could know something with certainty (Descartes, 1996). He postulated that the only thing he knew with certainty was that he was a thinking being. He dismissed the empiricist position that says things exist because the senses tell people they do. He demonstrated the fallibility of empirical knowledge by heating up a piece of wax. He argued that when it melts, the wax takes on a different form, and so, if people rely only on their senses, they can be fooled as to the nature of reality. For him, then, thinking, or rather the fact that 'I am thinking' was the only certainty that humans have. His position has been referred to as a **rationalist** position because he focused his investigations on thought, and he challenged knowledge gained through empirical methods by appealing to reason as the only criterion for judging truth. In response to his question about what he could know for certain, Descartes famously said: 'I think therefore I am (*cogito ergo sum*).' This position led to Descartes rejecting perception as a method for knowledge acquisition and proposing a **deductive** method for acquiring knowledge.

Rationalist
philosophical position stating people do not learn empirically, but come to knowledge because born with an innate capacity to think

Deductive
deductive reasoning refers to drawing inferences about specific things from a general law

In opposition to this rationalist approach, the philosopher John Locke (1632–1704) focused his studies on an empiricist method, suggesting that knowledge is acquired through sensory methods. According to Locke, children are not born with innate knowledge or concepts. Rather, they acquire knowledge as a result of experience. This empiricist position formed the basis for the behaviourist field of research in the mid-twentieth century. The implication of this viewpoint is that knowledge and concepts develop only through instruction and experience.

The contrary viewpoint that children are born with knowledge and concepts that unfold through maturation was supported by Jean-Jacques Rousseau (1712–1778). The implication of this **nativist** position is that children cannot be taught concepts but must be allowed the freedom to explore.

Nativist
referring to the nature side of the nature versus nurture debate, indicating that thinking is innate

Empiricism and rationalism in the twentieth century

Chapter two will look at modern developmental theories in some detail. This chapter looks briefly at the nature versus nurture debate as a continuation of the historical debates discussed earlier in the chapter. The nature versus nurture debate hinges on whether development can be explained as arising from external, environmental factors (nurture), or is best explained in a nativist way, as innate in the form of genetic predispositions (nature). The most famous twentieth century poles of this debate are behaviourism and cognitive psychology. The empiricist position outlined by Locke in the eighteenth century was redeveloped in the twentieth century in the field of behaviourist psychology.

Behaviourists, such as John B. Watson and B. F. Skinner, whom we will investigate in depth in chapter two, researched the impact the environment has on the developing child. For behaviourists, the only data researchers can study is empirical data. This psychological theory accepts that children are born blank slates upon which life's experiences 'write'. This is the nurture side of the nature versus nurture debate that was so topical in psychology in the twentieth century. On the one hand, researchers such as Watson and Skinner illustrated the primary importance of empirical experience on development. On the other hand, cognitive psychologists such as Noam Chomsky (1965) postulated a nativist view of development, claiming that children are born with a **language acquisition device**.

Language acquisition device
predisposition that enables a child to acquire language

For Chomsky, a child is born with an innate capacity to learn language. Consider, for example, a puppy and a small child. Exposed to language, the child will always learn to talk. The puppy, however, will never speak. Chomsky labelled the predisposition that enables the child to acquire language the language acquisition device. This is not literally a 'device' in the child's head, but is, rather, a hypothesised capacity that enables children to acquire language.

How do psychologists study development?

Developmental psychology studies children, and this requires the use of novel scientific methods. Studying a pre-verbal child, for example, requires methods of investigation that do not rely on language. Working with children, and people in general, provides many ethical challenges. This chapter will investigate these later. The methods you chose to investigate a developmental question will depend entirely on the question you want to answer.

Case studies

Teaching mathematics in grade six: Mrs Brandt (Hardman, 2008, p. 157)

Mrs Brandt is a grade six teacher in a rural primary school in the Western Cape. She has 47 students in her class. She is teaching her students about fractions. Yesterday she introduced the students to the notion of fractions, focusing on which part of the fraction is the numerator and which is the denominator. She begins the lesson by writing $\frac{1}{2}$ on the board and saying the following:

Teacher: This is what we call a fraction. Now all of you … [Points at blackboard: $\frac{1}{2}$ is written on the blackboard.]

Pupils: Fraction

Teacher: Fraction

Pupils: Fraction

Teacher: Fraction

Pupils: Fraction

Teacher: Right, this is the top [Points at the numerator]. The top of the?

Pupils: Fraction

Teacher: Right. Then if you go down you see this [Points at the denominator] part, it is what we call what?

Pupils: We call it denominator.

Teacher: Denominator, denominator, denominator, denominator. Right.

Teaching mathematics in grade six: Mr Abel (Hardman, 2008, p. 158)

Mr Abel teaches grade six mathematics at a farm school in the apple-growing district of the Western Cape. He has 42 students in his class. He has just been teaching children about fractions: in particular, he is teaching about the function of the denominator. He teaches fractions by cutting up apples that he has brought to the class. He is about to move on to a task, when he asks the class whether they have any questions.

Teacher: Question?

Wayne: Explain the denominator again sir. [Puts up his hand]

Teacher: Right, explain the denominator again.

Come let's go further. [Gets an apple from a bag of apples he has brought to the lesson]

Now, what is this? [Holds up an apple]
Students: *Whole*
Teacher: *Whole.*
And I cut him exactly, exactly, in how many parts? [Begins to cut the apple in half] *How many parts are there?*
Students: *Two*
Teacher: *Now, my denominator tells me how many parts I have divided my whole into* [Holds up parts]
In this case, it's two. [Holds up parts]
So my denominator in this case will be?
Students: *Two*
Teacher: *Two.*

ACTIVITY

What is happening here? The case studies about Mrs Brandt and Mr Abel teaching mathematics come from my research into the teaching and learning of mathematics in grade six classrooms in the Western Cape. I was asking the following question: How is the concept of fractions taught in disadvantaged primary schools in the Western Cape? These two case studies tell me something about each teacher's teaching methods.

1   How would you go about answering the question I posed?
2   What can you tell about each teacher's method of teaching from these extracts?

Research methods in developmental psychology

Qualitative and quantitative paradigms

Different research questions require different approaches to collecting data. While some questions lend themselves to the collection of quantitative data, others lend themselves to the collection of qualitative data. So, for example, if researchers wanted to know how many children in the Western Cape suffer from fetal alcohol spectrum disorder (FASD), they would collect data from clinics and schools that record numbers of children with this syndrome. However, if they wanted to know how children with FASD learn in a classroom situation, they would have to collect data on observations of behaviour.

Qualitative studies involve the non-numerical assessment of observations. In this approach, theory and data collection are interlinked, with theory influencing what data is collected and data influencing how the theory grows (Babbie & Mouton, 2001). Consider, for example, the following question: How does the use of computers in mathematics lessons impact on the cognitive development of grade six children? In order to begin to study this question, you need, first, to have a theory that describes how children develop cognitively. Once you have selected a theory that explains cognitive development, you then have to decide on the data you need to collect to answer this particular question. The question you are asking is a 'how' question, so you are interested in the processes underlying the impact of computers on cognitive development. The data you collect needs to be sufficiently layered to get at the answer to your question. In this instance, in-depth interviews with the children would be useful, and so too would detailed observations, which you could perhaps record on video.

Now, imagine that you have carried out your research and have discovered that time on computer, coupled with children's social background, appears to be the major factor impacting on children's development when they use computers. Clearly, this finding relates to the small group of grade six students you studied. But imagine that you want to know whether this is true of all grade six students. In this case you would need to turn to a research design that could quantify your findings.

Quantitative research, sometimes called statistical research, is numerically based. It is sometimes used in developmental psychology to test the **generalisability** of qualitative findings. In this case, you might design a questionnaire that could be sent to every school in South Africa that uses computers. This questionnaire could be filled out by grade six pupils and would contain questions that have arisen from your qualitative work. When the schools returned the questionnaires, you would input them into a quantitative computer package such as statistical package for the social sciences (SPSS). Then you would be able to run statistical procedures on them in order to determine whether social background and time on computer do indeed account for cognitive development with computers.

Generalisability
the ability of findings to talk to the larger population

Naturalistic observation

In naturalistic observation, the researcher observes the behaviour under investigation as it plays out in a natural setting. For example, imagine you are interested in studying bullying. It is not ethical to pay someone to bully someone else, so you would have to study bullying in its natural setting. Naturalistic observation is very useful when researchers are trying to study behaviour in a real-world setting; they can use the data gathered from such observation in establishing the validity of their findings.

However, naturalistic observation is not suitable for all questions developmental psychologists investigate. A drawback of observing behaviour in its natural setting is that the observer cannot manipulate **variables**. This makes it very difficult to make any causal inferences from observations. Throughout an observation, the observing researcher has to be unobtrusive, because subjects react differently when they know they are being observed from when they do not know they are being observed, and this will bias the findings.

Because naturalistic observation does not rely on the manipulation of variables in a structured setting, it is possible that two observers faced with the same observed behaviour might describe it in different ways. A famous instance of successful naturalistic observation is Darwin's observations during his trip on HMS *Beagle*, which was mentioned earlier in this chapter. The observations he made became the basis for the theory of evolution.

Researchers can collect data in a number of ways in naturalistic observation:

- **Counts:** They can count how many instances of the behaviour happened over the observation time.
- **Researcher narrative:** They can write down a narrative account of the observed patterns of behaviour.
- **Video and audio:** In order to remind themselves about the behaviour they observe, they can take a video of it or make audio recordings of exchanges, for later transcription.

Sampling refers to selecting the event or behaviour or object of study that the researcher will be observing. The following are two types of sampling:

- Situation sampling refers to observing behaviour in different contexts.
- Time sampling requires the observation of behaviour at different times. The researcher can choose times **randomly** or **systematically**.

Cross-sectional and longitudinal designs

A cross-sectional study involves observations of a sample, or cross-section of a population, at a specific point in time. Researchers using this design would try to draw a sample of children, for example, who are similar in most ways but who differ on one variable, such as age, for example. This is common in developmental research where a researcher might want to find out how children learn differently at different ages.

A problem inherent in cross-sectional studies is the reliance on generalising to a population, based on a single period in time. If you want to study something over time, and get a picture of how something develops, a longitudinal design will be more useful.

A longitudinal study enables researchers to track the development of phenomena over time. A classic study focused on what happened to a UFO cult when its prophecy about the end of the world failed to

Variable
something that can vary and can be manipulated during experiments to see whether relationships exist between two or more things manipulated

Randomly
using chance procedures

Systematically
in a considered way

materialise (Festinger, Reicker & Schacter, 1956). In order to study this question, the researchers had to study the cult over time. Incidentally, when the prophecy failed, the cult did not close down but, instead, recruited more members!

There are various types of longitudinal study:

- **Trend study:** A trend study is a form of longitudinal research that tracks trends over time. For example, imagine you want to investigate how the South African population has changed over time. You would draw on census data over a number of decades, showing shifts in the national population.

- **Cohort study:** In a cohort study, the researcher investigates changes in a specific subpopulation, or cohort, over time. One such cohort could be determined by age group. For example, imagine you want to investigate how people born in the 1990s respond to novel technology. You could track this cohort – people born in the 1990s – over the decades to see how they integrate technology into their lives. You might even want to compare this group with, say, a group born in the 1970s, to see what differences in integration of technology into their lives exist between the two cohorts.

- **Panel study:** A panel study is similar to trend and cohort studies, but it involves studying the same set of people at each stage of the research.

Correlational design

ACTIVITY

What impact does the computer package MasterMaths have on examination results in grade 12? Garth is a senior school mathematics teacher. He often uses computer programmes to add to his teaching. He is very interested in discovering whether a particular mathematics programme, MasterMaths, has an impact on the mathematics marks of grade 12 students. That is, he is interested in the relationship between the use of this programme and students' performance. How would you investigate a question like this (Spencer-Smith & Hardman, 2011)?

Imagine that you want to investigate how two variables are related to each other, but you do not want to manipulate the variables. For example, you might want to know how height and weight are related to each other. Researchers use a correlational design in order to determine what relationship – if any – exists between two variables (Babbie & Mouton, 2001). In this case, you might find that height and weight are positively correlated: the taller the people in your sample are, the more they weigh.

This is a positive correlation, because the direction of the relationship indicates that as a person gets taller, so that person gets heavier.

It is important to note, however, that correlation does not imply causation. That is, while height and weight are positively correlated for your sample, you cannot say that being tall *causes* a person to be heavier. A negative relationship can exist between variables: as one variable increases, the other decreases. For example, in the course of some research, you might find that in your sample there is a negative relationship between television viewing and exercise: the more a person watches television, the less he or she exercises.

Experimental design

The strongest design in research in regard to making causal statements is the experimental design. In this design, the researcher manipulates the **independent variable** (that variable that the researcher believes will cause an effect) to ascertain its effect on the **dependent variable** (the variable that changes depending on the impact of the independent variable) (Babbie & Mouton, 2001).

For example, imagine that you want to study the effect violent video games have on children's aggression. You could randomly assign one group of children to an experimental group and a second group of children to a control group. (It is important that you split the groups randomly because you will then be able to attribute any differences you note after the split to the experimental condition.) The children exposed to the violent video games are in the experimental group; those not exposed are in the control group. In order to test your hypothesis about the effect of violent video games on aggression in children, you will run your experiment and then test the experimental and control groups on aggression tasks to see whether there is a difference in aggression levels across the two groups. If you find that there is a difference, then you could draw the conclusion that violent video games impact on levels of aggression in children.

Independent variable
variable that the researcher thinks will cause the effect

Dependent variable
variable that changes due to the manipulation of the independent variable

Reliability and validity

In conducting research in developmental psychology, it is important that the conclusions drawn are trustworthy and are not simply based on common sense or influenced by the researcher's opinions (Denzin & Lincoln, 2005). If researchers are to take results seriously, the research must meet three criteria for deciding whether something is scientific rather than merely commonsensical:

- **Objectivity:** Researchers must collect data objectively. The criterion of objectivity requires that researcher's preconceptions do not distort results.

- **Reliability:** This refers to the consistency of research findings. Data should be reliable in two senses. First, provided that research conditions are the same, investigators should be able to obtain the same results each time they collect the data. Second, different researchers should be able to agree on the description of the results.
- **Replicability:** This refers to an independent set of researchers being able to replicate the results – that is, come up with the same results as the initial researchers did. For example, imagine that you are studying infants' ability to track objects when they disappear from sight, and you find that nine-month-old children can do this under certain conditions. An independent researcher should be able to replicate your study and come up with the same findings.

Ethical concerns when working with children

As a researcher, your primary duty to any person you study will be to protect that subject's welfare. To protect the subject's welfare, the American Psychological Association (APA) sets ethical standards. Read the information in the box describing an experiment carried out on a baby in the 1920s by behaviourist John B. Watson. Chapter two will discuss behaviourism in some detail. For the moment, however, it is useful for you to learn about this experiment, which provides a vivid illustration of why ethical standards are necessary in research with children.

In the 1920s, the noted behaviourist John B. Watson carried out an experiment about classical conditioning with a nine-month-old called Albert (American Psychological Association, 2010). Watson observed infants become afraid in the presence of loud noises. He deduced that this fear was innate and sought to study whether the fear of loud sounds could be generalised to other objects. To do this, he introduced Albert to a white rat, masks, a rabbit and various other objects. Albert showed no fear of any of the objects. However, in order to see whether he could engender fear in Albert, Watson introduced a rat to Albert. Then, as soon as Albert approached the rat, Watson made a loud noise behind the baby's head. Obviously, Albert cried. Each time Watson introduced the rat after that, he would make a loud noise, leading Albert to cry and try to move away from the rat. Eventually, the mere sight of the rat was enough to make Albert cry. It appeared to Watson, therefore, that he had conditioned Albert to fear the rat. We have no way of knowing (and neither did Watson, who was not able to track Albert's progress) what lasting impact (if any) this experiment had on Albert.

What is wrong with scaring a baby? Nowadays, Watson's experiment would be considered unethical because researchers are duty-bound to protect the welfare of their subjects. Clearly, trying to frighten a young baby is not ethical. If research is to be ethical, subjects must give their **informed consent** to participate in the research and must have a reasonable expectation that their anonymity will be assured.

Informed consent
relates to giving participants sufficient information about research for them to make a decision about whether they want to participate or not in the study; this is an ethical principle that requires that researchers are transparent in their approach to studying people

CHECK YOUR PROGRESS

* If you want to investigate the relationship between watching violent video games and aggression in children, what is the dependent variable in this study?
* What is qualitative research?
* Imagine researchers want to study the effects of bullying on self-esteem. The researchers ask two boys to bully a smaller boy in the class so that they can record whether the smaller boy's self-esteem is lowered when he is bullied. Is this ethical? Why?

CASE STUDY

I teach a group of in-service primary-school teachers in a graduate programme at the university where I work. I have a class this afternoon, and I received the following email from one of my students to excuse herself from the lecture:

Hi Joanne, I have a bit of a problem. Gangsters are shooting in the community where I work and we were asked not to let the kids go until it has died down. I too have to travel through where they are shooting, so I may not make it to class today. Hope you understand.

Questions

1   Reread the case study 'Genie and language development' from earlier in this chapter. Now that you have read about Genie and language development, can you reflect on how you learnt language? Ask your parents or others who looked after you to tell you how you learnt to talk.

2   Now that you have been introduced to ethics in research, consider how you would approach (a) research with children and (b) findings that report on research where informed consent has not been obtained. How can researchers learn about small children, for example, in ways that are ethical?

Conclusion

South Africa has seen many changes, both politically and socially, over the past 18 years. Its society has developed from an authoritarian society built on racial inequalities into a more open, democratic society. However, South Africans still face enormous challenges in righting the wrongs of the past. The case study on the previous page featured an email from a teacher in her mid forties, who, because of gang violence in her area, could not attend a lecture that she needed to attend to complete her postgraduate degree. After what you have learnt in this chapter, you might well be asking: 'What impact does this violence have on the school children in this area?' This chapter made it clear that it can certainly be anticipated that this violence will indeed impact on the developmental trajectories of the children affected by it.

In this chapter you also learnt how to carry out research in developmental psychology, so you will be able, for example, to design a study that could uncover the relationship between violence and optimal development.

The chapter also looked at the central debates in developmental psychology. You learnt to appreciate that nature and nurture are responsible for optimal development. The chapter tracked the emergence of this central debate to the ideas of Plato and Aristotle, through the Enlightenment thinking of Descartes and Locke, to current debates in evolutionary theory.

In chapter two you will learn how to explain development using theories – frameworks that enable people to analyse the world.

References

American Psychological Association (2010). *Ethical principles of psychologists and code of conduct.* [WWW document]. URL http://www.apa.org/ethics/code/index.aspx. 2 February 2012.

Babbie, E. & Mouton, J. (2001). *The practice of social research.* Cape Town: Oxford University Press.

Barnes, Jonathan (Ed.) (1995). *The Cambridge companion to Aristotle.* Cambridge: Cambridge University Press.

Chiarelli, Antonio (1973). *Evolution of the primates: An introduction to the biology of man.* London: Academic press.

Chomsky, Noam (1965). *Aspects of the theory of syntax.* Michigan: MIT Press.

Darwin, Charles (1882). *On the origin of species by means of natural selection, or the preservation of favoured races in the struggle for life.* London: John Murray.

Descartes, René (1996). *Meditations on first philosophy* (J. Cottingham, Trans.). Cambridge: Cambridge University Press. (Original work published 1641)

Denzin, N. K. & Lincoln, Y.S. (2005). *The SAGE handbook of qualitative research.* Thousand Oaks: Sage publications.

Dobzhansky, Theodosius G. (1937). *Genetics and the evolutionary process*. New York: Columbia University Press.

Festinger, L., Reicker, H.W. & Schacter, S. (1956). *When prophecy fails.* University of Minnesota Press.

Hardman, J. (2008). New technology, new pedogogy? An Activity Theory analysis of pedagogical activity with computers. PhD thesis presented to the University of Cape Town, Cape Town.

Hardman, J. (2010). Variation in semiotic mediation across different pedagogical contexts. *Education as Change, 14*, (1), 91–106.

Henzi, Peter (1996). *Evolution: Psychology 1 resources package*. Natal: Juta.

Irwin, T.H. (2010). The Platonic Corpus. In G. Fine (Ed.). *The Oxford handbook of Plato* (p. 63–64 and 68–70). Oxford: Oxford University Press.

Kahn, Charles H. (2004). *Plato and the Socratic dialogue: The philosophical use of a literary form*. Cambridge: Cambridge University Press.

Macfarlane, D. (2011, March 29). *Mail & Guardian Online*. [WWW document]. URL http://mg.co.za/article/2011-03-29-report-portrays-a-tragic-picture-of-sas-education-system. 29 March 2012.

Muthivhi, A.E. (2008). A socio-cultural case study of the schooling system in Venda, South Africa. PhD thesis presented to the University of the Witwatersrand, Johannesburg. May 2008. Johannesburg: Wits University.

Muthivhi, A. & Broom, Y. (2009). School as cultural practice: Piaget and Vygotsky on learning and concept development in post-apartheid South Africa. *Journal of Education, 47*.

Ridley, Mark (1993). *Evolution*. Oxford: Blackwell.

Spencer-Smith, G. & Hardman, J. (2011). Investigating the impact of computer software on matric mathematics results in the EMDC East district of Cape Town: A quantitative analysis. Kenton Conference, Cape Town: October 2011.

Vygotsky, Lev S. (1978). *Mind in society: The development of higher psychological processes*. (M. Cole, V. John-Steiner, S. Scribner, & E. Souberman, Trans.). (Eds). Cambridge, MA: Harvard University Press.

CHAPTER TWO

THEORIES OF DEVELOPMENT

Joanne Hardman

CASE STUDY

Sipho is 10 years old and is in grade 5. He goes to an English-medium school, although his first language is isiXhosa. He has been referred to a psychologist for tests because he is doing badly in school. He is very disruptive and cannot finish any tasks he starts in class. He does not have many friends but often plays with his neighbour's child, who is six years old.

Sipho lives with his grandmother, who is 65 years old, and his two aunts and four nephews. They live in a two-bedroomed house in a disadvantaged area of Cape Town. He has never met his father, who separated from his mother when Sipho was eight months old. He has three younger sisters who live with his mother. His grandmother works three days a week doing ironing for a family in town. She is very seldom at home when he gets home from school. His grandmother has a grade-eight education and does not buy newspapers. She has a Bible, which she occasionally reads to him.

Psychological tests indicate that Sipho has attention deficit and hyperactivity disorder (ADHD).

LEARNING OBJECTIVES

By the end of this chapter you should be able to:

* Discuss the various theoretical positions in developmental psychology
* Develop an understanding of how a child develops into an adult
* Describe psychodynamic theory
* Understand behaviourism
* Use ecosystemic theory to situate a child in his or her wider social context
* Use socio-cultural theory to understand the influence of culture on development
* Discuss development from a biological perspective
* Situate your thinking in a theoretical perspective that accounts for development.

Introduction

Chapter one introduced you to the various debates in developmental psychology. This chapter will investigate theoretical perspectives, or ways of describing what you study.

Developmental psychologists are faced with trying to explain how children develop into adults. If researchers merely collect data on subjects that interest them, this will not tell them why or how a person comes to act the way they do. For example, imagine you are interested in bullying in schools. You collect data from naturalistic observations that indicate certain types of bullying in a school. What then? How do you explain why some children bully and others are bullied? What you need is a framework, or theory, that will help you interpret the facts.

Developmental psychology involves a very broad school of research. Psychologists adopt many different theoretical perspectives to explain empirical data. The theoretical perspective you select to explain the data will depend on your own experience and decisions about what theory best explains what you are studying. It is important to note that psychologists never approach the world without a theory: the theory with which researchers approach the world will influence what data they collect and therefore, what conclusions they can draw about the phenomena they are studying.

Consider the case study at the start of this chapter. Can you explain what is happening to Sipho? Why is it necessary to explain what is happening to Sipho? You would not be able to help him unless you had a framework that helped you to understand the challenges he faces. This chapter will discuss various ways of explaining development. These theories provide a framework with which to understand development and, consequently, to act in ways to promote optimal development.

Theories of development

This section will consider theories of development following broad categories:
- Biological views
- Psychodynamic views
- The behaviourist paradigm
- Cognitive development and learning.

Biological views

Before discussing specific theories of development, it is important to note that development necessarily happens against a biological backdrop. Recall what happens when you are afraid: your heart races and your mouth becomes dry. Fear or nervousness, which are psychological processes, produce physical responses in your body. Biological theories of development look at processes in the brain and central nervous system and study how these develop and change as a child grows.

The neuropsychological perspective is currently dominant amongst biological explanations of child development. It is well understood today that damage to certain portions of the brain can have significant developmental impacts. Neuropsychology (and neuropsychiatry, in particular) has introduced useful drug therapies for assisting certain psychological disorders related to chemical imbalances in the brain.

Psychodynamic views

One of the most well-known psychologists of the twentieth century was Sigmund Freud. He revolutionised psychology by proposing a cure – which he called the 'talking-cure' – for **hysteria**. Freud's patients presented with certain symptoms, such as paralysis, which had no biological **aetiology**. In order to explain these symptoms, Freud postulated that much of what people do in their waking life is determined by **unconscious** factors (Fancher, 1973). That is, although they think they act consciously all the time, people are in fact driven by unconscious motives. A person's unconscious is not easily brought into awareness, and functions to keep unacceptable ideas or impulses hidden from his or her conscious mind. Symptoms represent outward manifestations of unconscious, unresolved conflicts. **Repression** (the psychological process involved in keeping these impulses hidden to protect the conscious mind) fails when symptoms manifest themselves (Levy, 1996). The purpose of Freud's psychoanalysis, then, becomes trying to uncover the historical origin of the unconscious conflict through the use of the 'talking cure' (Hayes, 1996).

Freud's work showed that unconscious conflicts had their origins in a person's past, often in the person's childhood (Hayes, 1996). This realisation led him to describe a theory of development that focused on how children pass through various stages in order to reach adulthood. At each of these psychosexual stages, certain conflicts arise and have to be addressed for the child to develop optimally.

An understanding of psychoanalysis requires an appreciation of the dynamics of repressed unconscious desires. Unresolved childhood fantasies, experiences and desires do not simply disappear; they live on and strive for conscious expression. A frustrated or unresolved childhood wish or desire is invested with psychological energy. This energy continues to seek resolution and may well break through into consciousness in the manifestation of symptoms.

Freud's psychosexual stages of development

Freud proposed that children have to pass through various stages of development. At each stage, children are faced with a psychological conflict

Hysteria
hysteria was used to describe neurotic behaviour; in the nineteenth and early twentieth century, it was used almost exclusively to describe neuroses in women; hence the word 'hysteria', which relates to the womb

Unconscious
this part of the mind is not available to a person's conscious mind, yet it affects behaviour

Aetiology
refers to the cause of an illness; the root of the symptom

Repression
the psychological process involved in keeping unacceptable impulses hidden to protect the conscious mind

that they need to negotiate. Failure to negotiate the conflict will result in repression. Freud's theory is very specifically a psychosexual theory. Therefore, Freud's theory posits that instinctual libidinous desires need to be appropriately directed, through socialisation. At each stage, the child's focus is deriving pleasure from specific parts of his or her body. These pleasure zones are termed erogenous zones. The stages are as follows (see also Figure 2.1, which illustrates the stages):

- The oral stage (first year of life) sees infants' focus directed at the mouth, lips and sucking.
- The anal stage (two to four years) centres on the bowel and bladder.
- In the phallic stage (four to six years) the site of psychological interest is the penis, vagina, pubic hair, breasts, and differences between adults and children.
- In the latent stage (six to puberty) sexual feelings are dormant.
- In the genital phase (puberty to death) sexual interests mature.

While Freud's theory was extremely influential at the turn of the twentieth century, psychodynamic theory has largely moved on from his early work. Erik Erikson, a follower of Freud, constructed a theory of development that moved away from the largely medical and biological basis of Freud's theory, to account for social and cultural influences on development. Erikson still drew on Freud's notion of the unconscious

Figure 2.1 Freud's psychosexual stages of development

Oral (0–2)
Infant achieves gratification through oral activities such as feeding, thumb sucking and babbling.

Anal (2–3)
The child learns to respond to some of the demands of society (such as bowel and bladder control).

Phallic (3–7)
The child learns to realise the differences between males and females and becomes aware of sexuality.

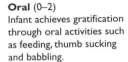

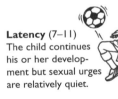

Latency (7–11)
The child continues his or her development but sexual urges are relatively quiet.

Genital (11–adult)
The growing adolescent shakes off old dependencies and learns to deal maturely with the opposite sex.

but, rather than focusing on the biological drives as the force of development, he proposed that social and cultural interaction was formative of personality (Cole, Cole & Lightfoot, 2005). He also went further than Freud by proposing that development did not end at sexual maturity (adolescence) but, rather, carried on throughout the lifespan of the person.

Erikson's psychosocial stages of development

Erikson proposed that the main aim of development was not biological survival but, rather, the formation of identity. According to him, a child passes through various stages of development, and at each stage a crisis must be negotiated. Successful negotiation of these crises develops a person's identity. The crises a child faces throughout development are not solely individual; children are shaped by other individuals, who in turn are shaped by their socio-cultural milieu (Cole, Cole & Lightfoot, 2005).

So, while maturation provides the timeline for personality development, individual cultural contexts provide different scenarios for development. Erickson's psychosocial stages of development are as follows:

- **First year – trust versus mistrust:** The first crisis an infant has to negotiate is how to trust someone to meet his or her needs.
- **Second year – autonomy versus shame and doubt:** In this stage an infant has to learn to control his or her own behaviour. Failure to meet the crisis posed here will lead to a child becoming doubtful and uncertain about him- or herself.
- **Third to sixth year – initiative versus guilt:** A child has to learn to become independent in this stage, through initiating and enjoying his or her own activities. If children are prohibited from initiating their own activities, they will begin to develop feelings of guilt for establishing their own independence.
- **Seventh year to puberty – industry versus inferiority:** In this stage a child has to learn to feel confident in his or her activities and feel competent in activities valued by others.
- **Adolescence – identity versus role confusion:** In this stage the peer group is extremely important as a child begins to develop a sense of identity in relation to his or her peer group.
- **Early adulthood – intimacy versus isolation:** The challenge here is to find an intimate life partner or risk loneliness.
- **Middle age – generativity versus stagnation:** Productivity in work enables a person to refine his or her sense of self and avoid stagnation.
- **Old age – integrity versus despair:** This is a difficult stage, when a person tries to make sense of the meaning of his or her life without becoming bitter and despairing over lost opportunities (Cole, Cole & Lightfoot, 2005).

Challenges to Freud's work

Freud's work has been challenged on various grounds.

The challenge that Freud's work is unscientific and too reductionist

Freud's work has been challenged for being unscientific and too reductionist. This type of critique does point to the difficulties Freud faced as he based his theory more on clinical impressions than on controlled empirical methods. But this type of critique does not offer a sufficiently tight academic critique of psychoanalytical methods that have had much success in treating neuroses. What this kind of critique does suggest is that Freud's work is less objective than he perhaps would have liked it to be, given his medical background.

However, it is important to note that the notion of the unconscious, as described by Freud, is a conceptual tool that can be used to understand neuroses. It is not an empirical reality existing somewhere in the brain but, rather, a concept to help psychologists explain neurotic behaviour. The notion of the unconscious has continuing explanatory use. Critiques that suggest that the unconscious is not capable of being studied empirically fail to recognise that Freud never postulated it as an empirical reality but, rather, as an explanatory principle.

The challenge to Freud's work by the feminist community

Freud has also been challenged by the feminist community over his claims about hysteria. These critiques, while interesting, often fail to situate Freud within his socio-historical context. Freud was working with women at a time when women did not have equal rights; they did not have the vote and in most cases could not work. That is, the historical climate Freud worked in was patriarchal. It is against this background, then, that psychologists need to read Freud.

The challenge that Freud's theory has limited validity

Perhaps more challenging to Freud's theory is the argument that the theory is essentially based on Freud's work with neurotic people, and that this limits the theory's validity in explaining normal development.

The challenge to Freud's theory of psychosexual development

Freud has also been critiqued on his theory of psychosexual development, most notably by Jeffrey Masson (1984) in his book *The assault on truth: Freud's suppression of the seduction theory*. Masson claims that Freud's theory of psychosexual development arises from the suppression of his earliest work, which suggested that many of Freud's neurotic clients had, in fact, been sexually abused as children, leading to neuroses in later life. Called the 'seduction theory', this portion of Freud's early work was very badly received. According to Masson, Freud chose to move away from this because of the chilly reception this theory received in medical circles.

Many have argued that Masson is incorrect in his conclusions. However, his critique was quite influential in the 1980s and 1990s and does pose some thought-provoking questions.

The behaviourist paradigm

Chapter one discussed the history of the nature versus nurture debate, illustrating how the strands of its argument were located in empiricist and rationalist philosophical traditions. Certainly the most widely used empiricist approach in the mid twentieth century was the behaviourist approach.

As chapter one mentioned, behaviourists such as John B. Watson suggested that a child is born as a blank slate or *tabula rasa* onto which life will draw: a person's empirical experiences are central in the development of his or her psychology. While developmental psychology has largely moved away from the narrowly defined behaviourist position, this theory still exerts influence in the field. It is important to understand the theory, as it describes how people learn empirical knowledge. This theory also, interestingly, underpins many adverts that seek to encourage people to buy some desired product by pairing it with either a desired lifestyle or a person the people watching the adverts aspire to be.

ACTIVITY

What do you think?

Give me a dozen healthy infants, well-formed, and my own specified world to bring them up in and I'll guarantee to take any one at random and train him to become any type of specialist I might select — doctor, lawyer, merchant-chief, and yes, even beggar-man and thief, regardless of his talents, penchants, tendencies, abilities, vocations, and race of his ancestors (Watson, 1930, p. 82).

1   Remember the nature versus nurture debate in chapter one? Where does this famous quotation from the notable behaviourist J. B. Watson situate Watson in that debate?
2   What do you think about Watson's statement?

3 Some people have argued that Watson's statement provides a liberating view of development: whatever the child brings into the world is incidental to who that child will become, given the right input. Do you think there is anything problematic with this way of thinking?
4 Imagine you were face to face with John B. Watson. Provide a counter-argument to this statement.

Classical conditioning

Ivan Petrovich Pavlov is generally regarded as the founder of behaviourism. Fascinated by the innate response (salivating) that dogs have when presented with food, Pavlov wanted to discover whether he could condition a dog to salivate in the absence of meat. He is best remembered for his work in **conditioned responses** (Pavlov, 1928).

Conditioned response response that has been learned in relation to a previously neutral stimulus

Classical conditioning involves pairing a neutral stimulus (such as a ringing bell) with an unconditional stimulus (for example meat, which evokes an instinctual response in a dog). If the ringing bell and the appearance of the meat are paired together for a sufficient amount of time, the dog will begin to associate the ringing of the bell with the appearance of meat. Eventually, the dog will begin to salivate when it hears the bell, even though no meat is paired with this ringing. That is, an unconditional stimulus (meat) elicits an unconditional response (salivating). It is possible to pair a neutral stimulus (bell) with the unconditional stimulus (meat) to elicit the response. The neutral stimulus is then termed a conditioned stimulus, which elicits a conditioned response.

Learning as a function of reinforcement: Skinner and Watson

Chapter one discussed John B. Watson's experiments using classical conditioning. There you learnt about how Watson managed to condition baby Albert to fear furry animals by pairing them with loud noises. Watson believed that children were essentially blank slates.

In contrast, B. F. Skinner, another prominent behaviourist, did not deny the existence of a mind. Rather, he focused his research on observable behaviours, because he did not want to make inferences about processes that could not be observed.

Operant conditioning a method of learning that occurs through rewarding specific behaviours that a person wants to see repeated; operant conditioning sets up an association between a behaviour and the consequence of that behaviour

Skinner is best known for his work in **operant conditioning** (Skinner, 1948). According to Skinner, behaviour that is reinforced will be repeated, and behaviour that is not reinforced will be extinguished. Hence he proposed **operant conditioning** as a mechanism for strengthening a desired behaviour through reinforcement. Reinforcement can be negative or positive. Positively reinforcing a behaviour refers to rewarding a behaviour to ensure that it is repeated. Negative reinforcement refers to reinforcing behaviour by taking away an unpleasant stimulus. The important aspect of this kind of conditioning, then, is that the desired behaviour is reinforced and, therefore, repeated.

Critiques of behaviourism

Few psychologists nowadays would advise adopting a purely behaviourist view of development, because psychologists now understand that nature and nurture are intricately interwoven. While Skinner did indeed recognise the importance of cognitive factors in development, he elected to focus his studies on observable behaviour, restricting this theory of development to external conditions.

Noam Chomsky provided what is perhaps the most famous critique of Skinner's work. Chomsky's review of Skinner's account of how language functions pointed to the fact that there are innate structures that pre-exist a child's interaction with a language context (Chomsky, 1959; Chomsky, 1965). Today, with new techniques such as functional magnetic resonance imagining (MRI), psychologists are able to observe brain processes in a way that was not available in Skinner's time.

ACTIVITY

1   Do you remember being in primary school? Did you ever get awarded stars for good work: a gold star, perhaps, for excellent work, or perhaps a silver star when you wished for a gold one? Did the star reinforce your behaviour?
2   What about negative reinforcement? What if your psychology lecturer asked you to pay R10 for every day your assignment is late? It is likely your lecturer does something like this – probably deducting 10 per cent from your assignment for every day that it is late. Well, such negative reinforcement certainly appears to motivate many students not to repeat late hand-in!

Cognitive development and learning

Piaget's stage theory

Jean Piaget is possibly the best-known and most influential developmental psychologist of the twentieth century. He approached the question of how children develop cognitively. He was interested in universal principles of development: that is, he wanted to explain developmental similarities rather than differences between children. Heavily influenced by Darwin's theory of evolution, which was discussed in chapter one, Piaget proposed that children learn through a process of biological adaptation to their world. Essentially biological in his thinking, he proposed that children develop thought through passing successfully through developmental stages.

Figure 2.2 Piaget

Unlike Freud, who theorised that children need to resolve unconscious conflicts at each developmental stage, Piaget's stage theory focuses
on how children construct knowledge through interacting with the
world. Like Freud, Piaget postulates that children pass through stages at
certain broadly defined ages, and that each stage represents a qualitative,
not merely quantitative, difference to the preceding stage.

One of Piaget's most profound contributions to the study of cognitive development is his assertion that children actively construct their
thought, through transacting with their environments. Prior to this assertion, the behaviourist notion that a child represented a *tabula rasa* held
tremendous sway in developmental circles.

ACTIVITY

*To know an object, to know an event, is not simply to look at it and make a mental
copy, or image, of it. To know an object is to act on it. To know is to modify, to transform the object, and to understand the process of this transformation, and as a
consequence to understand the way the object is constructed. An operation is thus
the essence of knowledge, it is an interiorised action which modifies the object of
knowledge (Piaget, 1964, p. 12).*

What do you think this quotation from Piaget means? Read the section below and return to this question. Give an example of coming to 'know' an object from your experience.

Piaget hypothesised that people are born with certain functions which help them to adapt to their environment. He termed these functions **assimilation** and **accommodation**. Assimilation refers to imposing existing cognitive structures onto unfamiliar knowledge in order to understand the novel information in terms of existing knowledge. Accommodation, in contrast, will happen if a person is faced with an event or object that is so unfamiliar that he or she cannot understand it using prior knowledge. This accommodation will result in changes in cognitive structures to make sense of the novel information (Miller, 1996).

These two processes, assimilation and accommodation, are continuously being balanced in a dynamic process of **equilibration** as a child develops and learns about the world. Equilibration refers to a biological imperative to maintain balance cognitively. A both realistic (accommodation) and meaningful (assimilation) rapport between subject and object is secured through this kind of balance. Assimilation and accommodation, then, are the mechanisms of equilibration.

Read the case study about a 22-month-old child named Isabella for an example of the active construction of knowledge.

Assimilation
incorporating new information into existing knowledge

Accommodation
adjusting thinking as a result of new knowledge

Equilibration
a biological imperative to maintain balance cognitively

Case study: An example of the active construction of knowledge

Isabella is 22 months old (she is, therefore, still in Piaget's sensorimotor phase of development – see below for a discussion of this stage). She has a dog. To her, all four-legged, furry animals have always been identified as 'doggie'; that is, her framework for understanding four-legged creatures is that of 'dog'. Faced with a cat for the first time, Isabella happily called with furry, four-legged creature 'doggie' and made her customary 'woof woof' sound to describe what a dog does. She assimilated the novel animal (cat) into her schema of four-legged animals (dog).

However, a cat is not a dog: it does not bark, it climbs trees, and, as Isabella found out, it moves very swiftly and, unlike her dog, scratches. How can Isabella make sense of this novel information? Some of the information clashes with her framework of what a four-legged creature does: climbing trees, for example, is not a feature of a dog's normal behaviour. She has to accommodate this new knowledge. Her framework of four-legged animals has to change now to incorporate a new creature – a cat.

The stages of development in Piaget's theory are as follows (these stages will be discussed in detail below):
- Sensorimotor stage (0–2 years of age)
- Pre-operational stage (between 2 and 7 years of age)
- Concrete operational stage (from about 7 to 11 years of age)
- Formal operational stage (older than 11 years of age).

Sensorimotor stage

The first developmental stage is the sensorimotor stage. It occurs from birth to two years of age. The central feature of this stage is the construction of knowledge based on action.

Pre-operational stage

The pre-operational stage, which occurs between two and seven years of age, sees a transition from understanding based on action to understanding based on symbolic representation (the ability to represent objects and events using mental symbols such as words or pictures). An important aspect of cognitive development in this stage is the appearance of the **semiotic function**. This refers to the child's developing ability to make something (a mental symbol, word or object) represent something that is not present (Piaget & Inhelder, 1969).

Semiotic function
a child's developing ability to make something represent something that is not present

The following are central features of the pre-operational stage (Miller, 1996):
- **Symbolic understanding:** This is an understanding based on symbols.
- **Egocentrism:** This refers to a child's inability to see a situation from a perspective other than his or her own. You can see egocentrism at play in nursery classrooms, where children engage in monologues. While they look as if they are talking to each other, in fact they are talking past each other. For an example of pre-operational monologue, read the box featuring Sipho and Nandi building a train.
- **Centration:** This occurs because the child can focus on only one aspect of a situation, to the exclusion of others.

An example of pre-operational monologue
Learning to build a train through communicative interaction
Sizwe and Nandi, pre-primary school children, are building a train using blocks of various shapes. The children are both four years old and are speaking while they work on the problem to be solved: the problem is trying to build the train that is hidden in front of Nandi in the absence of any more yellow round wheels. All the children have to use are green square and rectangular blocks. The children's words are translated from the original isiXhosa. All names used are pseudonyms.

Figure 2.3 Sizwe and Nandi, pre-primary school children, building a train using blocks of various shapes

Extract 1: Speaking in problem solving: first steps towards communicative interaction

Nandi says: 'You take this block. Green block. Uh. Green block for here and tyres'. And we can see Nandi trying to dislodge a green block which she then wants to use as a tyre for the train that is hidden in front of her. Sizwe is talking to Nandi (but also to himself!): 'The wheels is round silly!' Giggles. And tries to dislodge yellow round wheels from the truck he has in front of him. 'Not green (he seems to be referring to the square shape rather than the colour green). Did you ever see wheels like this (he points to the green blocks)? I (inaudible) wheels. Round. I take him off and then I put him. I put him here. Round wheels.' Sizwe is talking out loud while he takes the round wheels off the truck and puts them onto the train. Nandi continues for a while to fit the green square blocks to the undercarriage of the train but then emulates Sizwe and takes round wheels off the truck she has and fits them onto the train (Hardman, 2011, p. 27).

What we can see here is an example of egocentric speech. The children are not yet able to collaborate fully with each other and seem to be speaking to themselves, rather than actively communicating to solve a problem.

Concrete operational stage

The concrete operational stage runs from the ages of about 7 to 11 years, when children begin to develop a deeper understanding of operations like classification. Thinking here is still based on actual concrete situations, but it is beginning to move away from egocentrism and a child is now able to decentre. This shift from pre-operational thought to concrete operational thought is best captured in what Piaget called 'conservation experiments'.

Conservation refers to a child's ability to recognise that some properties of an object can remain constant even across physical transformations (Miller, 1996). Piaget illustrated this most famously in conservation experiments.

In a conservation experiment, the experimenter shows a child two identical glasses – glass A and glass B – which are both filled with the same amount of liquid. Then the experimenter introduces a third glass – glass C – which is shorter and wider than glass A and glass B. The experimenter pours the water from glass A into glass C. The child is then asked, 'Which glass has more water, glass B (longer and thinner) or glass C (shorter and fatter)?'

Obviously, it looks to the naked eye as if glass B has more water. Children in the pre-operational stage are unable to focus on more than one aspect of a situation. They will focus on the height of the water in the glasses and conclude that glass B has more water. However, children in the concrete operational stage will be able to say that both glasses have the same amount of water because nothing was added or taken away when water was poured from glass A into glass C.

Central features of the concrete operational stage are as follows (Miller, 1996):
- Egocentrism is absent.
- Children can classify (categorise at different levels – see the example on the next page) and conserve. They are not misled by visual appearance.
- Children can conserve because they can mentally reverse actions (reversibility; compensation; identity).

Conservation
ability to recognise that some properties of an object can remain constant even across physical transformations

- Children apply logic to actions and events. They are more flexible as they are not reliant or limited to the appearance of things. However, the children are still limited to actual (concrete) objects and events and cannot reason abstractly.

An example of classification

Figure 2.4 An example of classification using blocks that are black or white and round or square

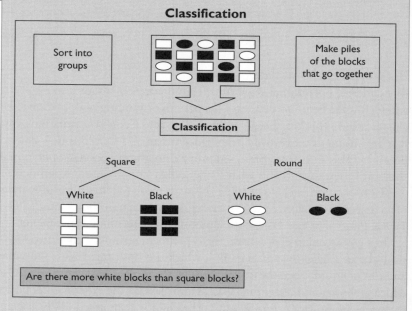

The important point about Piaget's stage theory is the *qualitative* differences between children at different stages. That is, it is not that a child in the concrete operational just knows more; rather, Piaget's point is that each developmental stage represents a *transformation* of a child's previous ways of understanding and organising information. At different developmental stages, children 'use different kinds of cognitive structures to solve problems and to adapt to new situations' (Piaget, 1964, p. 39).

Formal operational stage

Formal operational thinking is the final stage of development elaborated by Piaget, taking place at 11 years and older. This stage is characterised by a child's ability to reason abstractly and to think in a 'scientific way', that is, to develop hypotheses and reflect on causal mechanisms. A child in the formal operational stage is able to think theoretically.

ACTIVITY

... social transmission ... is fundamental ... But this factor is insufficient because the child can receive valuable information via language or via education directed by an adult only if he is in a state where he can understand this information. That is, to receive the information he must have a structure which enables him to assimilate this information (Piaget, 1964, p. 14).

Drawing on what you have learnt in this section, critically discuss this quotation.

While still extremely influential in educational psychology settings, Piaget's view of child development has been critiqued. Most significantly, recent research by neo-Vygotskians (the next section will discuss the theory of Vygotsyky) has illustrated that, with instruction, children can acquire relatively sophisticated concepts. According to Piaget, an effort to teach developmentally – that is, to develop a child's cognitive structures through instruction – would not be successful.

CHECK YOUR PROGRESS
- What are the processes of cognitive development, according to Piaget?
- What does it mean to say that intelligence is an act of equilibrium between assimilation and accommodation?

Vygotsky's socio-cultural theory

Although Vygotsky died rather early in the twentieth century (1934), his work continues to resonate strongly in the psychology of schooling. This is primarily because his work lends itself well to understanding how children learn in their cultural contexts. Of particular interest for South Africa is Vygotsky's focus on how mind is necessarily social.

The foundation of Vygotskian thought is captured in his '**general genetic law**', which states that higher cognitive functions – thinking, reasoning and problem-solving – begin as real relations between people, **interpsychologically**, before being internalised **intrapsychologically**. That is, a child's mind develops first as a relationship between the child and the significant other before turning inwards and becoming part of the child's psychology. This places a significant emphasis on the nature of interaction (Hardman, 2011). How a child is taught something will lead to how that child comes to think about that thing.

The process whereby external meanings become internal ones is called **mediation** (Vygotsky, 1978). Mediation refers to the active guidance of a more expert peer or teacher which moves a child from a state of not

General genetic law
foundation of Vygotskian thought; law that states that higher cognitive functions begin as real relations between people before being internalised

Intrapsychologically
the process of cultural development that refers to the internalisation of knowledge learnt interpsychologically

Interpsychologically
the process of cultural development that refers to learning as happening first between people

Mediation
active guidance of a more expert peer or teacher, which moves a child from a state of not knowing to a state of knowing

knowing to a state of knowing. Mediation is structured and is always aimed at developing what Vygotsky refers to as higher cognitive functions (HCF). These are the uniquely human structures that develop throughout a child's development. HCFs will not develop unless a child is actively taught them.

ACTIVITY

Vygotsky in South Africa

Vygotsky's work was developed in the 1920s and early 1930s in Russia. This was a time of immense social and cultural change in that country; the Tsarist regime had recently been toppled and a new, communist political structure was engaging in transforming Russia. At that time, Russia was a very unequal society, with a minority who were literate and well off and a majority who were poor and illiterate. Russia was also going through enormous social changes. This situation is not unlike that in South Africa currently. Vygotsky was interested in explaining cognitive differences that arose not from innate structures, but from immersion in different cultural contexts.

1   Why is Vygotsky potentially useful for South Africa today?
2   Go back to chapter one and read its opening case study again. Can you answer this question more fully now?

The zone of proximal development as a 'teachable' space

Vygotsky indicated in his work that learning, true learning (which leads to cognitive change), happens in what he called the zone of proximal development (ZPD). This is the space between what a child can accomplish on his or her own and what he or she can accomplish with the help of a more culturally knowledgeable peer or teacher. That is, mediation, structured guidance, takes place in the ZPD. Here are the buds of what will later bear the fruit of internalised knowledge.

It is important to remember that what is developed in the ZPD is a very specific kind of conceptual knowledge: what Vygotsky (1978) referred to as 'scientific concepts'.

Scientific and everyday concepts

To illustrate the difference between what can be learnt empirically and without mediation, and what needs to be learnt through mediation, Vygotsky (1997) made a distinction between, firstly, everyday, empirical or spontaneous concepts and, secondly, scientific concepts. Some commentators have referred to scientific concepts as 'schooled' concepts (Hedegaard, 1998; Daniels, 2001). Scientific concepts should not be thought of as relating narrowly to the field of science, but, rather, they should be seen as representing those kinds of concepts about which a person needs instruction in order to acquire. In the following quotation, Vygotsky explains how both the everyday and the scientific concepts are required for a child to understand his or her world:

The formation of concepts develops simultaneously from two directions: from the direction of the general and the particular ... the development of a scientific concept begins with the verbal definition. As part of an organised system, this verbal definition descends to concrete; it descends to phenomena which the concept represents. In contrast, the everyday concept tends to develop outside any definite system; it tends to move upwards toward abstraction and generalisation ... the weakness of the everyday concept lies in its incapacity for abstraction, in the child's incapacity to operate on it in a voluntary manner ... the weakness of the scientific concept lies in its verbalism, in its insufficient saturation with the concrete (Vygotsky, 1987, p. 163, 168, 169).

It might be said, then, that scientific concepts are learnt in school and require specific forms of instruction for a child to learn them. Scientific concepts are meaningful, and their meaning is not idiosyncratic and personal but, rather, social and general. Vygotsky's distinction between the 'sense' and 'meaning' of a word brings out the complex task of acquiring scientific concepts:

A word's sense is the aggregate of all the psychological facts that arise in our consciousness as a result of the word. Sense is a dynamic fluid, and complex formation which has several zones that vary in their stability. Meaning is only one of these zones of sense that the word acquires in the context of speech. It is the most stable, unified and precise of these zones. In different contexts, a word's sense changes. In contrast, meaning is a comparatively fixed and stable point, one that remains constant with all the changes of the word's sense that are associated with its use in various contexts (Vygotsky, 1987, p. 275–6).

How, then does a child go about acquiring a scientific concept? Vygotsky (1987) was quite clear that instruction was necessary for this process. The activity headed 'Mediation of scientific concepts' and the box headed 'What is mediated' contain important quotations in this regard.

ACTIVITY

Mediation of scientific concepts

The following quotation throws light on the concept of mediation of scientific concepts:

> *The development of the scientific ... concept, a phenomenon that occurs as part of the educational process, constitutes a unique form of systematic co-operation between the teacher and the child. The maturation of the child's higher mental functions occurs in this co-operative process, that is, occurs through the adult's assistance and participation ... In a problem involving scientific concepts, he must be able to do in collaboration with the teacher something that he has never done spontaneously ... we know that the child can do more in collaboration than he can do independently (Vygotsky, 1987, p. 168, 169)*

1 What portion of this quotation refers to mediation?
2 Can you spot any references to the ZPD in this quotation?

What is mediated?

Note, in the following quotation, how Vygotsky specifically indicates that mediation in the ZPD leading to the development of scientific concepts is to be distinguished from training in skills, such as typing:

> *We have seen that instruction and development do not coincide. They are two different processes with very complex interrelationships. **Instruction is only useful when it moves ahead of development**. When it does, it impels or awakens a whole series of functions that are in a stage of maturation lying in the zone of proximal development. **This is the major role of instruction in development.** This is what distinguishes the instruction of the child from the training of animals. **This is also what distinguishes instruction of the child which is directed toward his full development from instruction in specialised, technical skills such as typing or riding a bicycle.** The formal aspect of each school subject is that in which the influence of instruction on development is realized. Instruction would be completely unnecessary if it merely utilized what had already matured in the developmental process, if it were not itself a source of development (Vygotsky, 1987, p. 212) (emphasis added by author of this chapter).*

Vygotsky (1978; 1987) conveys a sense of how learning is not solely a maturational process, but that it is a fundamentally social and cultural practice.

Case study: How does mediation happen?

What follows is an extract taken from a grade 6 mathematics lesson in an underprivileged school on a farm 120 kilometres outside Cape Town in the Western Cape. The teacher, Mr Botha, has just been teaching a lesson on fractions and is about to move on to ask the students to practice what he has been teaching through completing an exercise. The exchange took place in Afrikaans (the language of instruction in the school and the first language of the students). It has been translated into English.

Teacher: Question? [Begins to hand out worksheets].

Wayne: Explain the denominator again sir. [Puts up his hand]

Teacher: Right, explain the denominator again.

Come let's go further. [Gets another apple]

Now, what is this? [Holds up an apple]

Students: Whole

Teacher: Whole.

And I cut it exactly, exactly, in how many parts?

How many parts are there?

Students: Two

Teacher: Now, my denominator tells me how many parts I have divided my whole into. [Holds up parts]

In this case, it's two. [Holds up parts]

So my denominator in this case will be?

Students: Two

Teacher: Two.

Teacher: You are clever

You are clever! [smiling]

But these … pieces show me, if I put them together, they are my whole. [Puts pieces together again]

But I want to know, what is my denominator?

And my denominator is going to tell me into how many parts

Students: Parts …

Teacher: And Bokaas told us very nicely that denominator stands ['staan']

Students: Under

Teacher: Under.

Denominator tells us how many parts we have (Hardman, 2008, p. 123).

ACTIVITY

How does mediation happen?

Draw on the Vygotskian concepts covered in the chapter to explain what Mr Botha is attempting to accomplish in the lesson featured in the case study headed 'How does mediation happen?'.

Bronfennbrenner's ecosystemic theory

While Vygotsky's work provides the basis for understanding cultural development in context, it is not well developed beyond the notion of mediation. Drawing on Bronfenbrenner's (1979) ecosystemic theory allows a more nuanced understanding of the context surrounding the child as incorporating the following: the individual child; the microsystem; the mesosystem; exosystem; macrosystem; and chronosystem, as shown in Figure 2.5 (also see Figure 11.1).

This theory focuses on how individuals develop in context. It views different levels and groupings of social context as systems, which are interactive. The functioning of the 'whole' depends on the interaction of the parts (systems). A system you will be familiar with is a school; it is composed of various 'parts' (students, teachers, parents, management, administrators, etc.). For the system to function well, all elements must function. So, for example, if students disrupt classes, they impact on the entire school's functioning. Within systems there are various subsystems (for example, the governing body is a system within the school system). A system may also interact with other systems outside it (for example, the school may have a partnership with a university). At the core of systemic theory is the understanding that cause-and-effect relationships are viewed as cyclical. That is, when one part of a system impacts on another part of that system, the effects are not unidirectional. For example, a student may blame a teacher when the student fails a course; this unidirectional way of thinking doesn't take into account the student's role in failing the test (he or she may not have learned the work). Sometimes cycles of relating become so entrenched that they are repeated in patterns.

Figure 2.5 Diagram illustrating Bronfenbrenner's (1979) ecosystemic theory

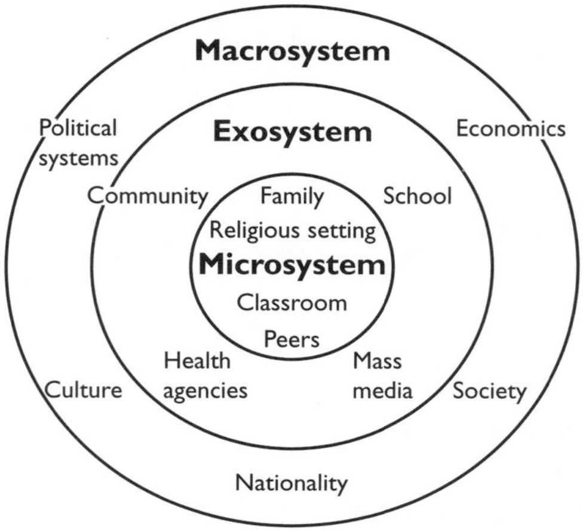

Source: Adapted from Bronfenbrenner, 1979

Given its focus on viewing the child as part of a larger system, this theory is particularly popular in family-therapy circles. A child presenting with oppositional behaviour, for example, will be engaged with as part of a wider system of family and community. In this sense, systems thinking is non-blaming, as it looks at multiple factors that impact on behaviour, rather than seeking to isolate one cause or allocate blame. Of course, this does not mean that individuals, communities or organisations do not own responsibility for their behaviour; it merely indicates that locating blame in any one space is futile. A consequence of this type of view of relationships as interactive and circular (rather than linear) is the understanding that interventions must be more complex, multi-level, holistic, and preventive. Chapter 11 will investigate how to use this model to explain violence.

CASE STUDY

Revisiting the opening case study about Sipho

Consider once more the case study about Sipho at the start of this chapter. How do the perspectives discussed in this chapter relate to the opening case study?

Biological

The biological paradigm seeks to explain development in terms of biological factors. So, in reference to Sipho, this perspective would describe his behaviour in terms of a neurological problem: attention deficit and hyperactivity disorder. This has been shown to be effectively treated with drug therapy: most recently and successfully it has been treated with the drug Ritalin. The question that now arises is: if Sipho takes Ritalin, will he be more successful in school? Reliance on the biological perspective alone does not inform psychologists about how the other factors in Sipho's life (for example living with an elderly grandmother, or attending a school where the medium of instruction is not his first language) shape his developmental trajectory.

Psychodynamic

A psychodynamic perspective would locate Sipho in the latent psychosexual phase. It would look at any potential unconscious conflicts that might have arisen in earlier stages, especially as Sipho's father was absent from his eighth month of life, and Sipho does not appear to have much male influence in his life.

Socio-cultural

Rather than locating Sipho's learning difficulties purely biologically, the socio-cultural theoretical perspective would take into account the various social, cultural and historical factors that have shaped Sipho's trajectory. What are these? Sipho comes from a disadvantaged community in Cape Town and lives with his elderly grandmother. There are not many books in the house; it is known that books are very important cognitive resources. Historically, the community that Sipho comes from has been marginalised by apartheid, and it continues to live in the long shadow cast by the inequality of that system. All these factors impact on Sipho's developmental trajectory. His learning problems cannot be located solely biologically, because this would fail to take account of other determining influences on his development.

Cognitive

Sipho is a concrete operational thinker. He needs to have access to concrete examples of what it is he is learning. Immersion in various different activities will help him to develop fully.

Behaviourist

Behaviourists would recommend a behavioural schedule for Sipho that can keep him focused on his work. This type of schedule would reward desired behaviour to ensure it is repeated.

Systems theory

Sipho's behaviour needs to be understood in the context of his interactions with his family and the wider community. His peer relations appear to be affecting his behaviour, as does his family unit. An intervention would involve his family as well as possibly widening his circle of friends. One suggestion could be an after-school club, where his energies can be directed into sport, for example.

Questions

1   Think about how you developed cognitively. Do you think you passed through the stages Piaget mentions? Can you remember anything from, for example, the concrete operational stage of your development? Write a few sentences about your memories of that time.

2   Now you have covered developmental theories, think back to the case study about Sipho at the start of the chapter. Imagine you are faced in your practice with a child who presents with learning difficulties. How would you go about working with that child, given what you have learnt in this chapter?

Conclusion

This chapter looked at how various theoretical perspectives inform how developmental psychologists answer questions about development.

The biological perspective tends to locate the aetiology of psychological distress within the brain. This is useful for helping psychologists to understand how a person's psychological world is influenced by brain chemistry.

The psychodynamic perspective explains development in terms of psychosexual stages. According to this perspective, a child needs to negotiate certain crises at each stage in order to avoid unresolved unconscious conflicts.

Behaviourists focus predominantly on observable behaviour. The behaviourist approach has been used successfully in schools to manage behaviour and to shape learning in terms of shaping behaviour.

Piaget proposed a radical departure from the behaviourist paradigm by suggesting that children actively construct knowledge through transacting with their environment. While he recognised the importance of the social and cultural context in development, Piaget viewed social and cultural context as necessary, but not sufficient, in explanation of development.

Vygotsky's work added depth to Piaget's perspective by highlighting the social, historical and cultural embeddedness of human consciousness.

References

Bronfenbrenner, Urie (1979). *The ecology of human development: Experiments by nature and design*. Cambridge, MA: Harvard University Press.

Chomsky, N. (1959). Review of Verbal Behaviour by B.F. Skinner. *Language, 35*, 26–58.

Chomsky, Noam. (1965). *Aspects of a theory of syntax*. Cambridge, MA: MIT Press.

Cole, M., Cole, S. & Lightfoot, C. (2005). *The development of children*. New York: Worth.

Daniels, Harry (2001). *Vygotsky and pedagogy*. New York: Routledge.

Fancher, Raul (1973). *Psychoanalytic psychology: The development of Freud's thought*. Michigan: Norton.

Hardman, J. (2007). Investigating pedagogical practices in relation to English language proficiency at pre-school level. Unpublished Ithemba project report (p. 1–27). Cape Town.

Hardman, J. (2008). New technology, new pedagogy? An Activity Theory analysis of pedagogical activity with computers. PhD thesis presented to the University of Cape Town, Cape Town.

Hardman, J. (2011). The developmental impact of communicative interaction. In D. D. Hook, B. Franks & M. Bauer (Eds). *Communication, culture and social change: The social psychological perspective* (p. 25–45). London: Palgrave.

Hayes, Grahame (1996). *Freud: Psychology resource pack*. Natal: Juta.

Hedegaard, M. (1998). Situated learning and cognition: Theoretical learning and cognition. *Mind, Culture and Activity, 5*, (2), 114–126.

Levy, Donald (1996). *Freud among the philosophers: The psychoanalytic unconscious and its philosophical critics*. New Haven, CT: Yale University Press.

Masson, Jeffrey (1984). *The assault on truth: Freud's suppression of the seduction theory*. New York, NY: Farrar Straus & Giroux.

Miller, Ronald (1996). *Piaget: Psychology I resource pack.* Durban: Juta.

Pavlov, Ivan P. (1928) *Lectures on conditioned reflexes, I.* London: Lawrence and Wishart.

Piaget, J. & Inhelder, B. (1969). *The psychology of the child.* London: Routledge and Kegan Paul.

Piaget, Jean (1964). *Six psychological studies.* New York: Vintage.

Skinner, B.F. (1948). Superstition in the pigeon. *Journal of Experimental Psychology, 38,* 168–172.

Vygotsky, Lev S. (1978). *Mind in society: The development of higher psychological processes.* (M. Cole, V. John-Steiner, S. Scribner, & E. Souberman, Trans.). (Eds). Cambridge, MA: Harvard University Press.

Vygotsky, Lev S. (1987). *The collected works of L.S. Vygotsky, I: Problems of general psychology.* (R. W. Rieber & A. S. Cartou). (Eds). N. Minick (Trans.). New York: Plenum Press.

Vygotsky, Lev S. (1997). *Educational psychology.* Boca Ratan: St Lucie Press.

Watson, John B. (1930). *Behaviourism.* Chicago: University of Chicago Press.

PART II

STAGES OF DEVELOPMENT

CHAPTER THREE

PRENATAL

Peter Hepper and Mokgadi Moletsane

CASE STUDY

Mary is forty years old, is married and has four children. She is unemployed and receives a government grant for her children. Her husband is a farm worker and does not earn much. Mary is three months pregnant, expecting their fifth child. Her pregnancy was not planned and she is contemplating an abortion, because her youngest child is only 18 months old. Mary's husband is against abortion and is happy that they will receive an additional grant by having another child.

Mary and her husband like to drink wine and smoke cigarettes. After discovering that she was pregnant, Mary continued drinking and smoking. When Mary and her husband are drunk, they have a tendency to fight and shout at each other.

The family gets milk and soup weekly from the nearby clinic, because the social workers discovered that sometimes they do not have food and their children go to school hungry.

Mary's husband abuses her verbally and physically. Mary has been admitted a few times to the nearby hospital for stress-related illnesses as well as physical injuries due to the beatings. She does not want to divorce her husband, because divorce is against her culture and beliefs, which in Sesotho are expressed as '*Lebitla la mosadi ke bogadi*', which roughly means 'Till death do us part'.

LEARNING OBJECTIVES

By the end of this chapter you should be able to:
- Show knowledge of the various prenatal stages
- Understand the beginning of human life
- Understand how the cells are formed and divided
- Distinguish between genetic and chromosomal abnormalities
- Understand the dangers of smoking and drinking alcohol during pregnancy
- Show knowledge of various environmental factors that can be harmful to an unborn child
- Understand the process of childbirth.

Introduction

Every human being goes through a sequence of phases in the course of life. This chapter focuses only on the prenatal developmental phase.

Life-cycle theories

Life-cycle theories, such as that suggested in the opening sentence of this introduction, make the following three assumptions (Kaplan & Sadock, 1988):

- **Development occurs in a sequence of successive, clearly defined stages:** This is the fundamental assumption of all cycle theories. These theories consider the sequence to be invariant – that is, it occurs in a constant order in every life, whether or not all stages are in fact completed.

- **The epigenetic principle applies:** The **epigenetic principle** of Erik Erikson (whose theory was discussed in chapter two) maintains that each stage of the cycle is characterised by events or crises that must be satisfactorily resolved in order for development to proceed smoothly. If such crises are not resolved within a given life period, the epigenetic model states that all subsequent stages reflect that failure in the form of physical, cognitive, social or emotional maladjustment.

- **Each stage contains a distinguishing dominant feature, complex of features or crisis point:** This dominant feature, complex of features or crisis point distinguishes the phase from phases that either precede or follow it.

Epigenetic principle
each stage of the life cycle is characterised by events or crises that must be satisfactorily resolved for development to proceed smoothly

The prenatal period

The **prenatal period** on which this chapter focuses is one of the most fascinating, yet least well understood, stages of human development. Its end is marked by a beginning: the birth of a baby. In most societies a newborn is given an age of zero, as if to imply that nothing of importance has occurred before this. But, as this chapter will demonstrate, the prenatal period is important for human development.

The prenatal period is the most rapid phase of development of a human life, beginning with a single cell and ending with a newborn baby emerging into the world. For many years, the prenatal period was viewed as simply one of growth and maturation, a time during which the body and organs were formed – in this context, the term 'maturation' refers to those aspects of development that are primarily under genetic control. Thus, development during this time was considered as proceeding largely under genetic control and immune to external influences.

However, as technology has advanced and scientists have become more sophisticated in examining the fetus, it has become clear that development

Prenatal period
the period beginning at conception and ending at birth

during the prenatal period is far from a simple question of genetically determined growth. Environmental agents may adversely affect the development of the fetus. Moreover, the environment may determine the functional capacity of the organs of the body. The actions and reactions of the baby will shape its own development. This chapter will provide an introduction to prenatal development and to how prenatal development acts as a foundation on which all subsequent development builds. The chapter will examine the physical development of an individual before birth. It will explore the impact of the environment on development. It will discuss the behaviour of the fetus and how this behaviour may be important for future development. It will consider the processes initiating birth and the reflexes of the newborn infant.

Taking into account the influence of culture

Culture has a significant influence on people's thoughts, feelings and behaviours, as well as over how they define health, growth (Bojuwoye, 2003), births and life cycles. In African culture, a person has a strong connection with his or her ancestors. The ancestors are important, especially with regard to such things as families, marriages, and births. In the event that a developmental stage is characterised by crises such as miscarriage or illness during pregnancy, these crises may be interpreted as follows: 'the ancestors turned their backs on the pregnant woman and her family', which is expressed in, for example, Sesotho as *'Ba fase ba re furaletse'* and isiZulu as *'Abaphansi ba si folathele'*.

Such crises might be regarded as resulting from failure to perform the traditional practices. The failure to perform traditional practices or rituals as instructed by ancestors is expressed in, for example, Sesotho as *'Go lahla maseko/setso'* and isiZulu as *'ukulahla amasiko in isiZulu'* (Kekae-Moletsane, 2004).

Example
Due to Western cultural influences, people might not believe in African rituals. This, according to African traditional healers and counsellors, might anger the ancestors and cause ill-health or other types of problems in a person's life (Kekae-Moletsane, 2004).

ACTIVITY

1   Critically analyse the three assumptions of life-cycle theories.
2   Explain how African culture, or any culture with which you are familiar, can play a significant role in human development and childbirth.
3   Critically analyse the connection between ancestors and health.

Key issues

Three key, related issues have dominated discussion of the prenatal period:
- The nature versus nurture debate
- The question of whether development is continuous or discontinuous
- The function of fetal behaviour.

The nature versus nurture debate

Chapters one and two have already introduced and referred to this debate. A dominating question has been this: how much is development during the prenatal period determined by genes and how much by the environment?

Traditionally, the prenatal period has been viewed as largely under the control of genes that direct the physical growth of the individual. However, environmental influences contribute more to development than was previously thought. Development during the prenatal period is an interaction between genes and environment.

The question of whether development is continuous or discontinuous

For many years, the event of birth was considered a new beginning, and events before were ignored and not considered as having any meaning for future development. However, this view is now changing. As progress has been made in understanding the abilities of the newborn, the question of when newborn abilities begin has arisen.

It is logically possible, although unlikely, that at the moment of birth the behavioural, sensory, and learning abilities of the newborn are suddenly switched on. It is more plausible that these abilities have their origins in the prenatal period, which implies a continuity of development across the birth period.

The function of fetal behaviour

Questions regarding the function of fetal behaviour have arisen as studies have begun to unravel the behavioural abilities of a fetus. Why does the fetus exhibit the behaviour and reactions it does? Are they a by-product of its maturation, or do they serve a function? These questions will be discussed as this chapter describes the prenatal development of the fetus.

Physical development

There are many cultural myths about the beginning of life and origin of children. Some parents find it difficult to tell their children about where children come from. When asked about this by children, some parents – and this was especially so in the past – reply that the babies are delivered by aeroplane or stork. It was, and can still be, embarrassing for some parents to tell their children the truth about their formation and the birth process.

The three stages of the prenatal period

The prenatal period, beginning at conception and ending at birth, is divided into three stages:
* The conceptual or germinal period
* The embryonic period
* The fetal period (Moore & Persuad, 2003).

The germinal period

The **germinal period** begins with the fertilisation of the egg by the sperm and concludes with the establishment of the pregnancy, approximately two weeks later. At ovulation, a mature egg is released from the ovary and enters the fallopian tube. Sperm travel up the tube to meet the egg, and fertilisation takes place in the fallopian tube.

Germinal period
first stage of the prenatal period; starts with fertilisation of the egg by the sperm and ends with the establishment of the pregnancy

The fertilised egg (the zygote, a single cell) now begins to divide. The first division to produce two cells takes place 24–36 hours after fertilisation. The cells divide, first to form a ball of cells (the morula), and then, with the formation of a cavity within the morula, the blastocyst. The cells, in the course of dividing, travel down the fallopian tube and enter the womb, where the blastocyst implants itself into the wall of the uterus (five to six days after fertilisation).

During the next five to seven days, the blastocyst establishes a primitive placenta and circulation. In this way it ensures the supply of nutrients and oxygen essential for continued development. Two weeks after fertilisation, pregnancy is established.

As well as developing a placenta, the blastocyst must also ensure pregnancy continues, and it secretes hormones, for two purposes:
* First, to prevent menstruation and thus stop the shedding of the lining of the uterus and consequent loss of the pregnancy
* Second, to prevent the mother's immune system from attacking the embryo or fetus.

Things can, however, go wrong during this process. The fertilisation process may occur in the abdominal cavity or the ovary (Mackay, 1988). This is an example of primary abdominal or ovarian ectopic pregnancy.

With ectopic pregnancy, the fertilised ovum embeds in the tube, having failed to reach its uterine destination. According to African traditional healers, this type of occurrence can be due to, for example, *boloi* in Sesotho or *ubuthakathi* in isiZulu. This can be described as sorcery or witchcraft or the use of superhuman power to harm or even kill someone, usually an enemy (Kekae-Moletsane, 2004).

ACTIVITY

1   Critically discuss why the process of 'conception' is regarded as the beginning of life.
2   Distinguish between the possible biological and African traditional causes of ectopic pregnancy.

Multiple conceptions

Although most babies are conceived singly, multiple births of varying numbers do occur. It is well known that the techniques used to treat infertility increase the incidence of multiple conceptions; 10 per cent of all fertilisations at the fertility clinic of the University of Bloemfontein lead to twins (Louw & Louw, 2007). Factors that may increase the prevalence of twins are a family history of twins, high maternal age, and large maternal size.

What leads to multiple conceptions?

In the case of identical (monozygotic) twins, triplets and other multiple births, the zygote divides into two or more separate entities after the ovum has been fertilised by the sperm. Each of the developing organisms then has the same genetic material, and the children should therefore be identical in those characteristics determined by genetic factors.

The embryonic period

Embryonic period
second stage of the prenatal period, beginning during the middle of the second week and concluding at the end of the eighth week

Embryo
an organism in the early stages of growth and differentiation, from fertilisation to the beginning of the third month of pregnancy (in humans); after that point in time, an embryo is called a fetus

The **embryonic period** begins during the middle of the second week and concludes at the end of the eighth week, at which time the physical appearance of the embryo is clearly human (see Figure 3.1). It is during this time that all the major organs of the body begin to form. It is a time of specialisation, when cells divide and differentiate to form specific organs, for example the heart and lungs. One of the mysteries of development is how cells 'know' to become a heart or lung cell, given that they are all identical at the start of the differentiation process. The local environment of surrounding cells and chemical messages is undoubtedly important, but exactly how one cell becomes a toenail, another a hair, is unknown.

During this period the individual is called an **embryo**. The heart, although only two-chambered, begins to beat, and blood is circulated around the embryo by the end of the third week. This enables the removal of waste and the acquisition of nutrients. As all the body's organs begin

Figure 3.1 At the end of the eighth week, at the conclusion of the embryonic period, the physical appearance of the embryo is clearly human

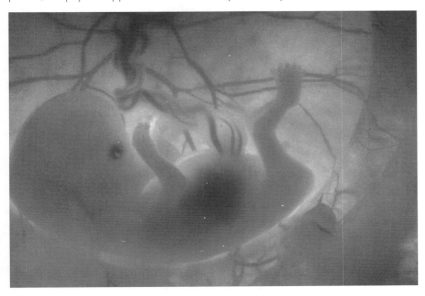

to form during this period, it is considered the most critical stage of development.

The umbilical cord and the placenta develop early during the embryonic stage. The umbilical cord is the 'lifeline' that connects the embryo to the placenta. Oxygen and nutrients from the mother pass through the umbilical cord to the embryo. The placenta is a structure that grows on the inner wall of the uterus and supplies the mentioned oxygen and nourishment to the embryo. It also removes embryonic waste.

The fetal period

The **fetal period** follows from the end of the embryonic period, beginning at nine weeks and ending with the onset of labour and birth of the baby. The individual is referred to as a **fetus** during this period.

The period is marked by the continued development and differentiation of structures that emerged during the embryonic period. Basic structures that were laid down in the embryonic period are refined and grow to their final form. Very few new structures appear. Particularly noticeable is the rapid rate of growth during the third and fourth month, with the fetus growing from about 2.5 cm at 8 weeks to 13–15 cm at 16 weeks. It is during this period that the origins of motor, sensory, and learning behaviour are to be found (as will be discussed in due course).

Fetal period
third stage of the prenatal period, following from the end of embryonic period, beginning at nine weeks, and ending with onset of labour and birth of baby

Fetus
an unborn offspring, from the embryo stage (the end of the eighth week after conception, when the major structures have formed) until birth

During the third month after conception, the penis and scrotum of the male fetus and the labia of the female fetus appear. The male sexual organs develop faster than those of the female. During this month, the connection is formed between the nervous system and the muscles, with the result that spontaneous movement of the arms and legs occurs.

During the fourth month, the face of the fetus becomes more human. The body lengthens so that the head is no longer out of proportion to the body. The mother is able to feel the movements of the fetus. During the fifth month, the movement of the fetus becomes stronger. By the sixth month, the eyes are fully formed and they look about in all directions.

The seventh month is a very important milestone in the development of the fetus. The seventh month is boundary between survival or not outside the uterus. There is a fairly strong possibility that the child will be able to survive should he or she be born. This is so because the fetus's nervous system, circulatory system, respiratory system and other body systems are reasonably well developed.

During the eighth month, fatty tissue is formed beneath the fetus's skin to protect it against the temperature change that will occur at birth. Development and maturation continue during the ninth month. More fatty tissue is formed, and the heart beats faster. More waste matter is excreted, and the body systems function more effectively. Antibodies are transferred from the mother to the child in order to reduce the risk of the child catching disease. The fetus begins to change its position; the head is situated in a downward position in preparation for the birth process.

Principles that guide prenatal development

Three major principles seem to guide prenatal development:
- **Development proceeds in a cephalocaudal direction (from head to foot):** That is, at any specific time, structures near the head are more developed than those near the toes.
- **Development proceeds from the basic to the more specialised:** Thus, organs do not initially appear as a miniature version of their final form. Rather, they first develop their basic characteristics, and then detail is added as development proceeds. For example, the heart is initially a two-chambered structure, and its final four-chambered form develops later.
- **Development proceeds in order of importance:** Thus, development begins with the 'more important' organs for survival, and the less important ones develop later. For this reason, the brain and heart are amongst the first organs to develop.

Brain development

The brain begins its development at 18 days after fertilisation. It is one of the slowest organs to develop, with development continuing for many years after birth. The relative proportion of brain to body decreases as development proceeds; the brain comprises some 25 per cent of body weight in a 9-week fetus, 10 per cent in a newborn, and only 2 per cent in an adult.

The brain develops from a layer of cells from the embryonic disc, the neural plate. This plate folds to form the neural tube, which closes, beginning in the middle and progressing to each end. Look at Figure 3.2, which illustrates this.

Figure 3.2 shows the following:
- At approximately nine days, the blastocyst has nearly fully implanted itself into the endometrium (see 'a' in Figure 3.2). The embryonic disc forms between the primary yolk sac and amniotic cavity. The individual develops from the cells of the embryonic disc. Initially formed as a layer of two cells thick, the embryonic disc undergoes a process of **gastrulation**. This begins at the end of the first week and continues to the third week, by which time three layers of cells, the primary germ layers, are formed: the ectoderm, mesoderm, and endoderm.
- At around 16–18 days (see 'b' to 'd' in Figure 3.2), cells in the ectoderm thicken to form the neural plate (see 'b'). A groove appears in the neural plate at around 18 days (see 'c'), and begins to close over,

Gastrulation
the development of the gastrula in lower animals and the formation of the three germ layers in the embryo of humans and higher animals

Figure 3.2 Formation of the neural tube

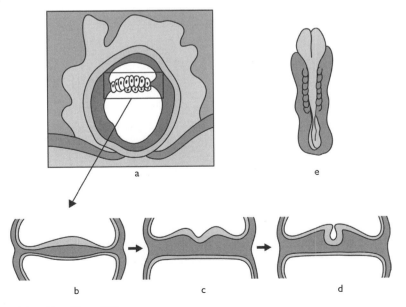

Source: Adapted from Moore, 1988

forming the neural tube (see 'd'). The walls of the neural tube will thicken and form the neuroepithelium, from which all the cells of the brain – neurons and glia – develop.

- A view of the embryo and closure of the neural tube in embryo at around 22 days (see 'e' in Figure 3.2). Closure of the tube begins in the middle and moves to each end. The neural tube is fully closed by the end of the fourth week. Failure to close properly may lead to defects such as spina bifida (see chapter 12).

Neural tube defects
a group of birth defects that affect the backbone and sometimes the spinal cord

Neural tube defects arise as a result of the failure of the neural tube to close properly. Examples of such neural tube defects are spina bifida or anencephaly. The neural tube has closed by the fourth week, and the walls begin to thicken (Müller & O'Rahilly, 2004). The walls of the neural tube contain progenitor cells which will give rise to the neurons and glia cells of the brain.

The development of the brain may be considered at two levels:

- First, at the gross level considering how the neural tube develops to form the main structures of the brain, hindbrain, midbrain, and forebrain.
- Second, at the micro level examining how the complex organisation of cells within the brain is achieved.

The development of the brain at gross level

Development of the brain

The brain begins its development following the closure of the neural tube. The rostral end, destined to become the brain, enlarges to form three swellings, the forebrain, the midbrain and the hindbrain.

During the fourth week the forebrain further subdivides into the diencephalon and telencephalon. Towards the end of the fourth week the hindbrain divides into the metencephalon and myelencephalon.

By the fifth week this five-part structure of the brain is clearly visible. Although much more complexity is added as the brain develops, this basic five-part organisation remains throughout the rest of life.

By the eleventh week the telencephalon has greatly developed and covered the dienecephalon to form the cerebral hemispheres. Although the cerebral hemispheres are initially smooth in appearance, future development will see a massive increase in their surface area. The cerebral hemispheres become folded and assume their adult-like appearance, with many grooves (sulci) and convolutions (gyri).

Look at Figure 3.3, which shows the development of the brain at gross level. The hindbrain, the midbrain, and the forebrain are formed during the fourth week, as one end of the neural tube expands to form three primary vesicles (Müller & O'Rahilly, 2004). The forebrain further subdivides during the fifth week into the

Figure 3.3 Development of the brain

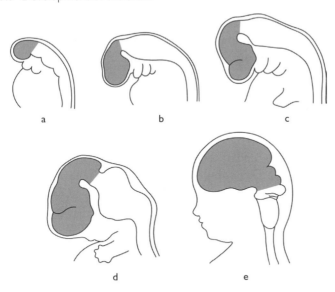

Source: Adapted from Carlson, 1994

telencephalon and diencephalon. The telencephalon gives rise to the neocortex (cerebral cortices).

The hindbrain and brain stem develop first, followed by the midbrain (Mai & Ashwell, 2004). This sequence probably reflects the need for basic biological functions controlled by the hindbrain and forebrain – for example breathing and digestion – to be operational at birth. The cerebral cortices involved in mental processing (often called the gray matter) develop later, a process that continues well after birth.

The development of the brain at micro level

At the micro level, all the neurons a person will ever possess have been generated by the end of the second trimester (Caviness et al., 1996). Between the tenth and twenty-sixth weeks, cells are produced at an extremely rapid rate; up to 250 000 cells are produced each minute. The adult brain contains an estimated 100 billion cells.

Initially there is massive overproduction of cells, and part of the development of the brain includes natural death of cells. Although mainly occurring after birth, this cell death (pruning or apoptosis) is a key element of the developmental process: it removes neurons that have not made connections or have made inappropriate connections. It is estimated that as much as 50 per cent to 70 per cent of brain cells initially produced are pruned in the postnatal period. Although development is often seen as an additive process, the development of

Ontogenesis
the development of an individual organism or anatomical or behavioral feature from the earliest stage to maturity

Proliferation
production of nerve cells during the cellular development of the brain

Migration
movement of progenitor cells from where they are formed in the wall of the neural tube during the cellular development of the brain

Myelination
process of forming a fatty coating around neurons; myelination increases the speed at which neurons can send messages to other neurons

Myelin
fatty coating that insulates neurons and increases the speed at which they can send messages (in the form of electrical impulses) to other neurons

Synaptogenesis
process by which nerve cells communicate with each other or with end organs, during the cellular development of the brain

the brain involves cell death as a central element in its **ontogenesis** (Oppenheim, 1991).

The cellular development of the brain comprises three main stages:

• **Proliferation: Proliferation**, the production of nerve cells, is completed by the end of the second trimester.

• **Migration of cells:** Cells are formed from progenitor cells in the wall of the neural tube. The **migration** of these cells involves them moving from here to their final location. Other cells, the radial glia cells, are produced alongside the neurons and serve as guides forming pathways along which the nerve cells migrate to their final position. Migration takes place between the fourth and ninth months of gestation.

• **Myelination and synaptogenesis:** The final stage involves myelination and synaptogenesis. **Myelination** is the process whereby the nerve cell is insulated from other cells by the development of a fatty sheath, **myelin**, around it. This greatly enhances the transmission of nerve impulses along the nerve. **Synaptogenesis** is the process by which nerve cells communicate with each other or with end organs, for example muscles, to enable the transmission of neural impulses across the brain and from the brain to other organs, and vice versa. These latter processes continue for some time after birth.

The development of the brain is a highly complex process in which timing of events is crucial to ensure that development proceeds normally (Mai & Ashwell, 2004). Numerous factors control the organisation of neural development. It is largely under genetic control. Some of the genes involved are now known (Des Portes et al., 1998). However, understanding of the processes that enable the progenitor cells in the neural tube to form the most highly complex organ in the human body – the brain – is poor.

Genetic abnormalities

Genetic abnormalities do happen, but it is important to realise that they are the exception, rather than the rule. Only 2 per cent or 3 per cent of live births show a significant defect. There are two types of genetic abnormalities: gene abnormalities and chromosomal abnormalities.

Gene abnormalities
Gene abnormalities are the result of faulty genes. Faulty genes may convey distorted messages, and the result is defects of various kinds. Examples are sex-linked abnormalities such as haemophilia, and ethnically linked gene abnormalities. Ethnically linked gene abnormalities are abnormalities that have a higher frequency among certain ethnic groups, because one of the progenitor (origin/ancestral) parents of a particular

ethnic group had a faulty gene. The faulty gene is therefore transmitted from generation to generation. In genetics, the first affected individual in a family who brings a genetic disorder to the attention of the medical community is termed the **proband**. For a genetic illness, first-degree relatives (mother, father, siblings) are more likely to have the disorder of the proband than are more distant relatives (Kaplan & Sadock, 1988).

The box below details the most common genetic abnormalities in South Africa.

Proband
first affected individual in a family who brings a genetic disorder to the attention of the medical community

Most common genetic abnormalities in South Africa

- **Porphyria amongst Afrikaners:** One in three Afrikaners carry the gene for porphyria variegate. This is the highest prevalence for this disorder in the world. Porphyria variegate is a metabolic disturbance characterised by blisters and scars, usually on parts of the skin exposed to sunlight. The disease, which is inherited dominantly, has been traced back to two Dutch immigrants who were married in the Cape in 1688.
- **Tay–Sachs disease amongst Jews:** Approximately 1 of out every 25 South African Jewish people carries the gene for this disease, while the general incidence is about 1 in 2 500. It is a serious, recessively inherited disease that affects the brain and the spinal cord. Death always occurs before the age of five.
- **Albinism amongst black South Africans:** About 1 in every 4 000 black South Africans suffers from albinism, while about only 1 in 15 000 white South Africans is affected. Albinism is a recessive condition characterised mainly by the absence of pigmentation in the skin, hair and eyes. The skin and eyes are very sensitive to bright light.
- **Thalassemia amongst South Africans of Greek or Italian descent:** Approximately 10 per cent of South Africans of Greek or Italian descent carry the gene for thalassemia. This is a recessive disorder characterised mainly by anaemia (deficiency of red blood cells) (Louw & Louw, 2007).

Chromosomal abnormalities

In 40 per cent of abortion patients, the cause of the abortion is a chromosomal defect (Mackay, 1988). The most common manifestation of chromosomal abnormality is Down's syndrome (formerly known as mongolism). This condition is characterised by mental retardation, particular facial characteristics, a stocky physique and a pleasant nature. In more than 90 per cent of such cases, the condition arises as a result of the presence of an extra chromosome at the twenty-first pair – hence the name trisomy-21 being given to the most common form of the syndrome. Such a person has 47 chromosomes. Diagnosis of the anomaly may influence the options regarding the type of delivery (Mackay, 1988).

Environmental influences on development

Prenatal physical development appears to proceed largely under instruction and direction from the individual's genes. However, this does not mean that it is immune to external influences that may alter the course of development. Environmental factors may influence the individual's ontogenesis. Indeed, environmental factors may be crucial for establishing the functional capabilities of the various organs of the body.

Teratogens

Teratogens
substances that exert an adverse influence on development

The clearest example of environmental influence is presented by **teratogens** – substances that exert an adverse influence on development. Initially it was thought that, while developing within the womb, the fetus was safe from external influences that could harm its development. However, it is now appreciated that the developing individual is at risk from environmental influences even in the womb (Kalter, 2003).

Teratology
the study of adverse consequences of exposure to environmental agents

The study of adverse consequences of exposure to environmental agents is termed **teratology**. Note that teratogenic effects are caused not only by substances external to the embryonic or fetal environment, for example alcohol through maternal drinking. Teratogenic effects are also caused by deficiencies of substances, for example vitamin deficiencies and other dietary deficiencies such as malnutrition, which may also lead to adverse development, as is discussed below.

As Feigenbaum and Veit (2003, in Du Preez, 2004) point out, human diseases represent changes in the normal structure or function of the human body. During pregnancy, an illness will generally not affect the unborn child, because the viruses and bacteria cannot enter the placenta. In some cases, however, viruses and bacteria are so small that they *are* able to enter the placenta. This will affect the unborn child.

The diseases that are likely to be transmitted from mother to child include the following:

• **Rubella (German measles):** The first agent to be identified as a teratogen was rubella (the medical term for German measles), when it was noticed that children born to women who had German measles during their pregnancy often suffered eye anomalies (Gregg, 1942, in Du Preez, 2004). Maternal rubella during the first trimester has been associated with severe mental retardation, deafness, and microcephaly in 50 per cent of infants born to those mothers (Kaplan & Saddock,

1988). In South Africa and in many other countries, pregnant mothers have access to the vaccine at clinics to develop immunity to rubella.

- **Aids (acquired immune deficiency syndrome):** Each year, many children are newly infected with HIV, mainly through mother-to-child transmission. An overwhelming majority – more than 90 per cent – of HIV infections in infants and children are passed on by mothers during pregnancy, labour, delivery or breastfeeding. Without any intervention, between 15 per cent and 45 per cent of infants born to mothers living with HIV will become infected (5–10 per cent during pregnancy, 10–20 per cent during labour and delivery, and 5–20 per cent through breastfeeding). During the birth process when the umbilical cord separates from the placenta, it results in an exchange of blood between the mother and child. Aids weakens a person's immune system such that a person is more vulnerable to a wide variety of diseases. Approximately 6 000 infected babies are born monthly in South Africa, and almost one in three pregnant women attending prenatal care clinics in South Africa are living with HIV (UNAIDS, 2011).
- **Syphilis:** Syphilis can lead to miscarriages, stillbirths or death of the baby after birth. Syphilitic infection of the fetus usually takes place only after four or five months. Early treatment can prevent fetal infection. The incidence of syphilis in Western countries is less than 1 per cent, whereas in Africa it is between 1 per cent and 17 per cent (depending on the geographical area), with an average of about 4 per cent in sub-Saharan Africa (World Health Organisation, 2001).
- **Genital herpes:** Genital herpes is an infection that is usually transmitted during sexual contact, usually through the skin and nervous system. It causes sores on the sexual organs. Although the virus can penetrate the placenta and infect the fetus, most infections occur during the birth process when the baby comes into contact with the mother's birth canal. According to Santrock (2004), 30 per cent of such babies die, while up to 25 per cent suffer brain damage.

It was not until the thalidomide tragedy in the 1950s and 1960s that it was finally accepted that environmental agents could severely affect an individual's development. (Thalidomide was a supposedly safe tranquilliser or sedative that mothers took during pregnancy. Its use resulted, most noticeably, in the birth of children with severe limb abnormalities.)

The range of effects of teratogens is great, and includes spontaneous abortion of the fetus, major and minor structural defects, growth retardation, developmental retardation, and behavioural disorders. Some effects are readily apparent at birth, for example the major structural anomalies resulting from exposure to thalidomide. Others, for example behavioural anomalies arising from exposure to alcohol, may not become apparent until later life.

One crucial factor determining the impact of any teratogen is the time of exposure. Generally speaking, exposure during the embryonic period – that is, the period of organogenesis (when the major organs of the body begin to form) – results in major impairments and malformations. Exposure during the fetal period (from about nine weeks from conception) results in growth impairments and delay. Many organs have specific periods – often just two to three days – during which they are especially susceptible. Exposure to teratogens at this time will have major effects on their formation; outside these times the effects will be more limited. For example, a crucial period for development of the arms is 27–30 days, and exposure to thalidomide at this time resulted in malformation of the arms. At other times the severity of the drug's effect on the arms was reduced or non-existent.

Many substances have been identified as having harmful effects on a fetus (see Table 3.1). The length of the period during which the brain is developing makes it particularly vulnerable to the effects of teratogenic agents. Substances may result in abnormalities in brain development in the absence of major physical structural abnormalities; these effects are much more difficult to detect, as they may become apparent only years after birth.

Table 3.1 Teratogens and some of their main effects (duration and timing of exposure play a key role in determining the extent of any effect)

Type of teratogen	Adverse effects
Prescription drugs	
• Thalidomide (sedative)	• Arm and leg malformation
• Warfarin (anticoagulant)	• Mental retardation, microcephaly (abnormally small head)
• Trimethadione (anticonvulsant)	• Developmental delay, 'V'-shaped eyebrow, cleft lip and/or palate
• Tetracycline (antibiotic)	• Tooth malformations
Substances of abuse	
• Heroin	• Fetal/newborn addiction, slower growth
• Cocaine	• Growth retardation; possible long-term behavioural effects
• Solvents	• Microcephaly
Social drugs	
• Alcohol	• Fetal alcohol syndrome, fetal alcohol effects
• Tobacco (smoking)	• Spontaneous abortion, growth retardation
• Caffeine	• Few human studies; high doses induce abnormalities in animals

Table 3.1 *(Continued)*

Type of teratogen	Adverse effects
Disease	
• Rubella	• Cataracts, deafness, heart defects
• Herpes simplex	• Microcephaly, microopthalmia (abnormally small or absent eyes, associated with blindness)
• Varicella (chickenpox)	• Muscle atrophy, mental retardation
Radiation	
	• Cell death, chromosome injury, mental and growth retardation (depends on dose and timing of exposure)
Maternal issues	
• Altered metabolism (for example diabetes)	• Increased birth weight, increased risk of congenital abnormalities
• Stress/anxiety	• Evidence pointing to effects on birth weight, behavioural development; risk of congenital abnormalities and growth retardation (depends on timing of exposure to her problems)

Source: Reprinted from *Early Human Development*, Vol. 12, no. 2, J.I.P. de Vries, G.H.A. Visser, H.F.R. Prechtl, The emergence of fetal behaviour. II. Quantitative aspects, pp. 99–120, Copyright © 1985, with permission from Elsevier.

Many teratogens are freely taken by mothers, for example alcohol, the products of cigarette smoking, and drugs. These teratogens as associated with the following syndromes and effects:

- **Fetal alcohol spectrum disorder (FASD):** Recall that chapter one introduced this topic. According to Viljoen et al. (2005), the highest prevalence of FASD worldwide was found among children in a wine-growing area in the Western Cape and Northern Cape. The case study of Mary at the beginning of this chapter offers a clear example of a pregnant woman resorting to alcohol as a coping mechanism; that is, trying to cope with the abuse from her husband. A study conducted by Croxford and Viljoen (1999) revealed that FASD has been a problem in the Western Cape for many years. The study reported higher rates of stillbirth and of neonatal death, and an increasingly poor outcome in successive pregnancies, due to alcohol intake during pregnancy. The symptoms of FASD include a small head, an abnormal facial appearance, growth retardation, learning disabilities, and behavioural disorders. At lower doses, the individual may manifest **fetal alcohol effects** – facial appearance may be normal but learning and behavioural problems are present in later life (Abel, 1989). Alcohol exhibits what is called a **dose-dependent effect**: the greater the exposure, the greater the effect on the fetus. It appears that even small amounts of alcohol may exert an effect on a developing individual (Hepper et al., 2005). Teratogenic effects are not simply the result of environmental exposure. In many cases the effect(s) is a result of an interaction between the individual's genes and the environmental agent. For example, not all women who drink the same amount of alcohol during pregnancy will have babies with identical syndromes. Some will be more affected than others, depending on the interaction between the environment and the individual's genes.

- **Fetal tobacco syndrome:** Fetal tobacco syndrome is evident in children born to mothers who smoke five or more cigarettes a day during pregnancy. This causes retarded growth in babies and may later negatively affect the cognitive performance in children. Nicotine penetrates the placenta and blocks the supply of oxygen to the fetus. Nicotine therefore has an adverse effect on the growing fetus. Nicotine can be found in the milk of mothers who smoke; as a result, nicotine can cause restlessness in babies and an unpleasant taste in the milk. According to the Medical Research Council (2006), an average of more than 20 per cent of pregnant women in South Africa smoke, and in certain groups more than 50 per cent smoke.

- **Effects of drugs:** Drugs such as heroin, morphine and tik cause physical dependency. A child born to a mother who uses such drugs during pregnancy may experience withdrawal symptoms, such as respiratory problems and convulsions, shortly after birth and may die. Such withdrawal symptoms arise because the baby's regular supply of the drug from the mother is cut off when he or she is born.

Fetal origins hypothesis

Postnatal health may be influenced by prenatal factors; this is the **fetal origins hypothesis** (Gluckman & Hanson, 2005). This hypothesis argues that the environment experienced during an individual's prenatal life 'programs' the functional capacity of the individual's organs, and this has a subsequent effect on the individual's health. When the fetus experiences a poor nutritional environment, it develops its body functions to cope with this. The environment experienced prenatally is the one that the fetus expects to continue experiencing, so its body develops to cope with it – a predictive adaptive response (Gluckman & Hanson, 2005).

Fetal alcohol effects
learning and behavioural problems due to lower doses of alcohol in pregnancy than the doses that result in FASD

Dose-dependent effect
the greater the exposure, the greater the effect on the fetus

Fetal tobacco syndrome
a syndrome in children born to mothers who smoke five or more cigarettes a day during pregnancy; causes retarded growth in babies and may later negatively affect cognitive performance in children

Fetal origins hypothesis
hypothesis that argues that postnatal health may be influenced by prenatal factors

Effects of nutrition on the fetus

An estimated 52 per cent of South African household incomes fall under the poverty line (Du Preez, 2004). Members of these households are more prone than other people to health and safety risks indicative of malnutrition and infection, and they may also be affected by many other factors. Many of these health and safety risks cause physical, cognitive, neurological or sensory problems that can also cause disability and learning difficulties (Donald, Lazarus & Lolwane, 2009).

Some foods are of good value to the body. Other foods, even though they are tasty, are of less value (Mackay, 1998). The unborn child is directly dependent on the mother for its nutritional needs. The baby obtains nutrition from the mother's bloodstream via the placenta. It is therefore important that the mother follows a healthy and balanced diet during pregnancy.

The most common nutrition-related abnormalities reported are a higher risk of stillbirth, low birth weight, premature births, deformities, retarded growth, and death during the first year of life. Recent studies have emphasised the important links between nutrition and optimum growth of the individual. Malnutrition can affect the child's brain and, subsequently, cognitive development, and it can lead to retardation (United Nations Children's Fund, 2005). Apart from the direct effect of malnutrition on mental and physical development, there are other obstacles – such as increased susceptibility to bacterial, viral, and parasitic diseases – probably the result of impaired immunological function (Mackay, 1988).

When the fetus experiences poor nutritional status, this changes its rate of growth and the fetus develops according to its current environment. Resources may be redistributed away from body organs to develop the brain. If this happens, it influences the development of these organs, for example the liver (the organ responsible for regulating cholesterol levels). Decreased body size in babies is associated with increased cholesterol levels when they become adults. These babies with low birth weight experience a normal nutritional status, but one for which their organs are not programmed and with which the organs cannot deal. This is why the cholesterol levels increase when they become adults.

A number of functions may be programmed in the womb, including blood pressure, insulin response to glucose, and cholesterol metabolism. In situations of poor nutrition, these may be programmed incorrectly. This can possibly lead to subsequent health problems. Although researchers debate the extent of prenatal programming, evidence suggests that poor prenatal conditions have long-term effects. The evidence suggests that these effects result from the mismatch between the prenatal environment in which the organs were developed and the postnatal environment in which the organs must function. The prenatal environment may thus determine the functional capacity of various organs for the rest of life.

Age of the pregnant woman

Teenage mothers are susceptible to certain problems, for example premature births, stillbirths and birth problems. Mothers aged 15 and younger
are normally at risk. Women older than 35 who become pregnant for the
first time, and women older than 40 who have previously been pregnant,
tend to have longer and more difficult birth processes.

Emotional state of the pregnant mother

Researchers are also considering the potential 'teratogenic' influence
of maternal psychological state during pregnancy, and the influence of
this state on the fetus and longer-term outcome. Maternal anxiety or
depression influences the behaviour of the fetus and newborn infant.
Moreover, stress or anxiety in pregnancy has been linked to lower temperament ratings at four to eight months after birth (Austin et al.,
2005).

The influence of the mother's emotional state on the baby is illustrated in many South African folk-tales. Most women in rural areas fetch
wood from the nearby bushes to make fire. There are many tales of a
mother who was frightened by a jackal or baboon while fetching wood,
and who later gave birth to a child with the psychological and/or physical
characteristics that closely resembled a jackal or a baboon.

In the case of a pregnant woman who is anxious, hormones such as
adrenaline and noradrenaline are released into the mother's bloodstream
by the endocrine glands. Maternal anxiety may affect early development of the brain, enhancing the child's later susceptibility to disorders
such as hyperactivity and anxiety problems (Van den Bergh & Marcoen,
2004).

ACTIVITY

1   In this chapter's opening case study, Mary is three months pregnant. Discuss
    her pregnancy stage.
2   'You are what you eat or you are what you do not eat.' Based on this state-
    ment, elaborate on the importance of nutrition during pregnancy.
3   Some diseases are likely to be transmitted from the mother to the child.
    Discuss this and give examples of such diseases.
4   Share any stories or folk-tales you have heard regarding pregnant women
    who were greatly startled and how the fear affected the unborn child.
5   Discuss the important stages of the birth process.
6   Critically analyse the effect of alcohol and smoke on an unborn baby.
7   What are your views on abortion? Should it be legalised or not? Support
    your argument.

8 Discuss the effect of stress on Mary's unborn child.
9 Mary is in an abusive relationship but does not want to divorce her husband because of her cultural beliefs and norms, which are reflected in the words *Lebitla la mosadi ke bogadi*' ('Till death do us part'). Mary faces certain challenges in relation to this pregnancy. What are these? What are possible solutions to her problems?

Behaviour of the fetus

The behaviour of the human fetus has aroused much speculation, but only in recent years has it been the subject of scientific study. Views of the behaviour of the fetus have ranged from the fetus as a miniature human with all its abilities, to the fetus as an unresponsive, passive organism. As science has examined the prenatal period, a picture of an active fetus has emerged: a fetus that exists in an environment of stimulation and reacts to it. The following sections review evidence pertaining to fetal movement, fetal sensory abilities, and fetal learning.

Fetal movement

The advent of ultrasound technology (see Figure 3.4) has provided clinicians and scientists with a window through which to watch the behaviour of the fetus. Mothers feel their fetus move from around 18–20 weeks of

Figure 3.4 Ultrasound image of human fetus at 16 weeks

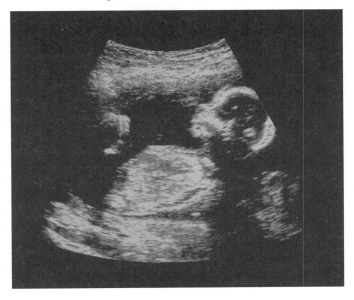

gestation (a time known as 'the quickening'), although there is much individual variation in the maternal perception of movements. Using ultrasound, however, researchers have observed fetal movements to emerge much earlier, at eight weeks (Prechtl, 1988).

These slow movements originate in nerve impulses from the spinal cord, and may result in passive movements of the arms and legs. Over the next few weeks a variety of different movements emerge (see Table 3.2). By 20 weeks, most of the movements the fetus will produce are present in its behavioural repertoire (Prechtl, 1988).

Table 3.2 Gestational age at which behaviours are first observed in the fetus

Behaviour	Gestational age (weeks)
Just discernible movement	7
Startle	8
General movement	8
Hiccup	9
Isolated arm movement	9
Isolated leg movement	9
Isolated head retroflexion[a]	9
Isolated head rotation	9–10
Isolated head anteflexion[b]	10
Fetal breathing movements	10
Arm twitch	10
Leg twitch	10
Hand–face contact	10
Stretch	10
Rotation of fetus	10
Jaw movement	10–11
Yawn	11
Finger movement	12
Sucking and swallowing	12
Clonic movement arm or leg[c]	13
Rooting	14
Eye movements	16

[a] retroflexion = head bends backwards
[b] anteflexion = head bends downwards
[c] clonic = short spasmodic movements)
Source: De Vries et al. (1985)

Behavioural states in the fetus

The fetus remains active throughout its time in the womb. However, as it develops, its movements become concentrated into periods of activity and periods of inactivity (James et al., 1995). Towards the end of pregnancy, **behavioural states** have been observed in the fetus. Behavioural states are defined as recognisable and well-defined associations of variables, which are stable over time and with clear transitions between each.

Researchers have identified four behavioural states in the fetus, based on the observation of behavioural states in the newborn (prebehavioural). Behavioural states are observed from 36 weeks of gestational age (Nijhuis et al., 1982). It has been argued that the emergence of behavioural states represents a greater degree of integration within the various parts of the central nervous system.

The following four states have been defined, using the variables of heart-rate pattern, the presence or absence of eye movements, and the presence or absence of body movements:

- **State 1F – Quiet sleep:** The fetus exhibits occasional startles, no eye movements, and a stable fetal heart rate. This occurrence of the state increases from about 15 per cent at 36 weeks of gestation to 32 per cent at 38 weeks, and 38 per cent at term.
- **State 2F – Active sleep:** This state is characterised by frequent and periodic gross body movements, eye movements are present, and the fetal heart rate shows frequent accelerations in association with movement. This is the most commonly occurring state, being observed in the fetus for around 42–48 per cent of time.
- **State 3F – Quiet awake:** No gross body movements are observed, eye movements are present, and the fetal heart rate shows no accelerations and has a wider oscillation bandwidth than in state 1F. This is a rare state to observe, as it occurs only briefly. In fact, its occurrence is usually represented by number of occurrences, rather than as a percentage of time.
- **State 4F – Active awake:** In this state, the fetus exhibits continual activity, eye movements are present, the fetal heart rate is unstable, and tachycardia (increased pulse rate) is present. This state occurs about 6–7 percent of the time between 36 and 38 weeks of gestation, increasing to 9 per cent just before birth, around 40 weeks of gestation.

Behavioural states recognisable and well-defined associations of variables, which are stable over time and with clear transitions between each

Fetal senses

All the senses adults have operate to some degree in the fetus (with the possible exception of vision; see below in the section headed 'Somatosensory stimuli'). However, in order for the senses to operate, a requirement is that stimulation penetrates the womb, to be received by the fetus's sensory receptors. The fetal environment is one of ever-changing stimuli, which the fetus can detect and to which it can respond.

Hearing

The fetus responds to sound from 22–24 weeks by exhibiting a change in its movement (Shahidullah & Hepper, 1993). The fetus's response is influenced by the frequency, intensity, and duration of the sound presented (Hepper & Shahidullah, 1994). For example, louder intensities elicit a greater response.

The fetus's hearing begins in the low-frequency part (250 Hz, 500 Hz) of the adult hearing range (20–20 000 Hz), and as it develops the range of frequencies it responds to increases (Hepper & Shahidullah, 1994). As well as simply responding to sounds, the fetus is able to discriminate between different sounds, for example spoken words such as 'babi' and 'biba' (Lecanuet et al., 1987).

The environment of the fetus is quite noisy. Sounds from the mother's heartbeat, blood flow, and digestive system will permeate the fetal environment (Querleu et al., 1988). All the sounds a person in the room with the mother can hear can also penetrate the mother's womb and stimulate the fetus's hearing. However, sounds from the external environment are attenuated by the mother's skin and other tissues. High-pitched sounds over 2 000 Hz are attenuated by as much as 40 decibels, and thus are probably not be experienced by the fetus (Querleu et al., 1989). To make them audible to the fetus would require a sound level that would damage the hearing of the mother! Interestingly, there is little attenuation around 125–250 Hz, the fundamental frequency of the human voice. Thus, the fetus will readily hear the mother talking and other speech sounds in the environment.

Chemosensation

The senses of smell and taste are difficult to separate in the womb, because the amniotic fluid bathes both receptor types and may stimulate both sensory systems. For this reason, the fetal responses to smell and taste are usually considered under the same heading: **chemosensation**.

Chemosensation
fetal responses to smell and taste

The fetus is able to discriminate between sweet and noxious substances added to the amniotic fluid. Fetuses increase their swallowing when a sweet substance (sugar) is added to the amniotic fluid by injection; however, fetuses decrease their swallowing when a noxious substance (iodinated poppy seed) is added. Newborns show a preference for the odour of their mother compared to that of another woman, and fetuses orient to their own amniotic fluid, further suggesting experience of odours or tastes in the womb (Schaal et al., 2004).

The fetus swallows amniotic fluid from around 12 weeks of gestation, so the fetus will experience substances that diffuse into the fluid – for example from the mother's diet (Schaal et al., 2004). Moreover, as the mother's diet changes, so will the stimulation the fetus receives.

Somatosensory stimuli

Pain

The question of whether the fetus feels pain is at the centre of many scientific and political debates. Answering this question is made more difficult by the fact that pain is a subjective phenomenon, and it can be difficult to examine. Pain responses have been observed in premature infants from around 24–26 weeks, and neural pathways for pain are formed around 26 weeks of gestation (Fitzgerald, 1993).

Researchers have observed behavioural reactions to possibly painful stimuli, for example if the fetus is touched by the needle during amniocentesis (a test for chromosome abnormalities in the fetus), or following fetal scalp blood sampling (to assess fetal status during labour). From 23 weeks of gestation, researchers have observed biochemical stress responses to needle punctures during blood transfusions. These, however, are all indirect measures of pain experience. There is still a debate as to whether the fetus feels pain.

Temperature

Anecdotal reports suggest that mothers feel more fetal movements as they take a hot bath. However, in the normal course of pregnancy, the temperature of the mother's womb is regulated and maintained, so there will be little variation for the fetus to experience.

Touch

Touch is the first sense of the fetus to develop, at around eight weeks. If the fetus's lips or cheeks are touched at 8–9 weeks, it responds by moving its head away from the touch (Hooker, 1952). Later in pregnancy, this response changes, and during the second trimester the fetus now moves towards the touch. By 14 weeks of gestation, most of the body, excluding the back and top of the head, is responsive to touch. The fetus's arms will make contact with its face from about 13 weeks of gestation, providing a source of stimulation. For twins and other multiple pregnancies, there will be much tactile stimulation from other womb partners.

Vision

Vision is the sense least likely to be stimulated during the normal course of pregnancy (Hepper, 1992). At best, the fetus may experience some general change in illumination. When tested under experimental conditions, the fetus, from around 26 weeks of gestation, exhibits a change in heart rate or movement when a bright light is flashed on the mother's abdomen, demonstrating that the visual system is operating to a certain extent.

Fetal learning

The ability of the fetus to learn is perhaps the most fascinating of all fetal abilities, because learning is often seen as the pinnacle of adult achievement. The ability to learn also has implications for the functioning of other abilities. For example, the ability to learn requires a sensory system able to detect and discriminate stimuli, and a memory system able to store information.

Habituation

The presentation of a loud, discrete sound initially elicits a large reaction (change in heart rate or movement) in the fetus. As this sound is repeated, however, the fetus's response wanes and eventually disappears – this waning of response is termed **habituation**.

Habituation
waning of response to stimuli

The fetus habituates to auditory stimuli from around 22–24 weeks of gestation. Researchers have observed that female fetuses habituate faster than male fetuses at any particular gestational age; this finding may indicate that female fetuses are developmentally more advanced than male fetuses (Hepper & Leader, 1996).

Exposure learning

Most studies examining fetal learning have studied whether newborns respond differently to sounds they have been exposed to before birth, compared to sounds to which they have not been exposed (Hepper, 1996).

Two aspects of interest here are the following:

- **Mother's voice:** Newborns prefer their mother's voice to that of an unfamiliar woman (DeCasper & Fifer, 1980). Some very elegant experiments were performed to reveal this remarkable ability. These studies used the newborn's ability to suck. Newborns sucked on a dummy in the absence of any stimulation, to establish a baseline sucking rate. Once this was established, researchers gave the newborn two choices: if it sucked faster than the baseline, it received the sound of its mother's voice through headphones, whereas if it sucked slower than the baseline, it received the voice of an unfamiliar woman. Newborns sucked faster to hear their mothers' voices. If researchers reversed the contingencies, and sucking slower than the baseline led to hearing the mother's voice, newborns sucked slower than the baseline. What is clear is that this ability to recognise the mother's voice is acquired before birth (Fifer & Moon, 1989).

- **Music:** Newborns prefer music they have heard prenatally, compared to music they have never heard. Interestingly, this preference can be observed at 36 weeks of gestation, but not at 30 weeks of gestation; this may indicate that learning of familiar sounds or tunes occurs after 30 weeks (Hepper, 1991).

Functions of behaviour

The fetus exhibits a complex and varied behavioural repertoire. But why does the fetus exhibit these behaviours? This section will explore a number of possible reasons.

Practising for life outside the womb

One key role of prenatal behaviour is to practise behaviours that will be essential for survival after birth; fetal breathing movements are an example of this. These movements are observed from 9 to 10 weeks of gestation (De Vries et al., 1985). Although there is no air in the womb, these movements – motion of the diaphragm and ribcage – would result in breathing after birth. This is why these movements are termed fetal breathing movements. At 30 weeks of gestation these movements occur around 30 per cent of the time (Patrick et al., 1980).

Later in pregnancy, fetal breathing movements increase during periods of fetal activity. Practising before birth ensures the neural pathways responsible for breathing are fully mature, thus ensuring a fully operational system when required, at the moment of birth.

Ontogenetic adaptations

Although fetal behaviour research currently emphasises the continuity of development, it is best to remember that the embryo and fetus exist in a very different environment from that which will be experienced after birth. It may thus be expected that the fetus would exhibit behaviour designed to ensure its survival in the womb, and such behaviours are termed **ontogenetic adaptations** – that is, adaptations to its life in the womb.

Although the concept of ontogenetic adaptations is well accepted, few studies have examined fetal adaptations to life in the womb. Some reflexes may be important for the process of birth and labour. An example of these is the kicking movements that appear near the end of pregnancy. These reposition the head of the fetus so that it is in the position for safe delivery (vertex presentation).

Ontogenetic adaptations
a fetus's adaptations to its life in the womb

Recognition of mother

The learning abilities of the fetus may be crucial for its survival and development in the first weeks after birth, by enabling it to recognise its mother and begin the process of attachment and exploration. Many studies have demonstrated the ability of the newborn infant to recognise its mother by auditory and odour cues, an ability acquired prenatally (DeCasper & Fifer, 1980; Porter & Winberg, 1999).

The mother is a crucial figure for the newborn's survival. In terms of recognising items in its environment, the newborn is a blank canvas, and has to learn what objects are in its environment as it develops. It makes good sense to provide one object, and a very important one at that, that the individual may recognise at birth. Prenatal learning may serve to ensure that the newborn recognises its mother at birth.

Breastfeeding

Prenatal learning may also be important for the establishment of breastfeeding. The same processes that flavour the mother's breast milk also flavour the amniotic fluid (Schaal et al., 2004). The fetus may learn about the flavour of the amniotic fluid while in the womb, and when placed to the breast for the first time, it recognises a familiar flavour and sucks readily. Successful breastfeeding is crucial for the newborn's survival; prenatal learning may ensure the successful establishment of breastfeeding (Hepper, 1996).

Developing physical form and developing the brain

The behaviour of the fetus is important for shaping the development of its body. The movements of the fetus are important for its structural development. The formation of the body's joints and the development of muscle and muscle tone all rely on the fetus moving its limbs during development. Joints do not form properly when their movements are restricted (Moessinger, 1988).

The behaviour of the fetus may also influence the long-term development of the brain. Sensory experiences may shape the development of its sensory system. It is well established that visual experience after birth shapes the development of the visual system (Blakemore & Cooper, 1970). For those senses active and stimulated before birth – for example audition – stimulation may influence the development of these sensory systems. The potential for experiential factors to influence the development of the brain is great.

Birth and labour

For most of pregnancy, the aim is to keep the baby within the womb until it is sufficiently mature to survive outside. Once this time is reached, however, the fetus can leave its uterine environment for life in the postnatal world.

Preparation for birth

The activity of the uterine muscles is inhibited during pregnancy by the hormone progesterone (the hormone found in the ovaries which helps to maintain pregnancy). However, the muscles of the uterus are not completely inactive. During pregnancy, mothers often feel a tightening of the uterus at regular intervals, known as Braxton Hicks contractions. These contractions play an important role in preparing the uterus for delivery by developing its muscle tone. These are different from the contractions that the mother feels during labour, which are shorter in duration and occur every few minutes, increasing in frequency and intensity as labour progresses.

As the time of birth approaches, the fetus's brain signals for more production of new chemicals, for example adrenocorticotrophin (ACTH) and cortisol. These chemicals act to convert progesterone to oestrogen. Oestrogen, in contrast to progesterone, promotes muscle activity in the uterus. The inhibitory control exercised over the muscles from the beginning of pregnancy is removed. Mothers may now feel a 'tightening' in the uterus, and they may experience contractions in the days leading up to delivery. These changes also stimulate the breast to prepare for the production of milk – a process completed when the baby begins to suck.

Labour and birth

Labour and birth involve a constant interaction between the baby and mother. For example, as the fetus's head presses against the cervix, this stimulates the mother's pituitary gland to release oxytocin. This in turn stimulates the muscles of the uterus to contract, forcing the fetus's head into the cervix and continuing the cycle of contraction. Moreover, oxytocin also stimulates the release of prostaglandins, which increase the strength of uterine muscle contractions. This process continually escalates during labour, contractions becoming more forceful, and eventually resulting in the birth of the baby.

Exactly what determines the onset of labour is unknown. However, somehow the fetus 'knows' when it is ready to be born, and it starts a series of processes that culminate in its birth.

The actual birth process is divided into three stages.

- **Stage 1:** The first stage, usually the longest, begins with uterine contractions, each maybe lasting up to a minute, occurring every 15–20 minutes. As this stage progresses, the contractions become more frequent and more intense. These contractions enable the mother's cervix to expand and stretch and enable the baby to move from the womb to the birth canal. At the end of the first stage, the cervix has dilated to about 9 cm. The length of this stage generally decreases after the mother's first baby, but there is huge variability between individual mothers in the duration of this stage of pregnancy. In first pregnancies, it may last 8–24 hours.

- **Stage 2:** Once the baby's head passes through the cervix and into the birth canal, the second stage of labour has begun. The mother bears down at the time of contractions in an effort to push the baby from her body. This stage culminates when the baby is born, free from the birth canal but attached to the mother by the umbilical cord and placenta.
- **Stage 3:** The third stage is the afterbirth. In this stage contractions expel the placenta.

Survival after birth

Two important changes need to take place after birth, as a result of the umbilical cord being cut and the baby having to survive on its own:

- First, the baby must now breathe for itself. The previous 25 weeks spent practising breathing movements now reap benefits as the baby starts breathing and obtaining oxygen through its own actions.
- Second, there is a change from the fetal pattern of blood circulation to the adult pattern of circulation. This is triggered by the fact that the baby now oxygenates its blood from the lungs and not the placenta. Perhaps the most important change is the closure of the foramen ovale, which prevents the blood, now deoxygenated blood, from flowing from the right atrium to the left atrium of the heart. These changes in blood flow occur over the first few days and weeks after birth (Moore & Persaud, 2003).

Reflexes

Reflexes
involuntary movements elicited in response to stimulation; inborn, automatic responses to a particular form of stimulation

A newborn's motor repertoire consists mainly of **reflexes**, which are involuntary movements elicited in response to stimulation, for example touch, light, change in position (see Table 3.3). Neural structures below the level of the cortex control these motor behaviours. These reflexes are present at birth and disappear in the months after birth. The normal exhibition and disappearance of these reflexes is an important indicator of the functioning and integrity of the baby's brain. Reflexes that persist beyond the time when they usually disappear, or are weaker than normal, may indicate underlying neural impairment, such as cerebral palsy.

Table 3.3 Some of a baby's reflexes

Reflex	Description	Developmental time course
Rooting	Touch the side of the mouth or cheek and the baby turns towards touch.	Birth to 4–5 months
Sucking	Touch the mouth or lips and the baby begins to suck.	Birth to 4–6 months
Grasping	When the baby's palms are touched the baby grasps the object.	Birth to 4 months
Moro	In response to a sudden loud sound or 'dropping', the baby suddenly startles, throws its head back and stretches out arms and legs, and then rapidly brings them back to the centre of the body.	Birth to 4–6 months
Babinski	Stroke the bottom of the foot and the toes fan out and then curl.	Birth to 9–12 months
Swimming	When the baby is placed in water, it holds its breath and makes swimming movements with arms and legs.	Birth to 4–6 months
Stepping	If the baby is held above a surface and its feet allowed to touch the surface, it begins to show walking movements.	Birth to 3–4 months
Labyrinthine	When the baby is placed on its back, it extends its arms and legs, or when placed on its stomach, it flexes its arms and legs.	Birth to 4 months

Reflexes are important for the survival of the newborn infant. Reflexes also serve as the basic building blocks on which future motor development is based. Some reflexes are essential for survival, for example breathing and swallowing. To enable breastfeeding, the newborn infant has a rooting and sucking reflex. Touch on the side of the mouth or cheek stimulates the newborn to turn towards the touch, to locate the nipple: this is rooting. Once the newborn has located the nipple, sucking – another reflex initiated by stimulation on the mouth or lips – enables the newborn to grasp the nipple and stimulate it to produce milk, and thus obtain nutrients essential for growth.

Rooting and sucking disappear at about 4–6 months, to be replaced by voluntary eating behaviour. Some reflexes remain throughout life, for example blinking and yawning. In the normal course of events, reflexes may disappear or become incorporated into more voluntary gross motor movements and fine motor movements – for example the grasping reflex of the infant.

Newborn senses

As this chapter has discussed, all of an individual's senses are functional to a certain extent in the womb; the baby's arrival in the world makes little difference in the baby's abilities, but rather marks a difference in the quality of sensation to which it is exposed. The biggest change is in the visual stimuli experienced by the baby. The visual system of the fetus will be unstimulated during pregnancy, other than by a diffuse orange glow, yet from birth a newborn is exposed to the same visual stimuli as adults. However, of all the senses, the visual sense is least well developed.

A newborn has poor visual accommodation and an underdeveloped pupillary reflex. Visual accommodation is the process whereby small muscles attached to the lens change the shape of the lens, thus bringing objects at different distances from the eye into focus. The newborn infant has limited visual accommodation. It can see objects most clearly about 20–50 cm away from its eye – an excellent distance for viewing the mother's face when feeding.

The pupillary reflex controls the amount of light entering the eye. After birth, this ability is poor, further inhibiting the ability of the baby to focus. Both processes develop rapidly. These processes, along with the development of other crucial processes for accurate vision – eye movements, tracking, and scanning – enable the infant's vision to improve with age. Audition, chemosensation, and various somatosensory senses have been operating since before birth and continue their development after birth to provide the baby with information about its new environment.

CASE STUDY

At the age of six Rose was told by her parents that her younger brother was delivered by an aeroplane at the hospital. She was not told the truth about where children come from. She is 13 years old and is menstruating. She likes to go out with friends and come home late. Rose's mother had an ectopic pregnancy at the age of 16, and the family thought she was bewitched. Rose's aunt, who is an alcoholic, had a child at the age of 45, and the child was diagnosed with Down's syndrome.

Rose's parents are concerned that she might have a boyfriend and fall pregnant. Rose's mother wants Rose to have information before she can have a sexual relationship. However, Rose's mother thinks it is taboo to discuss such issues with a child. She asked Rose's grandmother to talk to Rose on her behalf. Rose's grandmother told Rose that they arranged a meeting to guide her about sex and sexual relationships. Rose replied by saying that they do not have to bother because the Life Orientation teacher at school teaches them about sex education, and diseases such as HIV/Aids.

Rose's mother and grandmother were relieved that schools provide learners with such valuable information that they did not have when they were of Rose's age.

Questions

1 When you were a child, did your parents explain to you where children come from? Is it accepted in your culture to discuss conception issues with children? Reflect back during your childhood and explain your experience in this regard.

2 Explain the effects of genetic abnormalities and how they can be transmitted from generation to generation. Give an example of someone you know – or have found out about – who is affected by genetic abnormalities.

3 Imagine that an aunt of yours has an ectopic pregnancy. She keeps on blaming other people and thinks that she is bewitched. Explain the cause of ectopic pregnancy to her by distinguishing between the biological and other cultural beliefs.

4 Imagine that a friend of yours continues partying and drinking alcohol during pregnancy. Explain to her the effects of alcohol on a fetus during pregnancy.

5 Imagine that a pregnant woman asks you about nutrition and pregnancy. Explain to her how the fetus depends on her for its nutrition, and explain the importance of following a healthy and balanced diet during pregnancy.

6 Discuss how maternal anxiety can affect early development of the fetus's brain.

Conclusion

The prenatal period is a crucial period of development of a person's life. It is the formative period for all the body organs and plays a role in establishing their functional capacity. There is potential for severe disruption

to the normal developmental process from environmental agents. However, for the vast majority of pregnancies, the environment exerts a positive effect, shaping an individual's development. The fetus is an active
participant in its own development. Its behaviour is important for progressing normal development within the womb, and for its life in the
postnatal world. It is the foundation on which all future development
after birth is built.

References

Abel, E.L. (1989). *Fetal alcohol syndrome: Fetal alcohol effects.* New York: Plenum Press.

Austin, M.P., Hadzi-Pavlovic, D., Leader, L., Saint, K. & Parker, G. (2005). Maternal
trait anxiety, depression and life event stress in pregnancy: Relationships with infant
temperament. *Early Human Development, 81,* (2), 183–190.

Blakemore, C. & Cooper, G.F. (1970). Development of the brain depends on the visual
environment. *Nature, 228,* 477–278.

Bojuwoye, O. (2003). Mental health care delivery practices among traditional African
cultures – nature, process and virtues. In N.S. Madu (Ed.). *Contributions to
psychotherapy conference in Africa* (p. 188–206). Turfloop: University to the North.

Carlson, B.M. (1994). *Human embryology and developmental biology.* St Louise: Mosby.

Caviness, V.S., Kennedy, D.B., Bates, J.F. & Makris, N. (1996). The developing
human brain: A morphometric profile. In R.W. Thatcher, G.R. Lyon, J. Rumsey &
N. Krasnegor (Eds). *Developmental neuroimaging* (p. 3–14). San Diego, CA:
Academic Press.

Croxford, J. & Viljoen, D. (1999). Alcohol consumption by pregnant women in the
Western Cape. Foundation for Alcohol related Research (FARR). *South African
Medical Journal, 89,* (9), 962–965.

DeCasper, A.J. & Fifer, W.P. (1980). Of human bonding: Newborns prefer their
mothers' voices. *Science, 208,* 1174–1176.

Des Portes, V., Pinard, J.M., Billuart, P., Vinet, M.C., Koulakoff, A., Carrie, A. et al.
(1998). A novel CNS gene required for neuronal migration and involved in X-linked
subcortical laminar heterotopia and lissencephaly syndrome. *Cell, 92,* (1), 51–61.

De Vries, J.P.P., Visser, G.H.A. & Prechtl, H.F.R. (1985). The emergence of fetal. *Brain
and Cognition, 16,* 151–179.

Donald, D., Lazarus, S. & Lolwana, P. (2009). *Educational psychology in social context*
(3rd ed.). Cape Town: Oxford University Press.

Du Preez, C.S. (2004). Health and well-being. In E. Eloff & L. Ebersohn (Eds). *Keys to
Educational Psychology* (p. 44–63). Cape Town: UCT Press.

Fifer, W.P. & Moon, C. (1989). Psychobiology of newborn auditory preferences.
Seminars in Perinatilogy, 13, 430–433.

Fitzgerald, M. (1993). Development of pain pathways and mechanisms. In
K.J.S. Anand & P.J. McGrath (Eds). *Pain research and clinical management*
(p. 19–38). Amsterdam: Elsevier.

Gluckman, P. & Hanson, M. (2005). *The fetal matrix: Evolution, development and
disease.* Cambridge: Cambridge University Press.

Gregg, N.M. (1942). Congential cataracts following German measles in the mother.
Transactions of the Ophthalmological Society of Australia, 3, 35.

Hepper, P.G. (1991) An examination of fetal learning before and after birth. *Irish
Journal of Psychology, 12,* 95–107.

Hepper, P.G. (1992). Fetal psychology: An embryonic science. In J.G. Nijhuis (Ed.). *Fetal behaviour: Developmental and perinatal aspects* (p. 129–156). Oxford: Oxford University Press.

Hepper, P.G. (1996). Fetal memory: Does it exist? What does it do? *Acta Paediatrica Suppl., 416,* 16–20.

Hepper, P.G., Dornan, J.C. & Little, J.F. (2005). Maternal alcohol consumption during pregnancy may delay the development of spontaneous fetal startle behaviour. *Physiology and Behavior, 83,* 711–714.

Hepper, P.G. & Leader, L.R. (1996). Fetal habituation. *Fetal and Maternal Medicine Review, 8,* 109–123.

Hooker, Davenport (1952). *The prenatal origin of behavior.* Lawrence, Kansas: University of Kansas Press.

James, D., Pillai, M. & Somlenic, J. (1995). Neurobehavioural development in the human fetus. In J.-P. Lecanuet, W.P. Fifer, N.A. Krasnegor & W.P. Smotherman (Eds). *Fetal development: A psychobiological perspective* (p. 101–128). Hillsdale, NJ: Lawrence Erlbaum Associates.

Kail, R.V. & Cavanaugh, J.C. (1996). *Human development.* Boston: Brooks/Cole.

Kalter, H. (2003). Teratology in the 20th century: Environmental cause of congenital malformations in humans and how they were established. *Neurotoxicology and Teratology, 25,* 131–282.

Kaplan, H.I. & Sadock, B.J. (1988). *Synopsis of psychiatry: Behavioural sciences clinical psychiatry* (5th ed.). Baltimore: Williams & Wilkins.

Kekae-Moletsane, M. (2004). The efficacy of the Rorschach among black learners in South Africa. Unpublished thesis. University of Pretoria.

Lecanuet, J.-P., Granier-Deferre, C., DeCasper, A.J., Maugeais, R., Andrieu, A.J. & Busnel, M.C. (1987). Perception et discrimination foetale de stimuli langagiers, mise en evidence apartir de la reactivite cardiaque: Resultats preliminaries. *C-R de l'Acad Sci Paris, Serie III 1987,* 305, 161–164.

Louw, D. & Louw, A. (2007). *Child and adolescent development.* Bloemfontein: University of Free State, South Africa.

Mackay, B. (1988). *Obstetrics and the new born: An illustrated textbook* (2nd British ed.). London: British Library Cataloguing in Publication data.

Mai, J.K. & Ashwell, K.W.S. (2004). Fetal development of the central nervous system. In G. Paxinos & J.K. Mai (Eds). *The human nervous system* (p. 49–94). Amsterdam: Elsevier.

Medical Research Council (2006). *Smoking cessation during pregnancy project.* [WWW document]. URL http:/www.sahelthinfo.co.za/motivational/smoking.htm.

Moessinger, A.C. (1988). Morphological consequences of depressed or impaired fetal activity. In W.P. Smotherman & S.R. Robinson (Eds). *Behavior of the fetus* (p. 163–173). Caldwell, NJ: The Telford Press.

Moore, K.L. & Persuad, T.V.N. (1988). *The developing human: Clinically oriented embryology* (4th ed.). Philadelphia: Saunders.

Moore, K.L. & Persuad, T.V.N. (2003). *The developing human: Clinically oriented embryology* (7th ed.). Philadelphia: Saunders.

Moore, K.L. & Persuad, T.V.N. (2008). *The developing human: Clinically oriented embryology* (8th ed.). Philadelphia: Saunders.

Müller, F. & O'Rahilly, R. (2004). Olfactory structures in staged human embryos. *Cells Tissues Organs, 178,* (2), 93–116.

Nijhuis, J.G, Prechtl, H.F.T., Martin, C.B. & Bots, R.S.G.M. (1982). Are there behavioral states in the human fetus? *Early Human Development, 6,* 177–195.

O'Connor, T., Heron, J., Golding, J., Glover, V. & the ALSPAC team (2003). Maternal antenatal anxiety and behavioural/emotional problems in children: A test of a programming hypothesis. *Journal of Child Psychology and Psychiatry, 44*, 1025–1036.

Oppenheim, R.W. (1991). Cell death during development in the nervous system. *Ann Rev Neurosci, 14*, 453–501.

Patrick, J., Campbell, K., Carmichael, L., Natale, R. & Richardson, B. (1980). Patterns of human fetal breathing during the last 10 weeks of pregnancy. *Obstetrics and Gynecology, 654*, 24–30.

Porter, R.H. & Winberg, J. (1999). Unique salience of maternal breast odors for newborn infants. *Neuroscience and Biobehavioral Reviews, 23*, (3), 439–449.

Prechtl, H.F.R. (1988). Developmental neurology of the fetus. *Clinical Obstetrics & Gynaecology, 2*, 21–36.

Querleu, D., Renard, X., Versyp, F., Paris-Delrue, L. & Crepin, G. (1988). Fetal hearing. *European Journal of Obstetrics, Gynecology and Reproductive Biology, 29*, 191–212.

Querleu, D., Renard, X., Boutteville, C. & Crepin, G. (1989). Hearing the human fetus? *Semin Perinatol, 13*, 409–420.

Santrock, J.W. (2004). *Life-span development* (9th ed.). New York: McGraw-Hill.

Schaal, B., Hummel, T. & Soussignan, R. (2004) Olfaction in the fetal and premature infant: Functional status and clinical implications. *Clin Perinatol, 31*, 261–285.

Shahidullah, S. & Hepper, P.G. (1993). The developmental origins of fetal responsiveness to an acoustic stimulus. *Journal of Reproductive and Infant Psychology, 11*, 135–142.

Shahidullah, S. & Hepper, P.G. (1994). Frequency discrimination by the fetus. *Early Human Development, 36*, 13–26.

UNAIDS (2011). *Global HIV/AIDS response, 2011 report. Epidemic update and health sector progress towards universal access. Progress report 2011. Joint monitoring tool on the health sector response to HIV/AIDS*. Geneva.

United Nations Children's Fund (UNICEF) (2005). *Maternal nutrition*. [WWW document]. URL http://www.unicef.org.

Van den Bergh, B.R.H. & Marcoen, A. (2004). High antenatal maternal anxiety is related to ADHD symptoms, externalizing problems and anxiety in 8 and 9 year olds. *Child Development, 75*, (4), p. 1085–1097.

Viljoen, D.L., Gossage, J.P, Brooke, L., Adams, C.M., Jones, K.L. & Robinson, L.K. (2005). Foetal alcohol syndrome epidemiology in South African community: A second study of a very high prevalence area. *Journal for Studies on Alcohol, 66*, (5), 593–604.

World Health Organization (2001). *Global prevalence and incidence of selected curable sexually transmitted infections: Overview and estimates*. Geneva, Switzerland: Word Health Organization.

CHAPTER FOUR

INFANCY

Lauren Wild

CASE STUDY

Siyanda and Andile are twin boys. They arrived at an orphanage in KwaZulu-Natal when they were just over a year old. Welfare authorities had found the twins on a single bed together with their mother. They did not have any clothes, were sucking on empty bottles, and were covered with flies. There was no food in the house. The twins' 12-year-old sister was trying to care for herself and her brothers, as well as their mother, who was seriously ill as a result of Aids.

When they first came to the institution, Siyanda and Andile were so tiny and skinny that they looked as though they were about three months old. They were malnourished and had not reached the expected developmental milestones for their age. The twins were also covered with sores and smelled bad. They were tense and irritable, and seldom stopped crying.

The staff assumed that Siyanda and Andile were HIV-positive and would die within a few weeks. They dealt with the twins' basic physical and medical needs, but otherwise avoided them.

There were also signs that the twins may have been abused by staff or older children. During this period, Siyanda and Andile would spend most of their time rocking back and forth in their cots, hitting their heads with their fists or against a wall. They cried when they were picked up. If someone tried to interact with them, they would either gaze emptily into the distance, or act in a hostile and aggressive way (Sandhei & Richter, 2003).

LEARNING OBJECTIVES

By the end of this chapter you should be able to:

- Describe the changes that occur in infants' bodies, brains, and motor skills as they develop
- Summarise the major cognitive developments of the sensorimotor stage

- Identify the main milestones of language development in infancy
- Understand individual differences in temperament
- Explain the importance of the early caregiver–child relationship
- Outline the development of self-awareness, self-control, and independence.

Introduction

The case study featuring Siyanda and Andile raises difficult questions about how best to care for children who have been affected by HIV and Aids. However, it also raises bigger questions about the experiences that are necessary to ensure infants' health and development. What kinds of experiences do you think are important for children's development during the first two years of life? Why do you think the twins' development was delayed? Do you think they will be permanently scarred by their experiences, or will they recover? This chapter will provide evidence that will help you to answer these questions.

Development occurs more quickly in the first two years after birth than at any other time after birth. During this two-year period, a child develops from a relatively helpless newborn with a few basic reflexes to a toddler who walks, talks and plays an active part in family life. This chapter will explore how an infant's body and mind grow during this period. The chapter will also examine the important role that interactions with others play in social and personal development.

Physical development

Enormous changes take place in children's bodies, brains and motor skills during infancy. Like other aspects of development, these changes result from a complex interaction between genetic influences and environmental influences.

Body growth

In the first few days after birth, most newborns lose between five and seven per cent of their body weight. As soon as they adjust to sucking, swallowing and digesting, however, they grow very quickly. By the end of the first year, infants are typically one-and-a-half times taller and three times heavier than they were at birth. By the age of two years, they are typically one-and-three-quarter times taller and four times heavier than they were when they were born.

This means that it is possible literally to watch a baby grow in a few weeks. But rather than growing gradually, infants and toddlers grow in little spurts or bursts. In one study, children who researchers followed over the first 21 months of life went for periods of 1–6 weeks with no growth. Then they grew a centimetre or more in a period of 24 hours or less (Lampl, Veldhuis, & Johnson, 1992). So when parents say that their child seems to have grown overnight, they may be right!

As the child's overall size increases, different parts of the body grow at different rates. Two growth patterns describe these changes in body proportions:

- The first growth pattern is called the **cephalocaudal trend**. Translated from Latin, it means 'head to tail'. During the prenatal period, the head develops more rapidly than the lower part of the body. So when a baby is born, the head takes up a quarter of the total body length, the legs only a third. Gradually, the lower portions of the body catch up. Look at Figure 4.1. Notice how as people grow older, the head becomes smaller and the legs become longer in relation to the rest of the body.

- The second pattern is the **proximodistal trend**, meaning growth proceeds from 'near to far', or from the centre of the body outward. In the prenatal period, the head, chest and trunk grow first, followed by the arms and legs, and finally by the hands and feet. During infancy and childhood, the arms and legs continue to grow somewhat ahead of the hands and feet.

Look at Figure 4.1, which illustrates changes in the proportions of the human body during development.

Cephalocaudal trend
tendency for development to proceed from the head downward

Proximodistal trend
tendency for development to proceed from the centre of the body outward

Figure 4.1 Changes in the proportions of the human body during development – the fractions listed refer to head size as a proportion of total body length at different ages from the fetal period through adulthood

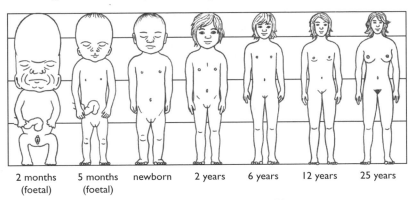

| 2 months | 5 months | newborn | 2 years | 6 years | 12 years | 25 years |
| (foetal) | (foetal) | | | | | |

Source: Adapted from Santrock (2005, p. 95) and Cole & Cole (2001, p. 182)

Motor development

Motor development refers to the sequence of changes in coordination of the muscles that are required for movements or physical activities. Many writers distinguish between two kinds of motor skills:

- **Gross motor skills: Gross motor development** refers to control over large muscle movements that help infants get around in the environment, such as crawling, standing and walking.
- **Fine motor skills: Fine motor development** has to do with control over smaller movements, such as reaching and grasping, and later eating with a spoon, tying shoe laces and writing.

The average age at which half of infants have mastered a particular skill is known as the **developmental norm** for that skill. Figure 4.2 shows the age norms for important gross motor milestones during infancy. For example, 50 per cent of infants can sit without support by the end of the fifth month, and can walk alone when they are about a year old. By this time they can also pick up small objects using their thumb and fingers and are well coordinated enough to eat with a spoon and drink from a cup.

Look at Figure 4.2, which illustrates age norms for important milestones in gross motor development.

The cephalocaudal trend and proximodistal trend can also be seen in motor development. For example, look at the developmental milestones in Figure 4.2: can you see the cephalocaudal (head-to-foot) trend in the way that control of the head and neck comes before control of the arms and chest, which comes before control of the legs? Can you also see the proximodistal (centre-outward) trend in the way that control of the head and trunk comes before control of the arms and legs, which in turn comes before infants learn to coordinate their hands and fingers? An example of this is the way in which infants initially reach for things by twisting their entire bodies, but gradually they learn to use just their arms.

The overall *sequence* of motor development tends to be similar for most children. However, it is important to note that large individual differences exist in the *rate* of motor progress; the timing of developmental milestones often varies by several months, especially among older infants. Therefore, a psychologist or paediatrician would be concerned about a child's development only if the child's motor skills were seriously delayed.

The similarities between the patterns of physical development and motor development suggest that maturation makes an important contribution to motor progress. Recall from chapter one the definition of maturation: the biological processes underlying development. But motor development is not simply determined by a person's genes. The world of interesting objects provides motivation for reaching, sitting, crawling, and so on, and infants develop increasingly complex motor skills as they learn through exploring and experimenting with the world around them.

Motor development
the sequence of changes in coordination of the muscles that are required for movements or physical activities

Gross motor development
control over large muscle movements that help infants get around in the environment

Fine motor development
control over smaller movements

Developmental norm
average age at which half of infants have mastered a particular skill

Figure 4.2 Age norms for important milestones in gross motor development – the left edge, interior mark and right edge of each bar indicate the age at which 25 per cent, 50 per cent and 90 per cent of infants have mastered each motor skill shown

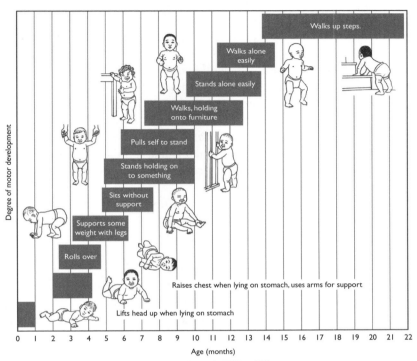

Source: Adapted from Weiten (2004, p. 433) and Santrock (2005, p. 171)

In fact, there is evidence that stimulation in the environment, and the opportunities that children are given for physical movement, can have an important impact on their motor skills. For example, mothers in Jamaica and in the Gusii culture of Kenya tend to encourage their infants' motor development by physically handling them in special ways (such as stroking, massaging, or gently stretching their arms and legs) or by encouraging energetic movement in their babies. These infants often achieve motor milestones earlier than those raised in cultures – such as that of the USA – that do not provide such opportunities for physical activities (Hopkins & Westra, 1988).

Brain development

At birth, the brain consists of most of the one billion nerve cells – or neurons – it will have in adulthood; however, it is only about one-quarter of its adult size, and it will continue to grow. This growth of the brain during infancy is crucial to future physical, cognitive and emotional development.

Major parts of the brain

At birth, the brain stem is one of the most highly developed areas of the nervous system. This is the part of the brain that controls things like breathing, sleeping, and basic reactions such as blinking and sucking. The cerebral cortex is much less developed – this is the outer layer of the brain, which controls a person's conscious thoughts, feelings, memories and deliberate actions (Zero to Three, 2012). As the cerebral cortex matures and becomes more efficiently connected to the brain stem and spinal cord, so the infant's abilities expand.

Different parts of the cerebral cortex develop at different times during infancy, childhood and adolescence (Gilmore et al., 2011):

- The primary motor area is the first area of the cerebral cortex to undergo development, allowing infants first to raise their heads while lying on their stomach, then to control their arms and trunk, and finally to control their legs.
- Important changes also take place in the first few months after birth in the primary sensory areas of the cortex. These areas, which include the areas responsible for touch, hearing and vision, are relatively mature by three months of age.
- The frontal cortex, which is important for making mental associations, remembering, planning, and producing deliberate movements, also begins to function during infancy. However, the frontal cortex remains immature for several years and continues to develop throughout childhood (Casey, Tottenham, Liston & Durston, 2005).

Brain cells

Synapses
tiny gaps between neurons, which are bridged with the help of chemicals called neurotransmitters

One of the reasons the brain grows in size after birth is that there is an increase in the number of **synapses**, or connections among neurons. Synapses are tiny gaps between neurons, which are bridged with the help of chemicals called neurotransmitters. Synapses enable neurons to communicate with one another and to store information.

Synaptic exuberance
the rapid development of connections between brain cells during infancy

At birth, the neurons in the brain are poorly connected. During infancy, there is a tremendous increase or 'blooming' in the number of synapses, in what is known as the period of **synaptic exuberance**. The number of synapses appears to peak at about age two. In fact, the infant brain has twice the number of synapses as it will have in early adolescence, and more than it will ever actually use. Over time, those connections that are used frequently are strengthened; those that prove unnecessary – that are not used – eventually die off (Huttenlocher & Dabkolhar, 1997). This cutting away or 'pruning' of unnecessary synapses during childhood and adolescence helps the brain function more quickly and efficiently.

The brain also becomes larger during infancy because of myelination, a process in which the neurons become covered with myelin (recall that chapter three defined myelin and described the process of myelination). As chapter three explained, myelin is a fatty coating that insulates the neurons and increases the speed at which they can send messages (in the form of electrical impulses) to other neurons. The lack of myelin is the main reason for the thought processes of babies being so much slower than the thought processes of adults. Myelination begins about halfway through the prenatal period in some parts of the brain, and it continues into adulthood in others. Visual pathways are myelinated between birth and five months of age. Myelination of pathways related to hearing begins during the prenatal period, but is not complete until about age four. The parts of the cerebral cortex that control attention and memory are not fully myelinated until young adulthood (Banich & Compton, 2011).

Early experience plays an important role in brain development

Until the middle of the twentieth century, scientists believed that brain development is solely the result of genetic factors. However, it is now widely believed – partly on the basis of animal studies – that early experiences can affect the structure and 'wiring' of the brain. As chapter one explained, when it introduced you to the concept, 'plasticity' is the technical term given to this capacity of the brain to change in response to positive and negative influences from the environment. Synaptic connections that are formed in the brain during infancy operate according to a 'use it or lose it' principle. Because of this, early experience plays an important role in determining which neural connections will form, which will remain, and which will die off. Positive, enriching experiences may lead to more synaptic connections in children. In contrast, abuse or deprivation – such as that experienced by Siyanda and Andile, who featured in the case study at the start of this chapter – can result in an 'over-pruning' of synapses. That over-pruning can leave the child with cognitive and emotional problems (Black, 1998; Nelson, 1999). This does not mean that a child who has a deprived infancy will be incapable of healthy later functioning: sometimes later stimulation can help to make up for early deprivation. Nevertheless, it makes sense to try to prevent problems in the first place by promoting healthy brain development during the first few years of life.

Feeding and malnutrition

Nutrition refers to the amount and kind of food that people eat. Because infants grow so quickly, adequate nutrition consumed in a loving and supportive environment is one of the most important requirements for healthy early growth of the brain and body. Today, many paediatricians recommend that parents feed their newborn babies as often as every two to three hours. By seven to eight months of age, babies (much like adults) usually feed about four times per day.

Most experts agree that breastfeeding is better for the infant's health than bottle feeding with formula, unless the mother has viral or bacterial infections such as HIV/Aids or tuberculosis (TB) or is taking drugs that can be passed on to the baby. Breast milk is ideally suited to infants' growth needs and offers protection against disease (Hanson et al., 2002). Early weaning of infants from breast milk to inadequate sources of nutrients (such as a cow's milk formula) can cause protein deficiency and malnutrition in infants. However, experts believe that malnutrition is not just a matter of insufficient food or nutrients; it is often linked to difficulties in the parent–infant relationship. Children are more likely to become malnourished when their caregivers are emotionally unavailable, insensitive or unresponsive to the baby's needs. Malnourished children may be more challenging to rear than healthy children, making it even more difficult to establish warm and nurturing parent–child relationships (Richter, 2004).

The World Health Organization has estimated that malnutrition is directly or indirectly responsible for approximately half of all deaths of children under the age of five in developing countries. In South Africa, protein-energy malnutrition was responsible for 4,3 per cent of deaths of children under five in 2000. It was the fifth leading cause of death for this age group, resulting in a total of 4 564 deaths (Bradshaw, Bourne & Nannan, 2003).

Even if it is not fatal, severe and lengthy malnutrition has a number of negative effects on a young child's physical, cognitive, and social development. Children who are malnourished during the prenatal period and infancy – as Syanda and Aidile from the opening case study are – do not grow adequately, either physically or mentally. Their brains are smaller than normal, and they have little resistance to infectious diseases. They also lack energy, have poor attention spans, and are less likely to explore their environment. Over time, this can result in lasting behavioural, social, and cognitive deficits, including slower language and fine motor development, lower IQ, and poorer school performance (Zero to Three, 2012; Richter, 2004).

It is, however, possible to improve the outcomes for malnourished children. One study, conducted between 1969 and 1989 in rural Guatemala, found that giving malnourished infants or children protein supplements and increased calories had long-term benefits for the children's knowledge, number skills, reading, and vocabulary (Pollitt, Gorman, Engle, Martorell & Rivera, 1993). These effects were particularly strong for the poorest children, and those who received supplements before they were two years old. Nowadays, health professionals are taught that treatment programmes for malnutrition should also provide physical and psychological stimulation for children and therapeutic interventions for parents and families (World Health Organization, 1999).

Sleeping

The immaturity of the infant's brain is thought to be one of the reasons that babies sleep so much – newborn babies usually sleep about 16 to 17 hours a day, although some sleep more than others (Thoman & Whitney, 1989). Sleeping allows infants to take a break from the constant rush of new sights, sounds, smells, tastes, and textures with which their brain is bombarded when they are awake. Unfortunately for parents, these 16 hours do not come in one lump, but are broken up into many naps that may last anywhere from a few minutes to a few hours, with periods of wakefulness in between. Thus, newborn infants may be awake at any time of the day or night. As infants develop, the amount of sleep they need gradually decreases. In addition, they begin to sleep for longer periods that begin to coincide more and more with adult day–night schedules.

The age at which babies take on adult-like sleep–wake cycles is influenced both by the maturation of the infant's brain and by the culture in which he or she grows up. Infant sleeping arrangements vary widely from one society to another. Middle-class parents in the USA and many European countries, for example, typically put their infants to bed at set hours – often in a room of their own – and try to get them to adopt an adult routine and to sleep through the night at an early age. However, in most parts of the world – including much of Africa, Asia and Central America – infants usually sleep in the same bed as their mothers (a practice referred to as **co-sleeping**). Often, these infants are fed on demand whenever they wake up, and they typically take a few months longer to sleep through the night (Super & Harkness, 1982).

Co-sleeping
the practice of infants sleeping in the same bed as their mothers

ACTIVITY

1   When you were a baby, did you sleep in the same room as your parents?
2   Did you share your parents' bed, or did you sleep in your own cot or bed?
3   Find out why your parents used these sleeping arrangements.
4   Would you use the same sleeping arrangements with your own children? Why (or why not)?

There is no firm evidence that either co-sleeping or sleeping alone is 'better' or 'worse' for infants. However, cultural differences in sleeping arrangements are important because they show how infant-care practices vary in different parts of the world as a result of different beliefs about what babies are, what they can do, and what they will need to do in the future. Separate sleeping arrangements for mothers and infants are common in societies that place strong emphasis on independence, self-reliance, and respect for the individual. The USA is an example of such a society. In contrast, co-sleeping is the norm in societies which place more value on teaching children to be interdependent, cooperative and sensitive to the needs of others (Shweder et al., 1998). In some traditional African infant-care practices, babies are kept close to their mothers (carried on their backs during the day, sharing their beds at night) and fed or soothed quickly when they cry. These practices can be seen in part as a reflection of the value placed on *ubuntu* – a spirit of community, connectedness, cooperation, and compassion.

CHECK YOUR PROGRESS
- What broad trends or patterns underlie physical development in infancy? Give examples of each trend.
- What are the main changes that take place with regard to brain cells during infancy?
- What are the effects of malnutrition during infancy?
- How do infant sleeping arrangements reflect cultural beliefs and values?

Cognitive development

As infants' brains develop, and as they actively explore the world around them, so their ability to think systematically and to remember their experiences improves. Much of what psychologists know about cognitive development in infancy can be credited to Jean Piaget, who has probably stimulated more research on how children think than anybody else.

Piaget's theory of cognitive development

Chapter two introduced Piaget's theory. This chapter will focus on Piaget's first stage of cognitive development, which covers the age range from birth to two years.

ACTIVITY

How does a baby think?
Imagine that you are a six-month-old infant. How do you think about the people and objects around you, when you don't yet have words for them and cannot speak?

You probably found the exercise of imagining yourself to be a six-month-old infant very difficult. Hardly anyone can remember what it was like to be a baby. However, Piaget's research has helped psychologists to understand how babies think.

Piaget's sensorimotor stage

Piaget called his first stage of cognitive development 'sensorimotor' because infants use their senses (vision, touch, taste, hearing, and smell) and physical actions (motor activity) to learn about the world (Piaget & Inhelder, 1969). In other words, Piaget believed that babies and toddlers 'think' with their eyes, ears, hands, etc. They cannot yet carry out many activities inside their heads.

As chapter three explained, a reflex is an inborn, automatic response to a particular form of stimulation, and at birth, much of the baby's behaviour consists of reflexes. The following are some examples of reflexes (chapter three mentioned some of these):

- **Rooting reflex:** Stroke a newborn baby's cheek (near the corner of the mouth), and the baby will turn his or her head in your direction (the rooting reflex).
- **Palmar grasp reflex:** Put your finger in a baby's palm, and she or he will grab on tightly.
- **Sucking reflex:** Place your finger in a baby's mouth, and he or she will suck it.

Newborn babies suck, grasp and look in much the same way, no matter what kind of experiences they have. For example, they will suck a finger or a ball in the same way that they suck the breast. During the sensorimotor period, they gradually learn to coordinate their sensations and perceptions with their physical movements and actions. They also begin to build up mental pictures of objects in their environment, according to what they can do with the objects. By about one month old, infants will open their mouths differently for a nipple than for a spoon. By about four months, they sit up, reach for, and manipulate objects. By about eight months, babies come to recognise that they can 'make things happen' through their actions. They begin to act intentionally – for example, by shaking a rattle to make a noise, or dropping toys out of their cots and watching them fall to the floor. At this age, babies often think that throwing things is a great game.

During this period, babies gradually also achieve what is known as **object permanence**: the realisation that things continue to exist even when they are not being perceived – that is, when they are out of sight or not present to the senses.

Object permanence
the realisation that things continue to exist when these things cannot be seen, heard, or touched

Object permanence

Have you played the game of Peek-a-boo with a baby, when you cover your face with your hands or hide it behind an object? Then you suddenly show your face and say 'Boo!' Many babies find this hilarious. They love this game, and will play it over and over again. Yet if you tried to play this game with your friends they would probably not be particularly amused. Why is this?

It is probably due to the fact that the baby is just starting to understand the idea of object permanence. He or she is therefore surprised and delighted to find that you are still there. Your friends, however, mastered the idea of object permanence a long time ago. They take it for granted that you are still there behind your hands, and are therefore not at all surprised when you reappear.

Piaget studied babies' reactions to objects that they could see, and which were then hidden from them. For example, imagine that a four-month-old is looking at a rattle. While the baby watches, you slowly cover the rattle with a pillow. Although the baby has seen the pillow, he or she will probably lose all interest in the rattle. Piaget concluded that infants behave as though they believe that an object that is out of sight no longer exists.

By 8 to 12 months, babies will look for a hidden object, but they will look for it in the place they first found it after seeing it hidden, even if they later saw it being moved to another place. Piaget called this **the A, not B, error.** Piaget noticed the A, not B, error when his son Laurent was nine-and-a-half months old. Piaget placed the baby on a sofa, with a small blanket (A) on his right and a woollen jersey (B) on his left. As the baby watched, Piaget hid his watch under the blanket (A). His son lifted the blanket and retrieved the watch. After repeating this game several times, Piaget placed the watch under the jersey (B) instead of under the blanket. The baby watched closely, then again lifted the blanket (A) and searched for the watch there. Piaget reasoned that the baby must believe that the object's existence is linked to a particular location (the location where the object was first found) and to the infant's own actions in getting it back from that location. According to Piaget, it is only by about 18 months of age that the concept of object permanence is fully mastered.

Understanding the concept of object permanence is an important milestone in cognitive development: it is the basis for language and thought. Adults don't have to point at things to get other people to understand them. They use symbols such as words to stand for, or mentally represent, the ideas they have.

Consider using a word to stand for something. Before you can use a word to stand for something, you need to be able to separate the idea

The A, not B, error
the tendency of infants to search for a hidden object in the location they last found it (A), rather than in a new place to which they saw it being moved (B)

of something (for example a sandwich) from the actual object. You can think about a sandwich, have a picture of one in your mind, talk about it, without a sandwich actually being anywhere in the room. Object permanence is the very beginning of thought. By the time the sensorimotor stage comes to an end, infants are able to use symbols in their thinking: that is, they are able to think in ideas, and to use words to express those ideas.

Does research support Piaget's theory?

Although some research has supported Piaget's theory, nowadays there is also growing evidence that Piaget may have underestimated infants' cognitive abilities. For example, some researchers suggest that infants may develop at least some understanding of object permanence much earlier than Piaget claimed. These researchers have used an alternative method known as **violation-of-expectations research**. This method is based on what infants look at, and for how long. Because it doesn't require any motor activity, it can be used with infants as young as three months.

In violation-of-expectations research, infants first get used to seeing an event happen as it normally would. This process is known as **habituation**. Habituation involves learning not to respond to a stimulus that is repeated over and over – or in other words, learning to be bored by the familiar. For example, you might not notice the continual ticking of a clock, because you are so used to it. Once an infant has been habituated to a familiar event, the event is changed in a way that conflicts with (violates) normal expectations or the laws of physics (an impossible event). An example of an impossible event would be a person walking through a brick wall. If you were to see a person walk through an open door, you would probably not pay this event much attention. However, if you were to see a person walk through a solid wall, you would probably stare in amazement. Thus, if the infant looks longer at the impossible event, this is interpreted as evidence that the infant recognises it as surprising.

In one experiment (Baillargeon & De Vos, 1991), infants who were three-and-a-half months old watched a short carrot and then a tall carrot slide along a track, disappear behind a screen, and then reappear (see Figure 4.3). After the infants became used to seeing these events, the solid screen was replaced by a screen with a large gap or window at the top. The short carrot did not appear in the gap when passing behind the screen. This event is a possible event, because the short carrot was shorter than the bottom edge of the gap. However, the tall carrot, which should have appeared in the gap, also did not. This event is an impossible event, because the tall carrot was taller than the lower edge of the gap. The babies looked for longer at the tall than at the short carrot event, suggesting that they expected the tall carrot to reappear, and were surprised when it did not.

Violation-of-expectations research a method in which researchers show infants a possible event (one that follows physical laws) and an impossible event (a variation of the first event that conflicts with normal expectations or the laws of physics)

Habituation learning not to respond to a stimulus that is repeated over and over

Figure 4.3 An illustration of the short carrot event, tall carrot event, possible event, and impossible event

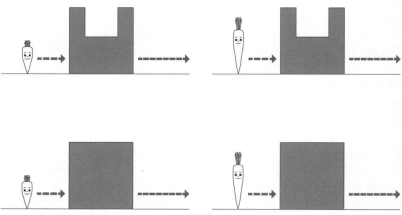

Source: Adapted from Baillargeon, R. & De Vos, J. (2008) Object permanence in young infants: Further evidence. *Child Development, 62*, 1230. Copyright © 2008, The Society for Research in Child Development, Inc. Reprinted by permission of John Wiley and Sons.

How do researchers interpret the findings of Baillargeon & De Vos (1991)? Findings of violation-of-expectations research have led some researchers to believe that infants are born with some understanding of the properties of objects. However, this interpretation is still controversial. Critics of violation-of-expectations research argue that an infant's responses are not due to innate or inborn knowledge, but rather to processes such as perception, attention, memory, and increasing experience of the world that simply allow the infant to tell that 'something is different' or 'something is familiar'. These critics ask the following questions (Haith & Benson, 1998):

- Why, if infants as young as three-and-a-half months have a concept of object permanence, does infants' search for something they have seen hidden begin only several months after they can grasp objects?
- Why do they make the A, not B, error when they search?

Elizabeth Spelke (1998) has suggested one possible answer. She argues that a very basic knowledge of object permanence may exist in early infancy, and may become more sophisticated as infants have more experience in reaching for and handling objects, and translating what they know into a successful search strategy.

Early memory

In order to master the concept of object permanence, an infant has to be able to remember the location of a hidden object. When do infants become capable of remembering their experiences? Since infants cannot tell researchers what they remember, researchers have had to find ways to let them show it.

Researcher Carolyn Rovee-Collier (1999) tied a ribbon to a baby's ankle, and attached the other end to an attractive mobile (a toy that can be hung over a baby's cot). Rovee-Collier found that within a few minutes, the infant learnt that kicking her leg made the mobile move. In order to test infant memory, Rovee-Collier showed the baby the mobile again days or weeks later (without the ribbon attached), to see whether he or she would kick again. To succeed at this task, the infant must first recognise the mobile, and then recall that in order to make it move, he or she needs to kick. Two-month-old infants can remember how to make the mobile move for up to two days; three-month-olds can remember for about a week; and six-month-olds can remember for more than two weeks. This is clear evidence that infants of two-to-six months old are able to recognise what they have experienced before.

However, young infants' memory of a behaviour seems to depend on specific cues, or reminders of what they have learned. Between two and six months of age, infants will kick only when they see the original mobile: they have trouble remembering what to do when researchers show them a different mobile (for example one that has different toy animals hanging from it). After long delays, infants of this age also have difficulty remembering what to do when they are in a different setting or context from the one in which they originally learned the behaviour.

By about six to nine months, infants become capable of moving beyond recognition memory to being able to deliberately recall ('call to mind') objects and events, without any clear reminder. Around this age, infants become capable of **deferred imitation**: remembering and imitating a sequence of behaviours that they learnt through observation alone, and have not practised. An example would be seeing a researcher put a teddy bear in bed, cover him with a blanket, and read him a story. As infants get older, they become capable of remembering and imitating such events for longer. Six-month-olds are capable of deferred imitation for a day at most, 13-month-olds can remember and imitate behaviours they learned as long as 3 months before, and infants aged between 16 and 20 months are capable of deferred imitation for a whole year after observing a new behaviour (Bauer, Herstgaard, Dropik & Wewerka, 2000).

In summary, there is evidence that infants and toddlers are capable of learning and storing memories over fairly long periods of time.

Deferred imitation
a child's ability to remember and copy new actions he or she has previously observed another person perform

Why, then, do most people remember so little of their first years of life? The next section will explore this issue.

ACTIVITY

1 Write down what you think is your first or earliest memory.
2 How old do you think you were when you experienced this event?
3 How much detail can you remember?

Infantile amnesia

In thinking about your first or earliest memory, you probably found that you could remember little if anything that happened during the first three years of your life. This inability of adults and older children to remember events that occurred before the age of about two or three years is called **infantile amnesia**. How do psychologists explain infantile amnesia? One suggestion is that infants store memories in a 'pre-verbal' form that people find it difficult to access once they become capable of using language to talk about events (Simcock & Hayne, 2002). Alternatively, it may be that what is lacking is a sense of self around which memories of events can be organised as 'events that happened to me' (Howe & Courage, 1993). There are a number of other ideas about why infants' early memories don't last, but currently there is still no firm explanation of why most people have no recollection of a period of life that is very important to later development.

Infantile amnesia
inability of adults and older children to remember events that occurred before the age of about two or three years

Social interaction and cognitive development

Piaget viewed children as little scientists, independently exploring the world. Vygotsky (1978), in contrast, believed that cognitive development occurs as a result of children's social interactions. Chapter two introduced you to a special Vygotskian concept: the zone of proximal development (ZPD). The ZPD is the gap between what a child can accomplish on his or her own and what he or she can accomplish with the help of a more knowledgeable or skilled member of his or her culture. Shared activities with adults and peers on tasks that are in the child's zone of proximal development allow children to participate in activities that are beyond their capacities when working alone. Over time, children are gradually able to internalise the skills that they practised with adult support: that is, to make those skills their own.

Jerome Bruner has built on Vygotsky's work using the concept of **scaffolding**. Scaffolding is the metal or wood structure workers stand

Scaffolding
Bruner's term for a form of teaching in which the level of support offered is adjusted to fit the learner's current level of performance

on when painting a house or doing construction work; the scaffolding doesn't do the work for them, but it holds them up so they can do it. Bruner pointed out that adults can support children's thinking in the same way by providing them with the words for an experience they are having, by teaching them strategies for solving problems, and so on. The less able a child is to do a task, the more support and direction – or scaffolding – an adult must give. As children become more skilled, the adult helps less and less until finally the 'scaffold' is unnecessary (Wood, Bruner & Ross, 1976).

Rogoff (1991) illustrates how learning takes place in the ZPD by describing how an adult and a 12-month-old worked a jack-in-the-box toy together. First, the adult performed all the actions (turning the handle to get the toy rabbit out of the box, and pushing the toy rabbit back into the box), while the baby watched. In the second episode of play, the baby attempted to push the toy rabbit back into the box, with the help and encouragement of the adult. In the third episode, the baby began to participate in turning the handle. Eventually, the baby participated in winding the handle, pushing the toy rabbit back into the box, and closing the box, while the adult helped by winding the handle to near the end of its cycle and helping to hold the lid down on the springy toy rabbit. Thus, interactions with adults may help to advance infants' cognitive skills.

CHECK YOUR PROGRESS

- What did Piaget mean by the terms 'assimilation', 'accommodation' and 'object permanence'?
- How has violation-of-expectations research challenged Piaget's views on the development of object permanence?
- How did Rovee-Collier assess infant memory? What did she discover about infants' memory capacities?
- Using Vygotsky's and Bruner's ideas, explain how adults can support infants' cognitive development.

The beginnings of language

Language is a form of communication – whether spoken, written or signed – that is based on a system of symbols such as letters or dots and dashes. In order to learn a language, a person must master a number of skills and rules. For example, he or she must learn to recognise and produce the basic sounds of that language, to understand the meaning of words, and to combine these words into grammatical sentences. Whatever language they learn, people all over the world follow a similar path in language development. This section will take a look at some important early milestones in this process.

Before the first words

Long before babies say their first words, they communicate with their caregivers and other people. Their sounds and gestures go through this sequence during their first year:

- **Crying:** Babies cry even at birth. Crying can be a sign of distress, but parents soon learn that there are different types of cries that mean different things, such as hunger, sleepiness or anger.
- **Cooing:** Babies first coo at about one to two months. These are vowel-like sounds such as 'oooh'. These sounds usually occur when the infant is interacting with the caregiver.
- **Babbling:** Babbling first occurs between 6 and 10 months of age, and includes strings of consonant–vowel combinations such as 'ma, ma, ma, ma'. These sounds are the building blocks of true speech.
- **Gestures:** Infants start using gestures, such as showing and pointing, at about 8 to 12 months of age. They may wave goodbye, nod to mean 'yes', or hold up their arms to show that they want to be picked up.

Recognising language sounds

From birth up to about six months, infants are 'citizens of the world'; they can recognise when sounds change, no matter what language the sounds come from. But over the next six months, infants get better at perceiving the changes in sounds from the language their caregivers speak, and they gradually lose the ability to recognise sounds that don't exist in their home language. For example, infants from English-speaking homes can tell the difference between the 'r' sound (ra) and the 'l' sound (la) when they are 6 months old, and get better at it by 12 months of age. However, in Japanese there is no 'r' or 'l'. Six-month-old Japanese babies are just as good as babies from English-speaking homes at recognising the ra and la distinction, but by 12 months of age they lose this ability (Kuhl et al., 2006). This process is thought to be due to the 'blooming' and 'pruning' of brain connections, which you learnt about earlier in this chapter. Read the box headed 'Bilingual babies' to see how the brain reacts when infants are exposed to two languages, rather than only one.

Bilingual babies

In South Africa – with its eleven official languages – being able to speak more than one language is an advantage, and often even a necessity. In households where two different languages are spoken, children have an excellent opportunity to become bilingual. But what are the effects of learning two languages at the same time?

Some people worry that growing up bilingual will confuse a baby and delay language development. However, the research evidence suggests that babies are just as prepared to learn two languages from birth as one. Bilingual children reach the main language milestones (such as babbling and speaking the first word) at the same age as monolingual children (Grosjean, 2010). Bilingual babies may take a little longer than monolingual children to distinguish sounds in different languages. However, the brains of bilingual babies remain flexible to language for a longer period of time.

Adrian Garcia-Sierra et al. (2011) found that babies growing up in monolingual English homes could detect changes in sounds in both English and Spanish at six to nine months of age. But at 10–12 months of age, these babies could distinguish only changes in English sounds. Babies growing up in bilingual English and Spanish homes showed a different pattern. At six to nine months, the bilingual babies did not respond when sounds changed in either language. But at 10–12 months, they could detect when sounds changed in both English and Spanish.

This ability to switch between languages may help bilingual children to develop particularly flexible ways of thinking and learning (Kovács & Mehler, 2009). Researchers agree that the best way for infants to learn a second language is through social interaction and daily exposure to each language.

Another important task for infants is to pick out individual words from the non-stop stream of sound that makes up ordinary speech. To do so, they must find the boundaries between words. This is very difficult, because adults don't usually pause between words when they speak. Still, infants begin to spot word boundaries by eight months of age. In one experiment (Saffran, Aslin & Newport, 1996), eight-month-old infants listened to two minutes of speech consisting entirely of random combinations of syllables that were run together in the following way: Dapikutiladotupirogolabu … dapikutupirotiladogolabu … tupirodapi-kutiladogolabu.

At the end of the two-minute period, the experimenters played some made-up three-syllable 'words' for the infants. Some of these 'words' were new, but some – like 'tupiro' – had been in the original passage (three times, in fact). Surprisingly, the children were more likely to turn their heads in response to items that had been in the passage than to ones that hadn't. Since head-turning in infants is a sign of noticing, it is clear that the children were somehow able to recognise the syllable combinations that were in the two minutes of nonsense to which they had been listening.

The first words

At about 8–12 months of age, infants often show their first understanding of words. On average, infants understand about 50 words at about 13 months of age, but they can't say this many words until about 18 months. So, an infant's receptive vocabulary (words the child understands) is much larger than his or her spoken vocabulary (words the child uses).

The infant's first word usually occurs at about 10 to 15 months of age, and on average at about 13 months. An English-speaking child's first words usually include those that name important people (for example 'daddy'), familiar animals (for example 'doggie'), vehicles ('car'), toys ('ball'), food ('milk'), body parts ('eye'), clothes ('hat'), household items ('clock'), and greeting terms ('bye-bye') (Nelson, 1973). These first words are closely linked to objects the child can act on and to those objects that get the child's attention by moving or changing. For example, the words 'shoes', 'socks', 'toys' and 'cars' are more common than words referring to objects that are 'just there', such as tables or houses.

Once infants start to speak, their spoken vocabulary quickly increases from about 50 words at the age of 18 months, to about 200 words by the age of 2 years. This rapid increase in vocabulary that begins at approximately 18 months is called the **vocabulary spurt** (Dapretto & Bjork, 2000).

Children sometimes overextend or underextend the meanings of the words they use (Kay & Anglin, 1982). **Overextension** is the tendency to apply a word to objects that are not related to the word's meaning, or are inappropriate for it. For example, when children learn to say 'dog', they often also apply the word to other four-legged animals. With time, overextensions decrease and eventually disappear. **Underextension** is the tendency to apply a word too narrowly; it occurs when children fail to use a word to name a relevant event or object. For example, a child might use the word 'bottle' to describe the plastic bottle he or she drinks from, but not to describe other kinds of bottle.

Telegraphic speech

By the time they are 18–24 months of age, toddlers start to put two or more words together to express one idea (for example 'See doggie', 'More milk'). At first, children typically use **telegraphic speech**, which uses only a few words that are essential to get the child's meaning across. The phrase 'telegraphic speech' comes from telegraphs, machines that were used to transmit written messages (telegrams) quickly over long distances before email and faxes were available. Telegrams were generally charged by the word, so people using this method of communication would leave out any words that were not absolutely necessary.

Vocabulary spurt
rapid increase in learning new words that begins at approximately 18 months of age

Overextension
applying a word too broadly

Underextension
applying a word too narrowly

Telegraphic speech
simplified speech in which only the most important words are used to express ideas

Explaining language development: Biological and environmental influences

Although language is vitally important in everyday life, most people take it for granted – at least until they have to learn a new language. Adults who learn a new language often find that they struggle to tell the difference between similar sounds and to pronounce words correctly. They find it difficult to remember all the new words they are learning, and cannot understand what other people are saying, as they talk too fast. Yet by the time toddlers reach their second birthday, they already know the meaning of approximately 200 words, can pronounce them correctly, and are able to put them together in the proper order. When you think about it, this is really an amazing achievement. How do infants actually learn language, and how do they do it so quickly? Theorists have provided a variety of different answers to this question, but nowadays most researchers believe that both biology and the environment influence language development.

Biological influences

Some language scholars believe that language learning is innate and biologically based. One such linguist is Noam Chomsky, whose work was first discussed in chapter one. Chomsky (2002) believes that children are born into the world with a **language acquisition device (LAD)**, which is an inborn biological system that prepares the child to detect and learn the sounds and rules of language.

Language acquisition device
an inborn biological system that helps children learn language

There is some evidence that supports the idea of a biologically based capacity to learn language. For example, there are certain areas of the brain that are specialised for language functions: Broca's area – in the left frontal lobe of the brain – controls speaking, whereas Wernicke's area – a region of the brain's left hemisphere – is involved in understanding language (Papathanassiou et al., 2000). In addition, there is evidence that children all over the world learn language in the same stages. These stages occur in the same order and around the same ages, regardless of what language children learn to speak.

Does this mean that the environment doesn't matter? No! It seems that learning also plays a role in language acquisition, if only because children acquire the languages they hear around them.

Environmental influences

Learning theorists argue that language develops through imitation and reinforcement. Children listen to others and imitate what they hear. They are also praised by parents and other adults for meaningful speech, and corrected when they make mistakes. Imitation and reinforcement alone cannot explain how children learn grammatical rules and create sentences they have never heard before. Nevertheless, many theorists nowadays believe that interactions with older companions help children to learn the rules of language and communication.

What is important in the environment to promote language development? First, there is evidence that children need to hear live language. Children cannot learn language solely from listening to the radio or watching television (Ervin-Tripp, 1973). In order to work out what a sentence means, they need to be able to link it with what they can see happening around them. Second, not only do children need to hear lots of live language, but they also learn better if they are actively involved in social interactions, and people talk to them (Locke, 1997). Children like Siyanda and Andile, from the case study that opened this chapter, who have been neglected often show delays in both their receptive and spoken vocabulary (Allen & Oliver, 1982).

Although children do not need any special teaching to learn language, there are several strategies that caregivers can use to help their infants learn language. Caregivers use most of these techniques automatically, and are often not even aware of what they are doing. One example of such a strategy is **child-directed speech** ('baby talk'), language spoken in a higher, more sing-song voice than normal, with simple words and sentences and a lot of repetition. To appreciate the notion of child-directed speech, imagine that you are taking a baby for a walk, and you pass a family of ducks. You probably wouldn't say, 'Look at that mother duck taking her ducklings for a walk.' Instead, you'd probably say something more like, 'Ducks! Look at the ducks. See? Mommy duck and baby ducks!' Child-directed speech helps to attract the infant's attention (Cooper & Aslin, 1990). It is hard to use child-directed speech when there are no babies around. As soon as you start talking to a baby though, you probably shift automatically into child-directed speech.

Other strategies that adults use to enhance the child's language include the following:

- **Labelling:** Labelling is identifying the names of objects.
- **Expanding:** Expanding is restating, in a grammatically complete form, what a child has said. For example, if the child says, 'Doggie bark', the adult might say, 'Yes, the dog is barking at the person delivering the post.'

Note that adults use these strategies naturally and in meaningful conversations with children. Even children who are slow in learning language do not need to be 'taught' to talk; turning language into work can do more harm than good. Instead, children usually benefit when parents or caregivers talk, read and sing to them, respond to and encourage the children's interest in language, and make the children feel that language is fun.

Child-directed speech
'baby talk'; language spoken in a higher, more sing-song voice than normal, with simple words and sentences and a lot of repetition

Labelling
identifying the names of objects – a strategy that adults use to enhance the child's language

Expanding
restating, in a grammatically complete form, what a child has said – a strategy that adults use to enhance the child's language

CHECK YOUR PROGRESS
- What is the typical course of language development before the first words?
- What are the major milestones of language development from birth to age two?
- What is the Language Acquisition Device (LAD)?
- Outline three strategies that parents or caregivers use to help babies learn to talk.

Psychosocial development

The physical, cognitive, and language changes that this chapter has looked at are shared by all typically developing children. Yet, even though all infants have certain things in common, each infant is a unique individual right from the start. Infants are also social beings who seem to be biologically prepared to interact with others and form relationships with them. During the course of the first year, infants usually develop close emotional ties to their caregivers. The nature and quality of these early attachments may have important implications for later social and emotional development.

This section will consider several aspects of psychosocial development:
- Temperament
- Early capacities
- Attachment
- Self-awareness and independence.

Temperament

Almost any parent who has had more than one child will be able to tell you that some babies just seem to be born more active, less irritable, or more sociable than others. One infant might be cheerful much of the time; another might cry a lot. These behaviours reflect differences in **temperament**, an individual's behavioural style and characteristic way of emotionally responding to events. Many psychologists believe that temperament is already present at birth.

Categories and dimensions of temperament

Temperament has been defined and measured in a number of different ways. Alexander Thomas, Stella Chess and their colleagues (Chess & Thomas, 1996) found that many babies could be classified into one of three temperamental categories:
- **Easy:** Easy infants are cheerful and even-tempered. They adapt easily to new experiences such as new foods or routines. They quickly develop regular sleeping and feeding schedules.

Temperament
an individual's behavioural style and characteristic way of emotionally responding to events

- **Difficult:** Difficult infants, in contrast, are active, intense and irritable. They are negative towards new experiences. They show irregular sleep and feeding schedules.
- **Slow to warm up:** Slow-to-warm-up infants are much less active and intense, but they take some time to adapt to new experiences.

Chess and Thomas (1996) also found that there was a fourth group of children who did not fit into any of these temperamental categories.

Other researchers feel that giving children a negative label like 'difficult' can be damaging. These researchers prefer to see temperament as dimensional. For example, Mary Rothbart (2007) has proposed that there are the following three basic dimensions of temperament, which interact with one another:

- **Surgency, or extraversion:** This involves the infant's tendency to approach new experiences actively and energetically.
- **Negative affectivity:** This refers to the tendency to be sad, easily frustrated, and irritable. Intense children who seem to be easily angered or upset would be described as having greater negative affectivity than those who are more laid back.
- **Effortful control:** This refers to the extent to which children are able to sustain their attention, control their behaviour and regulate their emotions. For example, some children are more effective than others at reducing feelings such as anger and fear, and at waiting for something they want.

Jerome Kagan (2003) has identified another temperamental dimension that he believes is very important: behavioural inhibition. Uninhibited children approach the world around them with confidence, eagerness, and a positive attitude. In contrast, inhibited children are shy, timid, and cautious.

Is temperament genetic?

There is evidence that early temperamental differences in sociability, shyness, and emotionality are rooted in inherited differences in the chemistry and functioning of the brain (Kagan, 2003). In other words, some of the temperamental differences between people can be traced to their genes. However, a child's experiences (which include parenting styles and broader cultural values) also seem to play an important role in shaping temperament-based behaviours (Sturm, 2004).

Does temperament remain the same over time?

There is some stability over time in measures of children's temperament; for example, inhibited infants are more likely than uninhibited infants to be shy and quiet in unfamiliar situations at the age of 11 (Kagan, 2003). However, not all inhibited infants become shy children or shy adults. Whether temperament will remain stable over time seems to depend on the way in which an infant's temperament interacts over time with his or her caregivers' parenting behaviours (Sanson, Hemphill & Smart, 2004). Thus, the personality of the adult is by no means set in stone in infancy.

ACTIVITY

Ask your childhood caregivers how they would describe your own temperament as an infant or toddler. Is your personality today similar to the temperament you displayed in early childhood?

Infants' early capacities

Human infants need the support and protection of their parents or caregivers in order to survive. Although babies are physically helpless, they are born with basic sensory and behavioural skills. These early capacities help infants and their caregivers to form close relationships with one another.

Newborn reflexes

Earlier in this chapter and in chapter three, you learnt that much of a newborn baby's behaviour consists of reflexes such as rooting, sucking, and grasping. Many of these inborn behaviours are important for the newborn's survival. For example, the sucking and swallowing reflexes are necessary for feeding.

However, some reflexes also help parents and infants to interact with one another and strengthen the relationship between them. For instance, a baby who searches for and successfully finds the nipple, sucks easily during feeding, and grabs when the hand is touched encourages parents to respond lovingly and feel competent as caregivers.

Sensory abilities

Newborn babies respond to touch, especially around the mouth, on the palms, and on the soles of the feet. They can distinguish several basic tastes (sweet, sour, bitter) and smells. By 4–10 days of age, breastfed babies prefer the smell of their own mother's breast milk to that of another woman (Porter, Makin, Davis & Christensen, 1992).

As chapter three mentioned, newborn infants can also hear a variety of sounds. They can tell sounds of the human voice apart from other kinds of sound. Newborn infants can recognise their mother's voice, and apparently prefer it to those of other women. DeCasper and Fifer (1980) found that, in order to hear their mother's voice rather than that of another female, newborns learnt to suck faster or slower on a special dummy connected to a tape recorder. This probably happens because the infant can hear the mother's voice in the uterus before being born, and is therefore familiar with it.

Vision is the least developed of the senses at birth. Newborn babies cannot focus their eyes as well as an adult can, and images such as the parent's face, even from close up, look quite blurred. Newborns are also very short-sighted. Nevertheless, they are able to see objects about 30 centimetres away – more-or-less the distance of the parent's face when an infant is feeding – which allows them to make eye contact. A newborn baby's eyes are particularly attracted to moving objects. Newborns also seem to prefer to look at forms that resemble human faces rather than at other patterns (Mondloch et al., 1999). Within the first few hours after birth, infants can mimic certain facial expressions (Meltzoff & Moore, 1977). They don't do this consciously, but they are able to translate what they see into similar actions of their own. Imitation is one of the best learning strategies babies have.

The baby's appearance

Babies are usually physically appealing; they look 'cute'. 'Babyish' features – a large head, a prominent forehead, large eyes, and round cheeks – seem to appeal to adults (especially women) and to bring out caregiving behaviours in them (Fullard & Reiling, 1976).

Fullard and Reiling (1976) found that adults prefer photographs of infant humans to photographs of adult humans, and also prefer photographs of infant animals to photographs of adult animals (see Figure 4.4).

Crying

Crying also helps to ensure that infants soon become the centre of family life, and is the key to their survival. Crying triggers increases in adults' heart rate and blood pressure, which are physiological signs of anxiety (Bleichfeld & Moely, 1984). Most adults find it almost impossible to ignore a baby's cry.

Smiling

Regardless of the culture in which they are raised, infants all over the world begin to smile in response to stimulation from the outside when they are about one month old. When an infant is about two-and-a-half to three months of age, these smiles become truly social: infants smile in response to others' smiles, and in turn draw smiles from other people. This helps to strengthen an infant's relationship with his or her caregiver. If a baby smiles in response to a caregiver's face, voice or touch, this suggests to the caregiver that the infant recognises and loves him or her. An infant's smiles also encourage caregivers to be more affectionate and stimulating in response.

Figure 4.4 Look at the two pictures below. Which do you like best?

(a)

(b)

Thus, it seems that human beings have evolved in ways that help to ensure that infants will receive the care, protection, and stimulation they need to survive and thrive. Contrary to what many people believe, however, close attachments between infants and their caregivers do not happen immediately or automatically when an infant is born.

Attachment

John Bowlby (1974) used the term 'attachment' to refer to the close, affectionate relationship that develops between the infant and one or a few specific caregivers such as mothers, fathers, grandparents, and child-minders. Attachment also refers to the realisation that one person in the world is special among all others.

Attachment develops during the first year of life. Newborn babies are not particularly choosy about people. However, they soon come to show preferences for some people over others. By the age of six to eight months, infants typically show a clear attachment to one, or a few, familiar care-givers. At this age, they may also show **stranger anxiety** – expressions of fear or discomfort, such as clinging to the mother in the presence of strangers. How can you know that a baby is attached to someone? A baby who is attached to a caregiver will try to remain near to the caregiver, will become upset if separated from the caregiver (**separation anxiety**), and will be happy or comforted when reunited with the person to whom he or she is attached.

The formation of attachment depends partly on cognitive develop-ment (including memory development), and particularly on the under-standing of **person permanence**. Person permanence is a special form of object permanence – the understanding that a person exists even when he or she can't be perceived. Before infants can develop attachment, they must have some understanding that people are permanent, that their caregivers exist even when they leave the room and can't be seen.

Although attachment depends on cognitive development, attachments don't form automatically. According to Bowlby, whether an attachment forms and how secure it is will be influenced by the ongoing interac-tion between infant and caregiver, and by the ability of each partner to respond to the other's signals. It is only in rare circumstances (for exam-ple in an overcrowded and understaffed orphanage) that a child will fail to develop an attachment relationship. If there is somebody to attach to, the infant will become attached to that person. However, some attach-ment relationships are more secure than others.

Patterns of attachment

Mary Ainsworth, an American developmental psychologist, took up and extended Bowlby's work. On the basis of work with infants in Uganda and the USA, Ainsworth developed a way to assess differences in the qual-ity of the attachments between parents and their 12- to 24-month-old infants (Ainsworth, 1979). This is known as the **strange-situation test**.

In this test, the infant and caregiver are brought to a playroom, and an observer notes how the infant reacts to a series of mildly stressful events, including the approaches of an adult stranger and the departures and

Stranger anxiety
the distress that infants experience in the presence of strangers

Separation anxiety
the distress that infants experience when they are separated from a primary caregiver

Person permanence
a special form of object permanence – the understanding that a person exists even when he or she can't be perceived

Strange-situation test
test assessing the quality of an infant's attachment to a parent

returns of their parent. Depending on these reactions, the quality of an infant's attachment to a parent can be placed in one of four categories:

- **Securely attached:** These babies use the parent as a secure base and are comfortable exploring when he or she is present. They often become upset when the parent leaves the room, but greet the parent when he or she returns, are quickly comforted by the parent, and then continue playing. In all cultures that have been studied, most infants show secure attachments to their caregivers.

- **Insecurely attached – resistant:** Resistant infants are fearful of the stranger and don't explore the environment, even when the parent is present. Resistant infants get very upset if the parent leaves the room but are not comforted by the parent's return. They seem to resent the parent for having left, and may resist the parent if he or she tries to make physical contact.

- **Insecurely attached – avoidant:** Avoidant infants seem fairly uninterested in the stranger and the environment of the playroom. These infants are not distressed by their parent's departure. They often ignore the parent when he or she returns.

- **Insecurely attached – disorganised/disoriented:** A small number of infants appear dazed and confused in the strange-situation procedure. These infants show strange behaviours when the parent returns after having left the room, such as moving away from the parent (instead of towards him or her), or freezing all movement. Because these children seem to lack any organised strategy for dealing with the stress they experience in the strange situation, Mary Main and her colleagues (Main & Solomon, 1990) described these children's attachment relationships as disorganised or disoriented.

Influences on the attachment relationship

The work of Ainsworth and others has helped to identify the factors that determine into which of the above four categories a particular attachment relationship will fall. These factors include:

- Quality of caregiving
- Infant characteristics
- The broader context.

Quality of caregiving

Although specific child-care practices vary from one culture to another, a secure attachment relationship in all societies seems to depend on two types of caregiving (Ainsworth, 1979):

- **Sensitive:** Sensitive caregivers treat the infant as a separate person with feelings and wishes, and are able to see things from the baby's point of view. A sensitive caregiver is able to read an infant's signals (for example facial expressions, body language, and crying). A sensitive caregiver is also able to use these cues to judge what the infant wants or needs – for example that the infant is hungry or tired, or has hurting teeth, or has found something interesting.

• **Responsive:** A responsive caregiver is quick, effective, and reliable at providing what the baby wants and needs (for example food, comfort, rest, and cuddles).

Insensitive, inconsistent, and rejecting caregiving tends to be associated with insecure attachments in children. More specifically, resistant attachments tend to be associated with inconsistent, unresponsive care; avoidant attachments tend to be associated with either rejection or over-stimulation (for example talking energetically to infants while they are falling asleep) (Isabella, 1993). Disorganised/disoriented attachments are associated with frightened (anxious and withdrawn) or frightening (intrusive and abusive) behaviour in parents (Hesse & Main, 2006).

The caregiver's age, knowledge about child development, and mental health can all affect his or her parenting abilities. For example, there is evidence that caregivers who are depressed often find it more difficult to be sensitive and responsive to infants. Infants of depressed mothers, in turn, are more likely than children of non-depressed caregivers to be insecurely attached (Murray, Fiori-Cowley, Hooper & Cooper, 1996).

Infant characteristics

Characteristics of the infant can also influence the sensitivity and responsiveness of the caregiver's behaviour and the quality of the attach-

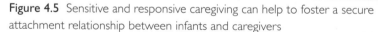

Figure 4.5 Sensitive and responsive caregiving can help to foster a secure attachment relationship between infants and caregivers

ment relationship. Sensitive and responsive caregiving can be more difficult if a baby has a difficult temperament, or is premature, disabled, or ill. The 'signals' of these babies may be more difficult to read, and they may be fussier, cry more, and be more difficult to soothe than other infants. These behaviours can make a caregiver feel incompetent and rejected.

However, parental treatment does seem to be more important than child characteristics in influencing the quality of the attachment relationship. Even infants who are temperamentally difficult or have special needs are likely to form secure attachments with caregivers who are patient and sensitive to their babies' particular characteristics (Mangelsdorf, Gunnar, Kestenbaum, Lang & Andreas, 1990).

The broader context

Characteristics of the broader context can also influence the sensitivity and responsiveness of the caregiver's behaviour and the quality of the attachment relationship. Infants are more likely to be securely attached when their parents have a positive, supportive relationship with each other, whereas marital difficulties are associated with insecure attachments (Howes & Markman, 1989).

Stressful living conditions associated with poverty can also undermine attachment by making sensitive and responsive caregiving more difficult (Diener, Nievar & Wright, 2003). These findings are particularly relevant for South Africa and other developing countries where poverty and unemployment is widespread. In South Africa, two out of three children live in poverty (Hall, 2009). Many people living in poor communities also face associated stressors, such as family and community violence, single parenthood, and high rates of HIV and Aids. Read the box headed 'South African research on attachment', which explores how parenting and attachment are affected in these conditions.

South African research on attachment

Mark Tomlinson, Peter Cooper and their colleagues studied attachment in 147 mother–infant pairs living in Khayelitsha, near Cape Town (Cooper et al., 1999; Tomlinson, Cooper & Murray, 2005; Tomlinson, Swartz, Cooper & Molteno, 2004). They assessed the mother's mood and observed her interactions with her two-month-old infant. They were able to track down 98 of these original mother–infant pairs when the infants were 18 months old, and again assessed the mother's mood and the quality of her interactions with the infant. They also assessed the infants' attachment security, using Ainsworth's strange-situation procedure.

The researchers found that nearly 35 per cent of mothers were clinically depressed 2 months after the birth of their baby. This is about three times as many as researchers would expect based on international figures for postnatal depression. The high rate of postnatal depression in Khayelitsha is probably related to the fact that all of the women in this study came from a very poor community, and many of these mothers were experiencing other life stresses on top of the stresses of becoming a mother. Mothers were more likely to be depressed when their infants were two months old under the following conditions:

- If the baby was unplanned or unwanted
- If the father had a negative attitude toward the baby
- If the father was not financially supporting the mother
- If the mother lacked social support from others.

Depressed mothers, in turn, were more likely to be insensitive in interacting with their babies than mothers who were not depressed.

Yet despite the high rate of maternal depression, the researchers found that most infants (62 per cent) were securely attached to their mothers at 18 months. They suggest that local childrearing practices (involving a lot of close physical contact between mothers and infants, co-sleeping, and breastfeeding on demand for at least the first year), together with support and compassion from the broader community (*ubuntu*), may have helped mothers and infants to form secure attachments, despite living in adverse conditions.

Of the infants who were classified as insecurely attached, only 4 per cent were classified as avoidant and 8 per cent as resistant. A fairly large group (26 per cent), however, were classified as disorganised. Attachments were more likely to be insecure if mothers had been intrusive (pushy and controlling) or remote (distant and withdrawn) in face-to-face interactions with their infants at 2 months, and were insensitive in playing with them at 18 months. Maternal depression was associated with insecure attachments only if mothers were insensitive in interacting with their toddlers at 18 months. Infants were more likely to be classified as disorganised if their caregivers had been either extremely remote ('frightened') or extremely intrusive ('frightening') in interacting with them at two months. Such parenting behaviours may be due to the difficult living circumstances that many women in Khayelitsha experience.

Why are early attachment relationships important?

From Freud on, a number of theorists have argued that the parent–child relationship has important implications for human development. Why do they believe that the earliest relationships people have are so crucial? Are these ideas supported by research? This section will explore these questions.

Bowlby's theory: Internal working models

Bowlby (1980) believed that the establishment of strong, secure emotional ties between the baby and the person (or people) who looks after the baby is crucial for healthy later life. He argued that the quality of the early parent–infant attachment has important effects on later development, including the kinds of relationship people have with friends, romantic partners, and their own children.

A basic assumption of attachment theory is that people's early experiences with caregivers shape their mental images or internal working models of themselves and other people, which, in turn, influence people's expectations about close relationships. According to attachment theory, children who experience sensitive and emotionally available caregiving early in life will, most probably, come to believe that they are worthy of love and attention, and that other people are essentially good and can be trusted and depended upon for support. Thus, such children are likely to have generally positive expectations of close relationships. In contrast, when early caregiving is inadequate, people are more likely to develop a feeling that they are difficult to love or unworthy of affection, and that other people are unreliable. They are likely to have much more negative expectations regarding relationships.

Erikson's theory: Trust versus mistrust

Chapter two introduced you to Erik Erikson's psychosocial theory of development. Erikson agreed with Bowlby's ideas about the importance of the early caregiver–child relationship. Erikson (1963) argued that development proceeds through eight stages, and that a special problem or crisis in social relationships dominates each of these stages.

Erikson's first psychosocial stage spans the period from birth to about 18 months. The psychosocial crisis here is one of basic trust versus mistrust. According to Erikson, if caregivers are warm and responsive, infants will gain a sense of trust that the world is good. As a result, they will feel confident about going out and exploring the world. Mistrust occurs when infants have to wait too long for comfort or are handled harshly. In this case, they are likely to become suspicious, insecure, and anxious, and to protect themselves by withdrawing from people and things around them. Erikson recognised that no parent can be perfectly in tune with a baby's needs all the time. But when the balance of care is sympathetic and loving, the psychological conflict of the first year – basic trust versus mistrust – is resolved on the positive side.

Research evidence: Early attachment and later development

Two main lines of research have tried to answer the question of how important the early caregiver–child relationship is for development. Some researchers have studied infants raised in institutions, where the infants never had the opportunity to form attachments. Others have focused on the later development of infants who were either securely attached or insecurely attached.

Studies of infants like Siyanda and Andile (from the case study at the start of this chapter) who grow up in orphanages and don't have the opportunity to form close, stable attachments to specific adults, have found that that they tend to show disturbed social and emotional adjustment later in childhood. Four-year-old children who were reared in deprived institutions in Romania for at least the first six months of life, and who were later adopted into British homes, were found to be much more likely than most children to show an abnormal pattern of insecure behaviour. Rutter and O'Connor (2004) called this abnormal pattern of insecure behaviour 'disinhibited attachment'. These Romanian adoptees tended to be indiscriminately friendly towards adults, and instead of being wary of strangers, approached them in a silly, overenthusiastic or overexcited manner. Generally, the longer children had been in the institution, the more likely they were to experience long-term difficulties.

What about infants who do form attachments to caregivers? Does the security or insecurity of their attachment relationships make a difference later in life? A number of studies suggest that it does: children who were securely attached as one-year-olds:

- Are later more cheerful and cooperative and less aggressive with adults
- Are more cooperative and sympathetic with peers
- Are more interested in exploring their environment
- Are more persistent at solving problems
- Do better on cognitive and language tests (Ainsworth, 1979).

Other researchers have found that adults who remember their early relationships with their parents as being warm and secure tend to have higher-quality romantic relationships in adulthood (Hazan & Shaver, 1987) and to be more sensitive in interacting with their own children (Van Ijzendoorn, 1995). However, note that these studies measured adults' perceptions or memories of their early attachment relationships. These studies did not measure what actually happened in those relationships. You should bear in mind that these perceptions may be changed by later events.

In summary, the evidence suggests that the quality of early parenting can have long-term consequences for development. This does not mean, however, that there is no hope for children who start their lives in institutions or who are insecurely attached to their caregivers: what happens after infancy is also important. There is evidence that the quality of attachment in infancy is unlikely to have long-term effects on development unless the same quality is maintained consistently over a reasonably long period of time (Waters, Weinfeld & Hamilton, 2000). In addition, an insecure relationship with one parent can be compensated for by secure attachments to the other parent, or to siblings, grandparents, childminders, and so on (Main & Weston, 1981; NICHD Early Child Care Research Network, 1997). Although psychologists don't know much about the effects of being reared by more than one adult, as is common in many developing countries, it is likely that a child benefits from having several attachment figures who can provide the child with comfort and security, as well as exposing the child to a range of interaction styles and learning experiences.

Day care and attachment

Does placing an infant in day care while his or her parents go out to work disrupt the attachment process? This question has been the topic of heated debate. Although the research findings are mixed, most of the evidence suggests that day care, in and of itself, is not harmful to children's attachment relationships. For example, results of a major study conducted in 10 cities in the USA (NICHD Early Child Care Research Network, 1997) suggested that a mother's sensitivity and responsiveness to her infant were much more important for attachment security than whether or not the infant was in non-parental care. In fact, under some circumstances, high-quality day care made up for the effects of insensitive parenting. However, infants were less likely to be secure when low levels of sensitivity and responsiveness from the mother were combined with poor-quality care, long hours in care, or more than one care arrangement. Overall, the research findings suggest that children generally do well when they receive good-quality care (whether it is provided within or outside the home); inconsistent or poor-quality care (again, regardless of who provides it) is more likely to be linked to poor outcomes.

Self-awareness and independence

In the previous section, it was clear that early social interactions are important for helping infants to gain a sense of trust and security. These social interactions – together with the developments in thinking, language, and motor skills that occur during infancy – also play an important role in giving infants a greater awareness of themselves as separate people. Self-awareness is not something that infants are born with; however, it starts to develop during the first few months of life.

Beginning at about four months of age, infants will touch a mirror image if something interesting is reflected there. Infants who are ten months old can use a mirror image to find a toy being lowered behind their backs. However, it is not until about 18 months that children begin to show self-awareness by recognising themselves in a mirror. At that age, if a red spot is painted on the child's nose, he or she will try to rub the spot off after seeing it on the mirror image (Lewis, Sullivan, Stanger & Weiss, 1989). This suggests that by 18 months, infants are capable of recognising the image in the mirror as their own, and know that they don't normally have red noses. By the age of two, children can typically identify the reflection in the mirror as 'me'.

Once infants begin to develop a sense of self, they start to show the first signs of self-control. Between 12 and 18 months, infants begin to become capable of compliance – they can obey simple requests and commands such as 'No. Don't touch!' (Kaler & Kopp, 1990). Of course, as every parent knows, they can also decide to do just the opposite! Once they have gained trust in their caregivers, toddlers become more concerned with autonomy and independence.

According to Erikson's (1963) theory, between the ages of about 18 months and 3 years, the central crisis is one of autonomy versus shame and doubt. Using new mental skills and motor skills, children want to choose and decide for themselves. As a result, toddlers often say things like 'No' and 'Do it myself'. One the one hand, if toddlers are restrained too much or are constantly criticised, shamed or punished when they fail at new skills (like eating with a spoon, using the toilet or helping pick up their toys), they may come to doubt their abilities and feel unsuccessful and inadequate to control events. On the other hand, a sense of autonomy and self-control is fostered when caregivers understand and support toddlers' attempts at independence, while also giving them suitable guidance and firm limits based on the child's level of maturation and development.

CHECK YOUR PROGRESS

- What categories and dimensions have been used to describe infant temperament?
- What are the characteristics of the four basic patterns or categories of attachment?
- How are caregiving styles related to attachment patterns in infancy?
- How is the early caregiver–infant attachment related to later development?
- What new behaviours that appear towards the end of the second year suggest that children have developed a sense of 'self'?

CASE STUDY

What do you think happened to Siyanda and Andile, the twins you read about at the beginning of this chapter? After the twins had been in the institution for a few months, their housemother was replaced by a trained care worker. She understood how important it was to stimulate the twins and integrate them with the older children and staff. The twins' behaviour began to improve enormously.

However, their physical and motor development remained severely delayed. When they were observed at the age of 3-and-a-half, the twins were about the size expected of an average 18-month-old. They could walk, but their steps were uncoordinated and unbalanced. They had difficulty starting and stopping movements and making their way around obstacles. They also found it difficult to control their fingers, and they often dropped objects. They were very active, found it difficult to focus on anything for more than a few seconds, and were easily distracted.

The twins' language development was also delayed. However, they were now very interested in people around them, and constantly sought attention and cuddles. When they were given affection, they laughed excitedly. They did not show attachments to any particular caregivers or older children, but indiscriminately enjoyed everyone's company. Unfortunately, some of the staff still believed that the twins were HIV positive and continued to keep their distance from them (Sandhei & Richter, 2003).

Questions

1   Linda Richter (2004) has pointed out that although most of the world is poor and underdeveloped, the majority of research on infant mental health and development that is published in journals and presented at international conferences comes from white, middle-class people living in the USA and Western Europe. Suggest why this is the case? What do you think are important issues, problems and concerns related to infant development in Africa that researchers should be trying to understand and respond to?

2   Imagine your friend Thabo wants to enhance his 18-month-old son's speech and language skills. How would you advise Thabo on this matter?

Conclusion

Physical development is rapid in infancy. Physical growth and motor development follow the cephalocaudal (head-to-foot) and proximodistal (centre-outward) trends. The brain also grows in complexity, and is very sensitive to environmental influences. Good nutrition consumed in a caring environment is one of the best ways of fostering healthy early growth of the brain and body.

Even in the early weeks, infants are capable of learning and remembering. However, their cognitive abilities expand during this period. According to Piaget, infants are in the sensorimotor stage of cognitive development. During this period, they learn through sensory and motor activity. Infants gradually acquire object permanence, and become capable of using symbols in their thinking. Their understanding and use of language also develops rapidly.

Along with these cognitive achievements, infants are developing self-awareness and showing signs of distinct temperaments. Infancy is an important period for forming attachments to caregivers. Research based on the strange-situation test has found four patterns of caregiver–infant attachment: secure, resistant, avoidant, and disorganised. These attachment patterns may have long-term implications for development. The key to good caregiving in the first two years of life is warm, sensitive, responsive parenting, combined with reasonable expectations for increasing self-control. According to Erikson, this should help to establish basic trust and a healthy sense of autonomy in the child.

References

Ainsworth, M. (1979). Infant-mother attachment. *American Psychologist, 34*, 932–937.

Allen, R.E. & Oliver, J.M. (1982). The effects of child maltreatment on language development. *Child Abuse and Neglect, 6*, 299–305.

Baillargeon, R. & De Vos, J. (1991). Object permanence in young infants: Further evidence. *Child Development, 62*, 1227–1246.

Banich, M.T. & Compton, R.J. (2011). *Cognitive neuroscience* (3rd ed., International ed.). Belmont, CA: Wadsworth, Cengage Learning.

Bauer, P.J., Herstgaard, L.A., Dropik, P.L. & Wewerka, S.S. (2000). Parameters of remembering and forgetting in the transition from infancy to early childhood. *Monographs of the Society for Research in Child Development, 65* (Serial No. 263).

Black, J.E. (1998). How a child builds its brain: Some lessons from animal studies of neural plasticity. *Preventive Medicine, 27*, 168–171.

Bleichfeld, B. & Moely, B. (1984). Psychophysiological response to an infant cry: Comparison of groups of women in different phases of the maternal cycle. *Developmental Psychology, 20*, 1082–1091.

Bowlby, John (1974). *Attachment and loss: Vol. 1. Attachment.* London: The Hogarth Press.

Bowlby, John (1980). *Attachment and loss: Vol. 2. Separation: Anxiety and anger.* London, England: The Hogarth Press.

Bradshaw, D., Bourne, D. & Nannan, N. (2003). *What are the leading causes of death among South African children?* (MRC Policy Brief No. 3). Cape Town: Medical Research Council.

Casey, B.J., Tottenham, N., Liston, C. & Durston, S. (2005). Imaging the developing brain: What have we learned about cognitive development? *Trends in Cognitive Sciences, 9*, 104–110.

Chess, S. & Thomas, A. (1996). *Temperament: Theory and practice*. New York, NY: Brunner/Mazel.

Chomsky, Noam (2002). *On nature and language*. Cambridge, England: Cambridge University Press.

Cole, M. & Cole, S.R. (2001). *The development of children* (4th ed.). New York, NY: Worth publishers.

Cooper, R.P. & Aslin, R.N. (1990). Preference for infant-directed speech in the first month after birth. *Child Development, 61*, 1584–1595.

Cooper, P.J., Tomlinson, M., Swartz, L., Woolgar, M., Murray, L. & Molteno, C. (1999). Postpartum depression and the mother–infant relationship in a South African peri-urban settlement. *British Journal of Psychiatry, 175*, 554–558.

Dapretto, M. & Bjork, E.L. (2000). The development of word retrieval abilities in the second year and its relation to early vocabulary growth. *Child Development, 71*, 635–648.

DeCasper, A. & Fifer, W. (1980). Of human bonding: Newborns prefer their mother's voices. *Science, 208*, 1174–1176.

Diener, M.L., Nievar, M.A. & Wright, C. (2003). Attachment security among mothers and their young children living in poverty: Associations with maternal, child, and contextual characteristics. *Merrill-Palmer Quarterly, 49*, 154–182.

Erikson, Erik (1963). *Childhood and society* (2nd ed.). New York, NY: Norton.

Ervin-Tripp, S. (1973). Some strategies for the first two years. In T.E. Moore (Ed.), *Cognitive development and the acquisition of language* (p. 261–297). New York, NY: Academic Press.

Fullard, W. & Reiling, A.M. (1976). An investigation of Lorenz's babyness. *Child Development, 47*, 1191–1193.

Garcia-Sierra, A., Rivera-Maritza, M., Percaccio, C.R., Conboy, B.T., Romo, H., Klarman, L. … Kuhl, P.K. (2011). Bilingual language learning: An ERP study relating early brain responses to speech, language input, and later word production. *Journal of Phonetics, 39*, 546–557.

Gilmore, J.H., Shi, F., Woolson, F.L., Knickmeyer, R.C., Short, S.J., Lin, W. … Shen, D. (2011). Longitudinal development of cortical and subcortical gray matter from birth to 2 years. *Cerebral Cortex*. Advance online publication. doi: 10.1093/cercor/bhr327

Grosjean, François (2010). *Bilingual: Life and reality*. Cambridge, MA: Harvard University Press.

Haith, M.M. & Benson, J.B. (1998). Infant cognition. In D. Kuhn & R.S. Siegler (Eds). *Handbook of child psychology: Vol. 2. Cognition, perception, and language* (5th ed.) (p. 199–254). New York, NY: Wiley.

Hall, Katherine (2009). *Income and social grants – children living in poverty*. Cape Town: Children's Institute, University of Cape Town.

Hanson, L.A., Korotkova, M., Halverson, L., Mattsby-Baltzer, I., Hah-Zoric, M., Silferdal, S.A. … Telemo, E. (2002). Breastfeeding, a complex support system for the offspring. *Pediatrics International, 44*, 347–352.

Hazan, C. & Shaver, P. (1987). Romantic love conceptualized as an attachment process. *Journal of Personality and Social Psychology, 52*, 511–524.

Hesse, E., & Main, M. (2006). Frightened, threatening, and dissociative parental behavior in low-risk samples: Description, discussion, and interpretations. *Development and Psychopathology, 18*, 309–343.

Hopkins, B. & Westra, T. (1988). Maternal handling and motor development: An intracultural study. *Genetic Psychology Monographs, 14*, 377–420.

Howe, M.L. & Courage, M.L. (1993). On resolving the enigma of infantile amnesia. *Psychological Bulletin, 113*, 305–326.

Howes, P. & Markman, H.J. (1989). Marital quality and child functioning: A longitudinal investigation. *Child Development, 60,* 1044–1051.

Huttenlocher, P.R. & Dabkolhar, A.S. (1997). Regional differences in synaptogenesis in human cerebral cortex. *Journal of Comparative Neurology, 37,* 167–178.

Isabella, R.A. (1993). Origins of attachment: Maternal interactive behavior across the first year. *Child Development, 64,* 605–621.

Kagan, J. (2003). Biology, context, and developmental inquiry. *Annual Review of Psychology, 54,* 1–23.

Kaler, S.R. & Kopp, C.B. (1990). Compliance and comprehension in very young toddlers. *Child Development, 61,* 1997–2003.

Kay, D.A. & Anglin, J.M. (1982). Overextension and underextension in the child's expressive and receptive speech. *Journal of Child Language, 9,* 83–98.

Kovács, A.M. & Mehler, J. (2009). Cognitive gains in 7-month-old bilingual infants. *Proceedings of the National Academy of Sciences of the United States of America, 106,* 6556–6560.

Kuhl, P.K., Stevens, E., Hayashi, A., Deguchi, T., Kiritani, S. & Iverson, P. (2006). Infants show a facilitation effect for native language phonetic perception between 6 and 12 months. *Developmental Science, 9,* (2), F13–F21.

Lampl, M., Veldhuis, J.D. & Johnson, M.L. (1992). Saltation and stasis: A model of human growth. *Science, 258,* (3880), 801–803.

Lewis, M., Sullivan, M.W., Stanger, C. & Weiss, M. (1989). Self-development and self-conscious emotions. *Child Development, 60,* 146–156.

Locke, J.L. (1997). A theory of neurolinguistic development. *Brain and Language, 58,* 265–326.

Main, M. & Solomon, J. (1990). Procedures for identifying infants as disorganized/disoriented during the Ainsworth Strange Situation. In M.T. Greenberg, D. Cicchetti & E.M. Cummings (Eds). Attachment in the preschool years: *Theory, research and intervention* (p. 121–160). Chicago, IL: University of Chicago Press.

Main, M. & Weston, D.R. (1981). The quality of the toddler's relationship to mother and to father: Related to conflict and the readiness to establish new relationships. *Child Development, 52,* 932–940.

Mangelsdorf, S., Gunnar, M., Kestenbaum, R., Lang, S. & Andreas, D. (1990). Infant proneness-to-distress temperament, maternal personality, and mother-infant attachment: Associations and goodness of fit. *Child Development, 61,* 820–831.

Meltzoff, A. & Moore, M. (1977). Imitation of facial and manual gestures by human neonates. *Science, 198,* 75–78.

Mondloch, C.J., Lewis, T.L., Budreau, D.R., Maurer, D., Dannemiller, J.L., Stephens, B.R. & Kleiner-Gathercoal, K.A. (1999). Face perception during early infancy. *Psychological Science, 10,* 419–422.

Murray, L., Fiori-Cowley, A., Hooper, R. & Cooper, P. (1996). The impact of postnatal depression and associated adversity on early mother-infant interactions and later infant outcome. *Child Development, 67,* 2512–2526.

Nelson, C.A. (1999). Neural plasticity and human development. *Current Directions in Psychological Science, 8,* 42–45.

Nelson, K. (1973). Structure and strategy in learning to talk. *Monographs of the Society for Research in Child Development, 38,* (1–2) (Serial No. 149).

NICHD Early Child Care Research Network (1997). The effects of infant child care on infant-mother attachment security: Results of the NICHD Study of Early Child Care. *Child Development, 68,* 860–879.

Papathanassiou, D., Etard, O., Mellet, E., Zago, L., Mazoyer, B. & Tzourio-Mazoyer, N. (2000). A common language network for comprehension and production: A contribution to the definition of language epicenters with PET. *NeuroImage, 11,* 347–357.

Piaget, J. & Inhelder, B. (1969). *The psychology of the child* (H. Weaver, Trans.). London, England: Routledge & Kegan Paul. (Original work published 1966)

Pollitt, E.P., Gorman, K.S., Engle, P.L., Martorell, R. & Rivera, J. (1993). Early supplementary feeding and cognition. *Monographs of the Society for Research in Child Development, 58*, (7, Serial No. 235).

Porter, R.H., Makin, J.W., Davis, L.B. & Christensen, K.M. (1992). Breast-fed infants respond to olfactory clues from their own mother and unfamiliar lactating mothers. *Infant Behaviour and Development, 15*, 85–93.

Richter, Linda (2004). *The importance of caregiver–child interactions for the survival and healthy development of young children: A review*. Geneva, Switzerland: World Health Organization.

Rogoff, B. (1991). The joint socialization of development by young children and adults. In P. Light, S. Sheldon & M. Woodhead (Eds). *Learning to think* (p. 67–96). London: Routledge.

Rothbart, M.K. (2007). Temperament, development, and personality. *Current Directions in Psychological Science, 16*, 207–212.

Rovee-Collier, C. (1999). The development of infant memory. *Current Directions in Psychological Science, 8*, 80–85.

Rutter, M., & O'Connor, T.G. (2004). Are there biological programming effects for psychological development? Findings from a study of Romanian adoptees. *Developmental Psychology, 40*, 81–94.

Saffran, J.R., Aslin, R.N., & Newport, E.L. (1996). Statistical learning by 8-month-old infants. *Science, 274*, 1926–1928.

Sandhei, M. & Richter, L. (2003). What does it take to care? *ChildrenFIRST, 47*, 3639.

Santrock, J.W. (2005). *A topical approach to life-span development* (2nd ed.). Boston, MA: McGraw-Hill.

Sanson, S., Hemphill, S.A. & Smart, D. (2004). Connections between temperament and social development: A review. *Social Development, 13*, 142–170.

Shweder, R.A., Goodnow, J., Hatano, G., LeVine, R.A., Markus, H., & Miller, P. (1998). The cultural psychology of development: One mind, many mentalities. In R.M. Lerner (Ed.). *Handbook of Child Psychology: Vol. 1. Theoretical models of human development* (5th ed.), (p. 865–938). New York, NY: Wiley.

Simcock, G. & Hayne, H. (2002). Breaking the barrier? Children fail to translate their preverbal memories into language. *Psychological Science, 13*, 225–231.

Spelke, Elizabeth. (1998). Nativism, empiricism, and the origins of knowledge. *Infant Behaviour and Development, 21*, 181–200.

Sturm, L. (2004). Temperament in early childhood: A primer for the perplexed. *Zero to Three, 24*, (4), 4–11.

Super, C.M. & Harkness, S. (1982). The infant's niche in rural Kenya and metropolitan America. In L.L. Adler (Ed.). *Parents' cultural belief systems: Their origins, expressions, and consequences* (p. 447–466). New York, NY: Guilford Press.

Thoman, E.B. & Whitney, M.P. (1989). Sleep states of infants monitored in the home: Individual differences, developmental trends, and origins of diurnal cyclicity. *Infant Behavior and Development, 12*, 59–75.

Tomlinson, M., Cooper, P. & Murray, L. (2005). The mother-infant relationship and infant attachment in a South African peri-urban settlement. *Child Development, 76*, 1044–1054.

Tomlinson, M., Swartz, L., Cooper, P. & Molteno, C. (2004). Social factors and postpartum depression in Khayelitsha, Cape Town. *South African Journal of Psychology, 34*, 409–420.

Van Ijzendoorn, M.H. (1995). Adult attachment representations, parental responsiveness, and infant attachment: A meta-analysis on the predictive validity of the Adult Attachment Interview. *Psychological Bulletin, 117*, 387–403.

Vygotsky, Lev S. (1978). *Mind in society: The development of higher psychological processes.* (M. Cole, V. John-Steiner, S. Scribner & E. Souberman, Trans.) (Eds). Cambridge, MA: Harvard University Press.

Waters, E., Weinfield, N.S. & Hamilton, C.E. (2000). The stability of attachment security from infancy to adolescence and early adulthood: General discussion. *Child Development, 71,* 703–706.

Weiten, W. (2004). *Psychology: Themes and variations* (6th ed.). Belmont, CA: Wadsworth/Thomson Learning.

Wood, D., Bruner, J.S. & Ross, G. (1976). The role of tutoring in problem solving. *Journal of Child Psychology and Psychiatry, 17,* 89–100.

World Health Organization (1999). *Management of severe malnutrition: A manual for physicians and other senior health workers.* Geneva, Switzerland: World Health Organization.

Zero to Three (2012). *FAQ's on the brain.* [WWW document]. URL http://www .zerotothree.org/child-development/brain-development/faqs-on-the-brain.html.

CHAPTER FIVE

EARLY CHILDHOOD

Louise Stroud, Joanne Hardman and Giulietta Harrison

CASE STUDY

Muriel, a 31-year-old convicted shoplifter, lives in the Johannesburg jail with her 18-month-old daughter Eva. Muriel was caught shoplifting when she was seven months pregnant. Eva was born while Muriel was in prison and has never been outside the prison. Muriel says many of her family members think that she is lucky because at least here, in prison, Eva has three meals a day and a warm bed to sleep in. But Muriel does not think that she is lucky: Eva has never seen a dog or a cat; she has never driven in a car; all she knows is people in uniforms. Muriel is due for release when Eva is two and she is very worried about how Eva will adapt to the outside world.

LEARNING OBJECTIVES

At the end of this chapter you should be able to
- Understand the cognitive development of pre-operational and concrete operational children
- Understand play as the 'leading' activity in early childhood
- Describe the basic avenues of learning proposed by the Griffiths Mental Development Scales
- Understand the six stages of moral development proposed by Lawrence Kohlberg
- Begin to explore strategies to assist children in their moral reasoning development.

Introduction

Muriel's story outlined in the case study above highlights the challenges that a child's environment can have on his or her developmental trajectory. At least Eva is with her mother; children are routinely removed from their mother's care in prisons when they reach the age of two. Chapter four discussed the importance of attachment in developing prosocial behaviour in children. Removing children from attachment figures is potentially fraught with long-term effects. This chapter looks particularly at early childhood, defined as from birth to eight years of age. Chapter three dealt with infancy, and this chapter does not cover that ground again; this chapter is concerned with a focus on children from one year old to eight years of age. The focus is on understanding how the developing child becomes socialised into his or her society.

It is well known that children's development involves an interaction between their maturation processes and the affects of the environment (Natanson, 1998). It is also true that everyone involved with the care and education of children will have observed their development in the practicalities of day-to-day situations. Those observations, combined with established common knowledge, form the basis for everyday understanding of where the child is in his or her development. While common sense assists an understanding of everyday interactions, this chapter will focus on core developmental theorists to enable an understanding of early childhood and the issues facing development in this developmental period.

The developing child

Pregnancy and birth reveal a baby's living architecture, which is stirring, beautiful, and wondrous. In every sense of the word – marvellous! The baby's unavoidable advent into the world brings with it epic changes for newborns and parents alike. At birth, the major fetal organs – such as the lungs, stomach, intestines, and kidneys – which have remained untested because there was no oxygen to breathe, food to digest, or waste to eliminate, must all start functioning at once – in some cases within seconds of delivery. Other organs already in use – such as the heart and brain – must adapt without hesitation to a world for which they have been meticulously designed and prepared, but which differs utterly from the one in which they have functioned. Blood coming into the heart must suddenly be shunted to the lungs; this means that the opening between the two upper chambers of the heart (necessary for circulation when oxygen enters the blood stream through the placenta) needs to be sealed at once. The nervous system immediately begins to make use of information from eyes that are almost blinded by a blizzard of incoming data. It is as if the child was constructed under the ocean, then thrust up onto dry land in perfect working order, and immediately pressed into service (Tsiaras, 2002). A baby, unlike a fetus, must sustain itself against many shocks, changes in temperature, and disease. Later in its life, as it develops into a child and an adult, it will have to sustain itself against the rough and tumble of school, work, dating, loss, and, probably, having children of its own. Starting at birth, a person has to negotiate each new terrain for him- or herself (Jackson, 1999; Tsiaras, 2002).

Unpacking developmental psychology

Developmental psychology deals with the intricate nature of human activities and the processes that transform 'substance', or the visible, tangible realities of the world into an invisible experience in a person's individual inner world. Individuals choose to make this private or invisible experience visible through various channels of expression. For example, language, which can be written or spoken, is often reflected in the use of metaphor and beliefs, but can also be identified through play, gesture, or body stances. People communicate their felt experiences as realities of the world they live in: this communication is received through the sensory channels and then individually understood through the mechanism of perception. As Preston (2005) indicates, it is in this way that learning and development take place.

The development of the mental processes of growing children can be seen to follow a natural progression line, often observed in the outward displays of behaviour and language use and skills of these children (Preston, 2005). This mental progression can be observed in expressions of performance, behaviour and language. Significantly, the progressive nature of these thinking processes can be identified in hierarchical stages of development, and often they do not follow a precisely chronological order (Preston, 2005).

Child development, particularly early childhood development, is a dynamic, moving target. Therefore, it is important always to take into account the particular situation of each child in a particular family and consider all his or her physical, social, intellectual, emotional and educational needs in that particular context, to understand fully the child and his or her development. In other words, understanding the child's avenues of learning is important.

The section that follows will describe the following:
* Trends that appear to be significant for mental growth
* The **basic avenues of learning**.

This description does not fall easily and smoothly into sequence. Rather, it has been garnered from many sources and people.

Basic avenues of learning
the basic means/channels through which children mentally develop and grow, such as using their eyes (sight) and hands (touch), as well as speech and hearing

ACTIVITY

What do you think?

1   Young children conduct experiments; analyse statistics; form intuitive theories of the physical, biological, and psychological realms; use language to tease out what they know and ask focused questions; and form relationships. In the light of this, give three activities that you might use in a child's playtime to assist his or her growth and exploration. Specify the developmental areas of growth you would wish these activities to encourage.

2   Do you agree with Preston (2005) that children's mental progression and development can often be seen in their outward displays of behaviour, language, and skill? Motivate your answer with practical examples from expressions of behaviour that you have observed in developing children.

Piaget's conception of cognitive development in early childhood

Pre-operational thought

Assimilation
understanding novel situations in terms of one's existing cognitive structures

Accommodation
altering one's existing cognitive structures because the novel situation is so unfamiliar it clashes with one's existing structures, forcing a change in the structure

Object permanence
the ability to recognise that something continues to exist even when it is not observed; an understanding that objects exist outside one's perception of them

Symbolic functioning
the use of mental symbols, words, or pictures which one uses to represent something which is not physically present

Chapter two discussed Piaget's theory of cognitive development in some depth. This chapter focuses very specifically on two stages of development: pre-operational and concrete operational thinking. For Piaget (1964), children learn through actively constructing knowledge by transacting with their world. That is, the child acts on his or her environment, the environment affords and constrains action, and the child actively constructs knowledge through the processes of **assimilation** and **accommodation**, passing through successive developmental stages as he or she does so. The first stage of development has already been covered in the chapter on infant development, namely the sensorimotor stage. In this developmental stage the infant develops **object permanence** and the foundations of **symbolic functioning** become evident, preparing the infant for the next developmental stage, where pre-operational thinking develops. The pre-operational stage (roughly between the ages of two to six) is characterised by a specific mode of thought where the developing child is able to focus on only one aspect of a task or situation to the exclusion of others. Piaget called this centration. This is manifested in egocentric thinking, where the child views the world or situation in terms of his or her own viewpoint, to the exclusion of others' viewpoints. Chapter two showed how two children engaged in monologues when solving a problem, rather than opening a dialogue to assist each other to solve the problem. This is most obvious when children are asked to perform a conservation experiment (see chapter 2; page 41). In the conservation experiment pre-operational children are unable to conserve because they can focus on only one salient aspect of the situation (namely the height of the water in the container, rather than the breadth of the container). Children at this developmental stage also confuse appearance and reality. So, for example, a straw that is placed into water and therefore appears bent, is actually perceived as bent in reality. Piaget gives a nice example of how children at this stage confuse appearance and reality when he records the following interaction between his two of his children:

> ...at 2:7(12), seeing Lucienne in a new bathing suit, with a cap, Jacqueline asked: 'What's the baby's name?'. Her mother explained that it was a bathing costume, but Jacqueline pointed to Lucienne herself and said: 'What's the name of that?' (indicating Lucienne's face) and repeated the question several times. But as soon as Lucienne had her dress on again, Jacqueline exclaimed very seriously: 'It's Lucienne again', as if her sister had changed her identity in changing her clothes (1954, p. 224).

Pre-operational thinking is also based on pre-causal reasoning. Children at this stage have difficulty grasping cause-and-effect relationships. A cemetery, for example, may be interpreted as causing death, rather than being one of the effects of death (Cole, Cole & Lightfoot, 2002). An achievement of this stage is the formation of mental symbols, an ability that lies initially in imitative behaviour. Initially entirely bodily based, imitation begins to become more symbolic during this stage.

Concrete operational stage

While the vast majority of early childhood development (ECD) work will fall outside this stage, it is worth noting this developmental stage as some children who fall within the ECD category will be in this developmental stage. This stage lasts from roughly the ages of 6 to 12 years. A major achievement of this stage is the ability to decentre. That is, a child in this stage is able to focus on more than one aspect of a situation. This is best illustrated in relation to conservation experiments where a child is able to spot that as nothing has been added or removed from the container, the identity of the water remains unchanged across the transformation of containers. The ability to decentre leads to declining egocentrism and children in this stage are able to listen to other's viewpoints, follow rules in games, and even begin to understand that a person may act in one way but feel another way; these are significant achievements and pave the way for hypothetical thinking that is required at a high-school level.

Piaget's body of work is still extremely useful today, but his theory paid insufficient attention to the impact of the socio-cultural milieu on the developing child. His work, however, provided a fertile ground for Vygotsky to develop a theory to account for the impact of history and the socio-cultural world on the developing child.

Vygotsky's socio-cultural or cultural–historical approach to development

Vygotsky's body of work is variously referred to as socio-cultural theory (Miller, 2011) or cultural-historical activity theory (CHAT) (Vianna & Stetsenko, 2011). The different names accorded to this theory arise from the different sites of engagement with his theory: in the West, Vygotsky's work has been referred to as socio-cultural theory, while in Russia, the vast body of Neo-Vygotskian work that builds on Vygotsky's original opus is generally referred to as cultural–historical activity theory. The differences in name are not of primary importance for this chapter: what is important is the emphasis on how the social, cultural, and histori-cal milieu impact on a child's developmental trajectory. Chapter two covered Vygotsky's theory, but here you need to remind yourself that the difference between Piaget and Vygotsky's work lies in the focus on the importance of social interactions in the development of thinking. For Vygotsky, a child develops uniquely human capacities to think in particular ways through interacting with others in the social world and internalising cultural tools, which have a history, rather than merely con-structing thought through interacting with the world, as the Piagetian epistemic subject does. This chapter focuses specifically on two aspects of Vygotsky's work that inform ECD: the development of self-regulation and the understanding that play is the leading activity of this devel-opmental phase. Neo-Vygotskians, such as Karpov (2003), have done

Self-regulation
the ability to attend selectively to specific aspects of a situation; to start something that one might not want to, and to stop an activity that one is enjoying

extensive research into **self-regulation**, illustrating that it is a necessary pre-condition for learning at school. Self-regulation, however, like all higher cognitive concepts, needs to be mediated to the developing child. The next section will discuss how play, the leading activity of early child-hood, forms the basis for developing self-regulation in children as they move from pre-school to school.

Self-regulation and 'play' as a leading activity

As with all higher cognitive functions, self-regulation is initially external, occurring between the mother and the child, before being internalised (remember Vygotsky's 1978 general genetic law – skip back to page 43 in chapter two to refresh your memory). The (m)other will initially regulate the baby's actions externally. So for example, when a baby cries because he or she is hungry, he or she may grasp for the bottle of milk the mother gives him or her. This grasping has no actual meaning to the child … yet. The mother, however, interprets the gesture for the child and gives the child the bottle of milk. The infant begins to realise that the grasping motion is being interpreted by the mother, who essentially regulates the child's grasping actions until these actions develop into actual pointing. The mother initially regulates the infant's behaviour before this regulation is internalised as self-regulation (Morris, 2012). What can be seen here is that an adult is essential to the development of self-regulation:

> *The correct organisation of the child's activity plays an important role in the development of voluntary attention. How clearly the task of action, its goals and conditions are specified and whether or not the situational elements, which are significant for the fulfilment of the activity, are adequately identified determines the level of the child's attention. The cultivation of voluntary, premediated attention is one of the important problems of preschool pedagogy and one of the important conditions in the child's preparation for training at school (Yendovitskaya et al., 1971, pp. 86–87).*

Moreover, Vygotsky indicated the central role that 'play' serves in developing self-regulation: 'Play creates demands on the child to act against immediate impulse', and 'A child's greatest self-control occurs in play' (Vygotsky, 1962, p. 99). 'Play' is structured by rules that must be followed and peers regulate a child's behaviour during play (Morris, 2012).

A child's ability to self-regulate is essentially linked to social activity, particularly at preschool level, which allows for profound developmental activity because it provides opportunities to 'test' new learning safely and establish appropriate dialogue.

In this chapter self-regulation refers to:

> *… a deep internal mechanism that underlies mindful, intentional and thoughtful behaviours of children. It is the capacity to control one's impulses, both to stop doing something (even if one wants to continue doing it) and to start doing something (even if one doesn't want to do it). Self-regulated children can delay gratification and suppress their impulses long enough to think ahead to the possible consequences of their action, or to consider alternative actions that would be more appropriate (Bodrova & Leong, 2005, p. 55).*

Karpov (2005) discusses how children acquire self-regulation by means of conscious mediation by the educator within a **fantasy corner** and general

Fantasy corner
an area in a preschool classroom that is set aside for children to engage in imaginative play; the area is structured and has spaces for 'make-believe' activities, dress-up areas, and various toys and/or materials that can be used in imaginative play

classroom environment. He suggests that it is only when the educator actively provides the necessary dialogue to resolve conflict, provides tools for problem solving, unpacks tasks into manageable steps, and sets up fantasy corners that stimulate learners to explore the adult world, that self-regulation will be optimised by the mediator.

The work done by Vygotsky – and his colleagues Luria, Leont'ev, Galperin, and Elkonin – has demonstrated that the dominant activity at preschool level is play. Play is significant at this level of development as it allows for imitation of adult behaviour; the development of language and meaning together with the opportunities to internalise generalisations which help to regulate behaviour within socially accepted norms (Elkonin, 1974). Vygotsky (1967) believed that meaning is constructed through a combination of language and its cultural context and that when children indulge in play they extend existing skills to new limits (Bruner, 1977).

Karpov (2005) suggests that the adult plays a key role in the child's ability to develop self-regulation because it is the adult who presents an attitude towards learning, provides stimulating objects, models situational language, and helps the child to develop their motivation to learn. This role is performed by the educator in the preschool classroom when he or she provides tools for learning. For example material that can be draped as a cape or used as a tent; when he or she gives the child the dialogue to resolve conflict, for instance, 'Please may I have a turn with the princess crown'; when he or she sets up creative activities that stimulate new learning and provide discussion, like planting beans and making a giant beanstalk. The importance of language and social interaction between the adult and the child is highlighted by Vygotsky's theory of how children learn.

Karpov (2005) explains that self-regulation occurs through the child in the course of mediation when the child acquires and masters new psychological tools, which result in the development of new mental processes: '… the learning of specific abilities in one domain transforms the intellectual functioning in other areas' (Van der Veer & Valsiner, 1991). These mental processes outgrow the child's current activity, which creates the basis for the child's switching to a new activity (Rowe & Wertsch, 2004).

Language is intimately tied to actions and this enables the child to internalise his or her new learning and develop levels of self-regulation (Karpov, 2005). Private speech together with reacting to peers and educators helps the child to learn to regulate behaviour and internalise new learning (Wertsch, 1979).

As an infant the child is initially interested in manipulating objects presented to him or her by the adult or primary caregiver on whom the child is largely focused (Bruner, 1977). The child changes from simply exploring his or her environment to observing the links between the objects he or she is manipulating and their purpose. The focus changes to one of object-orientated actions whereby the adult draws the child's attention to the context of the object. For example, a spoon is used for eating (Karpov, 2005, p. 86). At the preschool level, objects can be manipulated to represent all manner of things. For example, a wooden block could be a cellphone and a piece of netting a veil. Whilst indulging in fantasy play, the learners are continuously describing how the game will be played out. In this way, according to Vygotsky, they are organising their thinking and regulating their behaviour (Van der Veer & Valsiner, 1991). By engaging in play children are learning to regulate their behaviour because they are experiencing the need to regulate within their imagined roles (Bruner, 1997).

The problem solving aspect of external dialogue frequently requires intervention on the part of the preschool educator (Karpov, 2005). It is here that he or she must help provide the language necessary to lead to the internalisation of regulation: that is, self-regulation (Zeidner, Matthews, Roberts & MacCann, 2003). Adult mediation guides the child and gives him or her the tools to plan and direct his or her thinking, thereby becoming more logical, less impulsive, and better able to regulate his or her behaviour (Elkonin, 1974). Much of the self-talk by the preschooler occurs during fantasy play, which traditionally is an area where preschoolers in South African kindergarten classrooms are given the freedom to play without structure or intervention.

Self-regulation for Vygotsky (1978) is achieved through social interaction and begins with the child exploring his or her innate potential to imitate adult behaviour through 'adult watching' (Bruner, 1977, p. 179). The child's developmental potential is evidenced by the degree to which he or she benefits from external intervention (Glick, 1997). Learning will lead to development if it occurs within the child's **Zone of Proximal Development** (ZPD) where skills and concepts can come to fruition with the appropriate guidance of the educator, peers, or significant others (Bodrova & Leong, 2001). At preschool level, the year preceeding grade one, this guidance could take the form of mediation within fantasy play which provides the opportunity for the preschooler to learn how to delay gratification, listen to instructions, and plan a task (Karpov, 2005). In so doing the child is developing self-regulation (Elkonin, 1974). Bodrova and Leong (2007) argue that educators should allocate more time to play in the preschool programme because it is through play that the child moves forward and develops.

> ... *play contains all developmental tendencies in a condensed form; in play it is as though the child were trying to jump above the level of his normal behaviour* (Vygotsky, 1933, p. 16).

Zone of Proximal Development
the social space, or gap, between what a child can do on his or her own and what he or she has the potential to accomplish with the assistance of a culturally more competent 'other'

This would suggest that play has the potential to help the preschooler to regulate their behaviour. Rubtsov and Yudina (2010) argue that current studies show a tendency to spend the preschool years cramming knowledge of numbers, letters, and phonics into the daily programme and that the reason for this is the natural desire to learn that is exhibited by most preschool students and consequently exploited by policy makers: '... the child's development is artificially accelerated and the preschool education is made more "adult" ' (Rubtsov & Yudin, 2010, p. 8). Rubtsov and Yudin consider this a grave error on the part of educators and support the concept that play should be encouraged. Recognising the importance of fantasy play as a site for developing self-regulation, some schools in New York have begun to turn their programmes more towards a focus on play, than a narrow academic focus (*New York Times*, 2009). In South Africa, Harrison's (2011) work on self-regulation with a preschool class found that mediated fantasy play had a developmental impact on, amongst other things, children's organisational skills. While there is still a dearth of such work in South Africa, Harrison's work points to the importance of fantasy play in developing self-regulation.

So what can be concluded about play? Much of Karpov's work (2005) has illustrated that adult mediation, children's prior knowledge, and language are key factors that shape socio-dramatic play and influence the development of abstraction (Morris, 2012, p. 150). In particular, '... studies of the neo-Vygotskians have demonstrated that the development of children's ability to use object substitutes is crucially determined by adult mediation' (Karpov, 2005, p. 126). It is the adult, then, who must create a space for fantasy play in the preschool classroom, providing the objects or materials that can be used in imaginative play – a stick that becomes a sword, a broom that becomes a broomstick to fly on, a dress-up corner where children can 'become' anyone they want to be. It is the teacher (or engaged parent) who provides children with the vocabulary with which to manipulate objects into imaginative, fantastical things. Most importantly, however, we must not forget that without motivation, the desire to engage in the play, the child will not learn. Play, therefore, must provide an inviting space that children want to inhabit (Morris, 2012). Have you ever wondered why the big purple dinosaur called Barney on television is so appealing to children in this developmental phase? Well, next time you have an opportunity to do so, watch an episode of Barney and you will notice most of the fundamental features mentioned above: the focus on imaginative play ('live from your imagination'); the structured engagement with imaginative play; the provision of a vocabulary with which to engage with the imaginative space; the elaboration of rules or engagement. All these things have made Barney, a purple dinosaur, one of the most influential characters in ECD.

CHECK YOUR PROGRESS

From the moment of birth, children are in constant interaction with adults who actively seek to incorporate them into their culture and its historically accumulated store of meanings and ways of doing things. In the beginning, children's responses to the world are dominated by natural processes, namely those provided by their biological heritage. But through the constant intercession of adults, more complex, instrumental psychological processes begin to take shape. At first, these processes can operate only in the course of the children's interactions with adults. As Vygotsky phrased it, the processes are interpsychic; that is, they are shared between people. Adults at this stage are external agents mediating the children's contact with the world. But as children grow older, the processes that were initially shared with adults come to be performed within children themselves. That is, the mediated responding to the world becomes an intrapsychic process. It is through this interiorisation of historically determined and culturally organised ways of operating on information that the social nature of people comes to be their psychological nature as well (Luria, 1979, p. 45).

- What do you understand by the term 'mediation'?
- How is mediation important in the development of self-regulation?
- State the general genetic law in your own words.
- Provide an example from your own childhood of how someone helped regulate your behaviour and how you internalised this.

Case study: the 'hurried' child: are parental expectations stealing childhood?

Jessica is five years old. She attends nursery school from 8am until 12pm. Her mother, Sarah, fetches her at 12pm and then drives her to her ballet lesson, which begins at 12h30. After ballet, Jessica has her art lesson at 14h00. She eats her lunch in the car while her mother drives her to art. After art, Jessica has her 'Mozart for youngsters' class, where she is learning to play the violin. She gets home at 17h30. She eats dinner at 18h00 and is in bed by 19h45.

Sarah's mother worked throughout her childhood and Sarah regrets that she did not have access to various after-school activities because she attended an after-care class where all she did was her homework. Sarah gave up her job when Jessica was born because she wanted her daughter to have the opportunities that she had lost out on. Lately, Jessica has begun to exhibit features of exhaustion and this is why her mother has decided to consult a child psychologist to develop a schedule that meets Jessica's needs, while still giving Jessica the benefit of all the activities Sarah missed out on while growing up.

- Given what you have just learnt about the importance of play in this developmental phase, what kind of schedule would you draw up for Jessica?
- How would you approach the revised schedule with Sarah's mother, given her desire for her child to access activities she never had the opportunity to access?

The next section will discuss the development of a scale used to measure mental development. The Griffiths Scales of Mental Development take seriously the notion of 'play' as a necessary part of early childhood development.

The Griffiths Scales of Mental Development

Ruth Griffiths's view of child development is reflected in a philosophy based on the basic avenues of learning, the concept of play, and the need to assess with more confidence the development of young children. The thinking of Griffiths is in line with modern systemic approaches, in which the basic avenues of learning for the early developing child are strongly depicted. This is aptly reflected in the following quotation:

> Play for young children is not recreation activity. It is not leisure-time activity nor escape activity. Play is thinking time for young children. It is language time. Problem-solving time. It is memory time, planning time, investigating time. It is organization-of-ideas time, when the young child uses his mind and body and his social skills and all his powers in response to the stimuli he has met (http://www.enotes.com/famous-quotes/play-for-young-children-is-not-recreation-activity, 2008).

Studies suggest that when children play spontaneously ('getting into everything'), they are also exploring cause and effect and doing experiments. This has also been described as being the most effective way to discover how the world works (Gopnik, 2010). It has been suggested that the provision of interesting activities, choice in activities, and choice in how to complete activities improves children's persistence and thus attention to the task (Stewart, Rule & Giordano, 2007).

Various methods are available for assessing and understanding early childhood development. The Griffiths Mental Development Scales are among those that are recognised worldwide, particularly by pediatricians and psychologists, as they enable a thorough, holistic diagnosis through analysis of the development profile. The 1954 Griffiths Mental Development Scales originally covered the first two years of life, and assessed development in five areas – locomotor, personal–social, hearing and speech, eye and hand co-ordination, and performance. The Griffiths Extended Scales of Mental Development were developed in the 1960s and tested children aged two to eight years. A sixth sub-scale, practical reasoning, was introduced with the Extended Scales.

When the Griffiths Mental Development Scales were first introduced, the psychometric conceptions of intelligence were emerging and were to influence psychometric measurement for the next three generations. These narrow conceptions included verbal, visual–spatial, and mathematical abilities. The Griffiths Mental Development Scales brought with them an innovative system for developmental assessment, as Griffiths was keenly aware of the importance of interactions between the various avenues of learning. She advocated a broad-based approach to understanding mental development (that is, the processes and rates at which growth and maturation of a child's attributes and abilities takes place). She was aware of the importance of social and emotional developmental factors and the interplay between these and mental development.

Understanding early development in a child thus involves a comprehensive investigation of the child's abilities, including motor abilities, social abilities, and cognitive abilities. The rapidly shifting nature of young children's development poses problems when psychologists or other professionals assess them. Clinical skills and judgment are required to differentiate between what is intellectual and what may be primarily neurophysiological or socio-emotional. Through periodic re-examinations of young children, psychologists and researchers can bring to light developmental trends and establish developmental baselines.

The basic avenues of learning

According to Griffiths (1986), it would seem that the earliest beginnings of mental development rest primarily upon the physiological functions and a child's developing awareness of his or her physiological needs. The physiological functions are rhythmical, occurring regularly in time – for example ingestion and digestion, waking and sleeping. From the moment of birth, with the onset of breathing and the beginning of a separate existence, a child has to begin to adjust to the physical environment. Even before birth, a child has experienced at some level, probably mainly physiological, the various rhythms of life, for these are already laid down in the nervous system (refer again to chapter three for a detailed discussion on the prenatal period of development).

In earliest infancy, a baby begins to adjust to the rhythms of experience, to come to expect certain happenings at certain times and in certain places (refer again to chapter four for a detailed discussion of infancy). This ability to adjust is fundamental to habit formation, and with a child's growing awareness of his or her social environment, he or she learns to react in a twofold way, now positively and now negatively, the whole complex of activities and retreats from activity being in a sense an outgrowth of the child's natural (inborn) rhythms. Thus conative drives become gradually superimposed upon the basic vegetative rhythms, such as food intake, elimination, waking, and sleeping. For example, a hungry child cries, grows angry if neglected, and learns to vary his or her means of demanding attention.

But the human brain continues to develop and is constantly moving forward in its development. It is highly impressionable and has great latent potential for use. What a person can do cortically does not come fully 'on line' until the school years or adolescence (refer to chapters six and seven for a full discussion of these periods of development); the brain fully reaches maturation only in the early 30s. In this regard, Griffiths's thinking opened doors. Look at Figure 5.1, which illustrates Griffiths's holistic model reflecting the basic avenues of learning.

Figure 5.1 Griffiths's holistic model reflecting the basic avenues of learning

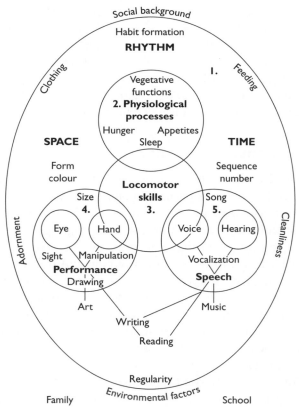

Source: Griffiths (1986, p. 29)

In Figure 5.1, the large oval (numbered '1') represents the social background in which a child is situated. The social background encircles the child from the beginning, modifying and influencing all his or her experiences.

The circle numbered '2' in Figure 5.1 represents the physiological functions and organic movements, awareness of which appears basic to experience. Superimposed on this physiological substrate, certain weak physical movements gradually become more gross and lead to differentiated attempts to move the body in various ways, of which the first in importance are those that lead on to locomotor development (see the circle numbered '3' in Figure 5.1). These, too, are rhythmical, resting back upon the gradual acquisition of certain habits. It is instructive to watch the energetic kicking of an infant, and then young child, whose limbs go vigorously one, two, one, two, alternately; these movements strengthen the muscles soon to be involved in more complicated movements such as rolling over, sitting up, crawling, walking, climbing, running, and, finally, riding a bicycle.

Arm and hand movements, at first vague and poorly directed – clutching at near objects, holding on to grasped objects – which develop later into more complicated manipulative acts, accompany and overlay the locomotor series (see the circle numbered '4' in Figure 5.1). For successful manipulative development, hand and eye must co-operate. These are the two basic avenues of learning. The eye, at first roving without fixating, gradually begins to follow moving objects and 'look at' still ones. The hand, coming into contact with near objects, soon supplements vision, and the two develop together in manipulative performances of growing complexity.

Meanwhile, a child is not silent. Almost from birth, a normal baby makes vague sounds (see the circle numbered '5' in Figure 5.1). These sounds are hardly voiced at first, but presently they become definite vocalisation and, later, babble and then speech. All this is in addition to the baby's expressive crying. The baby listens intently to sounds and to the voices around. Hearing (active listening) and voice together result in vocalisation and babble, which finally develop into speech. Hearing and voice are two further basic avenues of learning.

All this development takes place in time and space. The eye and hand co-operate in exploring the spatial surroundings, although even blind children build up their own conception of space and spatial relations out of their sense of touch and their concentration on manual exploration of the environment. Hearing, then listening to a sequence of sounds, such as involved in learning gradually to understand language, takes place in time rather than in space, and builds up in a child the expectation of meaningful sequences. Babies understand a great deal of the spoken language that flows around them long before their inexperienced vocal organs can frame a response.

The two broad sets of activities representing different types of experience – performance (the circle numbered '4') and speech (the circle numbered '5') – are the two main aspects of intellectual development, and together ultimately form the basis of formal education, both practical and verbal. A more advanced stage in this developmental process is reached when an older child learns to read and write, for then all four main avenues of learning, eye and hand together with voice and hearing, co-operate in the acquisition of the complex ability to understand and reproduce written language. As they develop, all these abilities form a complex and unified whole. The whole child acts in everything he or she does, directing his or her attention in rapid exploring and learning in relation to environment.

Stewart (2005) recognised that Griffiths's thinking was considerably advanced for that time and, significantly, it is still acknowledged as being in line with contemporary developmental theories. Stewart described Griffiths's contribution to child development in the following paragraph:

> Griffiths' theoretical approach may appear somewhat dated, but it remains fundamentally sound. Most of its features are consistent with current theory of child development, as Griffiths acknowledged the child within his social systems; she recognised the physiological aspect of child development; and she attributed equal importance to the psychological aspects of the child. She identified six domains of development, which she stated provided a thorough view of development. She maintained that the domains measured separate abilities, but emphasized that there is also considerable overlap between them. All these aspects are consistent with current thinking on child development (Stewart, 2005, p. 97).

Importantly, in the field of childhood development, the above-mentioned areas underpinning the Griffiths Mental Development Scales remain vital areas of child development, the culmination of which provides a holistic blueprint of mental development in infancy and early childhood. Child development is a dynamic, moving target. It is important to take a fresh look (from time to time) at the underpinning theories, philosophies, and principles of development to ensure that these stay relevant. When psychologists and other practitioners seek to understand the dynamics of the human mental process, they cannot ignore the evidence of its collective activities across time (Preston, 2005).

ACTIVITY

Using symbols, pictures, magazine cutouts, words etc., design your own diagram that illustrates your understanding of children's basic avenues of learning.

Moral development in children

The discussion that follows will consider moral development in children. Chapter six will also consider this topic in detail, and you should read the discussion here and that in chapter six as complementary sources of information on this topic.

Griffiths asserted that mental progression can be observed in expressions of performance, behaviour, and language (Preston, 2005). This assertion is similar to the assertions of many theorists who continue to influence the field of developmental psychology and psychometric assessments of child development (such as Piaget, Erikson, and Vygotsky, whose work earlier chapters discussed). Griffiths acknowledged that the interplay between social, emotional, and moral developmental factors significantly impacted on a child's mental development (Luiz et al., 2006).

Children's brains may be thought of as 'wet cement' in which formative relationships and experiential learning leave lasting impressions. When psychologists and other practitioners attempt to describe and plot children's physical, social, and emotional maturation, it is therefore important that they take into consideration the many cultural, socio-economic, and environmental factors that could shape and influence this development. The unfortunate reality is that many of the contexts in which children are raised today are less than ideal. Poverty, crime, disease, death, violence, human-rights violations, war, and conflict abound in many parts of the world. This means that as children explore and learn more about their environment – and in turn discover more about themselves – they are likely to face many external and internal challenges that could considerably stunt their emotional, social, and physical development. Of increasing concern to those in the helping professions is the far-reaching effect that such influencers could have on children's overall moral development. Posada and Wainryb express this concern eloquently:

More and more of the world's children are being sucked into a bleak moral vacuum—a psychological space devoid of basic human rights and values. How might children's development be altered by the violence, lawlessness, and deprivation to which they are exposed? (Posada & Wainryb, 2008, p. 882).

Research conducted into the moral development of children in countries affected by political violence has revealed that their moral development is likely to be truncated (Posada & Wainryb, 2008). When children are inadequately exposed to social interactions that help facilitate the development of moral concepts, they are likely to experience conflict between proposed moral principles (for example 'Don't hurt others' and 'It is wrong to steal, lie, cheat, etc.') and those considerations specific to their environments (such as the need to eat, or to be safe, or to see justice meted out for considerable wrongs against themselves and their families). However, research has also shown that young children are still capable of judging certain behaviour to be wrong, not merely based on how they or others might be punished for such behaviour, but according to their intrinsic concern with fairness and the overall welfare of others (Posada & Wainryb, 2008). This intrinsic ability to be able to label actions as 'good' or 'bad', 'unfair' or 'fair', even when submerged in environments that support conflicting norms and practices, shows that the development of moral concepts is not determined by merely cultural and societal conditions (Posada & Wainryb, 2008). Nevertheless, children still require that caregivers and others 'properly guide and equip them for a successful journey' (Wonderly, 2009, p. 3) as they explore and form opinions about life's moral terrains.

Read the box headed 'Discussing moral development', which will help you to tease out your own views on this topic.

Discussing moral development

Discuss the following questions:

- Do you feel that it is important for society to instil good morals in children, or is morality an outdated concept? Why do you feel this way?
- Have you noticed an increase or decrease in levels of morality among children in your community? Why do you think this is so?

Theory of moral development

Moral reasoning
a thinking process with the objective of determining whether an idea is right or wrong

Development theorists such as Piaget, whose work earlier chapters have discussed in some detail, and Lawrence Kohlberg (1927–1987) provide structured frameworks on which to hinge an understanding of the growth of **moral reasoning** in children. These frameworks in turn serve as springboards from which to form effective strategies for childhood moral development. Later chapters will return to discuss Piaget's work in further detail, and will also expand on the discussion of Kohlberg's work presented here.

Kohlberg's work on moral reasoning

While completing his doctoral dissertation, Kohlberg undertook a cross-sectional study of moral reasoning in 75 boys distributed in age from early childhood to late adolescence. From this study emerged Kohlberg's extended hypothesis of six stage-like positions in the development of moral reasoning.

Piaget's work strongly influenced Kohlberg's thinking. Piaget's focus on an active subject interacting with a dynamic environment shaped Kohlberg's approach. In addition, Kohlberg used Piaget's focus to harness an empirical psychological inquiry into some philosophical issues concerning ethics. However, where Piaget was content in his later work to restrict himself to how people construct and know the world mathematically and scientifically, Kohlberg studied how people structure their experiences of, and judgements about, the social world (Fowler, 1981).

By taking justice as the norm for moral judgement, Kohlberg argued, both empirically and philosophically, that moral reasoning develops through a succession of stages. He contended that the sequence of these stages is invariant and universal, and that 'higher' stages are more adequate (or more true) than the 'earlier' ones. In developing his theory, Kohlberg gave attention to how people in different stages construct and take account of the social perspectives of other people and groups.

A central thrust of Kohlberg's work is the claim that moral judgement and action are a rational choice. Kohlberg stated that moral choice is not simply a matter of feelings or values, but involves interpreting a moral-dilemma situation, constructing all the points of view of the various participants and affected parties, and weighing their respective claims, rights, duties, and commitment to the good (Sigelman & Shaffer, 1991). Kohlberg saw these all as cognitive acts. Like Piaget, he saw a stage of moral judgement as characterised by a formally describable pattern of thought or reasoning employed by a person in the adjudication of moral claims. And just as Piaget saw formal operational thinking as the most developed stage of cognition, so Kohlberg saw the universalising exercise of the principles of justice as the most developed stage of moral reasoning. Kohlberg held that the process of development of this cognitive core of moral judgement occurred in the interaction of people with the social conditions of their lives. He added that Piaget's succession of stage-like equilibrations are, in effect, more or less comprehensive 'moral logics' (Fowler, 1981).

Kohlberg's stages of moral development

Kohlberg's stages are hierarchical (that is, each builds on and integrates the operations of the previous stages) and sequential (that is, one comes after the other in logical fashion). Furthermore, the sequence is both invariant (that is, a person cannot skip over a stage) and universal (that is, common to the moral development of people worldwide). Kohlberg noted that there is variation in the rate at which people in different societies move from one stage to another, and in the point of arrest or final equilibration that is average for adults in given cultures. However, Kohlberg emphasised that the same series of stages (if formally described) seem to characterise the path of development in moral judgement in each society (Fowler, 1981). Kohlberg proposed that there are three levels of moral reasoning: preconventional morality, conventional morality, and postconventional morality. He further proposed two stages within each level, as described below. (The section of chapter six headed 'Moral development' also sets out and discusses Kohlberg's stages in some detail, and chapter seven returns to consider the theory. You will probably find it useful to read the information in chapters six and seven in conjunction with the explanation that follows here.)

Level one: preconventional morality

At the level of preconventional morality, rules are really external to the self, rather than internalised. A child conforms to rules imposed by authority figures in order to avoid punishment, or to obtain personal rewards. The perspective of the self dominates (that is, what is right is what a person can get away with, or what is personally satisfying) (Sigelman & Shaffer, 1991).

Stage one (punishment-and-obedience orientation) is part of level one. In stage one, the goodness or badness of an act depends on its consequences. A child will obey authorities to avoid punishment and may not consider an act wrong if it is not punished. The greater the harm done or more severe the punishment, the more 'bad' the act is (Sigelman & Shaffer, 1991).

Stage two (instrumental hedonism) is also part of level one. A person at the second stage of moral development conforms to rules in order to gain rewards or satisfy personal needs. There is some concern for the perspectives of others, but this stage is ultimately motivated by the hope of benefit in return. 'You scratch my back and I'll scratch yours' is the guiding philosophy (Sigelman & Shaffer, 1991).

Level two: conventional morality

At the level of conventional morality, the individual has internalised many moral values. He or she strives to obey the rules set forth by others (such as parents, peers, and the government) in order to win their approval and recognition for good behaviour, or to maintain social order. The perspectives of other people besides the self are clearly recognised and given serious consideration (Sigelman & Shaffer, 1991).

Stage three ('good boy' or 'good girl' morality) is part of level two. In stage three, what is right is now that which pleases, helps, or is approved by others. People are often judged by their intentions, 'meaning well' is valued, and it is important to be 'nice' (Sigelman & Shaffer, 1991).

Stage four (authority and social-order-maintaining morality) is also part of level two. In stage four, what is right is what conforms to the rules of legitimate authorities. The reason for conforming is not so much a fear of punishment as a belief that rules and laws maintain a social order that is worth preserving. Being dutiful and respecting law and order are valued (Sigelman & Shaffer, 1991).

Level three: postconventional morality

At the third and final level of moral reasoning, postconventional morality, the individual attempts to define what is right in terms of broad principles of justice that have validity apart from the views of particular authority figures. The individual may distinguish between what is morally right and what is legal, recognising that some laws violate basic moral principles. Thus, the person transcends the perspectives of particular social groups or authorities and begins to take the perspective of all individuals (Sigelman & Shaffer, 1991).

Stage five (morality of contract, individual rights, and democratically accepted law) is part of level three. In stage five, there is an increased understanding of the underlying purposes served by laws. There is also a concern that rules should be arrived at through democratic consensus so that they express the will of the majority, or maximise social welfare. Whereas the person at stage four is unlikely to challenge an established law, the stage-five moral reasoner might call for democratic change in a law that comprises basic rights (Sigelman & Shaffer, 1991).

Stage six (morality of individual principles of conscience) is part of level four. In stage six, the 'highest' stage of moral reasoning, the individual defines right and wrong on the basis of self-chosen principles that are broad and universal in application. The stage-six thinker does not simply 'make up' whatever principles he or she happens to favour, but instead arrives at abstract principles of respect for all individuals and their rights that all religions or moral authorities might view as moral. Kohlberg (1981) described stage six as a kind of 'moral musical chairs' in which the person facing a moral dilemma is able to take the perspective, or 'chair', of each person or group that could potentially be affected by a decision and arrive at a solution that would be regarded as just from every 'chair'. Stage six is Kohlberg's vision of ideal moral reasoning, but it is so rarely observed that Kohlberg stopped attempting to measure its existence (Sigelman & Shaffer, 1991).

The prominence of Kohlberg's theory

In sum, Kohlberg's theory of moral development has become prominent for a good reason. It describes a universal sequence of changes in moral reasoning extending from childhood through adulthood. Moreover, the evidence supports Kohlberg's view that both cognitive growth and social experiences contribute to moral growth. However, there is also some merit to criticisms of the theory. The theory may indeed be somewhat biased against people who live in non-Western societies, who hold values other than individualistic and democratic ones, or who emphasise a 'morality of care' rather than a 'morality of abstract rights'. Moreover, because Kohlberg's theory focuses entirely on moral reasoning, it is necessary to rely on other perspectives, such as social learning, to understand how moral affect and moral behaviour interact to make people the moral beings they ultimately become (Sigelman & Shaffer, 1991).

Kohlberg: concluding remarks

Piaget and Kohlberg focus their stage analyses on the structures and reasoning in their respective domains, and their approaches have been designated as belonging to the structural–developmental school (Fowler, 1981). The structural–developmentalists point out that the structures of thought are themselves a kind of unconscious, different from the dynamic unconscious of Freud and Jung, to be sure, but to be seen in relation to it. According to Fowler (1981), Erikson's eight stages of the life cycle (recall that chapters two and four discussed Erikson in some detail), closely correlate with biological maturation and chronological age – particularly in the first five stages. In contrast, the structural–developmentalist stages, while dependent on maturation and time, are not tied to them. Movement from one structural–developmental stage to another is not automatic or inevitable. A person can 'arrest' or equilibrate in one of Piaget's or Kohlberg's intermediate stages. Yet the person who so arrests in cognitive or moral developmental terms must still meet the life challenges or crises described in Erikson's stages (that is, it can be said that psychosocial crises come, 'ready or not').

When these perspectives on successive developmental eras are considered in this way, an assumption is made of parallelism in cognitive, moral, and psychosocial development that, if optimal, may be the exception rather than the rule. In other words, people's ways of meeting and dealing with the developmental crises Erikson delineates may differ significantly, depending upon their operative stages of cognitive and moral-judgement development. In this regard, Sheehy has descriptively said, 'If you are aware that the fight of life is taking you somewhere, you can not only make the journey better, but also be more determined and resilient during the many battles' (Sheehy, 1997, p. 239).

Read the box headed 'Application of Kohlberg's theory of moral development', which discusses the Just Community Approach, which applies Kohlberg's theory in practice.

Moral reasoning
a thinking process with the objective of determining whether an idea is right or wrong

---

ACTIVITY

Personal reflection

1   In which stage of Kohlberg's theory of moral development would you place yourself currently? Why?
2   Think of an event in your childhood when you were clearly operating out of one of Kohlberg's proposed stages of moral development. This could have been when you were caught doing something disobedient, or when you observed an injustice towards another child. Record your feelings, thoughts, and actions from these events. Do these support one of Kohlberg's proposed developmental stages?

Application of Kohlberg's theory of moral development
The Just Community Approach

Kohlberg progressed from his early ventures into moral education, where he placed strong focus on developing a cognitive model of individual moral development (the six-stage theory), to the exploration of approaches that emphasised the development of community norms that could foster the growth of moral reasoning and behaviour in children. The outcome was the development of a strong educational intervention called the Just Community Approach (Rest, Narvaez, Thoma & Bebeau, 2000). Kohlberg came to believe that in order for children truly to learn concepts of justice, fairness, and morality, schools needed to become just environments in which students could be active participants in creating justice. Core to this approach of social and moral learning was the concept of student participation. Oser, Althof & Higgins-D'Alessandro explain that in schools adopting the Just Community Approach

> [s]tudents are invited to engage in ongoing reflections about the fairness of certain behaviour and of rules and policies and why their community needs a set of rules, thus developing their social-emotional and moral reasoning competence and their sense of responsibility and care for one another and for upholding the rules (Oser, Althof, & Higgins-D'Alessandro, 2008, p. 2).

Kohlberg realised that there was a limitation to moral-dilemma discussions that were grounded in literature and history alone. Therefore he developed a model in which moral development and progress could be assessed and measured in real-life school environments where young students' decisions had an impact (Oser, Althof & Higgins-D'Alessandro, 2008). Students' participation within these school environments includes helping to detect unsolved latent problems within the school, which concerns the rights and duties of each student and the whole community. They are encouraged to come up with joint solutions to these problems and are required to defend publicly their solutions and stances. Students and teachers are elected to special committees (the fairness committee, for example) that assist with the democratic running of the school. Students also vote for or against solutions raised, and they jointly develop and enforce norms, rules, and policies at their school (Oser, Althof & Higgins-D'Alessandro, 2008).

In encouraging children's active participation in the just and fair running of their school environments, Kohlberg aimed to strengthen their moral-reasoning capacities to the point that their future decisions and behaviour would reflect a well-navigated understanding of the value of creating and sustaining morality and justice in their immediate environments. Through their exposure to the practices of the Just Community Approach, these children would ideally adopt and develop moral-reasoning capacities that would go beyond a mere adherence to (or rejection of) indoctrinated theory and societal expectations.

ACTIVITY

1   Identify examples from your own community where there is a lack of positive role-modelling and community norms for adequate moral development in children.

2   How might you adapt and apply the principles of the Just Community Approach to work with young children in this context? (Describe the environment that you would establish to incorporate these principles. Which individual or community activities could you implement to encourage moral reasoning development in children?)

Empathy
the feeling of emotionally putting oneself in the place and experience of another

Developing empathy in children

Read the box headed 'Case study: Alice and Jonathan', which relates to the issue of developing **empathy** in children.

Case study: Alice and Jonathan

Alice refuses to share her toys with her friend, Jonathan, during a play date at his home. A clearly distressed Jonathan approaches his mother for assistance. Instead of trying to compel Alice towards less selfish behaviour by resorting to offers of reward or threats of punishment, Jonathan's mother decides to harness the power of Alice's vivid imagination by helping her empathise with Jonathan's feelings on the matter. 'Imagine if Jonathan refused to share his toys with you,' she says. 'How would that make you feel, Alice?'

Parents, guardians, and teachers have historically practised systems of punishment, reward, and role-modelling to encourage favourable behaviour and discourage unfavourable behaviour in children. To help move children beyond value indoctrination to true moral reasoning, alternative approaches to moral instruction now lean towards practises that, instead, help children develop a sense of empathy towards others, and identification with others. In appealing to children's sense of empathy (that is, their understanding of morality and justice on a personal and felt level), it is believed that children can better develop judgements that will uphold favourable responses, norms, and values as important when they are faced with moral and ethical issues (Wonderly, 2009). The facilitation of Alice's identification with Jonathan's pain in the short case study above could potentially assist Alice in arriving at the conclusion that causing such pain is wrong and that she should, instead, share her toys with Jonathan (Wonderly, 2009). Developing and strengthening children's sense of empathy is believed to be important for the development of their moral reasoning skills.

Film as an instrument of moral development

Children's film is one tool that researchers have identified as an effective instrument in eliciting empathetic responses from children (Wonderly, 2009). While didactic narratives have been used for many years to teach children lessons in morality, helping children to identify the moral messages in stories is of little consequence if they do not feel a level of respect towards those imperatives being taught (Wonderly, 2009). As the human condition is vividly and realistically portrayed to children through the medium of film, their identification with the main characters can evoke feelings of empathy that can be easily accessed for future discussion and application in home environments and learning environments (Wonderly, 2009).

Film is also a beneficial tool to stimulate moral imagination in children who experience learning barriers. Unlike literary figures, cinematic characters are often easily accessible, which makes them highly instructive (Wonderly, 2009). Children with limited reading-comprehension skills can readily access the dominant themes and emotions present in films. Also, depending on the simplicity of the film, language barriers can also be transcended as children relate instead to the visual cues and auditory stimulation present in the film's narrative.

While many parents lack the time to work adequately through moral themes found in their children's stories or novels, they can generally spare a few hours to view and create discussion around the ethical dilemmas present in a film. For educators, film can also serve as a convenient alternative to sourcing texts and literature that adequately portray themes of moral significance (Wonderly, 2009). Such films can then be used as points of departure for discussion and application in the classroom setting.

ACTIVITY

1   Do you agree that children's film can be used as an effective tool to evoke empathetic responses in children towards others?
2   Can you identify a film from your own childhood that had significant impact on your own ability to empathise with your peers or a particular social group?
3   List three contemporary examples of children's film that could be easily used by parents to create discussion with their children about issues of morality.

CHECK YOUR PROGRESS

- List and describe the three levels of moral reasoning, as proposed by Kohlberg.
- Draw a diagram that best illustrates/summarises the sequence of Kohlberg's six stages of moral development.
- Describe, in your own words, three benefits of using film as a tool to stimulate moral imagination in children.

Conclusion

Early childhood development is now acknowledged as 'a bidirectional transactional process in which genetic and environmental influences continuously alter each other in a dynamic manner' (Sharma, 2011, p. 163). Furthermore, theorists explain that multiple contexts such as parenting, socioeconomic status, and social relations interact with one another and with genetic expression, resulting in long-lasting consequences for development (Sharma, 2011; Shonokoff & Phillips, 2000). Environmental factors are considered important determinants of a child's future. Family and social environment most strongly, but not exclusively, influence emotional regulation, cognitive, and language outcomes, with most negative influences occurring in infancy. Griffiths acknowledged the impact of such factors by incorporating them into her diagram (see Figure 5.1). These multiple domains of child development have also been found to be interlocked, recursively interacting and influencing each other over time (Bornstein et al., 2012; Elder & Shanahan, 2006; Lerner, Lewin-Bizan & Warren, 2011). For example, proper nutrition during early childhood is vital not only for healthy physical development, but also for the enhancing of socio-emotional development and cognitive growth (Bornstein et al., 2012). Further, responsiveness in the parent–child relationship encourages healthy socio-emotional development, leading to significant gains in physical and cognitive outcomes (Bornstein et al., 2012). Magnusson and Stattin support the importance of the context and the recursiveness of multiple interacting systems in children's development by proposing the following:

> The individual is an active, purposeful part of an integrated, complex, and dynamic person–environment system … Consequently, it is not possible to understand how social systems function without knowledge of individual functioning, just as individual functioning and development cannot be understood without knowledge of the environment (Magnusson & Stattin, 2006, p. 401).

Thus it is individuals, rather than variables, that develop (Magnusson & Stattin, 1998), and such development is constantly being shaped, both consciously and unconsciously, by children's abilities to adapt and respond.

CASE STUDY

Thabo is seven years old. He lives with his teenage sister and his younger sister, who is two years old. His older sister, Nandipha, is 18 years old and works at the parcel counter in a large supermarket. Their mother, who had been their sole parent, passed away from an Aids-related illness when Kanyiso, the baby, was three months old. Nandipha dropped out of school at that time to seek employment so that she could care for her siblings. Thabo did not attend pre-school. He has just started school this year and his teacher reports that he is having difficulty attending to lessons. He appears unable to focus his attention for any length of time and it is difficult to get him to start new tasks when he is engaged with a task, such as drawing, which he likes. The teacher is concerned that he has ADHD and she wants him to see a psychologist.

1   Given what you have learnt about self-regulation in this chapter, critically discuss Thabo's presenting problem.
2   Given the importance in early childhood of significant others, discuss a possible treatment plan for Thabo.

Questions

1   Now that you have read about Early Childhood Development, think back to the case study at the beginning of this chapter. Do you think Muriel's fears about Eva adjusting to life outside prison are justified? What suggestions can you make to assist Muriel in the transition from prison to life outside prison? Draw on Vygotsky's theory to answer this question.

2   What do you think of Kohlberg's notion that morals can be taught in school? Critically discuss how you would approach teaching about theft to children between the ages of six and eight years.

References

Bodrova, E. & Leong, D.J. (2005). Promoting student self-regulation in learning. *National Association of Elementary School Principals*, 85, 54–58.

Bodrova, E. & Leong, D.J. (2007). *Tools of the mind: The Vygotskian approach to early childhood education*. New Jersey: Pearson Prentice Hall.

Bornstein, M.H., Britto, P.R., Nonoyama-Tarumi, Y., Ota, Y., Petrovic, O. & Putnick, D.L. (2012). Child development in developing countries: Introduction and methods. *Child Development, 83*, (1), 16–31.

Bruner, J. (1977). The organization of early skilled action. In M.P.M. Richards. *The integration of a child into a social world* (p. 167–184). London: University Press.

Cole, M., Cole, S. & Lightfoot, C. (2002). *The development of children*. New York, NY: Worth Publishers.

Elder, G.H., Jr. & Shanahan, M.J. (2006). The life course and human development. In R.M. Lerner & W. Damon (Eds). *Handbook of child psychology: Theoretical models of human development* (6th ed.) (p. 665–715). Hoboken, NJ: Wiley.

Elkonin, D. (1974). *The psychology of preschool children*. Cambridge: MIT Press.

Fowler, James W. (1981). Stages of faith: *The psychology of human development and the quest for meaning*. San Francisco, CA: Harper & Row.

Glick, J. (1997). Prologue to R.S. Rieber (Ed.). *The collected works of L.S. Vygotsky: The history of the development of Fügher Mental Functions. Vol. 4*. Translated by Marie J. Hall. New York: Plenum.

Gopnik, A. (2010). *How babies think. Scientific American, July*, 76–81.

Griffiths, Ruth (1986). *The abilities of babies. A study in mental measurement*. High Wycombe: The Test Agency.

Hall, M.J., Glick, J. & Rieber, R.W. (1997). *The collected works of L.S. Vygotsky: The history of the development of higher mental functions*. New York: Plenum Press.

Harrison, G. (2011). Mediating self-regulation in a kindergarten class in South Africa: An exploratory case study. Unpublished master's dissertation. University of Cape Town: Cape Town.

Jackson, D. (1999). *With child: Wisdom and traditions for pregnancy, birth and motherhood*. San Francisco: Chronicle Books, Duncan Baird Publishers.

Karpov, Y. & Haywood, C.H. (1998). Two ways to elaborate Vygotsky's concept of mediation: Implications for instruction. *American Psychologist*, 53, (1), 27–36.

Karpov, Y. (2003). Internalization of children's problem solving and individual differences in learning. *Cognitive Development*, 18, 377–398.

Karpov, Y. (2005). *The Neo-Vygotskian approach to child development*. New York: Cambridge University Press.

Kohlberg, Lawrence. (1981). *Essays on moral development: Vol. 1. The philosophy of moral development*. San Francisco, CA: Harper & Row.

Lerner, R.M., Lewin-Bizan, S. & Warren, A.E.A. (2011). Concepts and theories of human development. In M.H. Bornstein & M.E. Lamb (Eds). *Developmental science: An advanced textbook* (6th ed.) (p. 3–49). New York: Taylor & Francis.

Luiz, D.M., Barnard, A., Knoessen, N.P., Kotras, N., Horrocks, S., McAlinden, P., Challis, D. & O'Connell, R. (2006). *Griffiths mental development scales – extended revised: Two to eight years administration manual*. Oxford: Hogrefe.

Luria, A.R. (1979). *The making of mind: A personal account of Soviet psychology*. M. Cole & S. Cole (Eds). Cambridge, Mass., and London: Harvard University Press.

Magnusson, D. & Stattin, H. (1998). Person–context interaction theories. In W. Damon (Series ed.) & R. M. Lerner (Vol. ed.). *Handbook of child psychology: Vol. 1. Theoretical models of human development* (5th ed.) (p. 685–759). New York: Wiley.

Magnusson, D. & Stattin, H. (2006). The person in context: A holistic-interactionistic approach. In R.M. Lerner & W. Damon (Eds). *Handbook of child psychology: Theoretical models of human development* (6th ed.) (p. 400–464). Hoboken, NJ: Wiley.

Miller, R. (2011). *Vygotsky in perspective*. London: Cambridge University Press.

Morris, A. (2012). An analytical reading of neo-Vygotskian theory towards deriving implications for teaching science to six-year-olds in the Grade R classroom. Unpublished master's thesis, University of Cape Town, Cape Town.

Oser, F.K., Althof, W., Higgins-D'Alessandro, A. (2008). The Just Community approach to moral education: System change or individual change? *Journal of Moral Education, 37*, (3), 395–415.

Piaget, Jean. (1964). *Six psychological studies*. New York: Vintage.

Posada, R. & Wainryb, C. (2008). Moral development in a violent society: Colombian children's judgments in the context of survival and revenge. *Child Development, 79*, (4), 882–898.

Preston, Phyllis (2005). *Testing children: A practitioner's guide to the assessment of mental development in infants and young children*. Oxford: Hogrefe & Huber Publishers.

Rest, J.R., Narvaez, D., Thoma, S.J., Bebeau, M.J. (2000). A neo-Kohlbergian approach to morality research. *Journal of Moral Education, 29*, (4), 381–382.

Rowe, S. & Wertsch, J.V. (2007). Vygotsky's model of cognitive development. In U. Goswami (Ed.). *Blackwell handbook of childhood cognitive development*. Malden, M.A.: Blackwell.

Rubtsov, V.V. & Yudina, E.G. (2010). Current problems of preschool education. *Psyjournals, 3*, 5–15.

Sharma, A. (2011). Developmental examination: Birth to 5 years. *Archives of Disease in Childhood – Education and Practice Edition, 96*, 162–175.

Sheehy, Gail (1997). *New passages: Mapping your life across time*. London: HarperCollins.

Shonokoff, J.P. & Phillips, D.A. (2000). *From neurons to neighbourhoods: The science of early childhood development*. Washington, DC: National Academy Press.

Sigelman, C.K. & Shaffer, D.R. (1991). *Life-span human development*. Pacific Grove, CA: Brooks/Cole.

Stewart, R. (2005). The Griffiths Scales of Mental Development: Proposed new items for the revision of Subscales A, B, C, D and E. Unpublished doctoral thesis, Nelson Mandela Metropolitan University, Port Elizabeth, South Africa.

Stewart, R.A., Rule, A.C. & Giordano, D.A. (2007). The effect of fine motor skill activities on kindergarten student attention. *Early Childhood Education, 35*, 103–109.

Tough, P. (2009, September 25). Can the right kinds of play teach self-control? *The New York Times*, p.142. Retrieved from http://www.nytimes.com/

Tsiaras, Alexander (2002). *From conception to birth: A life unfolds*. London: Vermilion, Edbury Press, Random House.

Van der Veer, R. & Valsiner, J. (1991). *Understanding Vygotsky: A quest for synthesis*. Oxford: Blackwell.

Vianna, E. & Stetsenko, A. (2011). Connecting learning and identity development through a transformative activist stance: Application in adolescent development in a child welfare program. *Human Development, 54*, (5), 313–338.

Vygotsky, Lev S. (1933). Play and its role in the mental development of the child. In Bruner, J.S., Jolly, A. & Sylva, K. (Eds). *Play: Its role in development and evolution* (1976). New York: Basic Books.

Vygotsky, L. (1962). *Thought and language*. Hanfinann, E. & Vakker, G. (Eds). Cambridge, Massachusetts: The Massachusetts Institute of Technology Press

Vygotsky, Lev S. (1967). *The history of the development of higher mental functions*. New York: Plenum Press.

Wertsch, J. (1979). From social interaction to higher psychological processes. *Human Development, 22*, 1–22.

Wonderly, M. (2009). Children's film as an instrument of moral education. *Journal of Moral Education, 38*, (1), 1–15.

[WWW document]. URL http://www.enotes.com/famous-quotes/play-for-young-children-is-not-recreation-activity. 10 December 2008.

Yendovitskaya, T.V. (1971). Development of memory. In A.V. Zaporozhets & D.B. Elkonin (Eds). *Psychology of preschool children*. Cambridge, MA: MIT Press.

Zeidner, M., Matthews, G., Roberts, R.D & MacCann, C. (2003). Development of emotional intelligence: Towards a multi-level investment model. *Human Development, 46*, 69–96.

CHAPTER SIX

MIDDLE CHILDHOOD

Lauren Wild

CASE STUDY

My name is Mpumelelo. I live in Maranathi. I live with my grandmother, my sister Malibongwe, my sister Senzelwe, and my cousin, my mother, my grandfather, my aunt, and my uncle. I go to school at Okhayeni. I am in grade five. I am 10 years old.

I am not slim. I don't have skinny legs. I am good-looking. I am dark in complexion. I have short hair. I have got a small mouth, and my friends at school are Scelimpilo and Sonnyboy.

I only like to rear goats. There's nothing else that I could imagine myself rearing. I like goats because they don't wander too much. What I like is keeping domestic animals and what I hate is when you're a boy who minds livestock and yet you don't have a goat. I like goats because if there is a ceremony/ritual that is being performed I bring them and they slaughter them and then we all eat meat at home. I also take care of them; I play with them, especially those that are black and white (Abaqophi BakwaZisize Abakhanyayo children's radio project (2010). Umfana nembuzi yakhe/A boy with a goat. © Children's Institute, UCT; Zisize Educational Trust, & Okhayeni & Ntabayengwe Primary Schools).

LEARNING OBJECTIVES

By the end of this chapter you should be able to:

- Summarise the physical changes associated with middle childhood
- Describe the advances that take place in children's thinking, learning, and memory
- Explain how the school, family, and peer contexts influence development
- Understand the changes that occur in children's moral reasoning
- Discuss the development of children's self-concept and self-esteem.

Introduction

Between the ages of 6 and 11, children's bodies become taller, slimmer, and stronger. Their baby teeth fall out and permanent teeth replace them. But it is not just their bodies that are changing; their minds are changing too. Children are better at remembering things during middle childhood than they were in early childhood, and their thinking is more logical. They can follow complex instructions, and need less help from adults. In all cultures, the new physical and cognitive abilities that appear around the age of six or seven lead adults to start to make new demands of children, and children are ready to benefit from these experiences. Like Mpumelelo in the opening case study, they begin to learn skills that will be important in the adult world, whether these be reading and writing, or taking care of livestock or younger children. In South Africa and many other countries, this is when children first go to school. They are now exposed to a wider range of influences, including teachers and peers. These new contexts of development stimulate further cognitive and social development, and have an important influence on how children think about themselves.

ACTIVITY

Can you remember what you were like between the ages of 6 and 11? Perhaps you can find some photographs or other mementoes to help jog your memory, as you think about the following questions:
1   What did you look like in middle childhood? For example, how tall were you?
2   When did you lose your first teeth?
3   What new physical or mental skills did you learn during this period?
4   What were some of the difficulties or stresses that you faced?
5   In what places did you spend most of your time? What did you do there?
6   Who were the most important people in your life? How would you describe your relationships?

Physical development

Physical development in middle childhood is relatively slow, but steady. Children's bodies and brains continue to grow, leading to improvements in attention, thinking, and motor skills. Nutrition and physical exercise play an important role in physical development during the middle childhood years.

Body growth

As children enter middle childhood, their height and weight increase steadily, although more slowly than they did during infancy and early childhood. During the primary school years, children grow about five to eight centimetres per year, and add about two to three kilograms per year.

By the age of 9, girls are typically taller than boys. Yet even within each sex, some children are bigger than others. Both genetic influences and environmental influences contribute to size differences among children. Nutrition is one of the most important environmental influences on growth. Both undernutrition and overnutrition are problems in South Africa.

Motor development

During middle childhood, children become stronger and their coordination, balance, and flexibility improve dramatically. This means that their gross motor performance improves as well (recall that chapter four discussed gross motor skills and defined them as physical skills that involve movement of large muscles and the arms, legs or whole body). Children become skilled at physical activities like running, climbing, skipping, bicycle riding, swimming, and playing sports. Fine motor development also improves during middle childhood (recall that chapter four discussed fine motor skills and defined them as physical skills that involve the small muscles and precise movements of the hands and fingers). Children's writing becomes clearer and easier to read, and their drawings become more organised and detailed.

Gender differences in motor skills increase during middle childhood (Thomas & French, 1985). Boys tend to do better than girls on most gross motor skills, particularly those that require power and force (for example throwing and kicking). Girls tend to be better at fine motor skills such as writing and drawing, and at activities that combine movement with balance (for example skipping). This is partly due to physical differences between the sexes. For example, boys are usually stronger than girls because they have more muscle cells. However, gender differences in motor skills are also influenced by cultural expectations and gender stereotypes: widely held beliefs or generalisations about what males and females are like. For instance, boys tend to get more encouragement to play sports than girls. But read the box headed 'Exercise and obesity', and you will see that physical activity in middle childhood is important for the growth and development of both sexes.

Figure 6.1 During middle childhood, improved physical coordination, strength, balance, and flexibility combine to enhance many gross motor skills

Exercise and obesity

Physical exercise during middle childhood:

- Improves strength and stamina
- Helps build healthy bones and muscles
- Reduces depression, anxiety and stress
- Increases self-confidence
- Helps to control weight
- Reduces the risk of developing **obesity**.

Obesity
the condition of having
excessive body fat

'Obesity' is a term for excessive body fat. It is assessed using a measure called the body mass index (BMI), which estimates a person's proportion of body fat by dividing their weight in kilograms by the square of their height in metres. The World Health Organization defines obesity as a BMI of >30 kg/m^2, and overweight as a BMI >25kg/m^2.

Obesity is a growing problem among both adults and children in South Africa. The National Household Food Consumption Survey of 1999 reported that 17 per cent of South African children aged between one year and nine years living in urban areas were overweight or obese (Goedecke, Jennings & Lambert, 2006). Being overweight during childhood can have serious consequences. Overweight children are more likely to become obese adults (Whitaker, Wright, Pepe, Seidel & Dietz, 1997), and obesity in adulthood is associated with a variety of illnesses and an increased chance of early death. Obese children are also more vulnerable to a number of serious health problems during childhood. These include heart disease, liver disease, diabetes, asthma, disrupted breathing during sleep, and problems involving the bones and joints (commonly known as orthopaedic disorders). In addition, obese children often have social and psychological problems. Compared to normal-weight children, obese children tend to be less popular with their peers and to have fewer friends, and are more likely to be depressed (Daniels, 2006).

Why do children become fat? Genetic factors play a role: children are more likely to become obese if their parents are obese. Children who were underweight at birth are also at risk of later obesity. But even children who are biologically predisposed to becoming overweight will become obese only if they eat more calories than their bodies need. Obese children tend to:

- Eat diets with a high percentage of calories from fats
- Be less active
- Watch more television than children of normal weight (Anderson & Butcher, 2006; Goedecke et al., 2006).

Increased urbanisation means that many South Africans are moving to a Western diet that has more fat and sugar and less fibre than a traditional African diet (Steyn et al., 2006). In addition, findings of the Birth to Twenty study conducted at the University of the Witwatersrand suggest that most South African children are not getting nearly enough exercise. Less than half of the nine-year-olds studied took part in physical-education classes at school. Children from poorer households and those living with single parents and less educated mothers tended to do less exercise and watch more television than others. These findings are important, because these children are at risk for later health and social problems (McVeigh, Norris & de Wet, 2004).

Brain development

Two major growth spurts take place in the brain during middle childhood. The first begins around the age of 6, and the second begins around the age of 10 (Somsen, Van't Klooster, Van der Moolen, Van Leeuwen & Licht, 1997). Both spurts involve the development of new synapses, creating more connections among neurons. Myelination also continues, particularly in the frontal lobes of the cerebral cortex (recall that earlier chapters discussed myelination and defined it as a process in which the neurons become covered with a fatty substance called myelin, which increases the speed with which they can communicate with other neurons).

These changes in brain structure result in greater coordination between the frontal lobes and other areas of the brain. The changes make it easier for children to control their attention and play an important role in the more organised and complex thinking that children become capable of during the primary school years (Fischer, 2008).

CHECK YOUR PROGRESS

- How do children's bodies, brains, and motor skills change during middle childhood?
- How do the motor skills of boys and girls differ during this period? Why do these differences come about?
- Explain why the low levels of physical exercise in South African children are a cause for concern.

Cognitive development

Along with the physical gains of middle childhood, between the ages of 6 and 11 children show dramatic improvements in learning, memory, and problem-solving. Their thinking, in turn, becomes more rational, complex, and adult-like.

Piaget's concrete operational stage

Operation
Piaget's term for the mental activity a person carries out 'inside his or her head' or in his or her imagination to reach a logical conclusion

Piaget used the term '**operation**' to refer to the mental activity that a person carries out 'inside his or her head' to reach a logical conclusion. Operations allow people to imagine what might happen if something else were to occur. Around the age of seven, children start to use operations in solving problems (Piaget & Inhelder, 1969).

Piaget called this stage of cognitive development 'concrete operational' because during middle childhood, children can think logically only if the problem or object they are thinking about is real, practical, and concrete, and if they can check what they are doing using actual objects. This means that primary school lessons are most likely to be successful if they focus on concrete things rather than abstract ideas, and if children are given the opportunity to try things out themselves. In chapter one, you saw how Mr Abel taught children in grade six about fractions by cutting up apples. Similarly, if you teach children in primary school how to measure the area and perimeter of a rectangle, you will probably be much more effective if you start with concrete examples (How many tiles do we need for the bathroom? How long a fence do we need to surround the soccer field?) than if you simply give them a rule or formula and expect them to apply it.

As children's thinking becomes more rational during middle childhood, so they become less **egocentric**, and have less difficulty than younger children have in recognising a point of view other than their own. During middle childhood children become capable of considering more than one aspect of an object or situation at a time – what Piaget referred to as **decentration**. For example, children of primary school age can understand that the length and width of a rectangle determine its area.

This ability to focus on two or more dimensions of a problem at the same time means that concrete operational thinkers acquire a skill known as **conservation**. This means that they realise that certain characteristics of objects – such as quantity, volume, weight, and so on – cannot be judged just on appearances. For example, they realise that the volume of water doesn't change when they pour it from a short, broad jar into a tall, thin jar, even though it 'looks' different. Look at Figure 6.2, which illustrates some common tests of conservation.

The ability to conserve shows that children are learning some very important mathematical principles. These include:

* **Identity:** A = A and A + 0 = A. Something equals itself, and anything plus zero still equals itself. For example, if there were nine Jelly Tots in a row before, and somebody didn't add any (or eat any), then there are still nine Jelly Tots there. It doesn't matter if somebody spreads them

Egocentric thinking
the difficulty that young children have in recognising a point of view other than their own

Decentration
the ability to focus on two or more aspects of an object or situation at the same time

Conservation
the realisation that certain characteristics of objects, such as quantity, volume and weight, stay the same when the outward appearance of the object is changed

Figure 6.2 Some common tests of conservation

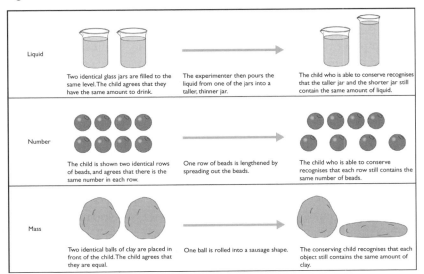

Source: Adapted from Sigelman & Rider (2006, p. 180) and Santrock (2005, p. 210)

out or moves them closer together; even if it looks as if there are more or less, the number of Jelly Tots has not changed.

- **Reversibility:** A – B + B = A. When somebody does something, whether it is squash a ball of clay flat or subtract a number, the person can do it in reverse and end up where he or she was before, with the same thing that the person had to begin with. For example, in the conservation-of-liquid experiment using the different-shaped jars, a child who is capable of reversibility knows that there would still be the same amount of liquid if the contents of the tall jar were poured back into the short jar. A preschool child, in contrast, shows irreversibility of thinking, and might insist that the water would overflow from the short jar if it were poured back.

- **Compensation:** (A – 1) + (B + 1) = A + B. Changes in one aspect of a problem can balance or make up for changes in another aspect of the problem. For example, in the conservation of volume experiment, a concrete operational thinker can understand that the increased height of the new container is compensated for by its smaller width: it is taller, but it is also thinner.

Memory

Many researchers believe that children's new ability to consider two or more aspects of a problem at once is due to increases in their memory abilities. Older children can learn faster and remember more than younger children can. For example, tests of visual memory show that 5-year-olds can remember the colour of one or two blocks they have just seen, whereas 10-year-olds can keep the colour of three or four blocks in mind (Riggs, McTaggart, Simpson & Freeman, 2006). But why do these improvements occur? John Flavell and Henry Wellman (1977) put forward four major explanations which, taken together, seem to explain why learning and memory improve in middle childhood:

- Changes in working memory capacity
- Changes in memory strategies
- Increased knowledge about memory
- Increased knowledge about the world.

Changes in working memory capacity

Information-processing approach
an approach to cognitive development in which the human mind is studied by comparing it to the workings of a computer

Theorists who adopt an **information-processing approach** believe that in order to understand the human mind, it is useful to compare it to a computer. A computer's hardware refers to the machine itself – its keyboard, its storage capacity, and so on. Similarly, the mind's 'hardware' is the brain. One reason that older children can remember more than younger children is that older children have more advanced hardware than young children have – just as today's computers have greater capacity than those of the past. As children get older, their brains have more space in working memory (so they can keep more information in mind at once), and they can process information more quickly.

Changes in memory strategies

In addition to its hardware, a computer has software – programs for word processing, analysing statistics, and so on. The mind also has 'software' – rules, strategies, and other mental 'programs' for taking in information, storing it in memory, and getting it out again. Older children have better 'software' than younger children. They have learned to use effective methods for getting information into long-term memory, and for retrieving the information when they need it.

To learn more about memory strategies, do the activity below.

ACTIVITY

The following is a memory task. Look at Figure 6.3, which contains 12 objects. Give yourself two minutes to memorise these objects. Now shut your textbook, and write down as many objects as you can remember.

Figure 6.3

Source: Adapted from Sigelman & Rider (2006, p. 263)

When you did the memory-task activity, what tricks or strategies did you use to make your task easier? Perhaps you helped yourself to remember the items in the picture by simply saying their names over and over, for example, 'Apple, chair, grapes …' Repeating items like this when trying to learn and remember is called **rehearsal**. Preschoolers rarely use rehearsal to move items into long-term memory, but most school-age children use this strategy (Flavell, Beach & Chinsky, 1966).

Another way you may have helped yourself to remember the items in the picture is by sorting them into meaningful groups such as 'food', 'animals', and 'furniture', and then rehearsing each of the groups. This memory strategy is known as **organisation**. Another organisational strategy, called chunking, is used when a long number (for example 0216854364) is broken into manageable sub-units (for example 021-685-4364 – a telephone number). The number of children using this strategy increases steadily through the primary school years (Kron-Sperl, Schneider & Hasselhorn, 2008).

The last strategy that children learn to use involves creating meaningful links between the items to be remembered by adding either words or images. This strategy is known as **elaboration**. For instance, you could help yourself to remember two of the items in the Figure 6.3 by picturing a horse eating a pear. Another example of elaboration would be children helping themselves to remember the location of the points of a compass by using a little rhyme such as 'Noddy Eats Silk Worms'.

Increased knowledge about memory

Older children may be able to remember more than younger children because they know more about memory than younger children know (Ghetti, Lyons, Lazzarin & Cornoldi, 2008). For example, older children know how much time and effort they must put in to learn things thoroughly, which strategies best fit different kinds of memory tasks, and so on. Knowledge of memory and memory processes is called **metamemory**. Metamemory is one aspect of **metacognition**, or a person's ability to think about his or her own thought processes.

Increased knowledge about the world

Older children know more about the world in general than young children know. Because school-aged children have an increased **knowledge base**, they are more likely to be familiar with the material to be learned, and familiar material is often easier to learn and remember than unfamiliar material. For example, imagine that you are reading a book about jazz. If you already know a lot about jazz, you can read quite quickly because you are able to link the information to what you already know. All you really need to do is to check for any new information, or for information

Rehearsal
memory strategy involving repeating items

Organisation
memory strategy involving sorting the items into meaningful groups or chunks

Elaboration
memory strategy involving creating meaningful links between the items to be remembered by adding either words or images

Metamemory
knowledge of memory and memory processes

Metacognition
a person's ability to think about his or her own thought processes

Knowledge base
how much a person knows about the content area to be learned

that contradicts what you already know. Learning about a highly unfamiliar topic is much more difficult.

Even young children appear to develop very effective memory strategies in areas that they know a lot about, whether the topic is, for example, dinosaurs or chess (Chi & Ceci, 1987). So it may be that older children can remember more words or numbers in lists than younger children simply because they are more familiar with language and numbers than young children are.

Problem solving

The development of children's memory is closely related to their ability to solve problems, as a person must draw on stored information in order to select appropriate problem-solving strategies (Zheng, Swanson & Marcoulides, 2011). How do children's problem-solving skills change as they get older? Piaget offered one answer to this question by arguing that children progress from one way of thinking to more complex ways of thinking as they mature. The information-processing theorist Robert Siegler, however, was not satisfied with this explanation. Siegler argued that cognitive development goes on all the time, not just during the shift from one stage to another.

Siegler (2000) proposed that children of all ages use a variety of problem-solving strategies. For example, given a subtraction problem such as 12 – 3, children sometimes count down three steps from 12 until they reach 9, but other times count up from 3 until they arrive at 12. Siegler's 'rule assessment' approach assumes that when children fail to solve problems, it is because they failed to take in all the important aspects of the task, or because they were following faulty rules. As they get older, they use less adaptive strategies less, and more adaptive strategies more, and occasionally totally new strategies may appear. Thus, cognitive development works much as evolution does, through a process of natural selection in which many ways of thinking are available, and the most adaptive survive.

Other cognitive development

Several other advances in thinking help children to carry out the everyday activities they are expected to perform during middle childhood:
- During middle childhood, children's ability to control their attention increases (Rebok et al., 1997). They can concentrate on a task more fully, and for longer.
- School-age children are more able than preschool children to plan in order to reach goals (Parrila & Das, 1996). They are better at deciding what to do first and what to do next in an orderly manner.

- Metacognition increases during middle childhood. This increase allows older children to weigh up how difficult a problem is and to choose appropriate strategies for solving it (Flavell, Green & Flavell, 1995).
- Children's language abilities increase strikingly during middle childhood. The average 6- or 7-year-old understands about 10 000 words; this increases to approximately 40 000 words by the time children are 10 or 11 (Anglin, 1993). Children also become better at keeping a meaningful conversation going. They also become better at taking into account the knowledge or viewpoint of the person to whom they are talking.
- Classification skills also improve during middle childhood. At about age seven or eight, children first understand the principle of **class inclusion**, the awareness that lower categories (known as subordinate classes) are included in larger, higher categories (known as superordinate classes) (Piaget & Inhelder, 1969). For example, school-age children understand that leopards are included in the class of mammals, and mammals are included in the class of animals. Preschool children understand that leopards are also animals, but they do not yet fully understand the relationship between the classes.

Class inclusion
the awareness that lower categories are included in larger, higher categories

Schooling and cognitive development

During middle childhood, children in South Africa spend much of their time in school. As in other countries, instruction in South African schools focuses on learning two basic symbol systems: written language and mathematics. The South African school curriculum is based on a learner-centred educational philosophy. Learner-centred education is based mainly on the work of Lev Vygotsky, but also draws on the ideas of Jean Piaget and John Dewey. The main ideas of learner-centred education are as follows:

- Children play an active role in their own learning.
- Learning builds on prior knowledge and experiences, which in turn are determined by the social and cultural context.
- Language is central to learning and cognitive development (Chisholm & Leyendecker, 2008).

What effects does schooling have on children's cognitive development? Researchers typically use one of two techniques to answer this question:

- **The school-cut-off strategy:** This technique involves comparing children of about the same age whose birth dates fall before and after the cut-off date for beginning school.
- **Cross-cultural research:** This technique examines the consequences of schooling in cultures where not all children go to school.

Overall, the results of these studies suggest that the basic cognitive developments associated with middle childhood (such as concrete operations) occur regardless of whether or not children go to school. However, schooling does improve children's logic, memory, and metacognitive skills by:

- Increasing their knowledge base and familiarity with certain tasks
- Teaching them specific strategies for remembering
- Increasing their ability to reflect upon and talk about their thought processes (Cole & Cole, 2001).

But perhaps the most significant effect of schooling on children's later lives is that it opens doors to more highly paid jobs and increased social status.

Mastering academic skills is therefore very important for children's future prospects. However, large numbers of children in South Africa – particularly those living in rural areas – do not go to school. The Eastern Cape has the highest percentage of children not in school (13 per cent), followed by KwaZulu-Natal (11 per cent) and Limpopo (10 per cent). Moreover, nearly one out of four South African children has to repeat grade one, and many learners drop out of school (Amoateng, Richter, Makiwane & Rama, 2004). Learning outcomes are also poor, on average, both in comparison to other developing countries and in relation to the goals of the South African curriculum (Chisholm, 2004).

What are the factors that influence school achievement? The following sections will discuss the influencing factors under the following broad headings:

- School characteristics
- Child characteristics
- Parenting practices.

School characteristics

International research has often approached the problem of what makes a school good or bad by identifying unusually effective schools. An effective school is defined as one in which learners show one or more of the following characteristics at higher rates than would be predicted, given the kind of families or neighbourhoods they come from:

- High scores on tests
- Good attendance at school
- Low rates of disruptive behaviour in the classroom and delinquency
- A high rate of later university attendance or college attendance
- High self-esteem.

When these successful schools are compared with others in similar neighbourhoods that have less impressive track records, certain common themes appear (Rutter & Maughan, 2002). Effective schools have clear goals and rules, good control, good communication, and high expectations for their students. They care about the overall well-being of the child, as well as having a focus on academics. Principals of effective schools provide clear and strong leadership, and they are dedicated to effective teaching. Teachers in these schools work well together and share the same goals. A large proportion of parents are involved in school activities.

Many primary schools in South Africa – particularly in informal settlements – do not meet these criteria of effective schools, and are of poor quality. Linda Chisholm (2004) has identified the following specific problems that need to be addressed:

- Large numbers of unqualified and under-trained teachers
- A lack of resources and facilities in poor (particularly rural) schools
- High levels of violence, sexism, and racism. Children who are abused or harassed at school often have difficulty concentrating, lose interest in school, and perform below their potential on their schoolwork.
- The language of teaching and learning. Although 90 per cent of learners in South Africa attend schools in which English is the language of learning and teaching, English is the home language of only 9 per cent of the population. Children who lack adequate English language skills – and whose teachers often also lack such skills – are likely to experience a delay in their academic achievement, sometimes with long-term effects (De Wet, 2002).

Such problems mean that while the goals of learner-based education are widely accepted in South Africa, they are often not reflected in actual classroom practice (Chisholm & Leyendecker, 2008).

Child characteristics

Children with specific learning disabilities do poorly in school, despite having normal intelligence test scores. The most common learning disability is dyslexia (difficulty learning to read). In South Africa, poor performance at school is also related to problems such as malnutrition, stunting, and fetal alcohol spectrum disorders which are common in poor communities (Fleisch, 2008).

Mastery orientation
tendency to seek challenges and to persist in the face of failure

Helpless orientation
tendency to avoid challenges and to give up in the face of obstacles or failure

A child's success in school can also be influenced by his or her beliefs about his or her own abilities. Learners who have a **mastery orientation** – who believe that they have the ability to succeed at schoolwork and control their own learning – are more likely to do well at school than students who doubt their abilities (Dweck & Leggett, 1988). Children who believe in their own abilities are more likely to set challenging goals and to use appropriate strategies to achieve them. They try hard, do not give up when they face difficulties, and ask for help when necessary. In contrast, learners with a **helpless orientation** are more likely to become frustrated and depressed, and to give up when they experience difficulties, which in turn makes success harder to achieve.

Parenting practices

Parents of children who are high in mastery motivation and do well at school tend to be authoritative (warm and caring, but also firm and consistent) rather than authoritarian or permissive. These authoritative parents encourage their children by praising them for ability and hard work, and are supportive without being overcontrolling (Ginsburg & Bronstein, 1993). Children whose parents encourage and support their academic learning in a positive manner are likely to enjoy new challenges and feel confident that they can handle them.

CHECK YOUR PROGRESS
- How, according to Piaget, is children's thinking in middle childhood different from their thinking in early childhood?
- Outline four major explanations for why memory improves during middle childhood?
- Explain how a child's success in school can be influenced by characteristics of the school, the child, and the child's parents.

The family

As important as school is in middle childhood, it is not the only significant influence in children's lives. During middle childhood, children occupy a much wider range of contexts than they did in early childhood, and spend more time unsupervised by adults and with peers. Nevertheless, the family's influence on their development remains very powerful.

Changing relations with parents

As children get older, their relationships with their parents change. By the age of seven, children often start to avoid open shows of affection with their parents in public, and parents in turn expect their children to behave in more responsible ways. Eleanor Maccoby (1984) points out that the issues that come up between parents and children also change; in middle childhood, parents worry more about children's work and behaviour at school, household chores, and their social lives and activities away from home.

Research findings suggest that, as was the case in early childhood, authoritative parenting tends to be associated with good cognitive and social skills in middle childhood, at least within middle-class communities (Kaufmann et al., 2000). However, as children develop, parents

Coregulation
the process in which control of the child's behaviour during middle childhood relies on cooperation and a sharing of responsibility between parents and children

Sibling
a brother or sister

use new and more indirect techniques to influence or correct their children's behaviour. Such techniques include appealing to reason, humour, self-esteem, or guilt. Maccoby (1984) has given the name **coregulation** to these techniques, in which control of the child's behaviour relies on cooperation and a sharing of responsibility between parents and children.

The influence of siblings

Sibling relationships in middle childhood are often ambivalent 'love–hate' relationships in which frequent conflict and rivalry exist alongside a great deal of affection, companionship, and kindness (Dunn, 2002). Although researchers have given far less attention to sibling relationships than to parent–child relationships, Gene Brody (2004) has shown that brothers and sisters can have important direct and indirect influences on each other's development.

Direct contributions of siblings to development
According to Brody (2004), most of the contributions that siblings make to development are positive. One of the most important functions of siblings is to provide emotional support. Brothers and sisters confide in one another and can protect and comfort one another during hard times.

In addition, older siblings often provide caregiving services for younger siblings. In many rural communities, older girls are the main caregivers for infants and toddlers, and are responsible for feeding them, comforting them, disciplining them, and so on. In other societies, older

Figure 6.4 Sibling rivalry is common in middle childhood – nevertheless, brothers and sisters also provide one another with emotional support and practical help

siblings play less of a role in caregiving, but girls particularly are often asked to babysit their younger siblings. Older siblings who take on a caregiving role learn more quickly to balance their own interests with others' needs than do older siblings who do not take care of their younger siblings. However, excessive caregiving duties may interfere with the older child's time spent on homework or school activities.

Older siblings also serve as teachers of new behaviour. Interactions with older siblings promote young children's language and cognitive development, and school-aged children who tutor their younger siblings may benefit as well: they score higher on tests of academic achievement than individuals who have not had these tutoring experiences. The mixture of closeness and conflict that often exists in sibling relationships can also play an important role in helping children to learn to understand other people's feelings and points of view.

Sibling influences can also be negative, however. Younger siblings growing up with aggressive older siblings are more likely to develop behaviour problems and school difficulties, and to have less positive peer relationships. This is particularly likely to be the case if they live in disadvantaged neighbourhoods where there are high levels of poverty and unemployment.

Indirect contributions of siblings to development

Brody (2004) discovered that siblings can also influence each other's development indirectly in the following ways:

- There is evidence that parents' positive or negative experiences with older siblings can influence what they expect from younger children, and what parenting strategies they use.
- Children who believe that they receive less warmth and more negative treatment from their parents than their siblings receive are more likely to develop emotional and behavioural problems. Adjustment problems are particularly likely if the child has a bad or distant individual relationship with his or her parents, and if the child perceives this differential treatment to be unfair. Children are less likely to be negatively affected by differential treatment if their parents treat them well (even if the sibling receives more positive treatment). If they understand why parents treat siblings differently from one another, they are also less likely to interpret differences in treatment as evidence that they are not valued or worthy of love. Possible reasons for parents treating siblings differently include differences in age, personality, and special needs.

Variety in family life

The research on parent and sibling influences on development assumes that most children grow up in a nuclear family consisting of a mother, a father, and their children. However, this nuclear family has never been

the most common family form in many parts of the world, and nowadays it is increasingly rare. Children are growing up in a greater variety of families than ever before, including, for example:
- Extended families like those of Mpumelelo (from the case study at the start of this chapter), in which relatives such as grandparents, aunts, uncles or cousins live in the same household as parents and their children
- Single-parent families
- Lesbian- and gay-headed families
- Reconstituted families with stepparents and stepchildren
- Families with parents who are unmarried but live together
- Sibling-headed families.

As a result of fostering or adoption, children are also growing up with parents to whom they are not biologically related. Families also change over time, and sometimes dissolve through separation, divorce, or death. What are the most common family forms in South Africa? Data from the population censuses in 1996 and 2001 suggest that the vast majority of children in South Africa live in one of two family types:
- Extended family households (54 per cent in 2001)
- Nuclear family households (nearly 38 per cent in 2001).

White South Africans are more likely to live in nuclear families. Extended families are more common in African, Asian, or coloured communities (Amoateng et al., 2004).

While the majority of children in South Africa live with their biological mothers, most do not live with their biological fathers. In 2002, the fathers of 11,5 per cent of South African children under the age of 16 were deceased. And in 2002, 45,8 per cent of South African children under the age of 16 had biological fathers who were alive but absent from the household. Again, there are differences among population groups: less than 40 per cent of all African children aged 15 years or younger were reported as living with their fathers in 2002, compared to almost 90 per cent of white children (Posel & Devey, 2006).

Single-parent families in South Africa

The vast majority of children in single-parent families in South Africa live with their mothers. According to South Africa's Central Statistical Services, about 42 per cent of children lived only with their mothers in 1998, in comparison to 1 per cent of children who lived only with their fathers at that time (Budlender, 1998).

Many single mothers were never married to their child's father. The 1996 census in South Africa found that 32 per cent of births among African people occurred outside marriage, compared to 24 per cent among coloured people, 3 per cent among Indian people, and 2 per cent among white people (Amoateng & Richter, 2003).

In other cases, these mothers became single as a result of divorce. In 2004, the divorce rate for South Africa as a whole was 5 per 1 000 married couples (Statistics South Africa, 2006). The divorce rate was highest among white people, followed by African people, and lowest among Indian people. In South Africa, marriages are more likely to dissolve through death than through divorce.

In recent years, increased numbers of adult deaths as a result of Aids have led to a rapid rise in the number of children who have experienced the death of one or both of their parents. According to information obtained in the 2004 General Household Survey in South Africa, 3,3 million children (18 per cent) had lost one or both of their biological parents. Twelve per cent of all children had lost their biological father only and 3 per cent had lost their biological mother only. A further 3 per cent had lost both biological parents (Meintjes, Leatt & Berry, 2006).

Does it make a difference to children if they grow up with only one as opposed to two parents, or if they lose contact with a parent as a result of divorce or death? Because these issues touch many people personally, people often have very strong – and sometimes opposing – views about these issues. But if the aim is to improve children's lives, it is vital that decisions about what is in their best interest are based on evidence, and not just on personal beliefs. The next section will therefore look at the research that has focused on the outcomes for children who are raised by unmarried single mothers, whose parents separate or divorce, and who experience the death of a parent during childhood.

Family structure and developmental outcomes

Most of the research on children raised in single-parent families has been conducted in the USA and Western Europe. This research suggests that the outcomes are similar for children whose parents divorce and for those whose parents were never married. On average, children born outside marriage and children whose parents divorce are more likely than children in two-parent families to have emotional and behavioural problems. They are less likely to perform well at school and to have good relations with their peers than children in two-parent families. Many of these difficulties apparently continue into adulthood. Children raised by single parents are more likely to have a lower educational level, to be unemployed or in low-status jobs, and to experience marital difficulties and symptoms of depression (Amato, 2005).

The international research findings on the effects of parental death on child adjustment suggest that experiencing the death of a parent also places children at risk for certain problems, although not as much as divorce or being born to an unmarried mother (Amato, 2005). South African research suggests that children whose parents have died from an Aids-related illness may be particularly vulnerable to developing emotional problems (Cluver, Gardner & Operario, 2007).

In order to understand these research results, it is important to note that the differences between children from single-parent and children from two-parent families are small, and average differences do not mean that all children in single-parent families are worse off than all children whose parents are, and remain, married. Overall, the research suggests that most children from single-parent families do not have psychological problems. However, more children from single-parent families are likely to have problems than those of continuously married parents. As a result, many researchers believe that rather than asking whether growing up in a single-parent family is harmful to children, they should rather be asking what factors in single-parent families contribute to children's adjustment difficulties, and what factors help children to adapt well.

Why might children do worse in single-parent families?

Paul Amato (2005) has discussed three possible explanations as to why growing up in a single-parent family poses risks to children's well-being:
- Economic hardship
- Exposure to stress
- Less effective parenting.

Economic hardship

Most children whose parents are unmarried, divorced, ill or deceased are economically disadvantaged. They often live in communities with high rates of crime, poor-quality schools, and few services.

Exposure to stress

Stress occurs when the demands of the environment exceed a person's ability to cope with them. Children living in single-parent families often face a series of stressful experiences. In addition to economic difficulties, these may include the following:
- The painful feelings associated with the loss of contact with a parent
- Having to move away from their home and familiar friends and neighbourhoods
- Disrupted schooling
- New routines and schedules
- Increased household chores and work responsibilities
- Stigmatisation and social isolation.

In many cases, these stresses do not have a clear beginning or end. For example, orphaned children may have had to deal with the physical and psychological effects of living with (and often caring for) an ill and dying parent; children whose parents are living with HIV and Aids have shown similar adjustment problems to those of orphans (Bauman et al., 2006). Similarly, children whose parents separate or divorce may be exposed to increased conflict between their parents both before and after one of the parents leaves the home. In fact, several researchers have suggested that it is conflict between a child's parents, rather than divorce itself, that poses the greatest risk for children. There is evidence that living in a conflict-ridden two-parent family can be more harmful to a child's development in the long term than living in a stable single-parent family (Harold, 2000).

Less effective parenting

The stresses associated with single parenthood, divorce, and the illness and death of family members can also have a negative impact on the quality of parenting. Single parents who have to cope with financial difficulties and other responsibilities without the support of a partner or other relatives are at risk of becoming stressed and depressed. And adults who are stressed and depressed are often not the most effective parents. They may become irritable, impatient, and less sensitive to their children's needs. They may also be inconsistent in their discipline – sometimes they tend to be too strict, and at other times too lenient. It doesn't help that children who are going through their parents' divorce, illness or death are usually not the easiest of children, because they are also suffering. They may become

Figure 6.5 Although divorce is stressful for children, living in a high-conflict two-parent family can be more harmful in the long-term than living in a low-conflict single-parent family

clingy or disrespectful and disobedient, which makes effective parenting even more difficult (Hetherington, Bridges & Insabella, 1998).

What can improve the outcomes for children in single-parent families?

Overall, the research evidence suggests that a parent's marital status is less important for children's well-being than what happens *within* families. The most important factor influencing children's adjustment is the nature of the relationships among all family members, and the quality of the care and support that children receive. For example, parental separation or divorce is unlikely to be damaging to children if parents can control their anger with one another, avoid exposing the child to arguments, and cooperate in providing the child with supportive, authoritative parenting (Kelly & Emery, 2003).

Another factor that can help single-parent families to fare better is adequate finances: research shows that children raised by single parents do better at school and have fewer behavioural problems when fathers pay child support (Amato, 2000). Social support from people such as relatives, friends, and school staff can also be very important (Amato, 2000).

As was noted above, many children in South Africa live in extended families. In households where biological fathers are not present, other men may assume the social role of father, or act as father figures. Support from extended family members and broader social networks is thought to play an important role in helping people to cope with stress. This type of support is also thought to help people to gain access to material resources and other opportunities such as jobs (Amoateng et al., 2004). Currently, however, very little is known about the effect of extended family members on child development in South Africa.

> ### CHECK YOUR PROGRESS
> * How do children's relationships with their parents change in middle childhood?
> * Outline the positive influences and negative influences of siblings on development.
> * Explain why growing up in a single-parent family increases the risk of negative outcomes for children.
> * Discuss the factors that help to promote positive outcomes in children growing up with single parents.

Peer relationships

Peer
a person who is of similar age and developmental level; a social equal

As important as family relationships are to development, some theorists argue that relationships with peers are at least as significant. **Peers** are people of approximately the same age and developmental level. Peer relationships are quite different from parent–child relationships. While parents have more power than their children do, peers are usually equals. This means that peers must learn to see things from each other's point of view. They also have to negotiate, compromise, and cooperate if they are to get along. Some theorists therefore believe that relationships with peers are particularly important for the development of many personal and social skills.

ACTIVITY

In 1998, Judith Rich Harris published a controversial book, *The Nurture Assumption*, in which she argued that parents do not have any important long-term effects on their child's personality, and that peers are in fact far more important in influencing how children turn out (Harris, 1998). Her critics have argued that while she makes important points about the fact that parents are not the only important influence on children, her conclusion is simply wrong. What do you think? Do you feel that your parents or your peers had a greater influence on the person you are today?

During middle childhood, children typically spend more and more time with their peers – particularly same-sex peers. Boys spend most of their time playing in groups, whereas girls mostly prefer to play with just one or two other girls at a time. Not all children prefer to spend time with members of their own sex, but this is the most common pattern in all cultures during middle childhood (Maccoby, 1990). As children spend more time playing together, three aspects of peer relationships become increasingly significant:

- Peer acceptance and popularity
- Friendship
- Bullying.

Peer acceptance and popularity

Some children in the peer group are better liked than others. Researchers study peer-group acceptance through sociometric techniques, in which children in a group are asked to state their feelings about other members of the group. For example, in a nomination procedure, a researcher might ask children in a classroom to choose three classmates whom they especially like and three whom they dislike. The researcher can then work out how popular each child in the group is by counting the number of times the child has been nominated as a 'liked' or 'disliked' individual.

Another way of measuring peer popularity is to use a rating scale. For example, a researcher will ask children to rate all of their classmates in terms of one or more dimensions, such as how nice or friendly they are, or how much they like to play with them. By finding out who is liked and who is disliked in a group, researchers can classify children into these four different categories of social status (Coie, Dodge, & Coppotelli, 1982):

- The popular (liked by most and disliked by few)
- The rejected (disliked by most and liked by few)
- The neglected (children who are neither actively liked nor disliked but seem instead to be invisible to their classmates)
- The controversial (children who are liked by many but also disliked by many).

Children who do not fall into any of the above groups are usually average-status children who are liked (or disliked) by a medium number of peers.

ACITIVITY

Think back to your years in primary school. Can you remember children who were popular? Rejected? Neglected? Controversial? What characteristics do you think contributed to the person's social status, in each case?

Why are some children more popular than others?

Evidence from a number of studies reviewed by Rubin, Bukowski and Parker (1998) suggests that positive social behaviours and negative social behaviours are the most important influence on children's social status in middle childhood. The kinds of behaviour that are associated with popularity may vary to some extent from one culture to another, depending on what kinds of behaviours are valued or seen as 'good' within that society. At least within Western cultural contexts, however:

- 'Popular' children tend to be those who are socially skilled, friendly, and cooperative.
- 'Rejected' children, in contrast, are often aggressive and disruptive, although some rejected children are extremely shy and withdrawn.
- 'Neglected' children are less sociable than their peers, but they are not aggressive. They tend to be fairly passive and unassertive, so other children don't really notice them.
- 'Controversial' children tend to have many of the characteristics of both popular and rejected children. For example, they may be aggressive and disruptive, but also helpful, cooperative, and good leaders.

Does peer status in childhood have long-term consequences?

Most children with poor peer relationships do not develop later adjustment problems. Nevertheless, children who are rejected by their peers are more likely to experience scholastic and psychological difficulties later in life than children who were accepted by their peers. Rejection by peers in childhood – particularly when related to aggression – has been linked to an increased risk of later academic problems, truancy, and school drop-out. Adolescents with a history of peer rejection are also more likely to abuse alcohol and drugs, to have psychological problems, and to be involved in delinquent or criminal behaviour (Rubin et al., 1998).

Why are poor peer relationships in childhood linked to later psychological problems?

The long-term problems shown by children who were rejected by their peers are probably not only or directly due to their poor relationships with peers. For example, children whose parents are harsh and punitive are more likely to have both peer difficulties and emotional difficulties (Kawabata, Alink, Tseng, Van IJzendoorn & Crick, 2011). Also, temperamental characteristics may play a role in social behaviours such as empathy, aggression, and conscience, which are responsible for poor relationships with peers and for other difficulties such as being in trouble with the law (Rothbart, 2007).

However, it does seem that in many cases a negative peer reputation (for example 'He is always hitting', 'She's mean') can set up a pattern of interactions that causes this reputation to be maintained or to get even worse (Mikami, Lerner & Lun, 2010). For example, imagine nine-year-old boys named Sipho and Lindela. Sipho has good social skills. As a result, his peers like him and he finds it easy to make friends. Through his friendships, he develops his understanding of other people, and improves his social skills further. This, in turn, should make him even more effective with – and usually more valued by – his peers. Lindela, in contrast, has less good social skills than Sipho to begin with. He is sometimes aggressive when he doesn't get what he wants. Even when he is not aggressive, Lindela's peers tend to avoid him and to exclude him from their games because they have come to expect negative behaviours from him. As a result, Lindela will probably have few opportunities to learn more socially appropriate patterns of behaviour. He is also likely to come to expect negative behaviour from his peers, which in turn is likely to encourage him to behave in negative ways towards them. A vicious circle then develops between Lindela and his peers, and his reputation is likely to get worse and worse.

ACTIVITY

Mpumelelo's self-description in the case study at the beginning of this chapter includes mention of two school friends. Think back to your middle-childhood years.
- Can you remember a significant friend from this time?
- What was special about this relationship that made it different from those with people you would not refer to as friends?

- Did the friendship last? Why or why not?
- How do you think you were influenced by this friendship at the time?
- Do you think this friendship has had any long-term effects on your life?

Friendship

Friendship
voluntary relationship involving an affectionate bond

Friendship is generally described as a voluntary relationship involving an affectionate bond (Ladd, 1999). Before age eight or so, friendships tend to be based around enjoying similar activities: a good friend is somebody who is fun to be with. For example, a preschooler might say, 'Andiswa is my friend, because she lives next door and she plays with me.' Between the ages of 8 and 10, however, children begin to describe friendships based on mutual loyalty, respect, kindness, and affection (Rubin et al., 1998). For example, a nine-year-old might say 'Andiswa is my friend, because we like each other and stick by each other no matter what.' Children in the middle-childhood years want their friends to be psychologically similar to themselves. They emphasise that friends must be sensitive to each other's point of view. In the context of these friendships, children share private jokes, develop secret codes, talk about their families, gossip, set out on adventures, and help each other in times of trouble. They also fight, threaten, break up, and make up.

Friendships of the middle-childhood years can be very close and affectionate. They are important for giving children a sense of belonging and social acceptance. In fact, close friends are the most important peers a child has. Popular children are more likely than unpopular ones to have friends, but even most unpopular children manage to find at least one friend. And regardless of whether they are popular or unpopular, children who have friends tend to be happier and more competent than those without friends, especially if their friends are well adjusted and supportive (Hartup & Stevens, 1997).

Bullying

Bullying
repeated, intentional, and organised acts of aggression directed towards particular peers (victims)

Relational aggression
behaviour intended to harm someone by damaging their friendships or reputation or deliberately excluding them from the group

Bullying is another aspect of social interaction that tends to appear in middle childhood. Bullying refers to repeated, intentional and organised acts of aggression that are directed towards particular peers (victims). The aggression may be physical (for example hitting), verbal (for example name-calling) or relational. **Relational aggression** (sometimes it is called covert, indirect or psychological aggression) involves harming another child's friendships, harming their reputation or deliberately leaving them out of the group. Physical bullying is more common among boys, while girls more often resort to relational bullying.

Bullies are children who act aggressively without being provoked, in order to dominate other children. Unlike other aggressive children, they are most likely to use force unemotionally, rather than in the heat of an argument. Bullies actually seem to have quite a good understanding of social interaction, but use this knowledge in an antisocial way, to control other people and get what they want (Olweus, 1995).

Why do some children become bullies? Dan Olweus (1995), a Norwegian psychologist who is a world expert on bullying, has found that children who are violent towards peers at school are likely to have:
* Been exposed to violence at home
* Had few limits placed by parents on aggressive behaviour
* Had insufficient love and warmth from their parents.

Bullies also tend to:
* Hold positive views of violence
* Show aggression towards both adults and children
* Have a strong need to dominate and feel more powerful than other children
* Feel little empathy for those they are bullying.

There is little evidence for the commonly held view that bullies are actually 'anxious and insecure' under the surface. It is true, however, that some children may turn to violence a way of defending themselves against others of whom they are afraid.

On average, it seems that around 1 in 10 schoolchildren are subject to persistent bullying. The **victimised** (children who are selectively and actively harmed, psychologically and physically, by bullies) tend to be:
* Anxious
* Insecure
* Lacking in self-esteem and self-confidence
* Isolated from the remainder of the peer group (Olweus, 1995).

Victims
children who are selectively and actively harmed, psychologically and physically, by bullies

These personality traits of victimised children are likely to be both a cause and a result of bullying. Children who are cautious, sensitive, and (in the case of boys) physically weak from an early age are likely to find it difficult to assert themselves in the peer group. At the same time, repeated harassment by peers must have considerably increased their anxiety, insecurity, and low self-esteem.

It is, however, important not to exaggerate the 'typical' characteristics of victims or bullies. Sometimes children can be both victim and bully, depending on the circumstances.

Effects of bullying
Until quite recently, adults tended to see bullying as playing or teasing which occasionally gets out of hand, or as an inevitable fact of school life, which children will eventually grow out of. However, bullying is now

recognised as a serious problem and seen as a form of violence against children. Bullying can have very damaging (and sometimes long-lasting) consequences. Being bullied can lead to a loss of self-esteem and confidence, depression, and, even, suicide (Olweus, 1995). And bullies, in turn, are at risk of becoming involved in criminal behaviour in later life.

What can be done to stop bullying?

Psychologists who specialise in studying bullying believe it is not enough just to protect the victims and rehabilitate the bullies. Rather, interventions must change the social climate of the entire school. All members of the school community – including educators, learners, and parents – should be made aware of what bullying is and how to respond to it. This whole-school approach has led to important reductions in bullying in a number of cases. However, it is not always effective. More research is therefore needed to determine how, and under what conditions, interventions are likely to be successful (Smith, Schneider, Smith & Ananiadou, 2004).

CHECK YOUR PROGRESS
- What are the four basic categories of social status?
- How does peer acceptance or rejection in middle childhood influence children's later lives?
- What are the characteristics of typical bullies?

Psychosocial development

As children move from early childhood to middle childhood, the changes that take place in their cognitive capacities and in their social lives contribute to important developments in the way they think about themselves and the world around them.

Moral development

One of the aspects that reveal these developments is children's thinking about moral issues. The term 'morality' implies an ability to tell the difference between right and wrong and to act on this distinction. But how do people actually decide whether something is right or wrong? Does children's thinking about moral issues change as they grow older? The American psychologist Lawrence Kohlberg developed the most comprehensive and best-known theory of how moral reasoning develops. Chapter five introduced you to this theory; the following sections restate the basic stages of the Kohlberg's theory, and also explain it in further detail.

Kohlberg's theory

Kohlberg studied moral reasoning in adolescents and adults as well as in children. Kohlberg's technique of studying moral reasoning was quite simple. He began by giving people a moral dilemma or problem, usually in the form of a story. Then he asked them questions about this dilemma. Kohlberg's moral dilemmas were problems that had two or more solutions, each of which is somehow 'wrong'. In each story, the listener has to make a choice between either obeying a law or rule or someone in authority, or doing something that conflicts with the rules but supports some deserving person whose needs were not being met.

Kohlberg's best-known story goes as follows: A woman is near death from cancer. A pharmacist has discovered a drug that doctors believe might save her. The pharmacist is charging 2 000 dollars for a small dose – ten times what the drug costs him to make. The sick woman's husband, Heinz, borrows from everyone he knows but can scrape together only 1 000 dollars. He begs the pharmacist to sell him the drug for 1 000 dollars or let him pay the rest later. The pharmacist refuses, saying, 'I discovered the drug and I'm going to make money from it.' Heinz, desperate, breaks into the man's store and steals the drug. Should Heinz have done that? Why or why not? (Colby, Kohlberg, Gibbs & Lieberman, 1983, p. 77).

Kohlberg carried out a number of studies on moral reasoning. He concluded that the way people look at moral issues reflects cognitive development. As chapter five explained, he proposed that there are three broad levels of moral reasoning, which he referred to as:
* Preconventional morality
* Conventional morality
* Postconventional morality.

Each of these three broad levels is divided into two stages. Kohlberg argued that the sequence of stages is the same for every individual; stages cannot be skipped or reversed. However, different individuals will progress through the stages at different speeds, and some individuals will never reach the later stages.

As children's ability to take (understand) the perspectives of others improves during middle childhood, so some children make a gradual shift from preconventional moral reasoning to conventional moral reasoning. The following sections will take a closer look at these two levels of moral reasoning, and the two stages within each level. Chapter seven will discuss postconventional moral reasoning.

As you read about Kohlberg's theory, it is important to remember that Kohlberg was interested in *how* and *why* people decide what to do when faced with a moral dilemma, not *what* they actually do. In other words, the reasoning underlying a person's response to a moral dilemma, not the answer itself, is what indicates the stage of moral development.

Level one: Preconventional morality
For most children up to the age of about 10 or so, the personal consequences of an action determine whether the action is judged good or bad: what is right is what the child can get away with, or what is personally satisfying. Moral reasoning at this level focuses on concrete factors such as reward and punishment, and is self-interested or egocentric.

Stage one: Punishment-and-obedience orientation
In the first stage of moral reasoning, the goodness or badness of an act depends on whether the act is rewarded or punished. Children obey rules in order to avoid punishment, but they might not consider an act wrong if it won't be punished. An example of a stage-one response to Kohlberg's 'Heinz dilemma' is: 'He shouldn't steal the drug because the police might catch him and he would have to go to jail.'

Stage two: Instrumental hedonism
A person at the second stage of moral development bases moral judgements on whether the consequences result in benefits for themselves or for their loved ones. The person obeys the rules in order to gain rewards or to satisfy personal needs. For example, a child at Kohlberg's stage two of moral reasoning might argue that Heinz should steal the drug because he wants his wife to live, or because some day he might have cancer and will want someone to steal the drug for him.

Level two: Conventional morality
Towards the end of middle childhood, some children become capable of a more sophisticated form of moral reasoning that Kohlberg referred to as conventional morality. At the conventional level, moral reasoning is guided by doing what family, society, or people in power expect. Children who are capable of conventional moral reasoning have internalised the standards of authority figures. In other words, they have made the moral principles that they have learned their own, and they follow these moral principles even when authority figures are not there to enforce them.

Stage three: 'Good boy' or 'good girl' morality
In this stage of moral reasoning, a child tries to be a good person in his or her own eyes and the eyes of others. At this stage, what is right is that which pleases, helps, or is approved of by others. An action is acceptable if the person involved has good intentions, but an action is wrong if the person is acting for selfish reasons. An example of stage-three moral reasoning in relation to Heinz's dilemma would be: 'He should steal the

drug. That is what a good husband should do. You can't blame him for doing something out of love for his wife. You'd blame him if he didn't love his wife enough to save her.'

Stage four: Authority and social-order-maintaining morality
At this stage of moral reasoning, the individual believes that moral people are those who do their 'duty' to keep society going and avoid the breakdown in the social order 'if everyone did it'. At this stage, what is right is what upholds the laws of society. An act is always wrong, regardless of motive or circumstances, if the act violates a rule or harms others. In terms of Heinz's dilemma, a stage-four response might be as follows: 'Heinz should not steal the drug, because stealing is always wrong. It's natural for him to want to save his wife, but he still knows that he's stealing and taking a valuable drug from the man who made it.'

Evaluating Kohlberg's theory
Was Kohlberg correct? Research has supported some aspects of Kohlberg's theory but questioned other aspects. Kohlberg and his colleagues followed a group of American boys through adulthood and found that they all progressed through Kohlberg's stages in order, and none of them skipped a stage (Colby et al., 1983). However, Kohlberg's theory has also been criticised on the following grounds:
- His stage model is too rigid.
- It is biased against females.
- It says a lot about moral reasoning, but little about how people actually behave when faced with moral dilemmas of their own.

The rest of this section will consider these criticisms.

The criticism that Kohlberg's stage model is too rigid
Some critics of Kohlberg's theory have argued that moral development may be gradual, rather than occurring in 'all or nothing' stages. For example, there is evidence that a person's stage of moral reasoning might vary depending on the topic. There is also evidence that young children are not trapped in preconventional thinking, but are sometimes capable of quite advanced forms of moral reasoning (Dawson & Gabrielian, 2003).

The criticism that Kohlberg's theory exhibits gender bias
An ex-student of Kohlberg's, Carol Gilligan, was concerned by the fact that Kohlberg's theory was developed from data provided only by male participants, and that some early studies found that most girls were at a lower stage of moral reasoning than boys. Gilligan (1982) suggested that perhaps what Kohlberg was actually measuring was a special kind of 'masculine' morality, and that his theory was therefore biased again women.

She conducted her own experiments on morality and discovered that when she told the story of Heinz stealing the drug for his dying wife to male and female children, they had different perspectives. For example, Jake (aged 11) said Heinz should steal 'because human life is worth more than money'. Amy (aged 11) said that Heinz should not steal the drug 'because he might have to go to jail and then his wife might get sicker ... They should talk it out to find some other way to get the money.'

Gilligan concluded that there are two basic approaches to moral reasoning:

- **The 'justice' perspective:** In this perspective, illustrated by Jake's answer, moral reasoning is based on a set of abstract, universal moral principles; this perspective is based on logic and rights.
- **The 'care' perspective:** In this perspective, illustrated by Amy's answer, moral reasoning is tied to concrete, specific situations with an emphasis on relationships, communication, and caring for others.

Because stereotypical women are tender and caring and stereotypical men are logical and rational, the justice perspective has been viewed as 'masculine' and the care perspective as 'feminine'. This has led to a lot of interest and research on whether men and women use different kinds of moral thought. At this point, however, the evidence suggests that any gender differences in moral orientations are small: both males and females bring a concern for caring and relationships and abstract ideas about right and wrong into their reasoning about real-life moral dilemmas. Moreover, there is little support for the claim that Kohlberg's theory is biased against women: more recent studies indicate that women reason just as complexly (or even more complexly) about moral issues as men do when their answers are scored by Kohlberg's criteria (Jaffee & Hyde, 2000). Nevertheless, Gilligan's theory and research have been important for broadening psychologists' view of morality by showing that both men and women often think about real-life moral issues in terms of their responsibilities for the welfare of other people. This is something that Kohlberg's model ignored.

The criticism that Kohlberg's theory fails to explain the relationship between moral reasoning and behaviour

Research has found that people who have higher levels of moral reasoning tend, in general, to behave more morally. But this relationship between moral reasoning and behaviour is not a very strong one: almost everyone has at some point done something that they knew to be wrong. Kohlberg's theory has been criticised because it does not explain how people actually behave in the 'real world' when faced with moral dilemmas of their own (Gibbs, 2003).

Critics claim that a cognitive approach to moral development gives too little attention to other factors that influence moral behaviour, for example:

- **Emotion:** The feelings that surround and motivate right or wrong actions, such as greed, hatred or guilt
- **Experience:** Has the child previously been rewarded or punished in similar situations? How has the child seen influential models such as parents and peers behave?
- **Empathy:** Does the child have the ability to take another person's perspective and understand that person's feelings? Does the child care about other people's troubles?
- **Ability to think ahead:** Can the child foresee and take into account the long-term consequences of his or her actions?

Kohlberg himself did recognise that non-cognitive factors such as emotional development and life experiences influence moral judgment. Moral thought is a very important part of children's moral development, but there is also a need to know something about how individuals actually behave when faced with moral dilemmas of their own. Kohlberg's theory is therefore most useful when it is combined with other theories that focus on the feeling or behavioural aspects of morality.

A new sense of self

The cognitive developments and social influences associated with middle childhood affect not only children's thinking about moral issues: they also have important implications for the way children think about themselves. Some researchers think that middle childhood is a particularly important time for the development of the self-concept, and that experiences during this period can have a major impact on children's self-esteem.

Changes in self-concept

Susan Harter has studied the development of the self-concept for more than 20 years. Harter (1998) provides evidence that when preschool children are asked to describe themselves, they tend to focus on concrete, observable characteristics (saying, for example, 'I'm six years old', 'I play soccer', 'I'm Muslim', 'I have two sisters'). Older school-aged children begin to describe themselves in terms of more general, stable traits. Instead of saying, 'I can kick a ball far,' they begin to emphasise both positive and negative characteristics and skills (saying, for example, 'I am good at sports', 'I get upset easily'). Note how 10-year-old Mpumelelo – introduced in the case study at the beginning of this chapter – describes himself as 'good-looking'. At some time between the ages of about 8 and 11 years, children also start to compare themselves to other children (saying, for example, 'I'm taller than most kids in my class', 'I'm not as pretty as my sister').

Social comparison
the process of judging the appearance, abilities, and behaviour of the self in relation to those of others

A major reason for this change in children's self-descriptions is that school-aged children often make **social comparisons**, judging their appearance, abilities, and behaviour in relation to those of others.

Why does social comparison begin to play a significant role in children's sense of themselves during middle childhood? For two reasons:

*   First, cognitive development and decreasing egocentrism mean that children are more able to understand others' thoughts and points of view.
*   Second, as children enter a much wider range of settings outside the family, they look to more people (including peers and teachers) for information about themselves. For many children, this is the first time that they are told that their efforts are not good enough, that another child did better, or that they failed. This means that children start to ask new questions about themselves, such as: 'Am I good at sports?', 'Do the other kids like me?', 'Am I good at maths?' Questions like these have no absolute answer because there are no fixed standards of success. Rather, success is measured in relation to the performance of others in the social group.

The development of self-esteem

Self-esteem
a person's overall evaluation of his or her worth

As school-aged children compare themselves with others in a wide variety of settings and receive feedback about their performance in different areas, so their **self-esteem** is also affected. Self-esteem refers to person's overall evaluation of his or her worth.

Erik Erikson (1963) proposed that the main psychosocial conflict of middle childhood is one of industry versus inferiority. He argued that at this stage in life, it is important for children to develop a sense of competence, of being able to do good work, and to keep up with their peers socially and academically, or they will feel inferior. Mpumelelo's self-description in the case study at the beginning of this chapter suggests that he is proud of his role in caring for the goats, and that he has a positive self-image. Why is this important? Research has shown that self-esteem is an important part of mental health. Low self-esteem has been linked to depression, anxiety, antisocial behaviour, and school drop-out (Swann, Chang-Schneider & McClarty, 2007).

Susan Harter's research has shown that preschoolers tend to have very high self-esteem: they evaluate themselves more positively than their teachers or peers do (Harter, 1998). Typically, self-esteem drops to more realistic levels during the first few years of primary school, so that children's self-evaluations begin to fit with the judgements of both their peers and teachers.

During middle childhood, children's self-evaluations also become more differentiated. Children become able to distinguish between academic competence, social competence, physical competence, and physical appearance. At the same time, older children become more capable of integrating or combining their separate self-evaluations into a general psychological image of themselves – an overall sense of self-esteem or self-worth (Harter, 1988).

Children attach greater importance to some self-judgements than to others. On average, however, perceived physical appearance is more strongly linked to overall self-worth than any other self-esteem factor (Harter, 2000). This is perhaps because society and the media put so much emphasis on physical appearance.

Does this mean that if parents want to boost their children's self-esteem, they should dress them in nice clothes in order to impress others, or tell them they look beautiful? Apparently not: Harter's (2000) research has shown that if children base their self-esteem on their appearance, they are more likely to feel dissatisfied with themselves and to be depressed. So what can parents do to build their children's self-esteem from the inside?

Harter (1998) summarises a growing body of research which suggests that three parental characteristics combine to produce high self-esteem in middle childhood:

- **Parents' acceptance and approval of their children:** Children who have closer, more affectionate and supportive relationships with their parents tend to feel accepted as competent and worthwhile. Parents can help to build their children's self-esteem by spending time with them, sharing their interests, and accepting them for who they are.
- **Parents' setting of clearly defined limits:** Children who like themselves tend to come from families with strong moral values or religious values. Their parents have high (but realistic) standards for their children's behaviour, and place appropriate limits on what they do. Appropriate expectations of children and limits on their activities seem to help children measure their own behaviour against reasonable standards.
- **Parents' respect for individuality:** Within the limits set by the parents' sense of standards, they show respect for their children's opinions and do not help their youngsters or make decisions for them when they don't need assistance.

Children whose parents love and respect them are more likely to love and respect themselves. And children who approve of their inner self as a worthwhile person are more likely to accept their outer self, or how they think they look.

CHECK YOUR PROGRESS
- What kinds of moral reasoning are typical of children in Kohlberg's stages one to four?
- How do the ways children describe themselves change during middle childhood?
- What parenting behaviours help to promote self-esteem?

CASE STUDY

My name is Sibusisiwe. I live in Maranatha. I go to Okhayeni. I am nine years old. My friends are Khululiwe and S'qinisiwe. When I was doing grade two we were learning under the trees. There were only two classrooms then so when it rained some children went into one classroom and others into the other classroom and they were very full. It was difficult.

I remember when I failed at school. Mother was not there when I came home. I cried because I had failed. Mum came and asked if I had passed and I said no. She said don't cry and she took books and taught me. I went back to school and I passed until now where I have arrived in grade five.

Now in the classroom we learn well and if you want to drink water you can go and drink. We learn in our own classrooms. Even if it is raining we don't get wet, also our exercise books don't get wet anymore, and we are not packed in the two classrooms – everyone is now in their own classroom (Abaqophi BakwaZisize Abakhanyayo children's radio project (2005). *Ukufunda ngaphansi kwezihlahla zomganu/*Marula trees for classrooms. © Children's Institute, UCT; Zisize Educational Trust, & Okhayeni & Ntabayengwe Primary Schools).

Questions

1   Think about your own experiences in primary school. How do you think your school, the parenting you received, and your own personal characteristics contributed to the challenges and achievements you experienced?

2   On the basis of what you have read in this chapter, what kinds of programmes and policies do you think would help to improve children's experiences in their families? Who should such programs target? For example, do you think the focus should be on strengthening marriage and decreasing family conflict, reducing rates of divorce, increasing the involvement of fathers, or improving the circumstances of children living in single-parent families? What difficulties do you foresee in trying to implement such interventions?

Conclusion

During middle childhood, physical growth slows, but strength and athletic skills improve. In the cognitive domain, children's thought processes become less egocentric. They can think logically about concrete problems as they enter Piaget's concrete operational stage. Their memory and language skills also increase. These cognitive gains allow children to benefit from formal schooling.

As Sibusisiwe's story in the closing case study illustrates, it is easier to understand the behavioural changes of middle childhood more clearly when these changes are considered in terms of the contexts in which development takes place. Adults in all cultures expect children aged six and seven to carry out new roles and duties. The children face Erikson's crisis of industry versus inferiority as they struggle to master the academic and social tasks of this period. Coregulation reflects a gradual shift in control over the child's behaviour from parents to child. Peer groups — including issues of acceptance, bullying, and friendship — become more important.

Children's increased cognitive abilities, together with their increased capacity to take the perspectives of others, lead some children to move from Kohlberg's preconventional level of moral reasoning to conventional moral reasoning. In addition, they develop a more complex self-concept, which affects self-esteem. Children whose experiences in middle childhood help them to develop a sense of competence and self-worth, as well as sensitivity to the needs and viewpoints of others, will be in a good position to meet the challenges of the next period of the life-span: adolescence.

References

Abaqophi BakwaZisize Abakhanyayo children's radio project (2005). *Ukufunda ngaphansi kwezihlahla zomganu/*Marula trees for classrooms [radio diary programme]. Cape Town, South Africa: Children's Institute, UCT; Zisize Educational Trust, & Okhayeni & Ntabayengwe Primary Schools.

Abaqophi BakwaZisize Abakhanyayo children's radio project (2010). *Umfana nembuzi yakhe/*A boy with a goat [radio diary programme]. Cape Town, South Africa: Children's Institute, UCT; Zisize Educational Trust, & Okhayeni & Ntabayengwe Primary Schools.

Amato, P.R. (2000). The consequences of divorce for adults and children. *Journal of Marriage and Family, 62*, 1269–1287.

Amato, P.R. (2005). The impact of family formation change on the cognitive, social and emotional well-being of the next generation. *The Future of Children, 15*, (2), 75–96.

Amoateng, A.Y. & Richter, L. (2003). The state of families in South Africa. In J. Daniel, A. Habib & R. Southall (Eds). *The state of the nation: South Africa 2003–2004* (p. 242–267). Cape Town: HSRC Press.

Amoateng, A.Y., Richter, L.M., Makiwane, M. & Rama, S. (2004). *Describing the structure and needs of families in South Africa: Towards the development of a national policy framework for families. A report commissioned by the Department of Social Development.* Pretoria: Child, Youth and Family Development, Human Sciences Research Council.

Anderson, P.M. & Butcher, K.F. (2006). Childhood obesity: Trends and potential causes. *The Future of Children, 16*, (1), 19–45.

Anglin, J. (1993). Vocabulary development: A morphological analysis. *Monographs of the Society for Research in Child Development, 58*, (10, Serial No. 238), 1–166.

Bauman, L.J., Foster, G., Silver, E.J., Berman, R., Gamble, I. & Muchaneta, L. (2006). Children caring for their ill parents with HIV/AIDS. *Vulnerable Children and Youth Studies, 1*, 56–70.

Brody, G.H. (2004). Siblings' direct and indirect contributions to child development. *Current Directions in Psychological Science, 13*, 124–126.

Budlender, Debbie (1998). *Women and men in South Africa*. Pretoria: Central Statistical Services.

Chi, M.T.H. & Ceci, S.J. (1987). Content knowledge: Its role, representation, and restructuring in memory development. *Advances in Child Development and Behavior, 20*, 91–141.

Chisholm, Linda (2004). *The quality of primary education in South Africa. Background paper prepared for UNESCO Education for All Global Monitoring Report*. Pretoria: Child, Youth and Family Development, Human Sciences Research Council.

Chisholm, L. & Leyendecker, R. (2008). Curriculum reform in post-1990s sub-Saharan Africa. *International Journal of Educational Development, 28*, 195–205.

Cluver, L., Gardner, F. & Operario, D. (2007). Psychological distress amongst AIDS-orphaned children in urban South Africa. *Journal of Child Psychology and Psychiatry, 48*, 755–763.

Coie, J.D., Dodge, K.A. & Coppotelli, H. (1982). Dimensions and types of social status: A cross-age perspective. *Developmental Psychology, 18*, 557–570.

Colby, A., Kohlberg, L., Gibbs, J. & Lieberman, M. (1983). A longitudinal study of moral judgment. *Monographs of the Society for Research in Child Development, 48*, (1–2, Serial No. 200).

Cole, M. & Cole, S.R. (2001). *The development of children* (4th ed.). New York, NY: Worth Publishers.

Daniels, S.R. (2006). The consequences of child overweight and obesity. *The Future of Children, 16* (1), 47–67.

Dawson, T.L. & Gabrielian, S. (2003). Developing conceptions of authority and contract across the lifespan: Two perspectives. *Developmental Review, 23*, 162–218.

De Wet, C. (2002). Factors influencing the choice of English as language of learning and teaching (LoLT). *South African Journal of Education, 22*, 119–124.

Dunn, J. (2002). Sibling relationships. In P.K. Smith and C.H. Hart (Eds). *Blackwell handbook of childhood social development* (p. 223–237). Oxford: Blackwell.

Dweck, C.S. & Leggett, E.L. (1988). A social-cognitive approach to motivation and personality. *Psychological Review, 95*, 256–273.

Erikson, Erik (1963). *Childhood and society* (2nd ed.). New York, NY: Norton.

Fischer, K.W. (2008). Dynamic cycles of cognitive and brain development: Measuring growth in mind, brain, and education. In A.M. Battro, K.W. Fischer & P. Léna (Eds). *The educated brain* (p. 127–150). Cambridge: Cambridge University Press.

Flavell, J.H., Beach, D.R. & Chinsky, J.M. (1966). Spontaneous verbal rehearsal in a memory task as a function of age. *Child Development, 37*, 283–299.

Flavell, J.H., Green, F.L. & Flavell, E.R. (1995). Young children's knowledge about thinking. *Monographs of the Society for Research in Child Development, 60*, (1, Serial No. 243), 1–96.

Flavell, J.H. & Wellman, H.M. (1977). Metamemory. In R.V. Kail & J.W. Hagen (Eds). *Perspectives on the development of memory and cognition* (p. 3–33). Hillsdale, NJ: Erlbaum.

Fleisch, Brahm (2008). *Primary education in crisis: Why South African schoolchildren underachieve in reading and mathematics*. Cape Town: Juta.

Ghetti, S., Lyons, K.E., Lazzarin, F. & Cornoldi, C. (2008). The development of metamemory monitoring during retrieval: The case of memory strength and memory absence. *Journal of Experimental Child Psychology, 99*, 157–181.

Gibbs, John C. (2003). *Moral development and reality: Beyond the theories of Kohlberg and Hoffman*. London: Sage publications.

Gilligan, Carol (1982). *In a different voice: Psychological theory and women's development.* Cambridge, MA: Harvard University Press.

Ginsburg, G.S. & Bronstein, P. (1993). Family factors related to children's intrinsic/extrinsic motivational orientation and academic performance. *Child Development, 64,* 1461–1474.

Goedecke, J.H., Jennings, C.L. & Lambert, E.V. (2006). Obesity in South Africa. In K. Steyn, J. Fourie, & N. Temple (Eds). *Chronic diseases of lifestyle in South Africa: 1995–2005. Technical report* (p. 65–79). Cape Town: South African Medical Research Council.

Harold, G. (2000, June). *Marital quality and children's wellbeing.* Review. London: One Plus One.

Harris, Judith R. (1998). *The nurture assumption: Why children turn out the way they do.* London: Bloomsbury.

Harter, Susan (1998). The development of self-representations. In N. Eisenberg (Ed.). *Handbook of child psychology: Vol. 3. Social, emotional, and personality development* (5th ed.) (p. 553–617). New York, NY: Wiley.

Harter, S. (2000). Is self-esteem only skin-deep? The inextricable link between physical appearance and self-esteem. *Reclaiming Children and Youth, 9,* (3), 133–138.

Hartup, W.W. & Stevens, N. (1997). Friendships and adaptation in the life course. *Psychological Bulletin, 121,* 355–370.

Hetherington, E.M., Bridges, M. & Insabella, G.M. (1998). What matters? What does not? Five perspectives on the association between marital transitions and children's adjustment. *American Psychologist, 53,* 167–184.

Jaffee, S. & Hyde, J.S. (2000). Gender differences in moral orientation: A meta-analysis. *Psychological Bulletin, 126,* 703–726.

Kaufmann, D., Ellis, G., Lucia, R.C.S., Salcedo, O., Rendina-Gobioff, G. & Gadd, R. (2000). The relationship between parenting style and children's adjustment: The parents' perspective. *Journal of Child and Family Studies, 9,* 231–245.

Kawabata, Y., Alink, L.R.A., Tseng, W.-L., Van IJzendoorn, M.H. & Crick, N.R. (2011). Maternal and paternal parenting styles associated with relational aggression in children and adolescents: A conceptual analysis and meta-analytic review. *Developmental Review, 31,* (4), 240–278.

Kelly, J.B. & Emery, R.E. (2003). Children's adjustment following divorce: Risk and resilience perspectives. *Family Relations, 52,* 352–362.

Kron-Sperl, V., Schneider, W. & Hasselhorn, M. (2008). The development and effectiveness of memory strategies in kindergarten and elementary school: Findings from the Würzburg and Göttingen longitudinal memory studies. *Cognitive Development, 23,* 79–104.

Ladd, G.W. (1999). Peer relationships and social competence during early and middle childhood. *Annual Review of Psychology, 50,* 333–359.

Maccoby, E.E. (1984). Middle childhood in the context of the family. In W.A. Collins (Ed.). *Development during middle childhood: The years from six to twelve* (p. 184–239). Washington, DC: National Academy Press.

Maccoby, E.E. (1990). Gender and relationships: A developmental account. *American Psychologist, 45,* 513–520.

McVeigh, J.A., Norris, S.A. & De Wet, T. (2004). The relationship between socio-economic status and physical activity patterns in South African children. *Acta Pædiatrica, 93,* 982–988.

Meintjes, H., Leatt, A. & Berry, L. (2006). *Demography of South Africa's children.* [WWW document]. URL *http://ci.org.za/childrencount/index.htm* (Children's Institute Children Count website).

Mikami, A.Y., Lerner, M.D. & Lun, J. (2010) Social context influences on children's rejection by their peers. *Child Development Perspectives, 4*, 123–130.

Olweus, D. (1995). Bullying or peer abuse at school: Facts and intervention. *Current Directions in Psychological Science, 4*, 196–200.

Parrila, R.K. & Das, U.N. (1996). Development of planning and its relation to other cognitive processes. *Journal of Applied Developmental Psychology, 17*, 597–624.

Piaget, J. & Inhelder, B. (1969). *The psychology of the child* (H. Weaver, Trans.). London: Routledge & Kegan Paul. (Original work published 1966.)

Posel, D. & Devey, R. (2006). The demographics of fathers in South Africa: An analysis of survey data, 1993–2002. In L. Richter & R. Morrell (Eds). *BABA: Men and fatherhood in South Africa* (p. 38–52). Cape Town: HSRC Press.

Rebok, G.W., Smith, C.B., Pascualvaca, D.M., Mirsky, A.F., Anthony, B.J., & Kellam, S.G. (1997). Developmental changes in attentional performance in urban children from eight to thirteen years. *Child Neuropsychology, 3*, 28–46.

Riggs, K.J., McTaggart, J., Simpson, A. & Freeman, R.P.J. (2006). Changes in the capacity of visual working memory in 5- to 10-year-olds. *Journal of Experimental Child Psychology, 95*, 18–26.

Rothbart, M.K. (2007). Temperament, development, and personality. *Current Directions in Psychological Science, 16*, 207–212.

Rubin, K.H., Bukowski, W. & Parker, J.G. (1998). Peer interactions, relationships and groups. In N. Eisenberg (Ed.). *Handbook of Child Psychology: Vol. 3. Social, emotional, and personality development* (5th ed.) (p. 619–700). New York, NY: Wiley.

Rutter, M. & Maughan, B. (2002). School effectiveness findings 1979–2002. *Journal of School Psychology, 40*, 451–475.

Santrock, John W. (2005). *A topical approach to life-span development* (2nd ed.). Boston: MA: McGraw-Hill.

Sigelman, C.K. & Rider, E.A. (2006). *Life-span human development* (5th ed.). Belmont, CA: Thomson Wadsworth.

Siegler, R.S. (2000). The rebirth of children's learning. *Child Development, 71*, 26–35.

Smith, J.D., Schneider, B.H., Smith, P.K. & Ananiadou, K. (2004). The effectiveness of whole-school antibullying programs: A synthesis of evaluation research. *School Psychology Review, 33*, 547–560.

Somsen, R.J.M., Van't Klooster, B.J., Van der Moolen, M.W., Van Leeuwen, H.M.P. & Licht, R. (1997). Growth spurts in brain maturation during middle childhood as indexed by EEG power spectra. *Biological Psychology, 44*, 187–209.

Statistics South Africa (2006). *Marriages and Divorces 2004. Statistical release P0307.* [WWW document]. URL *http://www.statssa.gov.za/publications/statsdownload. asp?PPN=P0307&SCH=3692.*

Steyn, N.P., Bradshaw, D., Norman, R., Joubert, J.D., Schneider, M. & Steyn, K. (2006). *Dietary changes and the health transition in South Africa: Implications for health policy.* Cape Town: South African Medical Research Council.

Swann, W.B. Jr., Chang-Schneider, C. & McClarty, K.L. (2007). Do people's self-views matter? Self-concept and self-esteem in everyday life. *American Psychologist, 62*, 84–94.

Thomas, J.R. & French, K.E. (1985). Gender differences across age in motor performance: A meta-analysis. *Psychological Bulletin, 98*, 260–282.

Whitaker, R.C., Wright, J.A., Pepe, M.S., Seidel, K.D. & Dietz, W.H. (1997). Predicting obesity in young adulthood from childhood and parental obesity. *New England Journal of Medicine, 337*, 869–73.

Zheng, X., Swanson, H.L. & Marcoulides, G.A. (2011). Working memory components as predictors of children's mathematical word problem solving. *Journal of Experimental Child Psychology, 110*, 481–498.

CHAPTER SEVEN

ADOLESCENCE

Lauren Wild and Sharlene Swartz

CASE STUDY

When I was younger...back then, it was just like: me. You know? My feelings and my mind and my stuff...But now, you're thinking of everyone around you...it's just, like, snowballed into this huge big picture of, like, everybody that I know: my family, my school, my friends, boyfriends, where am I going to work one day, what money will I get in... You know, all these things... You have to learn how to manage your feelings and stuff. Or else it just gets unmanageable ... (Leanne, girl, aged 17, Fish Hoek).

When I was 13 I moved to my aunt in Retreat because things were hectic at home in Ocean View.... I started high school near my aunt's house and I was really nervous because the place was totally different from Ocean View. I met a cool bunch of friends. We got on well because I could share my feelings with them and they with me. We would sing and dance around the school. One of my favourite days at school was a Friday; we would all throw money together and buy pies and chips. We would talk about where we would live and what we will be one day. (Brian, boy, aged 17, Ocean View) (Bray, Gooskens, Kahn, Moses & Seekings, 2010, p. 208, 224, 253).

LEARNING OBJECTIVES

By the end of this chapter you should be able to:

- Critically evaluate the view that adolescence is a period of 'storm and stress'
- Describe the physical changes associated with puberty, and the psychological implications of its timing
- Distinguish adolescent thinking from the thinking that is typical of middle childhood
- Describe the impact of parent–child relationships and peer relationships on adolescents
- Understand how adolescents think about moral issues
- Explain the significance of the adolescent period for the development of the self and identity.

Introduction

The quotations in the case study above illustrate the experiences of two adolescents growing up in different communities in Cape Town's Fish Hoek valley (Bray, Gooskens, Kahn, Moses & Seekings, 2010, p. 208, 224, 253). Adolescence is the period of transition from childhood to adulthood. It is a recognised stage of life in hundreds of societies across the world. The adolescent period begins around the onset of **puberty**, and ends with the adoption of adult roles such as employment and marriage (Schlegel & Barry, 1991). Although there is disagreement as to how exactly to define adolescence, it is often linked to the second decade of life. Some writers distinguish between early adolescence (11 or 12 to 14 years), mid-adolescence (15–17 years) and late adolescence (18–21 years). In South Africa, there are nearly 10,5 million people between the ages of 10 and 19, comprising more than 20 per cent of the population (Statistics South Africa, 2011). Adolescents are the largest age group not only in South Africa, but also in the world (Richter, 2006).

From a developmental perspective, adolescence is both an exciting and a challenging time. Physically, adolescents' bodies are maturing. Cognitively, they start to think about the world in new ways. Socially, changing relationships with families and peers play a central role in shaping their experiences. In Western societies, developmental tasks of the adolescent period include the following:
- Making a successful transition to high school
- Learning academic skills that are needed for higher education or work
- Achieving psychological autonomy
- Forming close friendships with those of the same and opposite sex
- Developing a sense of identity (Cicchetti & Rogosch, 2002).

However, expectations of adolescents are shaped by culture, and by historical and political events. The experience of adolescence, how long it lasts, and its impacts on later development and well-being are influenced by how a particular society thinks about young people, by what demands and pressure it places on them, and by what rights and opportunities it provides them with as they make their journey into adulthood.

The 'terrible teens'?: Views of adolescence

The early view of adolescence was that it is a time of emotional turmoil or 'storm and stress:' conflict with parents, moodiness, and reckless, antisocial behaviour (Hall, 1904). Anna Freud believed that this turmoil is universal and biologically based. She said, 'To be normal during the adolescent period is by itself abnormal' (Freud, 1958, p. 267).

Puberty
the period of human development in which a person becomes sexually mature and capable of producing a child

The 'storm and stress' idea continues to influence developmental research on adolescence. Nowadays, however, many researchers believe that this idea is incorrect, or at least exaggerated. Certain types of problems – such as conflict with parents, mood disorders, and risk behaviour – do occur more often in adolescence than earlier (Arnett, 1999). For examples, see the discussion in the box headed 'Adolescent risk behaviour'.

Nevertheless, most adolescents – like Leanne and Brian in the case study that opened this chapter – cope with the challenges of the adolescent period without developing serious social, emotional, or behavioural difficulties (Steinberg & Morris, 2001). Thus, the storm-and-stress view has given way to a more balanced view of adolescence as 'a period of development characterized by biological, cognitive, emotional, and social reorganization with the aim of adapting to cultural expectations of becoming an adult' (Susman & Rogol, 2004, p. 16).

Adolescent risk behaviour

Risk behaviour can be defined as any behaviour that places a person at risk for negative physical, psychological or social consequences. These consequences can play out in the short term or the long term. Rates of risk behaviour tend to peak in the late teens and early twenties (Arnett, 1999). According to the World Health Organization (2011), nearly two-thirds of premature deaths are associated with conditions or behaviours that began in adolescence.

A survey of South African adolescents in grades 8–11 (Reddy et al., 2010) showed that there is a high prevalence of risk behaviour in various domains:

- **Substance use:** 30 per cent had smoked cigarettes, 13 per cent had smoked dagga, and 29 per cent had engaged in binge drinking in the past month.
- **Sexual behaviour:** 13 per cent reported having had sex by the age of 13, and 69 per cent of sexually active learners did not use condoms consistently.
- **Violence:** 36 per cent reported having been bullied in the past month, and 15 per cent reported carrying weapons.
- **Traffic safety:** 38 per cent reported that in the past month they had been driven by someone who had been drinking alcohol.
- **Eating behaviours:** 20 per cent were overweight, and 8 per cent were underweight.
- **Physical activity:** 34 per cent had no physical education in schools, and 29 per cent watched TV or played computer games for more than 3 hours per day.
- **Suicide-related behaviours:** 21 per cent had attempted suicide.

Risk behaviours tend to cluster together: individuals who engage in one risk behaviour are more likely to engage in others. Most adolescents report low levels of risk behaviour. However, about 17 per cent of South African adolescents report high levels of risk behaviour (Reddy et al., 2010). Cognitive, emotional, biological, and social factors all play a role in whether or not a particular individual will participate in risk behaviour. For example, the following all increase the chances that an adolescent will engage in risk-taking:

- Ineffective decision-making strategies
- High emotionality and impulsivity
- Insecure attachments to parents
- Limited parental monitoring
- Association with antisocial peers (Boyer, 2006).

The international evidence suggests that information alone or 'scare tactics' are ineffective in preventing or reducing adolescent risk behaviour. However, life-skills programmes that develop adolescents' personal and social skills may work. Ideal programmes of this type involve not only adolescents, but also their families, schools, communities, and policy-makers (Flisher & Gevers, 2010).

Physical development

Adolescence is marked by dramatic physical growth and physiological changes. The biological changes associated with puberty have been a longstanding topic for research. More recently, the development of brain-imaging techniques has led to increased interest in, and understanding of, the developing adolescent brain. The biological changes associated with adolescence are universal. However, the timing and psychological implications of these changes vary across cultures and historical periods.

Puberty

Puberty involves a series of biological events that lead to an adult-sized body and sexual maturity (becoming capable of producing a child). Puberty is set in motion by hormonal processes – particularly the so-called sex hormones, androgens and oestrogens. Puberty takes place, on average, two years earlier in girls than in boys.

Adolescent growth spurt
the rapid increase in physical growth that occurs during adolescence

The adolescent growth spurt
The first outward sign of puberty is the **adolescent growth spurt**: rapid physical growth. Height and weight increase more quickly at this time

than at any other time since infancy. The adolescent growth spurt usually begins around the age of 10 or 11 in girls, and 12 or 13 in boys.

Chapter four explained that physical growth in infancy follows a cephalocaudal (head-to-foot) trend. In adolescence, this pattern of growth is reversed. At first, the hands, legs, and feet grow very quickly, and the trunk or body catches up only later (Sheehy, Gasser, Molinari & Largo, 1999). This is why young adolescents often appear gangly, awkward, and out of proportion, with long legs and big feet and hands. Sex differences also appear in the overall shape of the body. Boys' shoulders become wider, whereas girls' hips broaden relative to the shoulders and waist.

Changes in primary sexual characteristics

The primary sexual characteristics are those that involve the reproductive organs (ovaries, uterus, and vagina in females; penis, scrotum, and testes in males). As a result of the changes that occur in these characteristics during puberty, individuals become sexually mature and capable of producing a child. Around the age of 12 or 13, girls experience **menarche** (the first menstrual period) and boys start to produce viable sperm and experience their first ejaculation, or **semenarche**.

Menarche
a girl's first menstrual period

Semenarche
a boy's first ejaculation or discharge of semen

Development of secondary sexual characteristics

Secondary sexual characteristics are characteristics that are visible on the outside of the body and serve as additional signs of sexual maturity. Secondary sexual characteristics are not directly related to reproduction, which is why they are called secondary. They include things such as breasts in girls, pubic and underarm hair, and deepening voices, particularly in boys.

The timing of puberty

Like other aspects of development, the timing of puberty varies, depending on complex interactions between genetic factors and environmental factors. Many girls are reaching puberty earlier nowadays than in the past. In the 1950s, the average age of menarche for urban black girls in South African was between 14 and 15 years; today, it is between 12 and 13 years (Jones, Griffiths, Norris, Pettifor & Cameron, 2009). This change is probably due to improved nutrition and health care; menarche occurs earlier in heavier, well-nourished girls than in girls who are not well-nourished. Girls who experience stressful family lives are more likely to experience early menarche than those whose family lives are not stressful, perhaps because stress affects hormonal functioning (Chisholm, Quinlivan, Petersen & Coall, 2005). Poverty, malnutrition, and intense physical exercise can all delay sexual maturation.

Maturing either earlier or later than peers can affect a person socially and psychologically. The international research suggests that adolescents who mature very early are at increased risk of depression and behaviour problems (Negriff & Susman, 2011). In South Africa, boys and girls who are in a more advanced stage of puberty at age 13 are more likely to be smoking, experimenting with drugs, and having sex than are their less developed peers (Richter, 2006). Early-maturing adolescents may feel 'out of place' when they are with their age mates, and may form friendships and romantic relationships with older peers. Having older companions, in turn, provides adolescents with more opportunities to engage in risk behaviours such as sexual activity and substance use (Mendle, Turkheimer & Emery, 2007).

The disadvantages associated with early maturation appear to be greater for girls than for boys (Negriff & Susman, 2011). An early study found there are positive aspects to early maturation for boys. Early maturing boys tend to be viewed as self-confident, attractive, and popular. Late-maturing boys, in contrast, are more likely to be seen as anxious and attention seeking (Jones & Bayley, 1950). Late-maturing girls do not seem to be as disadvantaged as late-maturing boys. In fact, late-maturing girls tend to do better academically than their peers (Mendle et al., 2007).

This gender difference may be linked to how well the adolescent's body fits cultural ideals of physical attractiveness. Most of the research on the timing of puberty has been conducted in the USA or Western Europe. These cultures value a tall, muscular body shape for men, and a thin body shape for women. Early maturation brings boys closer to the male ideal, and may therefore improve their status. In contrast, early maturation moves girls further away from the thin ideal. This may explain why early-maturing girls are more likely than their peers to be dissatisfied with their bodies and to diet excessively (Mendle et al., 2007). People who live in poorer environments (for example rural Zulus) tend to prefer a heavier body shape for women than is considered attractive in Western cultures (Tovée, Swami, Furnham & Malgalparsad, 2006). However, a desire for thinness does seem to be increasingly widespread among adolescents in urban areas in South Africa (Caradas, Lambert & Charlton, 2001).

ACTIVITY

Think back to your early adolescence. As you reached puberty, how did your feelings about yourself and your relationships with others change?

Brain development

Neuroscientists once thought that brain development was essentially completed within the first few years of life. New findings, however, indicate that the brain continues to develop through adolescence and at least into a person's twenties. In chapter four, you learned how the early blooming and pruning of synapses and myelination of neurons helps the infant brain to function more quickly and efficiently. Brain-imaging research shows that pruning of unused synapses in the cerebral cortex continues in adolescence. At the same time, increasing myelination leads to stronger connections among various parts of the brain. These changes improve the organisation of the brain and strengthen cognitive skills such as reading and memory. A person's capacity to learn is greater in adolescence than at any other period in the lifespan (National Institute of Mental Health, 2011).

Brain scans also suggest that different parts of the brain mature at different rates. The parts of the brain involved in emotional responses are fully developed in adolescence, and even more active than they are in adulthood. However, the pre-frontal cortex – the part of the brain involved in planning and decision-making – is not yet mature. Some scientists believe that these changes contribute to making adolescents more vulnerable to risk behaviours and psychological disorders. Adolescents react more intensely than adults to stressful and pleasurable experiences, but have not yet developed the ability to control their strong emotional impulses (National Institute of Mental Health, 2011).

The changes that take place in adolescents' brains may also contribute to adolescents' tendency to go to sleep much later at night, and to wake later in the mornings. Adolescents need almost as much sleep as younger children – about 9 to 10 hours per night. Because most high schools have early starting times, adolescents may not get enough sleep. Inadequate sleep in adolescence has been associated with depression, behavioural problems, and poorer achievement in school. In South Africa, adolescents with sleep problems are more likely to smoke, drink alcohol, and use drugs (Fakier & Wild, 2011). Adequate sleep is therefore important for optimal physical, emotional, and cognitive functioning in adolescence.

CHECK YOUR PROGRESS
- What are the main physical changes that characterise puberty?
- How does the timing of puberty influence boys' and girls' psychological development?
- How does the brain change during adolescence?
- How might brain changes influence adolescents' behaviour?

Cognitive development

Recall that earlier chapters have mentioned the work of the renowned psychologist Jean Piaget. Piaget provided a useful theory for understanding adolescent cognitive development. Theories of cognitive development moves beyond the physical maturation of the brain seek to understand people's mental processes – how do people perceive, remember, think, speak, and solve problems? Theories of cognitive development are also concerned with how people, especially adolescents, develop the ability to think about thinking – what is known in psychology as metacognition.

ACTIVITY

Can you easily draw a diagram that shows how you come to make a decision? Has this ability improved over the years since you were a child, a teenager? Being able to 'think about thinking' is an important part of cognitive development. In a study conducted by Swartz (2009), young people aged 15 to 19, all living in an impoverished community, were asked to sketch out how they make decisions. Only a quarter of township-schooled youth were able to produce mind maps in which evidence of metacognitive ability was present.

Piaget's formal operations

Piaget helps psychologists to understand the cognitive development of adolescents by focusing attention on what can or cannot be grasped during the teenage years. Most importantly, he claims that adolescents construct their own cognitive worlds. They *are* affected by the physical development of their brain, but they do not thoughtlessly absorb the information they receive from the environment. Adolescent cognitive development develops from sensing and observing during infancy; to representing the world with words, images, and drawing (age 2 to 7); to a period of being able to think concretely about phenomena (age 7 to 11); culminating in adolescents' ability to apply what they know, think logically, and interpret abstract concepts. As chapter two explained, Piaget called this fourth stage in child development the formal operations stage, which, according to him, occurs between ages 11 and 15.

During this stage of development, adolescents make sense of their experiences and attempt to organise their worlds. They distinguish between important and less important ideas and ideals. They connect ideas, and allow their thinking to be changed by the introduction of new ideas. Recall from chapter two that Piaget (1954) called these two actions assimilation (incorporating new information into existing knowledge) and accommodation (adjusting thinking as a result of new knowledge). Recall also that Piaget speaks of 'equilibration' to explain how adolescents (or children) shift from one stage of thinking to the next. This movement occurs as they experience conflict or 'disequilibrium' and seek to find a balance or new equilibrium.

In summary, Piaget's fourth stage of cognitive development states that adolescents:

- Are able to think in abstract ways (able to do algebraic problems, for example)
- Are more idealistic and think about possibilities for themselves and the world
- Are able to reason logically and verbally (called hypothetical–deductive reasoning by Piaget).

There is some disagreement about whether all these goals are reached by the age of 15. Many psychologists argue that there is an early stage and a late stage of formal operations. Piaget (1972) himself later revised his theory to claim that the stage of formal operational thought is not completely achieved until as late as 20.

Read the box below to appreciate how poverty affects adolescents' cognitive development. This has considerable resonance in the South African context.

South Africa: Poverty and cognitive development

In the South African context, poverty affects cognitive development in various ways. Adolescents under continuous stress, who lack parental supervision and who are subject to low-quality education often lag behind those whose experience is the opposite. Adolescents' cognitive development, while related to brain maturation, also requires external stimulation in order to be fully and optimally achieved. There is growing evidence to support the fact that violent behaviour amongst youth in school may be due to impaired cognitive development; when this impairment is left undiagnosed and untreated, it leads to young people becoming bored and disruptive, and to them ultimately resorting to violence out of frustration (Lynam & Henry, 2001).

Information processing

It is common for adolescents to form images of ideal circumstances or roles. This is part of the process of replacing concrete experiences with a new-found ability to think abstractly and come to conclusions based on logical reasons. For example, adolescents might imagine what an ideal family may be like, or an ideal world. Their ability to solve problems also increases, since they develop the ability to choose between alternatives, construct scenarios, and test hypotheses. It is therefore not uncommon for an adolescent to become infatuated with a cause or to develop strong opinions on issues such as climate change, democracy, or war.

Factors affecting information processing

A number of factors are important in understanding how adolescents process information:

- What information are they receiving from the environment?
- How are they interpreting the data?
- What do they remember?
- What is forgotten?
- How is the information processed with regard to their own ideals, experience and values?
- What language do they use to express their thinking?

In addition, as adolescents are able to think more abstractly, their use of language changes. They become able to interpret meanings and understand various elements of language such as metaphors and irony. Their general writing and conversational skills also improve.

Read the box below, which outlines some of the implications of South Africa's multiple languages for tests of cognitive development in adolescents.

Use of multiple languages of learning in South Africa

In the South African context, the use of multiple languages of learning potentially causes problems for learners. The learners become fluent in their mother tongue and are able to display advanced cognitive development when speaking their home language, but many are called on to display their proficiency in a second language, since school exit exams (matric) are not written in indigenous languages. When adolescents in the South African context undertake tests to measure their levels of cognitive development, it is essential that these tests are language appropriate – since language and cognition are so closely related.

Environmental influences on learning

The ecosystemic theory of Urie Bronfenbrenner draws attention to the fact that adolescent development does not occur in isolation from multiple contexts in which a young person finds him- or herself. Bronfenbrenner proposed that human development be considered through a 'hierarchy of systems at four levels moving from the most proximal to the most remote' (Bronfenbrenner 1992, p. 226). These four contexts are:

- The *microsystem* (immediate context of work home and school)
- The *mesosystem* (interrelationships between microsystems)

- The *exosystem* (institutions and practices affecting youth)
- The *macrosystem* (social and cultural contexts).

Later Bronfenbrenner added a fifth context, that of the *chronosystem* (change over time). At the centre of this ecology is the developing individual young person – with all his or her 'cognitive competence, socio-emotional attributes, and context-relevant belief systems' (Bronfenbrenner 1992, p. 228). Chapter 11 will draw on Bronfenbrenner's work (you may wish to look at Figure 11.1 at this point, as it shows in a diagram the microsystem, the mesosystem, the exosystem, the macrosystem and the chronosystem).

The environments of home and school, culture, and political contexts of young people's lives therefore materially affect how they develop physically, cognitively, and emotionally.

Social learning

Albert Bandura, a leading social-learning theorist, outlined a simple but important theory of how adolescents learn. Bandura focuses on the reciprocal (rather than unidirectional) influences of behaviour, cognition, and environment. In Bandura's view, people learn by observing others; thinking, reasoning, imagining, planning, and valuing are social rather than individual in nature (Bandura, 1977, 1986). For Bandura, behaviour affects cognition, and vice versa, while a person's behaviour can affect the environment, and the environment can change a person's thought processes.

Schooling

As adolescents enter high school, they are faced with a number of changes that affect their cognitive development – for better or worse. As Brian and Leanne illustrate in the case study at the beginning of this chapter, school is a good place to discuss life and the future. However, it is a complicated process. Besides the psychosocial adjustment with which adolescent learners are confronted as they make new friends, they also have to put into practice their ideals and strive to both find out who they are and what they will one day do. At the same time, the pace at which learning happens is both increased and becomes more diverse as an adolescent enters high school.

Pace of learning and teaching styles

Adolescents naturally reason at varying speeds during this time of development, which can lead to differing rates of success in school. What is in no doubt is that adolescents reason at faster rates than younger children, and in many cases than older adults. One implication of this is that adolescents need to receive just enough stimulation in the school context to prevent boredom, but not so much that they find themselves unable to cope and become frustrated. In addition, teaching styles should ideally (but often do not) cater to this range of formality and abstraction, because, as you have already learned, there is variation in the rate at which adolescents acquire the ability for thinking abstractly and logically. Recall that Piaget's stage of formal operations states that people acquire the ability to think logically and interpret abstract concepts, and that this can occur from as early as 11 years of age to as late as 20 years – all of which is normal cognitive development.

Experiential learning

David Elkind (1981) has also shown that adolescents learn much better through experience, although there are a number of different learning styles. An overly rigid curriculum has the potential to dampen adolescents' creativity and to not hold their interest. This argument also applies to different learning styles and levels of development between boys and girls. Educators need to adapt learning to these variations as well.

Read the box below to learn about the importance of adult involvement in adolescents' learning.

Adult involvement in adolescents' learning is crucial to the cognitive development of adolescents. In South Africa, as in many places in the world, the time of high-school attendance introduces multiple teachers who teach specialised subjects, while at the same time parents, for various reasons, become less involved in their children's learning. One important reason for reduced parental involvement is that many parents feel less comfortable covering the content of subjects such as Maths and Science, especially if they have a low level of educational attainment and are aware of the rapid pace at which knowledge has changed 'since I was at school'.

The one thing that has not changed, however, is young people's need to be helped to reflect on what they are hearing and observing, and to make sense of it, question it, interpret it, and apply it. These are all functions that caring, interested, and involved adults can perform. This adult involvement in adolescent learning ultimately ensures good cognitive outcomes. This chapter will pick up this topic up again when it considers adolescents' moral development.

Caring schools

When adolescents have multiple teachers in high school, this may lead to a lack of attachment to teachers and to a non-caring school environment. Educational philosopher Nel Noddings (1984, 2002) argues that a caring schooling environment is essential for learning to take place. Noddings's vision for schooling is one in which school can, through provision of a **formative education**, encourage young people to be reflective and to be connected to others, and one which can exemplify democratic processes of living. At the core of such a formative education are teachers' caring and attentive relationships with adolescent learners.

For many adolescents in the South African schooling system, classes are too large, teachers are undertrained, and resources are too few to realise such an ideal. Schooling has a large role to play in adolescents' cognitive development, but schooling can also impair, rather than enhance this development, if conditions such as those in the current South African context prevail.

Formative education
one that attempts to shape, form or mould a person according to (hopefully) positive and healthy outcomes

---

CHECK YOUR PROGRESS
- How is adolescent thinking different from childhood thinking?
- What are the challenges to information processing during adolescence?
- How does the environment affect adolescent thinking?
- What theories, besides that of Piaget, help us to understand adolescent thinking, and what are their main contributions? (Consider, for example, the theories of Bandura, Bronfenbrenner, Elkind, and Noddings.)

Psychosocial development

Family relationships remain important in adolescence. At the same time, peer relationships become more mature and influential. At least in Western societies, adolescents face the task of becoming more independent from parents, and discovering who they really are.

The family

Most of the research on family relationships in adolescence has focused on parenting and the parent–child relationship. However, researchers are also starting to learn more about adolescents' relationships with their siblings and grandparents.

Relationships with parents

The popular media often portray relationships between parents and adolescents as extremely stressful and conflict ridden. However, psychological research conducted over several decades tells a different story. The evidence indicates that serious difficulties in parent–child relationships are the exception, not the norm. Only about 5%–15% of families experience extreme problems in parent–adolescent relationships, and these problems typically began in childhood (Smetana,

Campione-Barr & Metzger, 2006). In fact, about three-quarters of adolescents report having happy and pleasant relationships with their parents (Steinberg, 2001). Nevertheless, parent–child relationships do change during adolescence.

Parent–adolescent closeness

As children grow into adolescence, they tend to spend less time with their parents. The closeness of parent–child relationships also tends to decline (Smetana et al., 2006). Adolescents tend to be closer to their mothers than to their fathers (Steinberg & Morris, 2001).

Despite decreases in their closeness, most parent–adolescent relationships remain warm and supportive (Collins & Laursen, 2004). Adolescents who are securely attached to their parents tend to be better adjusted psychologically and more socially competent than their insecurely attached peers. They are less likely to engage in risk behaviours, and have better coping skills. Securely attached adolescents also find it easier to make the transition to high school (Moretti & Peled, 2004). In chapter four, you learned how a secure attachment between infants and their caregivers provides infants with a secure base from which they can explore the environment. Similarly, it seems that the support of parents provides adolescents with the confidence that they need to explore new experiences and relationships outside the family.

Parent–adolescent conflict

Declines in parent–child closeness in the adolescent years are often accompanied by more frequent conflicts with parents, at least temporarily in early and mid-adolescence (Steinberg & Morris, 2001). These conflicts are usually not severe; most often they are squabbles over things like disobedience, homework, or household chores. However, these arguments about seemingly trivial things may actually be expressions of larger conflicts over independence and responsibility. In most cases, conflict decreases again during late adolescence as adolescents and their parents gradually adjust their relationship in such a way that the adolescent is granted a more equal role in the family.

Interestingly, it seems that parent–adolescent conflict is often more stressful for the parents than the children. Adolescents tend to see their squabbles with parents as being unimportant. Parents, in contrast, tend to be upset by repeated, day-to-day bickering over mundane issues. This is particularly the case for mothers, who do most of the negotiating with teenagers. Many parents report a dip in self-esteem, life satisfaction, and psychological well-being during this time (Steinberg, 2001). High levels of parent–adolescent conflict are also detrimental to adolescent development. However, mild-to-moderate conflict is associated with

Figure 7.1 Parent–adolescent conflict often increases during adolescence, but it is generally about minor issues

better adolescent adjustment than either no conflict or frequent conflict (Smetana et al., 2006).

Parent–adolescent relationships across cultures

An increase in parent–child conflict has been seen in a diverse range of cultures, from Asia to the USA (Smetana, 2006). However, parent–adolescent conflict is more common in some cultures than in others. For example, there seems to be little parent–adolescent conflict in India. Indian adolescents spend much more time with their families than American adolescents do. They also enjoy this family time more than their American counterparts do (Larson & Wilson, 2004). How do researchers explain this difference?

In Western societies such as the USA, a major task of adolescence is to achieve psychological **autonomy**, or the ability to function independently as a separate, self-governing individual. In this context, declining closeness and increasing conflict between adolescents and their parents can play a positive role in the transition to adulthood: they lead to adolescents becoming more independent and autonomous. Indian culture, however, places the family at the centre of people's lives, and values interdependence rather than independence. In this context, the developmental task of adolescence is not to become autonomous, but rather to reduce separation. Thus, Indian adolescents focus on strengthening emotional

Autonomy
the ability to function independently as a separate, self-governing individual

bonds to their relatives, and on learning to put the needs of the family before their own individual needs (Larson & Wilson, 2004).

Even in Western cultures, researchers now appreciate that it is best for adolescents if they maintain a close attachment with their parents, even while they are gaining autonomy and becoming more independent. How is this balance achieved? The next section discusses which parenting styles seem best for achieving this balance.

Parenting styles and dimensions

Recall that chapter six mentioned three contrasting parenting styles: authoritarian, permissive, and authoritative. These styles were originally identified by Diana Baumrind (1967).

Like younger children, adolescents benefit from having at least one parent who is authoritative: warm, firm, and accepting of their needs for psychological autonomy. Adolescents with authoritative parents tend to do better in school, report less depression and anxiety and higher self-esteem, and are less likely to engage in antisocial behaviour and drug use. These benefits have been found across different cultural, ethnic, and socioeconomic groups (Steinberg, 2001).

In recent years, there has been a shift towards breaking down parenting styles into specific dimensions of parenting behaviour. Brian Barber and his colleagues have identified three central dimensions of parenting that appear to be particularly important in adolescence:

- Support versus rejection
- Firm behavioural control versus lax control
- Psychological autonomy versus psychological control.

Studies with adolescents in South Africa and a number of other countries have shown that parental support (warmth, acceptance, and affection) is associated with more social initiative and less depression. Firm behavioural control (supervision, monitoring, and limit-setting) is associated with less antisocial behaviour. In contrast, psychological control (intrusive parenting that does not permit the child to develop as a psychologically autonomous individual) is associated with more depression and antisocial behaviour (Barber, Stolz, Olsen, Collins & Burchinal, 2005). Thus, although patterns of interactions may change, parent–child relationships remain important for children's well-being during the adolescent years.

Relationships with siblings

Although most of the research on adolescents' family relationships has focused on their parents, there has been a recent increase in interest in adolescents' relationships with their brothers and sisters. How do the relationships between brothers and sisters change once siblings no longer live together in the same house and lead their own separate lives? Sibling conflict often increases when the first-born sibling enters early adolescence. From middle adolescence, however, both closeness and conflict between siblings decline. As brothers and sisters spend more time away from home and from each other, sibling relationships become less intense and more equal (Steinberg & Morris, 2001).

Although siblings have less influence on one another as they get older, they remain important. Better relationships with brothers and sisters are associated with fewer emotional and behavioural problems during adolescence. However, adolescents whose older siblings are involved in problem behaviours, early sexual activity, and drug use are at increased risk of also becoming involved in such behaviours (Smetana et al., 2006).

Relationships with grandparents

Grandparents have long been an important source of financial, practical, and emotional support in South African families. The Aids pandemic has made their role even more important. According to the 2001 population census (Statistics South Africa, 2005), 18 per cent of black South African adolescents aged 14–19 were living in a household where a grandparent or great-grandparent was the household head. Even when grandparents don't live with their grandchildren, they often play an important role in their lives.

The international research suggests that contact with grandparents tends to decline as children move into adolescence (Bridges, Roe, Dunn & O'Connor, 2007). Nevertheless, there is evidence that positive involvement from grandparents has the potential to benefit adolescents' psychological, physical, and academic well-being and development – particularly when their families are under stress (Attar-Schwartz, Tan, Buchanan, Flouri & Griggs, 2009; Yorgason, Padilla-Walker & Jackson, 2011).

Peer relationships

During adolescence, young people acquire skills needed to carry out adult roles, gain autonomy from parents, and recalibrate their relationships with members of the same sex and opposite sex (Elliott & Feldman, 1990). Consequently, peer relationships become prominent during this time. In landmark research in tracking US adolescents for a week using the **experience sampling method**, Csikszentmihalyi and Larson (1984, p. 222) found that adolescents spend 52 per cent of their time with peers, while spending only 21 per cent with adults and siblings, and 27 per cent of their time alone. These researchers conclude that friendships provides optimal conditions for growth amongst adolescents. However, others have questioned the influence of peers, friends, romantic partners, and **cliques** and **crowds** (or groups) in a teenager's life. Each will be discussed in turn.

Experience sampling method
a research technique that asks participants to stop at certain times and make notes of their experience or behaviour

Cliques
small groups of peers comprising 2 to 12 members, usually the same sex and age

Crowds
larger groups defined by reputation and stereotypes, and having social status in, for example, a school or community.

Adolescents choose friendships and reference crowds 'best suited to their needs for emotional support and exploration or reaffirmation of their values or aspirations [and so] peer groups promise to be a highly adaptive context in which to negotiate adolescence' (Brown, 1990, p. 180). The opposite applies too – 'for those who either falter in these tasks or choose a dysfunctional crowd, peer groups can have maladaptive consequences' (p. 185). Furthermore, given that adolescents make decisions focused largely on the here and now, because of their cognitive developmental stage, rather than thinking of the future, peer influence is especially important, especially with regard to young people's health and risk-taking behaviours.

Peer pressure and conformity

The key questions that interest those who parent and work with youth are:

- Do adolescents behave in particular ways because their peers are doing so?
- Are adolescents able to resist pressure to conform through other influences such as family, teachers, and youth leaders.

Of course, conformity can be both positive and negative. Young people can be pressurised into taking drugs as much as they can be pressurised into joining a youth project that looks after vulnerable children.

Research shows that peers have influence on some spheres, whereas families hold sway in others. Berndt (1979) shows that peers influence antisocial behaviour – most between ages 12 and 15 – while families have the highest influence towards prosocial activities at this time. The same applies to the age of young people. In early adolescence, families have more influence, then peers become more influential, until in late adolescence, youth act and reason with greater independence of both influences.

An important example of peer influence being put to positive effect and institutionalised is in the many peer-education programmes currently in operation in South Africa and throughout the world. These programmes are especially successful in helping adolescents develop and adhere to healthy behaviour with regard to sexual and reproductive health (Visser, 2007).

Cliques and crowds

In the same way as peers can be both negative influences and positive influences, the crowds and cliques in which young people locate themselves have similar effects. Groups satisfy adolescents' need for identity formation, for belonging, self-esteem, and information. However, these groups have norms and roles that adolescents have to navigate. The groups to which adolescents belong change from childhood to adolescence and over the course of adolescence. So, childhood groups are largely unisexual, then become mixed sex, and finally disintegrate into couples with looser affiliations to each other than before (Dunphy, 1963).

Groups generally predict behaviour. So, for example, in a study in the USA, athletic males ('jocks') were found to be more sexually active than those in other groups, while other groups – such as 'burnouts' and 'non-conformists' – were more likely to be taking drugs (Prinstein, Fetter & La Greca, 1996). Those who belong to cliques and crowds overall exhibit higher self-esteem than those who are rejected or excluded. However, youth who purposely avoid groups have been to shown to have the same self-esteem as those who are part of them.

In a South African study (Swartz, 2009), young people identified four kinds of youth in a local school, namely:

- **'Mommie's babies'**: Mommie's babies spent all their time at home or church.
- **'Skollies'**: Skollies were criminals and gangsters.
- **'Kasi boys and girls'**: Kasi boys and girls partied hard and experimented with petty thieving and alcohol.
- **'Right ones'**: Right ones did not separate themselves from their peers, but they partied and drank alcohol only to the extent that it did not affect their school work and, therefore, chances of success.

Friendship

Harry Sullivan (1953) is internationally renowned for his work on the nature and importance of friendship for adolescents. While all people require tenderness, playful companionship, social acceptance, intimacy, and sexual relations for their long term well-being, it is adolescent friendships that begin to meet these needs and teach young people the skills necessary to sustain these in long-term committed relationships and partnerships. According to Sullivan, the need for intimacy – defined as self-disclosure and the ability to share private thoughts – intensifies during early adolescence, motivating young people to seek out close friends. Furthermore, adolescents who report good friendships frequently go on to report prosocial behaviours and positive self-worth in adult life (Carlo et al., 1999). Close friendships also teach youth how to self-disclose appropriately, how to provide appropriate emotional support to others, and how to manage disagreements without damaging relationships.

In Swartz's study of young people's moral influences, friends were frequently cited as positive moral influences – friends were both 'good to me' and 'good for me' (Swartz, 2009). Youth reported that friends helped them see where they were 'going wrong', advised them on how to change, and, in the case of romantic partners, helped them to be less selfish and generally 'a better person'. These caring relationships provided youth with strong emotional ties and motivated young people to make sacrificial choices, such as voluntarily parting with money earned or won, keeping a job, and working hard at school in order to maximise the possibility of getting a job in the future.

Research has shown, however, that close friendships between adolescents with a large age gap frequently results in the younger peer becoming involved in age-inappropriate behaviour and sometimes in antisocial behaviour (Magnusson, 1988). This is in contrast to research with children that shows that mixed-age friendships at these younger ages have generally positive outcomes.

ACTIVITY

Looking back at your past friendships, what advice would you have valued as a younger adolescent in managing these friendships?

Romantic relationships and sexual activity

In the South African context, various studies (reported in Swartz, 2009) have shown that approximately one-third of young people have had sex by the time they reach the age of 15. Of these, 15 per cent are involved in an ongoing sexual relationship. This is roughly similar to other countries, although there are some groups of South African youth who are more at risk of early sexual activity than others. Those living in overcrowded communities and in communities where poverty affects both education and survival options are especially at risk in this respect.

In the context of sexually transmitted infections (including HIV and Aids), teenage pregnancy, and high rates of rape and coerced sex, it is desirable for adolescents to delay their first sexual encounter and the age at which they begin dating. Much research shows that young people who become involved in a dating relationship at a young age are more likely to become pregnant, or impregnate a partner, than those who are helped to delay individual (rather than group or crowd) dating. It has also been shown that dating amongst younger adolescents is egocentric and focused on recreation and status, whereas older youth date for intimacy and companionship.

However, little research reports on the role that romantic relationships can play in developing adolescents' identity and intimacy skills (Erikson, 1968). Studies have found that romantic relationships focus 'adolescents' attention ... on behaviors that foster and promote intimacy [such as] helping, caring ... sharing ... sympathy and empathy' (Fabes et al., 1999, p. 9).

The box headed 'Teenage pregnancy and parenthood' provides further information about adolescent sexual activity.

Teenage pregnancy and parenthood

The extent of teenage pregnancy (measured among young women aged 15 to 19) in South Africa ranges from 78 births per 1 000 in 1996, to an estimated 65 in 2001, and 73 in 2005 (Moultrie & McGrath, 2007). There are different rates of teenage fertility among each of the population groups in South Africa. In 1998 the *South African Demographic and Health Survey* (Department of Health, 2002) revealed that fertility rates for black teenagers and coloured teenagers were four times as high as those for white teenagers and Indian teenagers. In addition, rates of teen fertility (along with HIV infection) in informal settlements are significantly higher than in other communities (Shisana et al., 2005; Simbayi, Chauveau & Shisana, 2004).

Based on the 2001 census, Moultrie and Dorrington (2004) estimate that teenage fertility has decreased somewhat. This is an important counter-argument to those who claim that child-support grants from government act as a perverse inventive to teenagers who get themselves pregnant in order to access the child-support grant. If this were in fact true, the rates of teenage pregnancy would be increasing rather than decreasing. However, what is clear is that young women who become pregnant at an earlier age are at risk of adverse life outcomes. They are less likely to complete schooling, and therefore less likely to get good jobs or any employment at all. There is also a physical cost exerted on their bodies through early pregnancy.

A recent South African study (Swartz & Bhana, 2009) placed attention on adolescent boys who become fathers. The study showed that these young men have similar poor outcomes to young mothers, as well as delinquency. In addition, young fathers frequently have to overcome a number of challenges in being a present father to a child they have fathered whilst young. Some of these challenges include:

- Parental rejection (by the parents of the mother of their child)
- The cultural measure of money being equated with responsibility, resulting in fear and shame at being unable to provide – hence choosing to disappear
- The way in which parents sometimes commandeer young fathers' parental responsibilities
- The widespread failure of services and sex education for these young men.

In the South African context, there is currently an epidemic of absent fathers. Posel and Devey (2006, p. 47) estimate that among black households 63 per cent of fathers are 'disappeared' (12,8 per cent dead, 50,2 per cent absent). This is in contrast to 13,3 per cent disappeared white fathers (2,4 per cent dead and 10,9 per cent absent). It is not known what proportion of these disappeared fathers became fathers whilst still adolescents.

CHECK YOUR PROGRESS
• What positive and negative roles can friendship play in adolescents' development?
• What positive and negative roles can romantic relationships play in adolescents' development?
• Discuss the ways in which relationships and friendships improve or diminish self-esteem in adolescents?

Moral development

Young people's moral values, moral development, and moral education have long been the subject of numerous academic disciplines. However, it is psychology that makes the largest contribution to the academic study of morality and moral education. Psychologists are concerned with the various cognitive processes of moral development, as well as with emotional and social behaviour of adolescents. Specific contributions from psychology to the study of young people's moral functioning include:

• The role of empathy (Eisenberg, 2000; Hoffman, 2000)
• Intuition (Narváez, Getz, Thoma & Rest, 1999)
• The role of emotional intelligence in regulating moral emotions such as anger and shame (Goleman, 1995; Salovey & Sluyter, 1997).

Psychological studies have also considered:

• The importance of moral motivation (Eccles & Wigfield, 2002)
• Moral integrity (Blasi, 1980)
• The role of personality in moral formation (Damon, 1983; Glover, 2001)
• The process of translating belief into action (Blasi, 1980; Walker, 2004).

Piaget and Kohlberg

Perhaps the most well-known of all psychological contributions to the study of young people's morality is the developmental work of Piaget and Kohlberg (1981, 1984). In particular, Kohlberg, whose work was discussed at some length in chapters five and six, made the connection between increased levels of cognitive and psychosocial development and the ability to reason at increasing levels of moral complexity. Recall from chapters five and six that Kohlberg elucidated three developmental levels of moral reasoning, as follows:

• **Preconventional level (stages one and two):** Moral reasoning based on the avoidance of punishment, consequences, self-interest, and personal benefit marks people at this level.
• **Conventional level (stages three and four):** People reasoning at this level are marked by concern for interpersonal relationships, relational

influences, and social obligations. Adolescents begin to reason at stage four and show understanding of duties of justice and care.

- **Postconventional level (stages five and six):** Finally, people reasoning at this level are characterised by principled and impartial judgements made on the basis of a universally applicable social contract. At this level, morality becomes based on internal moral standards, rather than on external codes. Although the people reasoning at this level explore alternative options, they reach decisions autonomously. Adolescents may reach this stage of moral reasoning from an age as young as 12 – especially being able to distinguish between community rights and individual rights. Few adolescents, however, are able to reach stage six, where moral reasoning is based on universal human rights. In fact, according to Kohlberg, it takes a lifetime to get to postconventional moral reasoning, with most adults reasoning at the conventional level.

For the past 30 years, Kohlberg's work has dominated the field of moral development and materially influenced moral education. Chapters five and six discussed this influence in some detail. This section will complement the discussion in chapters five and six.

At least four broad approaches to moral education can be identified, as follows (some of these broad approaches incorporate Kohlberg's approach, while others react to it):
- A primarily cognitive emphasis on moral development and judgement
- An affective or emotional emphasis (see, for example, Hoffman (2000) on empathy; Eisenberg (2000) on guilt and shame; Rozin, Haidt and McCauley (2000) on disgust, anger, and hatred)
- Those having an activist emphasis on learning through doing (Coles, 1993; Damon & Gregory, 1997; Scales, 1999; Youniss & Yates, 1999)
- An emphasis on integrated character (Lickona, 1991).

The focus on cognitive development has eclipsed the other three approaches to moral education. Cognitive developmentalists maintain that autonomous choice, evolving judgement, and critical reflection are most important when educating young people in the moral domain. For cognitive developmentalists, the aim of moral education is to stimulate cognitive development and thereby help youth to develop moral judgement. Many of the techniques cognitive developmentalists use include the discussion of moral dilemmas, which proponents of this approach have shown is an effective way to improve moral reasoning. At least three educational strategies that have emerged from the academy have strong cognitive and developmental bases:
- 'Values clarification' (Raths, Harmin & Simon, 1966)
- 'Philosophy for children' (Lipman, 1991; Vardy & Grosch, 1994)
- 'Social perspective-taking' (Selman, 1971, 1980).

Selman's social perspective-taking

Harvard educationalist and psychologist Robert Selman, a colleague of Kohlberg, proposed a theory of social perspective-taking. He describes perspective taking as the ability to assume another person's perspective and understand that person's thoughts and feelings. In his theory, he describes the following sequential developmental stages of social perspective-taking from childhood though adulthood (Selman, 1971, 1980):

- **Stage 0, age 3–6:** In early childhood, an egocentric viewpoint is adopted.
- **Stage 1, age 6–8:** A social informational perspective follows.
- **Stage 2, age 8–10:** Then there is a more self-reflective stance.
- **Stage 3, age 10–12:** In early adolescence, youth are able to adopt a mutual perspective by stepping outside of the self–other interaction.
- **Stage 4, age 12–15:** Social and conventional system perspective-taking follows, during which the young person realises that complete understanding is not always possible and so social conventions must be used.

Following later empirical work, Selman concluded that the majority of youth on the brink of adolescence were at stage 2, while by age 16 most adolescents had reached stage 3 (but not yet stage 4). A number of factors account for the range of social perspective-taking abilities amongst youth. Among these are educational quality, home environment, and stimulation – similar factors to those that affect how children are placed on Kohlberg's scale. Apart from some of the wideness of age ranges in each stage, Selman's theory contributes to understanding how young people come to make moral decisions, especially those of an interpersonal nature.

Adolescents' increasing ability to take others' perspectives has implications for their self-understanding. This, in turn, impacts on their relationships with peers and family. Studies, for example Adams (1983), have shown that young people who are empathetic are more popular and that the quality of their friendships is improved.

Critiques of developmental approaches to moral development

Critiques of developmental approaches to moral education centre on two aspects:

- The elevation of the self to a sovereign position above that of the society in which an individual finds him- or herself (Hunter, 2000)
- An undue emphasis on individualism (Smith & Standish, 1997).

But the central criticism of developmental approaches centres on Kohlberg's work, which has been challenged on numerous fronts, for example:

- The use of fictitious dilemmas
- The gap between moral reasoning and moral behaviour

- The (disingenuous) way in which white middle-class men seem to always score higher on Kohlberg's scales than women or those from other cultures
- The conclusion that autonomous and individualistic moral judgement (characteristic of the postconventional level) is more advanced than a system of moral reflection based on a collectivist or communitarian orientation (characteristic of the conventional level)
- How young people's moral reasoning has little relationship with their functioning as moral people.

As a result of the challenges listed above, people have questioned the usefulness of Kohlberg's levels of moral reasoning. Some of these critiques have been covered in Chapter five on middle childhood, but will be discussed in more detail below.

The use of moral dilemmas

The use of fictitious moral dilemmas by cognitive developmentalists has been criticised because they are fictitious (and so do not help young people in real-life contexts) and because they are already flagged as moral dilemmas. Fictitious dilemmas do not measure participants' moral sensitivity, since they have already been judged to be moral dilemmas (Walker, 2002). Cognitive moral reasoning is significantly different when based on real, rather than hypothetical, dilemmas (Myyry & Helkama, 2002). Moral dilemmas also reinforce the perception that moral issues are something which is on the periphery of human life, rather than central to it (Smith & Standish, 1997). Walker (2002) adds that cognitive stimulation – the aim of moral dilemma discussion – is a simplistic approach to moral education. Research has also shown that talking about moral issues in the abstract is a poor predictor of what youth do in practice (Kuther & Higgins-D'Alessandro, 2000).

Feminist and cultural objections to Kohlberg

Carol Gilligan has shown that young women judge 'conflicting responsibilities rather than … competing rights' (Gilligan, 1982, p. 19) and consider collective rather than individualistic orientations as more important in their moral reasoning processes. Similar conclusions have been drawn for youth outside global Northern cultures, who privilege a collective conscience over individual conscience (Ferns & Thom, 2001; Snarey & Keljo, 1996). Not surprisingly therefore, women and collectivist cultures have been found to score lower on Kohlberg's scales. The study of Ferns and Thom (2001), for example, demonstrates how black South African youth consistently score below white youth on Kohlberg's scale of moral reasoning.

However, in a more nuanced study (Smith & Parekh, 1996) black South African youth between the ages of 10 and 12 scored higher on Kohlberg's schema than did their white counterparts, although older black youth scored lower. Snarey and Keljo comment that this result seems to align with that of Gilligan's study of young women, in that an initial 'strong voice of courage and honesty … [is replaced] by a strained voice of niceness and conformity' (Snarey & Keljo, 1996, p. 1089). Like those of young women, the scores of marginalised and oppressed groups appear to deteriorate over time.

Snarey and Keljo conclude that any form of oppression (sex, class, or 'race') contributes to stagnation in moral development. Possible reasons proposed for this difference include the following:

- Poor education resulting in diminished levels of high-order abstract thinking (Ferns & Thom, 2001; Snarey & Keljo, 1996)
- The way in which discrimination and oppression lowers esteem and silences strong voices (Maqsud, 1998; Snarey & Keljo, 1996)
- The finding that authoritarian parenting – usually found in contexts of poverty (Elliott & Feldman, 1990) rather than being related to 'race' or culture – seldom encourages autonomous thinking (Ferns & Thom, 2001).

Of course, an alternative explanation is that Kohlberg's research instrument is biased by language or towards masculine responses. However much this bias may have been unintentional, Kohlberg's work appears to have fuelled mistaken notions of inherent moral superiority. Ferns and Thoms (2001), for example, do not use Kohlberg's Moral Judgment Interview or Rest's Defining Issues Test (based on Kohlberg's schema) since it emerged (upon piloting) that the level of verbal proficiency required was unsuitable in a cross-cultural environment.

Critical absences in moral development

The first of these critical absences concerns the relationship between moral knowledge and moral practice, alluded to earlier as a key critique of Kohlberg's work. Robert Coles sums up a prevailing view:

> *The moral life is at once thought and action … [I] struggle…[between] strong respect for the work of Jean Piaget, Lawrence Kohlberg, Carol Gilligan, and yet a perplexity that sometimes slides into pique as I compare their ideas about 'moral development' with the thoroughly complicated matter of moral … behaviour (Coles, 1986, p. 286).*

This 'belief–behaviour' gap is one about which psychologists are increasingly writing (Bergman, 2002; Blasi, 1980; Lickona, 1976; Swartz, 2009; Walker, 2004). Augusto Blasi (1980) addresses this gap by focusing on the development of a moral identity – the integration of self with a sense of responsibility and integrity. For Damon (1984), the task is to investigate the 'person's understanding of self in relation to these moral beliefs' (p. 110). While both Blasi and Damon contribute to understanding the dynamics involved in this gap, neither pays attention to the role of context – the role of lived experience that occupies the space between moral belief and moral behaviour. Read the box headed 'Moral capital and moral ecology', which considers these issues further.

Moral capital and moral ecology

In a study done in Cape Town (Swartz, 2009), township youth aged between 14 and 20 were asked how they understood the concept of morality ('right' and 'wrong') and how their beliefs and contexts affected their action. Overall, the study provides an account of the moral lives of vulnerable young people from within a context of partial parenting, partial schooling, pervasive poverty, and inequality, in post-apartheid South Africa. The study introduced two important concepts into the discussion of youth morality, namely 'moral ecology' and 'moral capital'.

Moral ecology

Understanding youth moral development as an ecology draws on Urie Bronfenbrenner's 'ecological systems theory'. It helps to systematise the study of the environment's effects on people's lives by describing these influences as interconnecting systems. Considering contexts helps a researcher to see how the usual institutions that might inoculate youth against multiple negative influences exert less influence in poor environments than might be the case in a middle-class context. It shows how township youth have to choose to opt out of the current youth culture in favour of moral goodness, and how these youth construct a moral world in resistance to the existing culture. In Swartz's study, for example, it became clear that the socio-emotional effects of poverty influence young people's ability to reflect, and that employment is a moral necessity in the lives of poor youth.

Furthermore, the notion of a moral ecology helps moral educators consider moral life as more complex than only moral action. A definition of what it means to be good must surely include moral knowledge, moral identity, and moral desire, in addition to moral action. This has implications for where to concentrate the focus in moral education practice, when some elements are stronger than others in young people's lived experience.

Thimna's story

Thimna's story illustrates how an ecological lens helps to interpret young people's moral lives. Thimna is a tiny 19-year-old woman who struggled to concentrate at school, and showed clear signs of fetal alcohol spectrum disorder (FASD). She constantly dropped out of school due to her inability to focus on her studies. Thimna spoke of having grown up in a 'shebeen house' with her alcoholic mother selling alcohol, and that she (Thimna) had begun drinking at 14. Soon she was involved in a gang, and then incarcerated for stealing a cellphone in order to pay for her alcohol. She dropped out of school permanently after becoming pregnant, and currently struggles, due to her alcoholism, to hold down a job as a street sweeper. Thimna's moral ecology included physical manifestations of FASD, parental neglect, poor education and substance use – all of which are interrelated.

Applying moral ecology

What Thimna's story also shows is that neither is the moral life of young people living in a context of poverty linear and ordered, nor is their moral development directly related to physical maturation, as is often depicted in existing moral-development literature focused on youth living in the global North (Damon, 1984; Kohlberg, 1984). In more stable environments, moral growth is largely depicted as a series of deliberate choices within a series of narrow options. In the lives of township youth, while options are far wider, the act of choosing is more limited and immediate.

Using an ecological lens also shows how young people's moral reasoning ability, the role of personal responsibility for moral (or immoral) action, and the context of poverty are interwoven in complex ways. This interplay is crucial to understanding the chasm that exists between young people's stated moral beliefs and their subsequent behaviour. Swartz's study found that young people living in poverty lack not so much the ability to engage in high-order levels of cognitive reflection, but the opportunity and resources to do so. If, as various literatures suggest (Evans & English, 2002; Yehuda, Halligan & Grossman, 2001), poverty results in physical illness such as depression, despair, fatigue (from stress hormone overload), anxiety, apathy, a struggle to delay gratification, emotional blunting, the consequences of FASD, and **avolition**, then it is understandable that youth who live in poverty lack the resources to act on what they know and desire to be right, and toward which they aspire.

'Moral capital'

In the same study, young people regularly spoke of 'being good' as a form of capital – a resource that helps you get ahead. In other words the act of 'being good' resulted in them regularly attending school, completing their education, and accessing the job market. Having a job, in turn, enabled them to 'do good' things, like provide for family members. Being good therefore produces money – or economic capital.

Avolition
an inability to pursue goals or act on decisions; a lack of drive or motivation

In addition, these youth identified the necessary elements that would contribute to them becoming good people, which may also be described as assets or capital. Throughout Swartz's study, township youth made the connection between education and achieving future dreams and goals ('If you don't have any education, no future for you'), and they recognised school as

Figure 7.2 A schematic representation of the various components of 'moral capital'

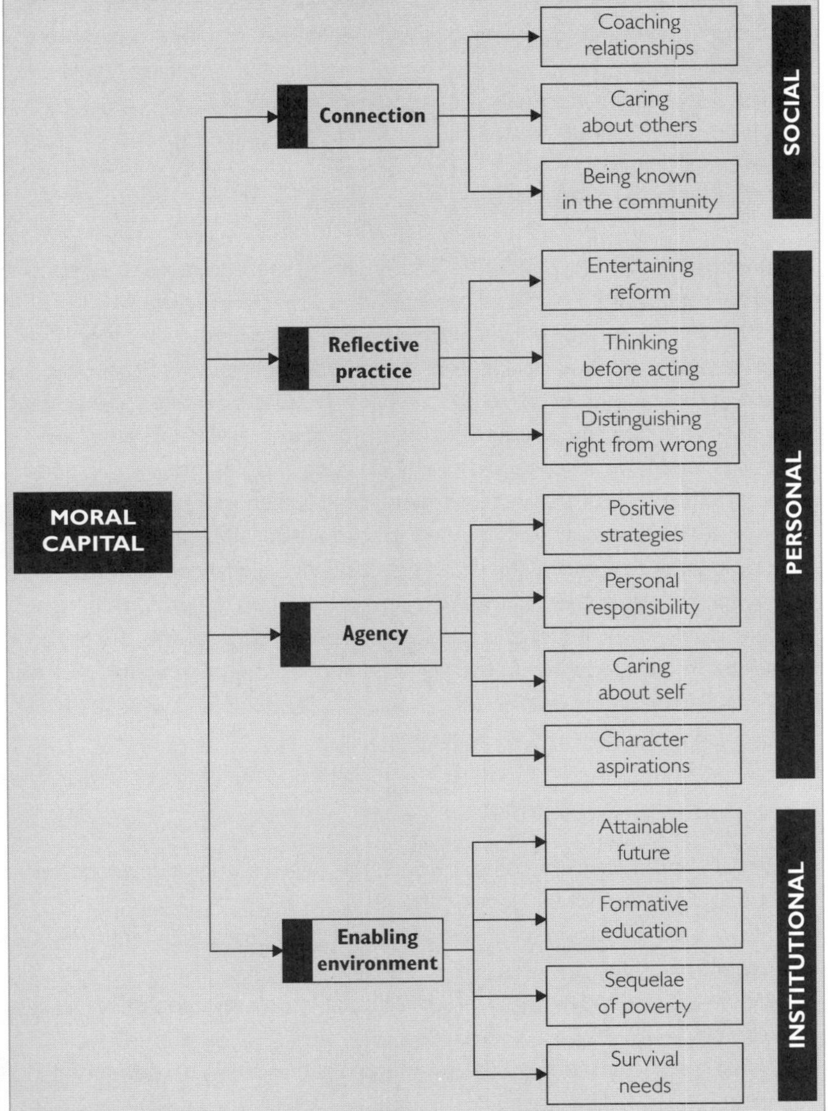

Source: Swartz (2009, p.149)

morally empowering, diversionary, a deterrent to crime, and the key to future success: 'School is very good, it takes you out of trouble, so if you don't want to be in trouble this keeps you out of trouble' (Ingwazi). Young people repeatedly made the connection between having a job and being a moral person ('becoming good people when they have got their own jobs'). In other words these youth saw morality as generating capital and capital generating morality. Being good provides young people with the opportunity to embark on the cycle of 'be a good person, complete school, get a job, be a good person.' In this sense, morality is seen as an instrumental good – it produces economic value.

From the research data, four overarching features of moral capital were identified:

- Relational connection
- Reflective practice
- Personal agency
- The importance of an enabling environment.

Look at Figure 7.2, which provides a summary of these four main elements of moral capital, with constituent components in each category.

The concept of moral capital provides a useful counterpoint to talk of moral panics and moral deficits. Moral capital shifts the focus from what is absent in the moral lives of youth to what is present. Educators and policy makers might now be encouraged to develop moral capital rather than complain about the absence of morality in young people. If the aim of moral education is to nurture or increase moral capital, then moral behaviour can be analysed with regard to the extent of moral capital already available to an individual or to a group. This could result in a more nuanced conversation between the 'blame the victim' and 'blame the system' schools of thought, since social and institutional factors will become part of the discussion, rather than solely focusing on the personal in questions of morality.

CHECK YOUR PROGRESS

- What are the main criticisms of Kohlberg's stages of moral development, especially in the South African context?
- How does social perspective-taking contribute to adolescents' moral decision making?
- What are the advantages of considering moral development as an 'ecology'?
- What are the components of 'moral capital' that might be developed in youth?

Development of the self

The development of abstract reasoning skills and changing social relations influence how adolescents think about the self. An important task for adolescents is to decide who they are, and to develop their own values.

The self-concept

Your self-concept refers to your perception of yourself, your understanding of what you are like. How do people's self-concepts change in adolescence?

In chapter six, you learnt that social comparison starts to play an important role in children's self-concepts during middle childhood. This tendency to compare the self with others continues in adolescence. In fact, younger adolescents are often very self-conscious and preoccupied with how others see them. But as young people move into late adolescence, they increasingly start to see themselves in terms of their own personal beliefs and values, rather than in terms of how they compare to others (Harter, 1998; Steinberg & Morris, 2001).

There is another important way in which the adolescent's self-concept differs from that of the child. The development of formal operational thought means that adolescents are more likely than children to use abstract labels such as 'intelligent' or 'extraverted' to describe themselves. In mid-adolescence, their self-descriptions vary across situations and across time. At this age, adolescents see themselves differently, depending on whether they are with their peers, parents or teachers (for example shy with peers, outgoing at home). By late adolescence, young people become better able to integrate their different or contradictory tendencies into a more general, coherent theory of the self. For example, a person who is sometimes cheerful and sometimes depressed might integrate these seemingly contradictory characteristics by using a higher-order abstract concept such as 'moody' or 'emotional' (Harter, 1998).

Self-esteem

Once adolescents begin to reflect on their own characteristics, they must deal with the question 'How much do I like myself?' One study investigated self-esteem from age 9 to age 90, using data collected from more than 300 000 individuals over the Internet (Robins, Trzesniewski, Tracy, Gosling & Potter, 2002). The findings showed that there was a drop in self-esteem in early adolescence, although self-esteem started to rise again in late adolescence. Girls' self-esteem dropped about twice as much in adolescence as boys' self-esteem.

The drop in self-esteem in early adolescence is probably due to a combination of factors. The transition to high school can be stressful, because it places new academic and social demands on children at the same time as it puts them at the bottom of the school social hierarchy. Having left grade seven as the big fish in a small pond, they must now start grade eight as the smallest fish in a big pond. In addition, girls in particular may become unhappy with their changing bodies. The increased cognitive capacities of adolescents also mean that they are more knowledgeable than children about their strengths and weaknesses.

Not all adolescents experience this dip in self-esteem, however. Adolescents who have the approval and support of parents and peers, and who do well in areas that are important to them, are likely to see themselves as worthy and capable (Steinberg & Morris, 2001).

Identity formation

Identity
a person's clear and consistent sense of who he or she is, what he or she believes and values, what he or she is going to do with his or her life, and where he or she fits into society

According to Erikson (1971), one of the main developmental tasks of adolescence is to develop a coherent sense of identity. The term '**identity**' refers to a person's clear and consistent sense of who he or she is, what he or she believes and values, what he or she is going to do with his or her life, and where he or she fits into society. The quotations from Leanne and Brian in the case study at the beginning of this chapter illustrate how adolescents become increasingly concerned with questions of who they will be and what they will do 'one day'. Identity formation involves three major issues: the choice of a career, the adoption of values to believe in and live by, and the development of a satisfying sexual identity.

Erikson proposed that adolescents experience the psychosocial crisis of identity versus role confusion as they struggle to determine who they are and where they are going in life. Young people who resolve this crisis in a positive way are able to formulate personal values, goals, and standards. They know who they 'really' are, and they have psychological strengths such as high self-esteem and an ability to form close relationships with others. In contrast, young people who resolve this crisis in a negative way remain confused over who they are and lack self-esteem. Their values are unclear and are easily influenced by others, and they have difficulty forming commitments and loyalties (Kroger, 2007). Erikson thought that such identity confusion is most likely to occur if earlier psychosocial crises were resolved in a negative way, or if society tries to force adolescents into roles that do not match their abilities or interests.

Individual differences and developmental trends in identity formation

James Marcia (1966) expanded on Erikson's theory and developed an interview that allows investigators to classify adolescents into one of four identity statuses based on what they say about making occupational, religious, and political choices. The key questions are whether or not the individual has experienced a process of *exploration* (or has seriously grappled

Figure 7.3 Questions around 'Who am I?' tend to become more frequent in adolescence, as young people face the task of developing a coherent sense of identity

with identity issues and explored alternatives) and whether or not he or she has achieved a *commitment* (that is, resolved the issues raised and made a personal investment in a set of goals, beliefs or values). Depending on whether or not there is a process of exploration and commitment, the individual is classified into one of the following four identity statuses:

- **Identity diffusion:** The **identity diffusion** status is characterised by a lack of both exploration and commitment. Adolescents in the diffusion status have not yet thought about their identity, or have given up the search. They have not established goals or values, and may take an 'I don't care' attitude. For example, consider an adolescent named Susan. When Susan is asked what she wants to do when she leaves school, she answers, 'I don't know. I haven't really given it much thought. I'm sure something will turn up.'

- **Foreclosure:** Individuals in the **identity foreclosure** status have committed themselves to goals and values, but without exploring an alternative. They seem to know who they are, but have uncritically accepted identities chosen for them by significant others, such as parents or teachers. For example, consider an adolescent named Nabeelah. Nabeelah plans to study medicine because her parents have always wanted her to become a doctor.

Identity diffusion
an identity status characterising individuals who have not given much thought to who they are, and have not committed themselves to particular goals or values

Foreclosure
an identity status characterising individuals who have committed themselves to an identity, but without much thought – they are becoming what others want them to become

Moratorium

an identity status characterising individuals who are actively exploring identity issues or experiencing an identity crisis, but who have not yet committed themselves to an identity

Identity achievement

an identity status characterising individuals who have seriously considered identity issues, resolved them, and made a commitment to particular goals and values

- **Moratorium:** Individuals in the identity **moratorium** status are in the process of searching for meaningful adult roles and values, but have not yet made a commitment. For example, consider an adolescent named Loyiso. Loyiso had planned to study engineering. However, he has discovered that he is also very interested in graphic design, and is now unsure about which career path to follow. He has started reading and talking to people in order to find out as much as he can about each career option.
- **Identity achievement:** An individual who has explored alternatives and made a commitment to personal goals and values is in the **identity achievement** status. For example, consider an adolescent named Philip. Philip has been enjoying his course in media and writing, and has managed to get a part-time job as a sub-editor at the *Cape Times*. He has given a lot of thought to journalism as a career, and is convinced that it is right for him.

Identity development follows many different paths. Many individuals remain in one status throughout adolescence, whereas others make one or more transitions from one status to another. Identity diffusion is considered to be the least developmentally mature status, and identity achievement the most mature. Most young adolescents progress from less mature statuses to more mature ones as they move into their late teens or early twenties. However, some move in the reverse direction (for example from achievement to moratorium) as they start to question decisions they had previously made (Meeus, Van de Schoot, Keijsers, Schwartz & Branje, 2010).

There is also evidence that identity development does not happen neatly, but in bits and pieces. Adolescents often achieve a sense of identity in one area (for example their career goals) while remaining confused about another area (such as their religious beliefs) (Archer, 1982). So certain aspects of identity may take shape earlier or remain more stable than others do. And decisions are not made once and for all, but have to be made time and time again. Nowadays, many researchers believe that the development of identity is a lifelong task. It begins with the development of a sense of self in infancy, and continues into old age. Questions around 'Who am I?' do tend to be particularly frequent in adolescence and early adulthood, but they are not exclusive to this age.

Influences on identity formation
Research has shown that the process of identity formation is influenced by at least the following six factors:
- **Cognitive skills:** The development of new cognitive skills associated with formal operational thinking allows adolescents to think in more abstract and flexible ways, and to imagine possible futures for themselves. Thus, adolescents who are more capable of complex, abstract

thinking, who actively seek information, and who have good problem-solving skills are more likely to raise and resolve identity issues than those who are less cognitively advanced (Kroger, 2007). From what psychologists already know about the development of the brain during adolescence (especially with regard to reflecting, deciding, and planning), it is easy to see the difficulties that young people might encounter in investigating possible futures including career choices, goals, and plans. Furthermore, if there is little stimulation and help with regard to developing cognitive skills such as planning, learning, and choosing, this can have a negative effect on an adolescent's overall life outcomes.

- **Personality:** Adolescents who are high in the personality traits of 'openness to experience' and 'conscientiousness' and low in the personality trait 'neuroticism' are more likely to explore alternatives and achieve an identity (Ozer & Benet-Martinez, 2006). These adolescents are curious, responsible, and emotionally stable.

- **Relationships with parents:** Identity formation is also influenced by relationships with parents. Adolescents tend to have difficulty forging their own identities when their parents are neglecting, rejecting, and emotionally distant from them, or overprotective and overcontrolling. Adolescents who have made the most progress towards achieving an individual identity tend to come from homes where high levels of warmth and support are combined with low levels of psychological control (Meeus, 2011). In these families, there is a solid base of affection, closeness, and mutual respect between children and parents (connectedness), but children are also given the freedom to disagree with their parents and be individuals in their own right (individuality) (Grotevant & Cooper, 1998).

- **Support from peers:** Social support from peers, including close friends and romantic partners, also has a positive impact on identity development during adolescence (Meeus & Dekovic, 1995).

- **Opportunities to explore:** Identity formation is also influenced by the extent to which adolescents are provided with opportunities to explore the world outside the home. Such opportunities can be provided by a variety of experiences, including those involved in work internships, volunteer projects, youth organisations, and attendance of university (Kroger, 2007).

- **The cultural and economic context:** The extent to which adolescents are provided with opportunities to explore is likely to depend on the broader cultural and economic context. Western industrialised societies that value individualism, personal choice, and responsibility allow adolescents a period of time in which to explore different roles before finally choosing an identity. Questioning and personal choice play a smaller role in traditional societies, or societies where educational and work opportunities are limited by racial, gender, political or economic barriers. In the South African context, where possible futures are limited by environmental constraints such as poverty and a lack of employment, this life stage is made more difficult for teenagers. In these cases, foreclosure may be more adaptive than identity achievement (Coté & Levine, 1988).

CHECK YOUR PROGRESS

* How does the self-concept change in adolescence?
* Why might a drop in self-esteem occur in early adolescence?
* What are the four identity statuses identified by James Marcia?
* What factors influence the process of identity formation?

CASE STUDY

In the case study at the beginning of this chapter, you were introduced to two participants in a study of adolescents growing up in Cape Town's Fish Hoek valley (Bray et al., 2010). Another participant in this study was Charney, a 17-year-old girl living with her parents in the working-class area of Ocean View. Charney stood out as being unusually successful at school and popular with her peers. She enjoyed spending time with her family, and described her mother as her best friend: a trusted companion with whom she could talk about anything. Yet her mother was also quite strict: she set clear boundaries for Charney's behaviour, and challenged her to use her talents and be the best she could be.

Charney was primarily responsible for the cooking and cleaning at home, but her parents were flexible with regard to domestic tasks, and willing to listen and negotiate. Their relationship with Charney was one of mutual respect, openness, and honesty.

Charney's mother also actively tried to build Charney's confidence and instil certain values in her, including that she did not need other people, such as friends or boyfriends, to define who she is. Charney spoke about some early experiences of giving in to peer pressure, but said that she now takes a strong stand against being persuaded to do things she does not wish to do. She was one of only two girls at her high school to pass matric with exemption in 2005 (Bray et al., 2010).

Questions

1 Based on what you have learned in this chapter, how would you describe the parenting behaviour of Charney's parents? How does this compare to the parenting that you received? How do you think your relationships with your parents in adolescence have influenced your academic achievement, behaviour, and social and emotional development?

2   Now that you have been introduced to the concepts of moral ecology and moral capital, what advice would you give to educators or policy makers who want to improve the moral behaviour of young people?

Conclusion

Adolescence is marked by dramatic physical growth and physiological changes, combined with important cognitive and social transitions. Genes, childhood experiences, and the environment in which a person reaches adolescence all influence behaviour. While family relationships remain important, friends and other peers become increasingly influential.

Development is also affected by the broader context in which adolescents live. In South Africa, poverty may reduce young people's opportunities to develop cognitive skills, to behave morally, and to explore possible futures.

Some adolescents find the challenges of this period stressful, and a small number have serious problems. Others, like Charney in the case study at the end of the chapter, cope well. Contrary to the popular 'storm and stress' view, most adolescents are reasonably happy and well behaved; find much to enjoy in their friendships, leisure activities, and family lives; and are hopeful about the future (Arnett, 1999; Graham, 2004).

References

Adams, G.R. (1983). Social competence during adolescence: Social sensitivity, locus of control, empathy, and peer popularity. *Journal of Youth and Adolescence, 12*, (3), 203–211.

Archer, S.L. (1982). The lower age boundaries of identity development. *Child Development, 53*, 1551–1556.

Arnett, J.J. (1999). Adolescent storm and stress, reconsidered. *American Psychologist, 54*, 317–326.

Attar-Schwartz, S., Tan, J.-P., Buchanan, A., Flouri, E. & Griggs, J. (2009). Grandparenting and adolescent adjustment in two-parent biological, lone-parent, and step-families. *Journal of Family Psychology, 23*, 67–75.

Bandura, Albert (1977). *Social learning theory.* Englewood Cliffs, NJ: Prentice Hall.

Bandura, Albert (1986). *Social foundations of thought and action: A social cognitive theory.* Englewood Cliffs, NJ: Prentice Hall.

Barber, B., Stolz, H.E., Olsen, J.A., Collins, W.A. & Burchinal, M. (2005). Parental support, psychological control, and behavioral control: Assessing relevance across time, culture, and method. *Monographs of the Society for Research in Child Development, 70*, (4), i,v,vii, 1–147.

Baumrind, D. (1967). Child care practices anteceding three patterns of preschool behavior. *Genetic Psychology Monographs, 75*, (1), 43–88.

Bergman, R. (2002). Why be moral? A conceptual model from developmental psychology. *Human Development, 45*, (2), 104–124.

Berndt, T.J. (1979). Developmental changes in conformity to peers and parents. *Developmental Psychology, 15*, 608–616.

Blasi, A. (1980). Bridging moral cognition and moral action: A critical review of the literature. *Psychological Bulletin, 88*, (1), 1–45.

Boyer, T.W. (2006). The development of risk-taking: A multi-perspective review. *Developmental Review, 26*, 291–345.

Bray, R., Gooskens, I., Kahn, L., Moses, S. & Seekings, J. (2010). *Growing up in the new South Africa: Childhood and adolescence in post-apartheid Cape Town.* Cape Town: HSRC Press.

Bridges, L.J., Roe, A.E.C., Dunn, J. & O'Connor, T.G. (2007). Children's perspectives on their relationships with grandparents following parental separation: A longitudinal study. *Social Development, 16*, 539–554.

Bronfenbrenner, U. (1992) Ecological systems theory. In R. Vasta (Ed.). *Six theories of child development.* London: Jessica Kingsley Publishers.

Brown, B.B. (1990). Peer groups and peer cultures. In S.S. Feldman & G.R. Elliott (Eds). *At the threshold: The developing adolescent* (p. 171–196). Cambridge, MA: Harvard University Press.

Caradas, A.A., Lambert, E.V. & Charlton, K.E. (2001). An ethnic comparison of eating attitudes and associated body image concerns in adolescent South African schoolgirls. *Journal of Human Nutrition and Dietetics, 14*, 111–120.

Carlo, G., Fabes, R., Laible, D. & Kupanoff, K. (1999). Early adolescence and prosocial/moral behavior II: The role of social and contextual influences. *Journal of Early Adolescence, 19*, (2), 133–147.

Chisholm, J.S., Quinlivan, J.A., Petersen, R.W. & Coall, D.A. (2005). Early stress predicts age at menarche and first birth, adult attachment, and expected lifespan. *Human Nature, 16*, 233–265.

Cicchetti, D. & Rogosch, F.A. (2002). A developmental psychopathology perspective on adolescence. *Journal of Consulting and Clinical Psychology, 70*, 6–20.

Coles, Robert (1986). *The moral life of children.* Boston: Atlantic Monthly Press.

Coles, Robert (1993). *The call of service: A witness to idealism.* Boston: Houghton Mifflin.

Collins, W.A. & Laursen, B. (2004). Parent–adolescent relationships and influences. In R.M. Lerner & L. Steinberg (Eds)., *Handbook of adolescent psychology* (2nd ed.) (p. 331–361). Hoboken, NJ: Wiley.

Coté, J.E. & Levine, C. (1988). A critical examination of the ego identity status paradigm. *Developmental Review, 8*, 147–184.

Csikszentmihalyi, M. & Larson, R. (1984). *Being adolescent: Conflict and growth in the teenage years.* New York: Basic Books.

Damon, William (1983). *Social and personality development: Infancy through adolescence* (1st ed.). New York: W.W. Norton.

Damon, W. (1984). Self understanding and moral development from childhood to adolescence. In W.M. Kurtines & J.L. Gewirtz (Eds). *Morality, moral behavior and moral development.* New York: Wiley.

Damon, W. & Gregory, A. (1997). The youth charter: Towards the formation of adolescent moral identity. *Journal of Moral Education, 26*, (2), 117–130.

Department of Health (2002). *South Africa demographic and health survey 1998: Full report.* Pretoria: Department of Health.

Dunphy, D.C. (1963). The social structure of urban adolescent peer groups. *Society, 26*, 230–246.

Eccles, J.S. & Wigfield, A. (2002). Motivational beliefs, values, and goals. *Annual Review of Psychology, 53*, 109–132.

Eisenberg, N. (2000). Emotion, regulation, and moral development. *Annual Review of Psychology, 51*, 665–697.

Elkind, David (1981). *The hurried child*. Reading, MA: Addison-Wesley.

Elliott, G.R. & Feldman, S.S. (1990). *At the threshold: The developing adolescent*. Cambridge, MA.: Harvard University Press.

Erikson, Erik H. (1968). *Identity: Youth and crisis*. New York: W.W. Norton.

Erikson, Erik (1971). *Identity, youth and crisis*. London: Faber.

Evans, G.W. & English, K. (2002). The environment of poverty: Multiple stressor exposure, psychophysiological stress, and socioemotional adjustment. *Child Development, 73*, (4), 1238–1248.

Fabes, R., Carlo, G., Kupanoff, K. & Laible, D. (1999). Early adolescence and prosocial/moral behavior I: The role of individual processes. *Journal of Early Adolescence, 19*, (1), 5–16.

Fakier, N. & Wild, L.G. (2011). Associations among sleep problems, learning difficulties and substance use in adolescence. *Journal of Adolescence, 34*, 717–726.

Ferns, I. & Thom, D.P. (2001). Moral development of black and white South African adolescents: Evidence against cultural universality in Kohlberg's theory. *South African Journal of Psychology, 31*, (4), 38–47.

Flisher, A.J. & Gevers, A. (2010). Adolescence. In I. Petersen, A. Bhana, A.J. Flisher, L. Swartz & L. Richter (Eds). *Promoting mental health in scarce-resource contexts* (p. 143–166). Cape Town: HSRC Press.

Freud, A. (1958). Adolescence. *Psychoanalytic Study of the Child, 15*, 255–278.

Gilligan, Carol (1982). *In a different voice: Psychological theory and women's development*. Cambridge, MA: Harvard University Press.

Glover, R.J. (2001). Discriminators of moral orientation: Gender role or personality? *Journal of Adult Development, 8*, (1), 1–7.

Goleman, Daniel (1995). *Emotional intelligence*. New York: Bantam Books.

Graham, Philip J. (2004). *The end of adolescence*. Oxford: Oxford University Press.

Grotevant, H.D. & Cooper, C.R. (1998). Individuality and connectedness in adolescent development: Review and prospects for research on identity, relationships, and context. In E.E.A. Skoe & A.L. von der Lippe, A.L. (Eds). *Personality development in adolescence: A cross national and life span perspective* (p. 3–37). London: Routledge.

Hall, G. Stanley (1904). *Adolescence: Its psychology and its relation to physiology, anthropology, sociology, sex, crime, religion, and education* (Vols. I & II). Englewood Cliffs, NJ: Prentice-Hall.

Harter, S. (1998). The development of self-representations. In N. Eisenberg (Ed.). *Handbook of child psychology (5th ed.), Vol. 3: Social, emotional, and personality development* (p. 553–617). New York, NY: Wiley.

Hoffman, Martin L. (2000). *Empathy and moral development: Implications for caring and justice*. Cambridge: Cambridge University Press.

Hunter, James D. (2000). *The death of character: Moral education in an age without good or evil*. New York: Basic Books.

Jones, L.L., Griffiths, P.L., Norris, S.A., Pettifor, J.M. & Cameron, N. (2009). Age at menarche and the evidence for a positive secular trend in urban South Africa. *American Journal of Human Biology, 21*, 130–132.

Jones, M.C. & Bayley, L.L. (1950). Physical maturing among boys as related to behavior. *The Journal of Educational Psychology, 41*, 129–148.

Kohlberg, Lawrence (1981). *Essays on moral development*. San Francisco: Harper & Row.

Kohlberg, Lawrence (1984). *The psychology of moral development: The nature and validity of moral stages* (1st ed.). San Francisco: Harper and Row.

Kroger, Jane (2007). *Identity development: Adolescence through adulthood* (2nd ed.). Thousand Oaks, CA: Sage.

Kuther, T.L. & Higgins-D'Alessandro, A. (2000). Bridging the gap between moral reasoning and adolescent engagement in risky behavior. *Journal of Adolescence, 23,* (4), 409–422.

Larson, R. & Wilson, S. (2004). Adolescence across place and time: Globalization and the changing pathways to adulthood. In R.M. Lerner & L. Steinberg (Eds). *Handbook of adolescent psychology* (2nd ed.) (p. 299–330). Hoboken, NJ: Wiley.

Lickona, Thomas (1976). *Moral development and behavior: Theory, research, and social issues.* New York, NY: Holt.

Lickona, Thomas (1991). *Educating for character: How our schools can teach respect and responsibility.* New York, NY: Bantam.

Lipman, Matthew (1991). *Thinking in education.* Cambridge, UK: Cambridge University Press.

Lynam, D. & Henry, B. (2001). The role of neuropsychological deficits in conduct disorders. In J. Hill & B. Maughan (Eds). *Conduct disorders in childhood and adolescence* (p. 235–263). New York: Cambridge University Press.

Magnusson, David (1988). *Individual development from an interactional perspective.* Hillsdale, NJ: Erlbaum.

Maqsud, M. (1998). Moral orientation of Batswana high school pupils in South Africa. *Journal of Social Psychology, 138,* (2), 255–257.

Marcia, J.E. (1966). Development and validation of ego-identity status. *Journal of Personality and Social Psychology, 3,* 551–558.

Meeus, W. (2011). The study of adolescent identity formation 2000–2010: A review of longitudinal research. *Journal of Research on Adolescence, 21,* 75–94.

Meeus, W. & Dekovic, M. (1995). Identity development, parental and peer support in adolescence: Results of a national Dutch survey. *Adolescence, 30,* 931–944.

Meeus, W., Van de Schoot, R., Keijsers, L., Schwartz, S.J. & Branje, S. (2010). On the progression and stability of adolescent identity formation: A five-wave longitudinal study in early-to-middle and middle-to-late adolescence. *Child Development, 81,* 1565–1581.

Mendle, J., Turkheimer, E. & Emery, R.E. (2007). Detrimental psychological outcomes associated with early pubertal timing in adolescent girls. *Developmental Review, 27,* 151–171.

Moultrie, T. & Dorrington, R. (2004). *Estimation of fertility from the 2001 South Africa census data.* Cape Town: Centre for Actuarial Research for Statistics South Africa.

Moultrie, T. & McGrath, N. (2007). Teenage fertility rates falling in South Africa. *South African Medical Journal, 97,* (6), 442–443.

Moretti, M.M. & Peled, M. (2004). Adolescent–parent attachment: Bonds that support healthy development. *Paediatrics and Child Health, 9,* 551–555.

Myyry, L. & Helkama, K. (2002). Moral reasoning and the use of procedural justice rules in hypothetical and real-life dilemmas. *Social Justice Research, 15,* (4), 373–391.

Narváez, D., Getz, I., Thoma, S. & Rest, J.R. (1999). Individual moral judgment and cultural ideologies. *Developmental Psychology, 35,* (2), 478–488.

National Institute of Mental Health (2011). *The teen brain: Still under construction* (NIH Publication No. 11-4929). Bethesda, MD: National Institute of Mental Health.

Negriff, S. & Susman, E.J. (2011). Pubertal timing, depression, and externalizing problems: A framework, review, and examination of gender differences. *Journal of Research on Adolescence, 21,* 717–746.

Noddings, Nel (1984). *Caring: A feminine approach to ethics and moral education.* London: University of California Press.

Noddings, Nel (2002). *Educating moral people: A caring alternative to character education.* New York: Teachers College Press.

Ozer, D.J. & Benet-Martinez, V. (2006). Personality and the prediction of consequential outcomes. *Annual Review of Psychology, 57*, 401–421.

Piaget, Jean (1954). *The construction of reality in the child.* New York: Basic Books.

Piaget, Jean (1968). *The moral judgement of the child.* London: Kegan Paul.

Piaget, J. (1972). Intellectual evolution from adolescence to adulthood. *Human Development, 15*, 1–12.

Posel, D. & Devey, R. (2006). The demographics of fatherhood in South Africa: An analysis of survey data, 1993–2002. In L. Richter & R. Morrell (Eds). *Baba: Men and fatherhood in South Africa.* Cape Town: HSRC Press.

Prinstein, M.J., Fetter, M.D. & La Greca, A.M. (1996). *Can you judge adolescents by the company they keep? Peer group membership, substance use, and risk-taking behavior.* Boston, MA: Society for Research on Adolescence.

Raths, L.E., Harmin, M. & Simon, S.B. (1966). *Values and teaching: Working with values in the classroom.* Columbus, Ohio: C.E. Merrill Books.

Reddy, S.P., James, S., Sewpaul, R., Koopman, F., Funani, N.I., Sifunda, S. … Omardien, R.G. (2010). *Umthente Uhlaba Usamila – The South African Youth Risk Behaviour Survey 2008.* Cape Town: South African Medical Research Council.

Richter, L.M. (2006). Studying adolescence. *Science, 312*, 1902–1905.

Robins, R.W., Trzesniewski, K.H., Tracy, J.L., Gosling, S.D. & Potter, J. (2002). Global self-esteem across the life-span. *Psychology and Aging, 17*, 423–434.

Rozin, P., Haidt, J. & McCauley, C.R. (2000). Disgust. In M. Lewis & J.M. Haviland-Jones (Eds). *Handbook of emotions* (2nd ed.) (p. 637–653). New York: Guilford Press.

Salovey, P. & Sluyter, D.J. (1997). *Emotional development and emotional intelligence: Educational implications.* New York: Basic Books.

Scales, P.C. (1999). Reducing risks and building developmental assets: Essential actions for promoting adolescent health. *The Journal of School Health, 69*, (3), 113–119.

Schlegel, A. & Barry, H. (1991). *Adolescence: An anthropological enquiry.* New York, NY: Free Press.

Selman, R. (1971). Taking another's perspective: Role-taking development in early childhood. *Child Development, 42*, (6), 1721–1734.

Selman, Robert L. (1980). *The growth of interpersonal understanding: Developmental and clinical analyses.* New York, NY: Academic Press.

Sheehy, A., Gasser, T., Molinari, L. & Largo, R.H. (1999). An analysis of variance of the pubertal and midgrowth spurts for length and width. *Annals of Human Biology, 26*, 309–331.

Shisana, O., Rehle, T., Simbayi, L. C., Parker, W., Zuma, K., Bhana, A. & Pillay, V. (2005). *South African national HIV prevalence, HIV incidence, behaviour and communication survey, 2005.* Cape Town: HSRC Press.

Simbayi, L. C., Chauveau, J. & Shisana, O. (2004). Behavioural responses of South African youth to the HIV/AIDS epidemic: A nationwide survey. *AIDS Care, 16*, (5), 605–618.

Smetana, J.G., Campione-Barr, N. & Metzger, A. (2006). Adolescent development in interpersonal and societal contexts. *Annual Review of Psychology, 57*, 255–284.

Smith, K. & Parekh, A. (1996). A cross-sectional study of moral development in the South African context. *Psychological Reports, 78*, (3), 851–859.

Smith, R. & Standish, P. (1997). *Teaching right and wrong: Moral education in the balance.* Stoke-on-Trent: Trentham.

Snarey, J. & Keljo, K. (1996). Revisiting a 'study of moral development in the South African context' by Smith and Parekh. *Psychological Reports, 79*, (3), 1089–1090.

Statistics South Africa (2005). *Stages in the life cycle of South Africans* (Report No. 03-02-46). Pretoria: Statistics South Africa.

Statistics South Africa (2011). *Mid-year population estimates 2011* (Statistical Release P0302). Pretoria: Statistics South Africa.

Steinberg, L. (2001). We know some things: Parent–adolescent relationships in retrospect and prospect. *Journal of Research on Adolescence, 11*, 1–19.

Steinberg, L. & Morris, A.S. (2001). Adolescent development. *Annual Review of Psychology, 52*, 83–110.

Sullivan, Harry S. (1953). *The interpersonal theory of psychiatry*. New York: Norton.

Susman, E.J. & Rogol, A. (2004). Puberty and psychological development. In R.M. Lerner & L. Steinberg (Eds). *Handbook of adolescent psychology* (2nd ed.) (p. 15–37). Hoboken, NJ: Wiley.

Swartz, Sharlene (2009). *Ikasi: The moral ecology of South Africa's township youth*. Johannesburg: Wits University Press.

Swartz, S. & Bhana, A. (2009). *Teenage tata: Voices of young fathers in South Africa*. Cape Town: HSRC Press.

Tovée, M.J., Swami, V., Furnham, A. & Malgalparsad, R. (2006). Changing perceptions of attractiveness as observers are exposed to a different culture. *Evolution and Human Behavior, 27*, 443–456.

Vardy, P. & Grosch, P. (1994). *The puzzle of ethics*. London: Fount.

Visser, M. (2007). HIV/AIDS prevention through peer education and support in secondary schools in South Africa. *Journal of Social Aspects of HIV/AIDS, 4*, (3), 678–694.

Walker, L.J. (2002). The model and the measure: An appraisal of the Minnesota approach to moral development. *Journal of Moral Education, 31*, (3), 353–367.

Walker, L.J. (2004). Gus in the gap: Bridging the judgment–action gap in moral functioning. In D.K. Lapsley & D. Narváez (Eds). *Moral development, self, and identity* (p. 1–20). London: Lawrence Erlbaum Associates.

World Health Organization (2011). *Young people: Health risks and solutions* (Fact Sheet No. 345). Geneva: World Health Organization.

Yehuda, R., Halligan, S.L. & Grossman, R. (2001). Childhood trauma and risk for PTSD: Relationship to intergenerational effects of trauma, parental and cortisol excretion. *Development and Psychopathology, 13*, (3), 733–753.

Yorgason, J.B., Padilla-Walker, L. & Jackson, J. (2011). Nonresidential grandparents' emotional and financial involvement in relation to early adolescent grandchild outcomes. *Journal of Research on Adolescence, 21*, 552–558.

Youniss, J. & Yates, M. (1999). Youth service and moral civic identity: A case for everyday morality. *Educational Psychology Review, 11*, (4), 361–376.

PART III

CONTEXTUALISING
CONTEMPORARY THEMES
IN CHILDHOOD
DEVELOPMENT

CHAPTER EIGHT

CHILDREN AND CHILDHOOD IN SOUTH AFRICA

Mokgadi Moletsane

CASE STUDY

Tshidi started school at the age of nine. Other children started school at the age of seven. Tshidi's start at school was delayed because the nearest school was 20 kilometres away from her home, and her parents wanted her to develop physically before walking to school. Only when she was nine years old did her mother and grandmother allow her to go to school because they then regarded her as fit to travel the distance to school and to deal with other challenges outside home. Tshidi repeated grade three because before she wrote the grade three examination, her mother suffered from migraines. Tshidi's mother asked her to drop out of school in order to help with house chores.

Tshidi lives with her single mother, two younger siblings, and grandmother in a one-bedroom house made from mud. When Tshidi was six years old, her mother gave her the chores of sweeping the yard and veranda. When she was seven and eight, washing dishes was added to the list of her chores. At the age of nine she was taught how to cook, fetch wood from the nearby bush, fetch water from the river, and carry a 10-litre bucket of water on her head.

Tshidi started menstruating at the age of 12 years. She was scared, but her mother and grandmother invited a few older women in their community to celebrate. They slaughtered the fattest sheep to celebrate her developmental milestone. During the celebration, she was given tips and advice by older women. She was also informed that she was an adult, and that she should stay away from boys because 'menstruation' meant she was ripe or ready to become pregnant.

Now, at the age of 16, Tshidi can do all the work done by adults, including washing and ironing clothes. During school holidays, she works as a domestic worker on the farm nearby that is also her mother's place of work, in order to augment her family's income.

Tshidi is friendly and has many friends. She performed well at school, despite the fact that she was older than other children in her class. She was chosen to be a class leader. Tshidi's dream is to become a medical doctor one day, in order to help her community. Tshidi is active in her community and church. She helps children with school work and is a church choir leader. She cannot wait to turn 18 in order to vote in the next election.

ACTIVITY

1   At what age did you start school?
2   What is the acceptable age of starting school?
3   What are the criteria of school readiness, in your view?
4   Analyse Tshidi's criteria of school readiness, according to her mother and grandmother, and give their reasons.
5   Do you think it is fair for Tshidi to be involved in home chores at a young age? Elaborate on your answer and support it with examples.
6   In your opinion, does menstruation signify adulthood? Support your view.

LEARNING OBJECTIVES

By the end of this chapter you should be able to:
- Conceptualise the terms 'children' and 'childhood'
- Understand childhood law, politics, and policies
- Understand children and childhood indicators
- Conceptualise childhood and child well-being
- Analyse fears as indicators of child well-being
- Explain children's vulnerability and resilience
- Know the family factors that influence child development and learning
- Understand children in families
- Understand children's rights.

Introduction

The construction of the terms 'children' and 'childhood' is interpreted differently in different cultures and by different generations. These concepts are often used interchangeably, yet the terms 'children' and 'childhood' represent different concepts and raise different analytical issues. In everyday discourse, people use them without difficulty, and, if need be, apply visual clues – for example the size or sexual maturity of a person – when these terms are used, as evidence upon which to make judgements (James & James, 2004).

Culturally based evaluation of these concepts is vital, however. For example, explanations such as young age, immature behaviour or exclusion from the world of work due to age are different in different cultural contexts. Tshidi's example, from the case study at the start of this chapter, highlights cultural and environmental factors that influence childhood. For example, Tshidi was allowed to go to school at the age of 9 when she was physically stronger than she was when she was 7; she was regarded as an adult at the age of 12 when she was menstruating; and she worked part time at the age of 16.

Some 250 million of the world's children aged between 5 and 14 are estimated to be economically active (James & James, 2004). This statistic highlights the inherent difficulty in trying to apply more culturally based criteria to the concepts of 'children' and 'childhood'. This chapter will undertake the important task of unpacking the concepts, and of indicating the distinctions between them, in order to provide a clear reference for these concepts.

Conceptualisation of children and childhood

Childhood is the structural site that is occupied by children as a collectivity (James & James, 2004). It is within this collective and institutional space of 'childhood' as a member of the category '**children**' that any individual child comes to exercise his or her unique agency. A singular term, '**child**', according to these authors, should be used only to refer to an individual young person. This term also refers to a young person's

Childhood
the structural site occupied by children as a collectivity; a developmental stage of the life course common to all children

Children
young people, between birth and the age of 18 years

Child
an individual young person, between birth and the age of 18 years

---

Figure 8.1 Within the collective and institutional space of 'childhood', as a member of the category 'children', any individual child comes to exercise his or her unique agency

developmental position in the life course and his or her collective category. The term 'child' is descriptive rather than analytic. Categories of childhood definition are highlighted below (James & James, 2004).

Social construction of childhood

Childhood is a developmental stage of the life course common to all children and characterised by basic physical and developmental patterns. The manner in which adults interpret, understand, and socially institutionalise childhood for children differs across and between cultures and generations, and also in relation to adults' engagement with children's everyday lives and actions (James & James, 2004). The social construction of childhood is depicted as the complex interweaving of social structures, political and economic institutions, beliefs, cultural mores, laws, policies, and everyday action of both adults and children in the home, street, and school.

Childhood and biological factors

The materiality of the biological base of childhood is a cultural universal. Childhood is a phase in the life course of all people and a period marked by rapid and common physiological and psychological development. Woodhead (1996) suggests that the ways in which biological facts are interpreted in relation to ideas about children's needs do vary between cultures. These varying ways of interpretation account for wide variety in the kind of social discriminations and legal differentiations made or not made between children and older people in any society (Woodhead, 1996).

'Children's needs' is the concept that is fundamental to the cultural politics of childhood. Woodhead (1996) argues that 'needs' form a spectrum from what might be called 'fundamental needs' — which have biological roots and therefore are universal, such as the need for food and water — to needs that are more socially constructed and therefore particular. These latter kinds of need are situational and culture bound, in that they are as much about the culture and society into which the child is growing as they are about the child. Consider the example in the box below.

According to Western planners, children need a certain amount of play space, and overcrowding is detrimental to their social development, leading to aggressive and non-cooperative behaviour (Woodhead, 1996). Regulations in England are in force to ensure the design of nurseries and playgroups does not exceed maximum allowable density levels. This regulation is contrary to the situation in some communities – especially disadvantaged communities – in Africa and South Africa. For example, most nurseries in informal settlements and townships are overcrowded. Play space is not a universal need but a socially constructed need.

The same may be said of living space. For example, recall the case study about Tshidi, at the start of this chapter: Tshidi, her mother, her grandmother and her two siblings share a one-bedroom mud house. They did not complain about living space. Instead lack of space brings the family members closer to each other.

The example in the box above indicates the contrast between a westernised model of childhood and a non-Western model of childhood prevalent where most people are poor and lack basic needs such as food and shelter. In relation to the implementation of the United Nations Convention on the Rights of the Clild (UNCRC) and its assertion of the universality of children's needs, rights, shared skills, and competences, in practice there is often considerable difficulty in making judgements about what children's best interests are in a particular culture and in a particular context (James & James, 2004).

Generational space and childhood

Another important fact about childhood is that eventually children do grow up, and, within a certain period, they leave their childhood behind. All adults have been, and remember being, children and will have some experiences in common (Qvortrup, 1994). The childhood of the current generation of children will be different from that remembered by their parents. Childhood's temporal location in generational history means that its character changes over time, shaped by changes in laws, policies, discourses, and social practices through which childhood is defined (Qvortrup, 1994).

Within one generation of children, in any society, each child's experiences of 'childhood' are affected by the uniqueness of their social circumstances. Patterns of material or cultural deprivation, for example, will ensure that in any given society, 'childhood' is experienced differently by different children.

As James, Jenks and Prout (1998) point out, being a child from a middle-class urban family in Rio de Janeiro, whose basic needs are met, is not the same as being a child of a poor share-cropping family in north-eastern Brazil, who struggles to access the basic needs. These children will have different experiences of life.

Children as social agents

Children's voices are of paramount importance. Children should be given an opportunity to express themselves, and adults should listen to what children say. The new paradigm in childhood studies suggests that the professionals working with children should be familiar with rights, principles and their use in advocating for change. Since the emergence of this new paradigm in childhood studies, psychologists can no longer regard children as the passive output of child-rearing practices, nor can they envisage the social development of children as the product of a simple biological determinism. Instead, psychologists have to acknowledge the diversity of children's childhoods and of children's own part as social agents in shaping their childhood experiences. The conceptualisation of social relationships and processes of the cultural politics of childhood have to be understood (James & James, 2004).

Children as citizens

Being a citizen involves having three types of right (James & James, 2004):
- Political rights include the right to vote or to strike.
- Civil rights include the rights to free speech, justice, property, and personal freedom.
- Social rights include such rights as access to welfare and education.

Children are excluded from political rights and have limited civil and social rights. As Cockburn (1998) explains, in the United Kingdom, this exclusion of children from full community membership as citizens became firmly institutionalised during the nineteenth century. This exclusion went hand in hand with the growth of the modern conception of childhood, and it was given empirical grounding through the introduction of numerous social policies designed to remove, under the guise of protection, children from areas of adult and public life.

In the nineteenth century, the establishment of children's rights to welfare and educational provision can be shown to have worked ironically to disable and disenfranchise children as citizens (Hendrick, 1997, in James & James, 2004). These progressive policies set children apart from the public world of adults and put in motion a very particular kind of age-based social exclusion (Hendrick, 1997, in James & James, 2004). Nowadays, for example, the classification of individual children as members of the social category 'children' continues to make them the targets for special welfare measures and renders them subject to specific legal constraints. While this process can be beneficial and benevolent (James & James, 2004), through bracketing all children together it does ignore children's individuality and uniqueness.

Childhood indicators

Indicators are at the heart of modern vocabulary (Ben-Arieh, 2006), be they related to the quality of the health system, educational institutions, or welfare arrangements, or connected to discourses of social exclusion or distribution of justice. Regarding children and childhood, indicators are used to assess standard of living, welfare support, marginalisation, and well-being and they measure distributive justice between age groups and between children of various ethnic and social groups. Indicators track trends along these dimensions; this makes indicators effective tools for evaluating policy implementation.

Like weather warning systems, **childhood indicators** such as social exclusion and dropout trends can point to what is coming economically and socially (Ben-Arieh, 2006). Recently there has been new emphasis on positive indicators (Moore & Limpman, 2005, in Ben-Arieh, 2006, p. 20) such as resilience or how certain factors develop a capacity in cope with risk factors (Ben-Arieh, 2006). Indicators are assigned meaning within the context of time and space. Indicators can also take on meaning through theories and models related to a particular domain and through the models of everyday life.

Although an individual child moves along the life cycle, demographic groups are as constant as social groups (Ben-Arieh, 2006). 'Being' refers to children in the present, whilst 'becoming' refers to what they might become in the future. Becoming has always been a core theme in child psychology and socialisation, a recognition that children are developing and growing and that parents, as well as the wider community, should support this process.

Childhood indicators indicators that assess children's standard of living, welfare support, marginalisation, and well-being and that measure distributive justice between age groups and between children of various ethnic and social groups; indicators track trends along these dimensions

> CHECK YOUR PROGRESS
> * What is your definition of children and childhood?
> * Give the main aspects of the universal and cultural definitions of childhood and give examples thereof.

Childhood and well-being

Well-being, as it relates to children, refers to the positions and experiences of individuals and groups in sets of domains. A number of reports on well-being refer to objective measurements and subjective measurements of domains such as health, economic security, education, behaviour, and social environment (America's Children, 2005).

The number of domains and indicators varies. Another study of the field over a period of time concludes with five dominating domains: physical, psychological, cognitive, social, and economic (Pollard & Lee, 2003, in Ben-Arieh, 2006, p. 22).

Standard of living is most often expressed by an index of measures. Measurements of well-being incorporate objective experiences and subjective experiences. Examples of such objective experiences are health or standard of living. Examples of subjective experiences are perceptions and evaluations of life and living conditions, satisfaction, and happiness (Ben-Arieh, 2006).

Indicators may be extracted from both the individual and the system, as when macro indicators on social cohesion illustrate the social environment of children. Child-centric measurements are now sometimes viewed as the voice of the child: the child's chance to express his or her own subjective opinions. For children, the indicators of well-being vary not only by context but also by life phase, making theorisation, conceptualisation, and measurement extremely complex.

Children's conceptualisation of well-being

A qualitative study conducted about children's definition of well-being indicated that the children who participated in that study defined well-being, and its components, as follows (Ben-Arieh, 2006):

- **Well-being:** Well-being is defined through feelings, in particular happiness, but integrating sadness is also relevant. Well-being is about feeling secure, particularly in social relations when relations are harmonious.
- **Autonomy and agency:** Well-being is the capacity to act freely and to make choices and exert influences in everyday situations. Children articulated the social relations upon which autonomy was premised, including stable, secure relationships with adults. Agency also included the capacity to act in ways consistent with being oneself.
- **Keeping safe and feeling secure:** According to children, fear and insecurity affects their well-being. Feeling safe and being safe are important parts of well-being. Safety included being with other people, having parents that protect the child and treat the child well, having a personal and safe place to be, and religion.
- **Sense of self:** Participants in the study used positive sense of self to define well-being. Feeling good about oneself could be linked with concrete achievements but also to a more general sense that things were going satisfactorily.
- **Material resources:** Children were aware that money provides increased and inequitable access to cultural activities and cultural capital. While children understood that money provides opportunities, and more money provides greater capacity to purchase goods and services, the overwhelming link between money and well-being is through having enough money to provide a decent standard of living for households and families, rather than individuals.

• **Physical environment and home:** Adequate physical shelter and home environments that are stable reference points are important to children's well-being. Home has several characteristics: it is a place defined through family; it is a place where children receive basic care; it is a place where children can relax and be themselves; it is a place where children have their possessions; it is, hopefully, a place where children can have fun; ideally, it is a place where children have space to do internal work and feel secure.

Fear as indicator of children's well-being

Fear is an integral part of insecurity. It is a psychosomatic and socio-emotional reaction to a certain situation (Rutter & Rutter, 1993, Ben-Arieh, 2004, p. 110, in Ben-Arieh, 2006). Despite the innate human capability to experience and express fears, fears are socially and culturally mediated and reinforced (Ollendick et al., 1991, 1996, in Ben-Arieh, 2004, p. 110); therefore fears reflect feelings of uncertainty inherent in the child's relationship to his or her surrounding world.

Fear is functional and protects humans against actual dangers. It is an emotion that functions as an important motivator for developing coping strategies in the face of threatening situations. Therefore fears are necessary for growth, but in excess they can inhibit and disturb growth (Craske, 1997, Ben-Arieh, 2004, in Ben-Arieh, 2006). Fears can disturb learning, concentration, creativity, or, even, play. Parents need to act as a protective filter between the child and the external world. The quality of child protection in society, managed by the parents and the authorities, is, in general, reflected in the fears of children.

The preschool years are a period in a person's life when fears are common and frequent. The study by Rutter and Rutter (1993, in Ben-Arieh, 2004) found that the most prevalent fears in the preschool period are fears of animals (at about three years or age), fears of the dark (at four to five years), and fears of imaginary creatures (at five to six years).

Other writers suggest that fears are modified by cultural factors. The cultural comparison of children's subjective well-being is required when researchers investigate the dependence of components of well-being on cultural and societal factors.

CHECK YOUR PROGRESS
• What are childhood indicators and what are they used to assess?
• Explain the term 'childhood well-being'.
• How can childhood well-being be measured?

Vulnerability

Children are more vulnerable than adults are to negative environments and situations. This can be due to the fact that they are still developing. They can be vulnerable due to negative social, political, and legal status. Children are dependent on their parents or adults; sometimes, those adults, instead of supporting the children, abuse or neglect them. Determinants that increase the possibility of negative effects on children are called '**risk factors**' (Louw & Louw, 2007). This section will explain certain risk factors: poverty, disease, illness, abuse, neglect, and family influences.

Risk factors
determinants that increase the possibility of negative effects on children

Poverty and neglect

Nearly 40 per cent of young children in South Africa are exposed to poverty and neglect (Du Preez, 2004). An estimated 52 per cent of South African households earn less than the poverty-line amount (Donald, Lazarus & Lolwana, 2009; Eloff, 2001, in Du Preez, 2004). The majority of these are households of black people from historically disadvantaged communities, and they are more prone than wealthier households are to health-and-safety risks associated with malnutrition, infection, and injury (Donald et al., 2009; Van Niekerk & Prins, 2001, in Du Preez, 2004). Many children from previously disadvantaged communities go to school hungry. Some of them do not have money to buy books and uniforms. Some teachers expect these children to perform well in school, despite their circumstances.

Disease and illness

Children from families who live in poverty are vulnerable to disease due to poor nutrition and lack of health-care facilities. As Freigenbaum and Veit (2003, in Du Preez, 2004, p. 55) explain, 'human diseases represent changes in the normal structure or function of the human body'. These changes can either be shown by specific symptoms or they can be asymptomatic until they have progressed sufficiently to show symptoms. Diseases can be contagious, generative, developmental, or, even, chronic.

Various factors can have an impact on illness. These factors include socio-economic factors, environmental factors, risk-taking lifestyles, and drug abuse, among others. Many children are orphaned by Aids in South Africa. Some Aids orphans are themselves infected with HIV. The risk of HIV infection in unborn children, girls, and young women is of great concern (Du Preez, 2004). Some orphans are forced by their circumstances to head their families and take care of their siblings. These children are deprived of their childhood as they are forced to take on adults' responsibilities.

Abuse and neglect

Some children are abused and neglected by the parents who should protect them at home. **Neglect** refers to failure to provide for basic needs.
The following are some types of neglect (Louw & Louw, 2007):

- **Physical neglect:** This is failure to provide for basic needs such as
  housing, nutrition, and medical care.
- **Emotional neglect:** This includes lack of care, love, and affection.
- **Educational neglect:** This involves failure to enrol a child in school.

Children may suffer various types of abuse in families:

- **Physical abuse:** They may be beaten, kicked, or, even, murdered by a
  parent or family member.
- **Sexual abuse:** This is the involvement of a dependent, developmentally immature child or children in sexual activities that they do not
  fully comprehend or to which they are unable to give their informed
  consent and which violate the social taboos of the culture and are
  against the law (Park and Khan, 2000, p. 326).

Resilience

Resilience is the ability to overcome negative factors, or the process
whereby people bounce back from adversity or risk factors (Louw &
Louw, 2006). Resilience is one of the focus points of positive psychology – a scientific study of strengths, virtues, and skills that enable individuals to thrive (Louw & Louw, 2006).

Different children can exhibit different resilience. Some children do
not react negatively towards traumatic situations, but, instead, show resilience, despite adversity. Children might grow up in the same house, and
be exposed to the same negative treatment and environment, but react
differently to that environment.

The following are strategies that can develop or improve resilience in
children (Dawes & Donald, 2000, Killan, 2004, Masten & Reeds, 2005,
in Louw & Louw, 2007):

- **Encouraging the child to establish and build positive relationships:**
  Children who enjoy positive relationships with others appear to be more
  resilient than their peers when exposed to current and future adversity.
- **Helping children make sense of their experience:** Children who can
  make sense of the adversity to which they are subjected appear to be
  affected less negatively by the experiences than children who cannot
  make sense of their experiences are.
- **Helping children exercise control over their experiences:** Children
  who experience some sense of control over their experiences appear to
  be less adversely affected by stressors than those who feel that stressors
  are beyond their control.

Neglect
failure to provide basic
needs

Resilience
A process whereby
people bounce back from
adversity

- **Providing the child with some routine:** Children benefit from a routine and structure, for example a planned regular study programme based on specific times.
- **Developing self-esteem and self-efficacy:** The creation of a supportive and facilitative environment, and specific opportunities to encourage a feeling of accomplishment and a sense of achievement in children, can help children's self-esteem and self-efficacy.

> **CHECK YOUR PROGRESS**
> - Explain possible factors that can lead to children's vulnerability. Give practical examples of these factors.
> - Critically discuss the possible strategies that can help to improve resilience in children.

Family and childhood

People define 'family' differently, depending on their culture and the time in which they live. The family is a social institution. In Western countries, the family is based on the organised and legally determined unit of father, mother, and a child or children – what is called a 'nuclear family'. Forms of family have changed tremendously. In South Africa, many people who have a background of previous disadvantage due to the apartheid system work a long way away from where they live. As a result, grandparents raise their grandchildren while parents work long hours far from home. A family comprising children and their parents, as well as grandparents and other relatives such as uncles and aunts, is called an 'extended family'. If a man marries more than one wife, this is called 'polygamy'. In South Africa and some other countries, same-sex couples can marry and become a family.

In South Africa and other countries in which HIV/Aids is prevalent, parental death as a result of HIV/Aids or Aids-related illnesses has left many orphaned children. This has led to a form of family called a 'child-headed family'. This family pattern requires children to take care of their siblings without adults' supervision (Moletsane, 2004).

Family environment can affect child development. The family factors that contribute to child learning and development will be discussed below.

Family factors that contribute to child learning and development

Socio-economic status

Many studies indicate that parental socio-economic status and education levels are highly predictive of children's developmental and academic outcome, as well as of their educational and occupational attainments as adults (Moletsane, 2004).

All of the following are related to social class: children's access to health-care facilities, nutrition, and education; children's physical environment, neighbourhood, and peers; and the child-rearing patterns experienced, the size of the family, its authority structure, and its stability (Hoffman, 1988, in Bornstein & Bradley, 2010). A major challenge for developmental science is to understand the links that connect socio-economic factors to child outcomes.

Parent–child interaction

A lack of parental interaction with children can compromise child development. Alcoholic parents, abusive parents, and parents who are absent from home for long periods of time are detrimental to children's intellectual, academic, and socio-emotional development. In contrast, a positive, stable, stimulating, and supportive relationship with parents or adults can render children resilient to the effects of a negative environment. The parent–child relationship is a two-way process. The relationship can also be hampered by the characteristics of the child (Moletsane, 2004).

Parent–child relationships, parental warmth, and attachment relationships certainly are essential to the health and well-being of children (Evans & Walsh, 2010). A systemic model of the parent–child relationship indicates that children are influenced by parenting through consistent exposure to supportive interactions or through direct contact; therefore, such features as sensitivity and warmth are essential (system theory will be discussed in some detail later in this chapter). Parents also produce and allocate resources that indirectly influence development by virtue of their effect on access to materials and protection from harm, for instance food, shelter, neighbourhood location, and educational materials. Whereas parenting may influence development at the proximal level through responsiveness and sensitivity, at the level of the family, time and allocation of time are valuable for development.

Physical environment

If children grow up in a family environment in which reading and writing materials are in abundance, and in which parents and caregivers make use of such material, they tend to develop an equal enthusiasm for reading and writing. Poverty can affect children's educational stimulation. For example, families who live in poverty cannot afford resources such as educational toys or writing and reading materials that stimulate children's interest in education. Children who grow up in such families often lack cognitive stimulation as well as interest in schoolwork.

Neighbourhood has an impact on a child's development. Children who grow up with neighbours who are interested in education and success are more likely to be successful than children who do not. In contrast, children who grow up in neighbourhoods where there are drug dealers, gangsters, and illiterate people are more likely than other children to experience what their peers are doing, and become involved in drugs.

Identification and modelling

Parents are their children's first teachers and, as a result, they should behave in an exemplary manner because children copy and learn from parents and caregivers. When parents are successful, children usually want to be like them. The process of identification and modelling should be fostered by warmth and support on the part of parents and caregivers; these foster in children such prosocial traits as kindness, honesty, generosity, obedience to rules, and consideration of the rights and welfare of others (Moletsane, 2004).

In order for parents and caregivers to promote modelling of appropriate behaviours, they need a favourable attitude towards their child and should also attract the child's attention to the processing of modelling behaviour. They can do this through overt or covert verbal rehearsal, encouragement of actual practice of the behaviour, and provision of incentives for adopting this behaviour.

Children exist in a system: System theory

System theory
a theory that views different levels and groups of people as interactive systems, where the functioning of the whole is dependent on the interaction between all parts

Children do not exist in a vacuum, but in families and in communities. They therefore exist within a system which consists of sub-systems. According to Donald, Lazarus, & Lolwana (2009), theories have applied system concepts to relationships between human beings and the interactions between groups of people in their particular social context. **System theory** sees different levels and groups of people as interactive systems where the functioning of the whole is dependent on the interaction between all parts. This is best illustrated in Bronfenbrenner's (1979) Ecological Systems theory (discussed again in chapter 11). For the purpose of this chapter, the relevance of this theory is in understanding children's development in families, communities, and other levels of the systems of which they are part. To understand the whole system, the relationships between subsystems must be examined.

Whole systems can interact with other systems around them, for instance a family may interact with other families, schools, and church, among other systems. All parts of systems affect the system as a whole (Donald, Lazarus & Lolwana, 2009). If a system and sub-system are affected, they will disturb the smooth functioning of other sub-systems, and if they are intact, the whole system will function well. This means sub-systems influence the entire system.

Read the box headed 'Sub-systems influence the entire system: The case of Thapelo', which illustrates these points.

Sub-systems influence the entire system: The case of Thapelo

Thapelo, who is a grade 10 learner, has a friend who abuses drugs. His friend was arrested by the police after they found drugs in his school bag during a drug search at school. The parents were informed about the incident. As a result, Thapelo's parents told him to stay away from his friend. Thapelo ignored his parents' guidance. After a month, Thapelo was also caught with drugs at school.

The incident described above affected the pattern of Thapelo's family functioning and other levels, as follows:

- **Family level:** Thapelo's drug-abuse problem affected his parents and their parenting style. His parents were shocked by the news and did not believe that their own child was involved in drugs. They had to deal with the shock and they had to strategise how to address Thapelo's situation. They had to seek information from professionals on how to deal with this shocking news. They changed the way in which they treated him because they had lost trust in him. They investigated why he abused drugs, who introduced him to drugs, where the drugs came from, when he started consuming drugs, and how to help him to stop abusing drugs. During that process, the parents' attention shifted from other siblings and was directed to Thapelo. Thapelo has two siblings, and they were also affected by Thapelo's drug problem because their parents' attention was on Thapelo. They felt rejected by their parents and started misbehaving in order to get their parents' attention back.

- **School level:** Thapelo's drug-abuse problem affected his learning. He was suspended from school for a month. This affected his progress and scholastic performance. He developed low self-esteem because his classmates started to isolate him. He started to hate school and as a result he failed Grade 10.

- **Community level:** Thapelo's parents were ashamed of what Thapelo had done. They were disappointed in him. The incident affected their relationship with the community and church. The parents kept Thapelo's drug abuse a secret from the neighbours, the priest, and the church congregation. Community members who heard about Thapelo's drug abuse did not want him to befriend their children, because they regarded him as a bad influence.

- **Government level – law enforcement:** Thapelo was arrested by the police. He was released on bail, which affected his parent's finances. He was later given a warning.
- **Medical and psychological help:** Thapelo consulted a psychologist and psychiatrist. He was referred to a rehabilitation centre to get professional help during the process of dealing with his drug problem. This process also affected his parents' finances, as this help cost a considerable amount of money.

CHECK YOUR PROGRESS

- Explain family factors that contribute to child development.
- Discuss how children's behaviour can affect the pattern of family functioning.

Law and childhood

Law is a key element in the process of social change (James & James, 2004). As James and James (2004) explain, law is integral to the production, regulation and reproduction of childhood over time. Law deals with childhood as a universal but specific, social, and legal category, which is distinguishable from adulthood. Law is regarded as an important element in the social construction of childhood because it is constituted through everyday actions and practices. It defines the key parameters of childhood: the age of consent in sexual relations, the age of school going, and the age of school leaving in any particular social and cultural context. In addition, law provides a mechanism whereby children in difficulty can be protected. It does this by articulating both principles and procedures through which the issues raised for individual children and their widely differing selves and circumstances can be addressed (James & James, 2004).

Children are politically excluded; for example, they are not allowed to vote. In South Africa, as in many other countries, people have to be 18 years old before they can vote. Some theorists have considered the extent to which – as a result of social, political, and economic developments – children are becoming increasingly excluded as a minority group from the adult social world through the tightening-up of generational boundaries. Others have suggested that childhood in Western contexts may be fast disappearing in the face of rapid technological and social change (Postman 1983, Buchingham, 2000, in James & James, 2004).

Universality of law

The law aids an understanding of the treatment of children within the legal system, but it also contains contradictions and paradoxes. As Fionda (2001, in James & James, 2004) points out, the conception of childhood adopted within any area of law can impact significantly on the way in which children are treated or in which their needs and interests are met. The universality of childhood as a life-space, in conjunction with the universalising tendencies of law, has in recent years triggered a profoundly important international discourse about childhood.

Such universalising tendencies in relation to childhood have been evident since the early part of the twentieth century with the promulgation of the Geneva Declaration on the Rights of the Child, followed by the United Nations Declaration on the Rights of the Child in 1959, and a plethora of subsequent international statements and declarations of varying levels of scope and significance (James and James, 2004). In terms of its impact on the international discourse about children and childhood, the most important of these is the United Nations Convention on the Rights of the Child (UNCRC), which was adopted by the United Nations General Assembly in 1989. This development was a reflection of the globalisation of child law.

Children's rights

When the United Nations introduced the UNCRC in 1989, this was the most significant international venture to protect children constitutionally. The UNCRC incorporates the full range of human rights, namely civil rights, cultural rights, political rights, and social rights. According to the UNCRC, the following are the basic human rights that children should have (UNICEF, 2007, in Louw & Louw, 2007):
- The right to survive
- The right to develop to the fullest
- The right to be protected from harmful influences, abuse, and exploitation
- The right to participate fully in family, cultural, and social life.

The four principles of the UNCRC are as follows:
- Non-discrimination
- Devotion to the best interest of the child
- The right to life, survival, and development
- Respect for the views of the child.

All the countries which agree with the Convention agree to abide by its obligations. South Africa officially joined this venture in 1995 (Louw & Louw, 2007), when it signed the UNCRC.

The introduction of the UNCRC not only attempted to create for the first time a truly international vision of childhood, but it also established the mechanism for the review of its implementation by signatories. Article 4 of the UNCRC (John, 1996, in James & James, 2004), stresses that children are to be seen as equals in that it gives children and teenagers the status of human beings with full rights, giving them the same value as adults. The UNCRC also has a theme on the 'best interest' principle. The theme emphasises that in all actions concerning children, the best interest of the child shall be a primary consideration.

The UNCRC highlights rights of freedom, rights of protection, and needs-based welfare rights. The problem with needs-based rights is that they are rooted in a perception of the developmental needs of children, and thus they are susceptible to being defined or moderated by political and cultural considerations. Unlike 'natural rights', needs-based rights are not fixed and universal but are highly contextual. The complication is that even the most extreme kind of needs have not traditionally been regarded as sufficient to justify a right.

Owing to the fact that one of the purposes of law is to protect the vulnerable and those living on the margins of society, the reason for the existence of the UNCRC (James & James, 2004) was to articulate the rights that were seen to be universal and central to the process of moving children from the margins to the centre of society. Articles 28 and 29 of the UNCRC recognise a child's rights to education, which should be directed at developing the child for active life as an adult and developing respect for the child's own cultural and national values and those of others (James & James, 2004, p. 85).

Children's rights, like human rights, refer to basic criteria or standards that are essential for developing people's potential and maintaining their dignity (Louw & Louw, 2007).

Read the box headed 'Children and South African law' for a South African perspective on the information above.

Children and South African law

In South Africa, some people who are unemployed beg for money, food or clothes at intersections. Some of them bring along children, who may be as young as two years old. The *Mail & Guardian Online* reported that in August 2010, the Gauteng Department of Health and Social Development, along with the police, removed children from people begging at the intersections (in most cases these people are the parents of the children). Even though the raid was widely publicised in advance, the officials did not obtain

Figure 8.2 Some of the adults who beg at intersections in South Africa are accompanied by children

court orders to remove the children and place them in temporary care homes (Parker, 'ConCourt deems', 2012).

The *Mail & Guardian Online* report said:

> *The Constitutional Court has ruled that parents of children who have been removed from their care by the state will now have access to an automatic review of that decision …*
>
> *Louise Du Plessis, an attorney for Lawyers for Human Rights …, said she was 'extremely pleased' with the ruling. She said social workers could have explored other options – such as investigating a family's situation while the child was still in the parents' care – if they needed to decide whether it was in the child's interest to remain with the family. Forced removal was extremely traumatic, she said, and was frequently abused by social workers ('ConCourt deems' parts of the Children's Act invalid' by Faranaaz Parker, Mail & Guardian Online. [http://www.mg.co.za/article/2012-01-11-concour-deems-sections-of-childrens-act-invalid] [Accessed 11 May 2012]).*

CASE STUDY

John is a 10-year-old boy. He is an orphan and lives with his grandmother, who is aged 75, and is unwell. The family does not have enough food. Unlike some boys of his age, John is unable to buy new fashionable clothes because the family depends on his grandmother's pension, which is R1 200 a month. John sells fruit and vegetables at the train station every weekend, in order to augment his grandmother's pension money. John is responsible for all the home chores, such as cleaning the house, cooking, and taking care of his sick grandmother. Unlike some boys of his age, he does not have the opportunity to play soccer and enjoy being in the company of his peers. His family situation has robbed him of his childhood.

Questions

1 'The terms "children" and "childhood" are interpreted differently in different cultures and generations.' Elaborate on this statement and give practical examples.

2 In the closing case study above, John is responsible for home chores that are normally done by adults. Critically explain John's case with regard to children's rights.

3 Critically explain the following categories of childhood definition, according to James & James (2004):
   a Generational space
   b Childhood
   c Children as citizens.

4 Briefly define 'childhood indicators' and explain their importance.

5 Explain and analyse 'fears as indicators of well-being'.

6 Who are vulnerable children? Explain and give practical examples.

7 Define resilience.

8 Discuss five strategies for developing or improving children's resilience.

9 Explain why law is regarded as an important element in the social construction of childhood.

10 Critically analyse the universality of law relating to childhood.

Conclusion

The terms 'children' and 'childhood' are conceptualised differently in different cultures and generations. For some people, childhood development is characterised by physical development, whereas for others, it is characterised by physiological developments and psychological developments. Children's standard of living, welfare, support, and marginalisation are assessed by means of childhood indicators. As citizens of the world, children have rights which should be protected. Negative environments can make children vulnerable. Children from families living in poverty are vulnerable to disease due to lack of nutrition and lack of health-care facilities. However, some children do not react negatively towards traumatic situations, but instead show resilience, despite adversity.

References

America's Children (2005). *Key indicators of well-being. Federal interagency Forum on Child and Family statistics.* [WWW document]. URL *http://www.childstats.gov/pdf/ac2005/ac_05.pdf.*

Ben-Arieh, Asher (2006). *Indicators of children's well-being: Theory and practice in a multi-cultural perspective.* Cambridge: Springler Publisher.

Bornstein, M.H. & Bradley, R.H. (Eds). (2010). *Socioeconomic status, parenting and child development.* Mahwah, NJ: Psychology Press, Laurence Erlbaum Associates.

Bronfenbrenner, Urie (1979). *The ecology of human development: Experiments by nature and design.* Cambridge, MA: Harvard University Press.

Cockburn, T. (1998). Children and citizenship in Britain. *Childhood, 5,* (1), 99–117.

Donald, D., Lazarus, S. & Lolwana, P. (2009). *Educational psychology in social context* (3rd ed.). Cape Town: Oxford University Press.

Du Preez, C. (2004). Health and well-being. In I. Eloff & L. Ebershon (Eds). *Keys to educational psychology* (p. 44–63). Cape Town: UCT Press.

Evans, G.W. & Wachs, T.D. (Eds). (2010). *Chaos and its influence on children's development. An ecological perspective.* Washington, DC: American Psychological Association.

James, A., Jenks, C. & Prout, A. (1998). *Theorising childhood.* Cambridge: Polity Press.

James, A. & James, L. (2004). *Constructing childhood: Theory, policy and social practice.* New York, NY: Palgrave Macmillan.

Louw, D. & Louw, A. (2007). *Child and adolescent development.* Bloemfontein: University of Free State, South Africa.

Moletsane, M. (2004). Families. In I. Eloff & L. Ebershon (Eds). *Keys to educational psychology* (p. 167–186). Cape Town: UCT Press.

Park, Y.J. & Khan, F. (2000). Helping the hidden victims. Sheltering children of abused women. In Y.J. Park, J. Fedler & Z. Dangor (Eds). *Reclaiming women spaces: New perspectives on violence against women and sheltering in South Africa* (p. 323–347). Johannesburg: Nisaa Institute for women's development.

Parker, F. (2012, January 11). ConCourt deems parts of Children's Act invalid. *Mail & Guardian Online.* http://mg.co.za/article/2012-01-11-concourt-deems-sections-of-childrens-act-invalid. 11 May 2012.

Qvorttrup, J. (1990). A voice for children in statistical and social accounting. In A. James & A. Prout (Eds). *Constructing and reconstructing childhood*. Basingstoke: Falmer.

Smith, A.B. (2008). *Children's rights and early childhood education. Children's Issues Centre, University of Otago*. [WWW document]. URL http://www.earlychildhoodaustralia.org.au/australian_journal_of_early_childhood/ajec_index_abstracts/childrens_rights_and_early_childhood_education.html.

Woodhead, Martin (1996). *In search of the rainbow: Pathways to quality in large-scale programmes for young disadvantaged children. Early Childhood Development: Practice and Reflections, 10*. The Hague: Bernard Van Leer Foundation.

CHAPTER NINE

CAREER DEVELOPMENT IN CHILDREN

Mark Watson, Mary McMahon and Louise Stroud

CASE STUDY

Devon's career development

Devon, when he was five years old, would say that he wanted to play for Bafana Bafana when he was asked 'What do you want to do when you grow up?' More than knowing he wanted to be a soccer player, he thought it would be a good job for boys; he was excited that he had just started playing junior soccer on weekends and he had scored his first goal. As Devon grew older, he realised that other children were better than he was at soccer. He had also grown to dislike the competitive and physical nature of the tackling element of the game.

When Devon was seven, his pet dog was hit by a car and was taken to the local vet. Devon visited the vet with his father, and he was excited that the vet could 'make my dog better'. Devon thought that he would really like to be able to help animals too. He told his parents that he wanted to be

---

Figure 9.1 Awareness of adult roles begins at a very young age through childhood experiences – at 11 years old, Devon wanted to be a lawyer when he grew up

a vet when he grew up. When Devon was in grade five, he learned from his friend that the vet had 'put her pet cat to sleep' because it had been very ill. The friend was upset. Devon decided that he would not like to do that, and he ruled out becoming a vet.

By the time Devon was 11 years old, his favourite show on TV was about crime, police, and lawyers. Devon thought being a police officer might be exciting, but he didn't want to have to 'fight bad people or use a gun'. From watching TV, he also saw that lawyers had 'nice cars and homes', and he learned that lawyers earned much more money than police officers. So he decided that he would be a lawyer instead. Devon's mother thought he would be a good lawyer because he had recently won a debating competition at his primary school.

LEARNING OBJECTIVES

At the end of this chapter you should be able to

- Understand the relationship between childhood development and career development
- Explain the key concepts of childhood career development
- Synthesise key findings from research about South African children's career development
- Consider children's career development in relation to socio-cultural and environmental contextual factors
- Explore the cawreer development of children by means of the prescribed assignment
- Apply career development concepts and research findings to the opening case study and closing case study.

Introduction

Childhood is referred to as the dawn of career development (Porfeli, Hartung & Vondracek, 2008). As reflected in Devon's story in the case study at the start of the chapter, awareness of adult roles begins at a very young age through childhood experiences. On a daily basis, children learn about adult life through seeing people going to work and being at work, and through their family lives, their school and community experiences, and their observation of media. Children make sense of their experiences by imagining themselves in certain roles to which they may or may not aspire. Through the experience of daily life, **childhood career development** is deeply embedded in the socio-cultural context in which it occurs (McMahon, Watson & Bimrose, 2010). Thus, the experiences and opportunities available to children vary according to their familial, socio-economic, and socio-cultural circumstances. The phenomenon of childhood career development is best understood through the lenses of

Childhood career development
the development of occupational awareness and occupational aspirations during childhood

two bodies of theory, specifically child development and career development (Watson & McMahon, 2007a). Child development theory has provided a foundation for career development theory by offering insight into the developmental tasks of childhood and the role of curiosity and exploration (Watson & McMahon, 2007a).

Understanding career development in childhood is critically important to a comprehensive understanding of the lifespan concept of career development (Hartung, Porfeli & Vondracek, 2005; McMahon & Watson, 2008; Watson & McMahon, 2005). Childhood provides foundational parameters that impact on later phases in the career developmental lifespan. For instance, failure to stimulate career curiosity in childhood can lead to adolescents making career decisions without sufficient exploration (Hartung, Porfeli & Vondracek, 2008). Watson and McMahon (2008) similarly suggest that career development in later life stages is 'too often grounded in a narrower, more stereotypical career awareness and exploration in childhood' (p. 82). For the purposes of this chapter, childhood is the period of 13 years of age and under (Watson & McMahon, 2005).

This chapter considers current theories of children's career development. The chapter also explores the relationship of such theory to more general theories of childhood development, thus filling a critical gap in the career literature to date (Watson & McMahon, 2007a). The chapter proceeds to describe more recent research that explores the interrelationship of developmental and career developmental tasks in South African children. Further, the chapter explores the growing body of research on the career development of children within a variety of South African contexts. Finally, the chapter considers the implications of career theory development and career research for the career development of South African children.

Childhood development and childhood career development

'What do you want to be when you grow up?' is a common question asked of children, and it is underpinned by an assumption that they will already be thinking about life as an adult. Despite this, career development tends to be regarded as relevant to adolescents and adults rather than children (for example, see Porfeli et al., 2008) even though it is widely accepted that career development is a lifespan process (for example, see Super, 1990). Many experts acknowledge that career development should be viewed holistically and that it has a focus beyond work or occupation because of the recursive relationship between work and all facets of life (for example, see Patton & McMahon, 2006).

Evidence of the occurrence of career development in childhood is found in the tasks and stages of long-established and highly regarded

Lifespan lifespace theory
a theory developed to conceptualise career development in terms of sequential life stages and different life roles over the lifespan

childhood development theories such as those of Erikson (1963, 1993) and Piaget (1977) and also in the socio-cultural theories of Vygotsky (1987) and Nelson (2007). And one of the most eminent theorists of career development, Super, in proposing his **lifespan lifespace theory** of career development, drew on child development theory, describing it as the 'only helpful literature' (Super, 1990, p. 231). Therefore, an examination of constructs from the child development literature related to career development will follow, in order to provide a foundation for the subsequent discussion of childhood career development from the perspective of career development theory. The examination will begin by considering relevant constructs from Piaget's theory. Then it will consider constructs from Erikson's theory. (Earlier chapters of this book have already provided detailed descriptions of each of these theories. This chapter will consider only sections of the theories relevant to the career development of children.)

Piaget (1977) focuses on the cognitive development of children and describes four major periods: the sensorimotor, pre-operational, concrete operational, and formal operational periods or stages. Of Piaget's four stages, the first three apply to children under the age of 12 years. Children under the age of seven years are egocentric in nature and they find it difficult to distinguish between fantasy and reality. Young children may imagine themselves in fantasy roles such as television stars, animals, or people they know; these children may be regarded as independent explorers and active constructers of their knowledge (Verenikina, 2003). Thus the aspiration of Devon, in the case study at the start of this chapter, at the age of five years, to be a Bafana Bafana soccer player may be based more on fantasy than on reality. As children grow older, they develop the ability to understand the world of work and the roles and occupations they observe around them. For example, they observe their parents in roles in the home and in the community, and they observe the occupations of others in their daily lives from experiences such as going to a shop, visiting a doctor or watching a tradesperson at work. Older children are more realistic in their thinking. Devon began to learn through his experience of playing soccer that his ability and his values might not be suited to a career in professional sport.

Erikson (1963, 1993) presents his theory of psychosocial development as a series of eight stages across the life cycle, as chapter two described. Five of these stages relate to childhood. Common to all the stages is the fact that individuals experience a crisis that needs to be resolved in order to progress to the subsequent developmental stage. The five stages that relate to children are:

- Trust versus mistrust (birth to 1 year of age)
- Autonomy versus shame and doubt (second year)

- Initiative versus guilt (third to sixth year)
- Industry versus inferiority (6 to 12 years of age)
- Identity versus role confusion (12 to 18 years of age).

From birth, children develop a sense of trust in themselves and their surrounding world through their experience of care from parents or other caregivers. Emanating out of this sense of trust, children begin to develop a sense of autonomy as they realise that they can determine their own behaviour and begin to act on their own initiative as a consequence of enhanced physical mobility. In the next stage, 'industry versus inferiority', children begin to develop work habits and skills through tasks at home and their attendance at school. Erikson regards this stage as an 'entrance to life' (1968, p. 172) and as a socially decisive period in which the broader societal environment becomes significant.

Implicit in the theories of Piaget and Erikson is the notion of learning. Vygotsky extended Piaget's notion of the child as an active learner by recognising the important role of their socio-cultural context (Verenikina, 2003). Vygotsky (1987) suggests that children learn in three ways:
- **Imitative learning:** Through imitative learning, children copy other people. For example, they may play games in which they imitate adults with whom they have interacted, such as doctors, nurses or teachers.
- **Instructive learning:** Teachers and other adults facilitate instructive learning.
- **Collaborative learning:** Through play and other activities such as classroom experiences and work in the home, children learn through collaboration with others. For example, by collaborating as a family member in the home, a child may learn about gender roles.

Figure 9.2 Collaborative learning: children learn through collaboration with others

In moving beyond Vygotsky's theory, Nelson (2007) emphasises learning as a two-way social process between children and their socio-cultural contexts. The case study of Devon at the beginning of this chapter illustrates Devon's career development in the context of his daily life.

In considering the foundational constructs of child development theory, it is evident that the development of skills, knowledge, and attitudes is embedded in the socio-cultural context in which a child lives. A critical element of the socio-cultural context that influences the learning process of children is that related to the world of work and the work-related roles of adults. Childhood development implicitly facilitates an increasing understanding of the world of work and children's potential future roles in it. The following section describes how career developmental theories of childhood account for this learning process.

CHECK YOUR PROGRESS

- What key features of each of the three stages of Piaget's cognitive development theory for children under 12 years of age may be applicable to children's career-development learning?
- What key features of each of the five stages of Erikson's psycho-social development theory for childhood may be applicable to children's career-development learning?
- How do the three forms of learning suggested by Vygotsky apply to children's career-development learning?

Childhood career development theories

As illustrated in child development theory and also in the case study of Devon at the beginning of this chapter, career development begins in childhood, and it is a relevant field of study worthy of inclusion in a text on childhood development. From a very young age, Devon had begun to think about his life as an adult. In essence, early in his life, Devon began to construct a concept of himself in adult work roles on the basis of the learning garnered from his experiences in the socio-cultural context in which he was growing up.

As Devon's story shows, much of his learning about career development was unintentional, inspired by experiences that he engaged in across his childhood. Most theory about childhood career development has focused on this unintentional learning about career development. In so doing, these theories have emphasised *what* is learned more than *how* learning takes place (Watson & McMahon, 2007a). An enhanced understanding of the foundational period of childhood career development could better inform understanding of career development in subsequent life stages. Further, such enhanced understanding could inform the nature of interventions that would encourage intentional learning about career development, as a foundation for the decisions and transitions of adolescence and adulthood.

At a theoretical level, childhood career development has been accounted for by a number of theorists, most notably Super (1990) and Gottfredson (2005), both of whom describe stages through which children pass. The following sections consider theoretical accounts of childhood career development. Where possible, they provide illustrative examples from the case study of Devon.

Super's lifespan lifespace theory

In Super's (1990) lifespan lifespace theory, the growth stage relates to children from birth to 14 years of age. Within the growth stage, there are 4 sub-stages, including:
- Curiosity (birth to 4 years)
- Fantasy (4 to 7 years)
- Interests (7 to 11 years)
- Capacities (11 to 14 years).

Within the growth stage, there are also nine dimensions of career development:
- Information
- Curiosity
- Exploration
- Key figures
- Interests
- Locus of control
- Perspective
- Self-concept
- Planfulness.

During childhood, there are four developmental tasks to be achieved:
- Becoming concerned about the future
- Increasing personal control over one's life
- Convincing oneself to achieve in both school and work
- Acquiring competent work habits and attitudes (Super, Savickas & Super, 1996).

In regard to these four developmental tasks to be achieved during childhood, Devon has clearly realised that adults work, and he has identified a possible future option for himself. His choice of soccer player is based on what he has learned by watching soccer on TV and also through his own experience of playing soccer. Thus Devon has begun to develop interests and a self-concept in relation to the future world of work. During the growth stage, young children's initial ideas may be fantasy related and become more realistic as they grow older. Critical to Super's theory is the development of self-concept, that is, the images children have of themselves in various life roles. Children may develop multiple self-concepts, including a vocational self-concept, particularly in terms of their increasing exposure to adult career roles and the future world of work.

Gottfredson's theory of circumscription and compromise

Theory of circumscription and compromise
a theory describing how children eliminate occupational aspirations on the basis of gender and social status as they grow older, leading them to choose from a range of acceptable occupations

A further account of the development of self-concept is provided through Gottfredson's (1981, 2005) **theory of circumscription and compromise**, which describes how individuals develop their occupational aspirations over time. To develop self-concept, Gottfredson conceptualises four stages of cognitive development, specifically orientation to size and power (3 to 5 years of age), orientation to sex roles (6 to 8 years), orientation to social valuation (9 to 13 years), and orientation to internal unique self (14 years and older). Thus from a young age Devon became aware that adults assume work roles and by the age of five he was beginning to identify occupations he regarded as good jobs for boys (that is, soccer player). At a later age, Devon was aware of the social benefits of the occupation of lawyer in comparison with that of police officer. Further, he was also beginning to align his own capacities and abilities with the occupation of lawyer. Thus, across his childhood, Devon's occupational aspirations became increasingly more realistic. As illustrated through the example of Devon, Gottfredson emphasises that as children grow older they circumscribe (that is, eliminate) occupational aspirations, first on the basis of gender and second on the basis of social status. Consequently, a range of acceptable occupations is created. Compromise is the process in which choices in later childhood and early adolescence need to be made from among the preferred alternatives.

More recent theories

Recursive interaction
how children influence and are influenced by the socio-cultural and environmental contexts in which they develop

The theories of both Super (1990) and Gottfredson (2005) introduce the notion of **recursive interaction** between children and the socio-cultural and environmental contexts in which they develop. While these two theories acknowledge several sources of career development learning – such as family, school, society, peer group and community – other theoretical formulations of children's career development have placed a greater emphasis on such contextual factors. Similar to the theories of child development, theories of the career development of children recognise the fundamental principle that human development 'is shaped by its historical–cultural context' (Sigelman & Rider, 2006, p. 9). For example, more recent theories (for example career construction theory; Savickas, 2002), take account of the embeddedness of people in their environments and the interaction between them and their environments. Yet there has been persistent criticism, especially in the South African context, that socio-cultural factors have not been adequately considered in career development theory (Maree & Molepo, 2006; Stead & Watson 2006; Watson 2009).

Further, theory of childhood career development is not yet adequately related to childhood development theory and other disciplines (Hartung et al., 2008; Schultheiss, 2008; Watson & McMahon, 2008). This limits people's understanding of children's career development and, in more recent times, it has led to research that may inform theory development. For instance, Schultheiss (2003) has explored several social and relational influences – such as the family – on children's career development.

Similarly, Howard and Walsh (2010) have explored children's reasoning about careers. Howard and Walsh (2010) propose a six-level developmental model in which the highest level of reasoning is based on children's systemic interaction with their environment.

In the South African context, research is needed to enhance the understanding of children's career development. The next section explores this.

CHECK YOUR PROGRESS

- How might Super's nine dimensions of career development in childhood be related to the four developmental tasks that need to be achieved in childhood?
- What is the difference between circumscription and compromise in Gottfredson's theory?
- How do you understand the concept of recursive interaction in relation to children and the environments within which they develop?

Research on childhood career development in South Africa

The limited research on children's career development has been acknowledged for more than half a century (Borow, 1964; Vondracek & Kirchner, 1974; Watson & McMahon, 2004a). Borow's original prediction that this gap in the career literature would become a significant focus of career research has largely been unrealised to date. The result is a limited body of research that lacks depth and cohesion (Watson & McMahon, 2004a, 2008). There have, however, been two significant reviews (Hartung et al., 2005; Watson & McMahon, 2005) and a meta-analysis (Porfeli et al., 2008) of childhood career development research in the international literature in the last decade. Besides re-emphasising the limited research on childhood career development, this literature demonstrates that an understanding of children's career development is more theoretically implied than researched.

Since the middle of the last century, career theory has focused on the lifespan from childhood through to old age. Yet most research on career development has remained 'lifespan limited' in its skewed focus on adolescents and adulthood (Watson & McMahon, 2008). International career research that has focused on children has also been skewed in its predominant exploration of **intra-individual influences** on children's career development, such as their age, gender, and interests (Watson, McMahon & Longe, 2011). Further, children's career development has been explored almost exclusively in the international literature in relation to children's occupational aspiration development.

The limited focus of such research has led to more recent calls for children's career development to be understood systemically (Schultheiss, 2003). Schultheiss (2008) suggests that career developmental processes in childhood are best researched 'rooted within life contexts' (p. 20), while others have argued further that research into children's career development needs to move beyond the traditional focus on the life contexts of middle-class socio-economic settings (Watson, McMahon, Foxcroft & Els, 2010). The need to embed the career research of children contextually is supported by Watson and McMahon's (2007b) suggestion that the career development of children represents a 'recursive process between children and a broad range of social, environmental and contextual influences' (p. 566). Watson and McMahon (2007b) believe that there is a need for research on the potential influence of the following on children's career development: society, socio-economic status, ethnicity, the media, the home environment, parents, and the school.

The career development of South African children remains an under-researched field, which has a similar skewed focus to that of the international research on children's career development. Thus the predominant focus in career research has been on white middle-class children in South Africa (Stead & Schultheiss, 2003, 2010; Watson & McMahon, 2004b, 2005, 2007b), with a resultant negligible body of research on black primary school children. Further, South African research on children's career development has largely focused on the development of their occupational aspirations (Watson et al., 2010).

Intra-individual influences

personal factors within individuals (such as their age, gender, and personality) that could impact on their career development

There has been a body of research on white, middle-class, urban South African children's career development. One research focus has been psychometric, with Stead and Schultheiss (2003, 2010) developing a Childhood Career Development Scale based on Super's nine dimensions of career development for children (Super, 1990). Other research has explored several career developmental behaviours of middle-class, urban, and English-speaking primary school children. For instance, several studies have explored the recursive relationship between children's career development and their contextual settings. Watson and McMahon (2004b) established that South African primary school children perceived their personal characteristics to be related to their occupational aspirations. However, how this matching of intra-individual factors with occupational aspirations takes place could not be adequately explained by the matching processes described in international career theories. McMahon and Watson (2005) explored the type of occupational information that South African children want. These authors established that the desired occupational information is related less to children's interests or to the nature of work, and more to broader concerns about their future lifestyle and the practical task of how to seek information. A more recent study explored whether children could relate their primary school activities to the future world of work (Watson & McMahon, 2007b). This research established that South African primary school children could make up to five connections between curricular, extra-curricular, and general school activities to future occupations that interested them.

Two recent studies have explored the career development of South African children from more diverse socio-economic and ethnic backgrounds. The first study to focus on the occupational aspiration development of South African urban, senior primary school, Xhosa-speaking children of low socio-economic status, reported that these children aspired more to occupations of social type – for example teacher, social worker, and nurse – and investigative type – for example doctor and lawyer (Watson, McMahon, Foxcroft and Els, 2010). An important finding of this research was that over 80 per cent of this sample of 274 grade five and grade six children aspired to high-status occupations, that is, occupations that would require professional training at a tertiary educational institution. There were few gender differences.

More recently, Watson et al. (2011) have provided baseline information on the career development occupational interests and aspirations of rural, black, senior primary school children of low socio-economic status. Similar to the findings on urban, Xhosa-speaking children, the results demonstrate that rural, black children were more interested in and aspired more to occupations at professional status level in social- and investigative-type categories. Several significant gender differences were evident, with girls aspiring more to social-type occupations and boys aspiring more to investigative-type occupations. The children's occupational aspirations also appeared to reflect gender traditionality, with girls aspiring towards nurse, teacher, and social worker, and boys towards police officer. Interestingly, such a finding is consistent with South African labour-market statistics that suggest that women are more dominant in the former occupations and males in the latter (Statistics South Africa, 2009). This finding may reflect the recursive relationship that children have with their environment, in which the gendered labour market influences the occupational aspirations of these children.

Linking childhood development and childhood career development in South Africa

While it is evident that career development is a process that spans the length of a child's natural development and that career development is influenced by many personal and contextual factors unique to each child's experience, childhood career development is a relatively new sphere of childhood development. Consequently, very little research has been conducted to date that sufficiently explores or describes the potential relationship between the two developmental domains (Kay, 2011; Van der Westhuyzen, 2011).

Some of the first research to describe the possible interrelationship of a child's career development and childhood development within the South African context specifically was conducted at the Nelson Mandela Metropolitan University (NMMU) in 2011. Here, two independent studies (Kay, 2011; Van der Westhuyzen, 2011) used the Griffiths Mental Development Scales–Extended Revised (GMDS–ER) and the Childhood Career Development Scale (CCDS) on 2 independent samples of 30 South African children between the ages of 8 years and 8 years and 4 months in order to establish any statistically significant relationships between childhood development and childhood career development tasks. To limit the possible influence of various gender differences and socio-economic differences, both sample groups included only one gender (that is, only male or only female), and participants were limited to those falling into the middle-to-upper class socio-economic status groups.

Although no statistically significant relationship between childhood career development and childhood development could be concluded from either study, the findings were nonetheless positive. Statistically significant relationships were found to exist between certain sub-scales of the GMDS-ER and CCDS, which would indicate an interrelationship between aspects of a child's career development and child development

(Van der Westhuyzen, 2011). For example, a correlation was found between the development of a child's eye–hand co-ordination (as assessed on the GMDS-ER) and the Key Figure sub-scale on the CCDS, which assesses how much value children place on influential role models during their development. Involved parents and teachers, aware of the importance of the development of fine motor skills in children, may encourage tasks such as drawing shapes and writing letters during playtime. They may also introduce toys specifically designed to develop fine motor skills, thus enhancing children's perceptions of parents and teachers as key figures in this specific area of their development (Van der Westhuyzen, 2011).

A weak positive correlation between childhood development and childhood career development was established from both studies, which would indicate the need for further study into the possible relationship between childhood development and childhood career development within the South African context (Kay, 2011; Van der Westhuyzen, 2011). Kay (2011) drew on Super's theory of career development as a gradual process to explain the overall weak correlation between childhood development and childhood career development. She proposed that, by contrasting Super's theory of career development with Erikson's theories of childhood development (which describe childhood development as a particularly rapid process), it could be hypothesised that 'career development and childhood development progress as separate but parallel processes that begin at different points and possibly proceed at different paces' (Kay, 2011, p. 147). These variations in 'starting points' and 'paces' in childhood development and childhood career development may explain the lack of a more significant relationship between the two developmental domains.

Despite no statistically significant relationship having been established between childhood development and childhood career development in either study, the possibility of a stronger relationship between the two cannot be ruled out; thus the potential interrelationship is important for practical consideration (Kay, 2011). As parents, educators, and individuals working in the helping professions in South Africa seek to guide children practically through the often tenuous transitions from early childhood to adulthood, they should consider how to incorporate career development opportunities practically into children's play environments and learning environments. Childhood career development needs to be appropriately addressed from as early as a primary school level, so as to enhance children's career exploration alongside their natural development and progress.

Read the box headed 'Concepts' for further exploration of key concepts, suggestions for further reading, and a consideration of some pertinent ethical issues.

Concepts

Think back to when you were a child. Get a clear picture in your mind about where you lived and who the significant people in your life were. Reflect on your likes and dislikes, your abilities and your hopes for the future at that time. Think about what you wanted to be when you grew up. You may remember your aspirations at different ages.

How did you learn about these aspirations? What did you know about these aspirations? What influenced you away from these aspirations?

Relate your reflections to the developmental stages of Super and Gottfredson.

Extra readings

Gottfredson, L.S. (2005). Applying Gottfredson's theory of circumscription and compromise in career guidance and counseling. In S.D. Brown & R.W. Lent (Eds). *Career development and counseling: Putting theory and research to work* (p. 71–100). Hoboken, NJ: John Wiley.

Super, D.E., Savickas, M. & Super, C. (1996). The life-span, life-space approach to careers. In D. Brown & L. Brooks (Eds). *Career choice and development: Applying contemporary theories to practice* (3rd ed.) (p. 121–178). San Francisco, CA: Jossey-Bass.

Ethical issues

Besides the standard ethical issues that are related to research with children, the socio-cultural context within which children live presents researchers with specific challenges. For example, in the context of South Africa, there is an increase in child-headed households. This raises the issue of the absence of appropriate adults to provide informed consent.

ACTIVITY

Assignment

Career conversations with children

Conduct a career conversation with at least two children that you know, preferably a child under the age of seven years and a child in the middle- to upper-childhood period. Ask them about what they want to do when they grow up, using a series of questions such as: What do you want to do when you grow up? How did you learn about that? What do you know about that job? What would you like about being a …? What would make you good at being a …?

Points to discuss

Subsequent to the completion of the conversations, reflect on each child's career development, guided by the following questions:

- How can the information the children provided to you be understood through the lens of the major developmental theories and career developmental theories?
- How would you describe the recursive relationship between socio-cultural influences and environmental influences on the two children's aspirations and learning about career development?

Critical thinking question

What is the relationship between childhood development and childhood career development? Consider this question in relation to the two children with whom you conducted your conversations.

Childhood career development for most South African children is systemically influenced by the environments in which they develop. Read the case study about Thathu, which demonstrates this.

CASE STUDY

Thathu's career development

Thathu was 13 years old and she lived in a rural area in one of the more impoverished South African provinces. Her mother worked as a cleaner, and she left for work early every morning and came home very tired late in the evening. Thathu walked with her siblings to school every day. Thathu liked going to school and loved her grade seven teacher, Mrs Mpofu. Mrs Mpofu 'was nice' to all of the children and encouraged them to work hard at school because it would help them 'get good jobs one day'. Thathu wanted to become a teacher, like Mrs Mpofu. Even though Thathu did very well at school, she worried about not being able to do her homework properly because she had to look after her younger siblings after school and do domestic chores in readiness for her mother's return in the evening.

Thathu's mother told Thathu that being a teacher would be a good job, but privately she wondered how this could happen because of the family's domestic and financial circumstances. Mrs Mpofu, however, had commenced a process of nominating Thathu, as a deserving student, for a bursary to a good high school in a nearby city.

Questions

1   Consider your own career development in childhood. In what ways could you have circumscribed and compromised your occupational aspirations?

2   Provide some examples from your own childhood development that would support the three forms of learning suggested by Vygotsky.

3   Describe how the socio-cultural and environmental contexts of South Africa's apartheid past could have had a negative recursive interaction with children's career development?

Conclusion

While career development in childhood may seem distant from the career decisions and transitions of adolescence and adulthood, there is clear evidence in the theories of child development and childhood career development that career development is relevant in the lives of children. Indeed childhood career development provides a foundation for career development across the lifespan. Consequently, childhood career development needs greater attention in research, theory, and practice.

The research reviewed in this chapter is the beginning of an evidence base for theory building within the South African context. Further, a more focused research and theory base will inform intentional interventions in the career development of children within the socio-cultural contexts in which they live. The case studies of Devon (at the start of the chapter) and Thatu (at the end) clearly illustrate how differently socio-cultural context can influence the career development of South African children. Watson and McMahon (2007a) suggest, in this regard, that children can learn from their socio-cultural context. They propose developing a greater awareness of childhood career development in families, schools, and community role models in order to stimulate intentional learning about career development. As this chapter illustrates, career development in childhood has received little attention, despite the fact that is highly relevant, and it warrants greater attention within the socio-cultural context of South Africa.

References

Borow, H. (1964). An integral view of occupational theory and research. In H. Borow (Ed.). *Man in a world at work* (p. 364–388). Boston, MA: Houghton Mifflin.
Erikson, Erik H. (1963). *Childhood in society* (2nd ed.). New York, NY: Norton.
Erikson, Erik H. (1968). *Identity, youth and crisis.* New York, NY: Norton.
Erikson, Erik H. (1993). *Childhood in society: The landmark work on the significance of childhood.* New York, NY: Norton.

Gottfredson, L.S. (1981). Circumscription and compromise: A developmental theory of occupational aspirations. *Journal of Counseling Psychology, 28*, 545–579.

Gottfredson, L.S. (2005). Applying Gottfredson's theory of circumscription and compromise in career guidance and counseling. In S.D. Brown & R.W. Lent (Eds). *Career development and counseling: Putting theory and research to work* (p. 71–100). Hoboken, NJ: John Wiley.

Hartung, P.J., Porfeli, E.J. & Vondracek, F.W. (2005). Child vocational development: A review and reconsideration. *Journal of Vocational Behavior, 66*, 385–419.

Hartung, P.J., Porfeli, E.J. & Vondracek, F.W. (2008). Career adaptability in childhood. *The Career Development Quarterly, 57*, 63–74.

Howard, K.A.S. & Walsh, M.E. (2010). Conceptions of career choice and attainment: Developmental levels in how children think about careers. *Journal of Vocational Behavior, 76*, 143–152.

Kay, L. (2011). Childhood development and career development in eight year-old South African boys. Unpublished master's thesis, Nelson Mandela Metropolitan University, Port Elizabeth.

Maree, K. & Molepo, M. (2006). The use of narratives in cross-cultural career counselling. In M. McMahon & W. Patton (Eds). *Career counselling: Constructivist approaches* (p. 69–81). Abingdon: Routledge.

McMahon, M. & Watson, M. (2005). Occupational information: What children want to know. *Journal of Career Development, 31*, 239–249.

McMahon, M. & Watson, M. (2008). Children's career development: Status quo and future directions. *The Career Development Quarterly, 57*, 4–6.

McMahon, M., Watson, M. & Bimrose, J. (2010, September). *Stories of careers, learning and identity across the lifespan: Considering the future narrative of career theory.* The Institute of Career Guidance. [WWW document]. URL *www.icg-uk.org/stories_ of_ careers.html*. 10 October 2010.

Nelson, Katherine (2007). *Young minds in social worlds: Experience, meaning and memory.* Cambridge, MA: Harvard University Press.

Patton & McMahon (2006). *Career development and systems theory: Connecting theory and practice.* Rotterdam: Sense Publishers.

Piaget, Jean (1977). *The development of thought: Equilibration of cognitive structures.* New York, NY: Viking Press.

Porfeli, E.J., Hartung, P.J. & Vondracek, F.W. (2008). Children's vocational development: A research rationale. *The Career Development Quarterly, 57*, 25–37.

Savickas, M.L. (2002). A developmental theory of vocational behavior. In D. Brown & Associates (Eds). *Career choice and development* (4th ed.) (p. 149–205). San Francisco, CA: Jossey-Bass.

Schultheiss, D.E.P. (2003). A relational approach to career counseling: Theoretical integration and practical application. *Journal of Counseling and Development, 81*, 301–310.

Schultheiss, D.E.P. (2008). Current status and future agenda for the theory, research and practice of childhood career development. *The Career Development Quarterly, 57*, 7–24.

Sigelman, C.K. & Rider, E.A. (2006). *Life-span human development* (5th ed.). Belmont, CA: Thomson Wadsworth.

Statistics South Africa. (2009). *Stats in brief, 2009* (1st ed.). Pretoria: Statistics South Africa.

Stead, G.B. & Schultheiss, D.E.P. (2003). Construction and psychometric properties of the Childhood Career Development Scale. *South African Journal of Psychology, 33*, 227–235.

Stead, G.B. & Schultheiss, D.E.P. (2010). Validity of Childhood Career Development Scale scores in South Africa. *International Journal for Educational and Vocational Guidance, 10*, 73–88.

Stead, G.B. & Watson, M.B. (2006). Indigenisation of career psychology in South Africa. In G.B. Stead & M.B. Watson (Eds). *Career psychology in the South African context* (2nd ed.). Pretoria: Van Schaik.

Super, D.E. (1990). A lifespan, lifespace approach to career development. In D. Brown & L. Brooks (Eds). *Career choice and development* (2nd Ed.) (p. 197–261). San Francisco, CA: Jossey-Bass.

Super, D.E., Savickas, M. & Super, C. (1996). The life-span, life-space approach to careers. In D. Brown & L. Brooks (Eds). *Career choice and development: Applying contemporary theories to practice* (3rd ed.) (p. 121–178). San Francisco, CA: Jossey-Bass.

Van der Westhuyzen, N. (2011). Childhood development and career development in eight year-old South African girls. Unpublished master's thesis, Nelson Mandela Metropolitan University, Port Elizabeth.

Verenikina, I. (2003). *Understanding scaffolding and the ZPD in educational research.* [WWW document]. URL *http://www.aare.edu.au/03pap/ver03682.pdf.* 15 March 2011.

Vondracek, S.I. & Kirchner, E.P. (1974). Vocational development in early childhood: An examination of young children's expressions of vocational aspirations. *Journal of Vocational Behavior, 5,* 251–260.

Vygotsky, L.S. (1987). Thinking and speech. In R.W. Rieber & A.S. Carton (Eds). *The collected works of L.S. Vygotsky* (Vol. 1) (p. 37–285). New York, NY: Plenum Press.

Watson, M. (2009). Transitioning contexts of career psychology in South Africa. *Asian Journal of Counselling, 16,* 133–148.

Watson, M. & McMahon, M. (2004a). Children's career development: A metatheoretical perspective. *Australian Journal of Career Development, 13,* 7–12.

Watson, M. & McMahon, M. (2004b). Matching occupation and self: Does matching theory adequately model children's thinking? *Psychological Reports, 95,* 421–431.

Watson, M. & McMahon, M. (2005). Children's career development: A research review from a learning perspective. *Journal of Vocational Behavior, 67,* 119–132.

Watson, M. & McMahon, M. (2007a). Children's career development learning: A foundation for lifelong career development. In V.B. Skorikov & W. Patton (Eds). *Career development in childhood and adolescence* (p. 29–45). Rotterdam: Sense.

Watson, M. & McMahon, M. (2007b). School and work: Connections made by South African and Australian primary school children. *South African Journal of Education, 27,* 565–577.

Watson, M. & McMahon, M. (2008). Children's career development: Metaphorical images of theory, research and practice. *The Career Development Quarterly, 57,* 75–83.

Watson, M., McMahon, M., Foxcroft, C. & Els, C. (2010). Occupational aspirations of low socioeconomic black South African children. *Journal of Career Development, 37,* 717–734.

Watson, M., McMahon, M. & Longe, P. (2011). Occupational interests and aspirations of rural black South African children: Considerations for theory, research and practice. *Journal of Psychology in Africa, 21,* (3), 413–420.

CHAPTER TEN

POVERTY, ADVERSITY, AND RESILIENCE

David Neves

CASE STUDY

Simpiwe was born to an impoverished black domestic worker in the 1970s, but raised by his maternal grandmother in the then rural Transkei homeland. Although he comes from a close-knit family, many of Simpiwe's memories of his childhood centre on the grinding poverty he and his five siblings endured, as they relied on small sums of money set back by their mother from the city, and a homestead garden they cultivated. Simpiwe recalls growing up in a rural village. He remembers both his poor-quality schooling and his first pair of shoes, received when he was 12 years old.

Showing some academic potential, Simpiwe was sent to live with an aunt in Soweto, where he attended a better-quality school. His determination saw him secure a scarce job as a packer at a supermarket, while he completed his schooling. However, dreams of further study were limited by his family's poverty. The odds remained stacked against Simpiwe: many of his siblings, extended family, and friends had succumbed to illness, criminality, or violence, or struggled with the sense of hopelessness of living in a severely resource-deprived context.

LEARNING OBJECTIVES

By the end of this chapter you should be able to:

- Explain the factors which create and perpetuate poverty in present-day South Africa
- Define poverty, and reflect critically on the limitation of income-based or asset-based definitions of poverty
- Be able to explain how poverty adversely impacts on human development
- Describe the manner and mechanisms by which poverty is reproduced from one generation to the next
- Describe the potential contribution that psychology can make to understanding and responding to poverty
- Describe the concept of resilience, and the factors that shape its effects.

Introduction

Poverty
a state of having insufficient resources to meet basic human needs; many accounts of poverty further expand on the notion of material deprivation, and stress both the relational aspects of poverty, including the absence of choice and opportunities

This chapter will consider the impact of **poverty** and adversity on human development. It seeks to examine how the negative experiences associated with poverty and adversity – such as hunger, deprivation, and violence – can shape the course of human development, and specifically child development. The chapter will do this with specific reference to the South African context.

The chapter begins by briefly looking at South Africa's history of racial dispossession and discrimination, and how the legacy of this has served to disadvantage black South Africans and their children. The chapter also briefly considers the way in which poverty continues and its ill effects endure, almost two decades since the formal end of apartheid. Against the backdrop of widespread poverty and adversity in South Africa, the chapter seeks to consider the nature of resilience, in other words the way in which many vulnerable individuals survive and even thrive under these conditions.

Examining these questions of poverty, adversity, and resilience allows the chapter also to consider larger conceptual issues within psychology, such as the relationship between an individual and the larger context (household, community, state, and economy) within which he or she is located. The chapter implicitly asks how to understand the dynamics between an individual and the context of the surrounding world.

In order to understand the effects of poverty and adversity, this chapter focuses attention on the interrelation between individual human development and the context more generally. The notion of the **socially embedded** nature of human development is particularly useful. The basic argument is that human development represents an internalisation and appropriation of the external world, and this argument helps in thinking about how the context comes to shape an individual's human development.

Socially embedded
firmly set or located in a social context, and therefore influenced by it

Poverty in South Africa

Upper middle-income country
a country classified by the World Bank, on the basis of several economic indicators, as ranking towards the top end of the middle-income countries

Between 500 million and a billion people across the world are trapped in poverty. Despite its status as an '**upper middle-income country**', South Africa has high and persistent levels of poverty. More than half the population is poor, with a third of the population below the international poverty line of two US dollars per day (Hoogeveen & Özler, 1996). The roots of poverty in South Africa can be traced from the beginnings of the colonial encounter between European settlers and indigenous African people more than 300 years ago, and through a long history of violence, dispossession, and racially based discrimination. Despite the end of race-based discrimination with the dismantling of apartheid in 1994, this legacy of disadvantage endures. In present-day South Africa, class divisions and socio-economic disadvantage still follow largely racial lines, and black people make up more than 95 per cent of the poor.

Poverty created by apartheid and colonialism and their legacies

Not only did apartheid and colonialism systematically impoverish black South Africans, but the onerous legacy of apartheid and colonialism also continues to recreate poverty in the present day.

Poverty exists for different reasons. Globally, the poor are often socially marginalised groups – such as nomads, indigenous people, low-caste groups, refugees or migrants – or people with impairments or illnesses. Frequently, the poor are also female and often older people (such as widows). In South Africa, poverty correlates with race because of the historical legacy of dispossession, and the workings of the economic order, which perpetuates poverty. This can be elaborated on in terms of four key legacies (Philip, 2010), described below.

Spatial legacies

The logic of apartheid spatial planning entailed clustering impoverished black people in outlying urban townships and far-flung former rural homelands (or 'bantustans'), typically located far from economic opportunity. Although the racist laws have been repealed, this exclusionary apartheid-era geography remains clearly evident in South Africa's cities and countryside to this day, underpinned by the market logic of property prices and by notions of urban planning that discourage informal economic activity. This spatial legacy continues to keep the poorest people furthest way from jobs and markets.

Asset legacies

Important assets (such as land, business ownership, and capital) continue to be distributed amongst South Africa's different racial groups in highly skewed ways. Despite transformative polices, black South Africans have disproportionately fewer of these assets than other racial groups. This is not to deny the existence of a growing group of black people who have managed to accumulate wealth; yet, in aggregate terms, black people remain significantly poorer than other population groups. Not only does this shortage of assets make black people poor in the present, but it also erodes their ability to escape their poverty in the future.

Figure 10.1 The spatial legacy of exclusionary apartheid-era geography continues to keep the poorest people furthest way from jobs and markets

Human-capital legacies

Human capital – such as good health and high-quality education – is, similarly, very unevenly distributed amongst the South African population. As a racial group, black people continue to lag behind on most of these measures of human development. On average, black people have lower life expectancy, higher morbidity (illness) rates, and lower levels of educational attainment than other racial groups (Bhorat & Kanbur, 2006), largely through a combination of their poverty and inferior access to resources and services.

Human capital
the aggregate capacity (including ability, knowledge, skill, and motivation) possessed by an individual, or a group of individuals, within a specific context

Economic legacies

The South African economy was historically built up on cheap, unskilled black labour, but has changed in the last three decades. The economy has become increasingly reliant on skilled employees and capital-intensive investment (in such things as machinery). Since 1994, employment and wages have therefore increased amongst high-income groups, while low-skill workers (who are disproportionately workers who are black) have lost jobs (Seekings & Nattrass, 2005; Banerjee, Galiani, Levinsohn & Woolard, 2006). Moreover the uneven nature of the South Africa's development path means that the powerful industrial economy exists amidst conditions of widespread underdevelopment and impoverishment. Unlike the econo-mies of many developing societies, the South African economy is domi-nated by a concentrated core of powerful and monopolistic firms, which makes it difficult for poor people to engage in or grow small and infor-mal enterprises. Similarly, the crowded rural labour reserves of the former homelands have long seen the decline of small-scale agriculture, and this decline limits the potential of impoverished people to subsist outside the realm of markets and money.

Against this economic backdrop it is unsurprising that many black people are impoverished, and that they rely on a variety of marginal activities to survive. These activities include part-time and informal work, support (borrowing and lending) from family and friends, and the state-provided social grants (for children, the disabled, and the elderly) received by more than a quarter of the population.

Poverty is not random and occurs in the context of inequality

Two additional points about poverty in South Africa need to be emphasised:
- **Widespread poverty in South Africa is not a random, accidental, and residual or even surprising phenomenon:** Pervasive, racialised poverty is the predictable consequence of racial dispossession, and of a capital-intensive, job-shedding economic-growth path. South Afri-ca's poor are, therefore, not poor *despite* the presence of an advanced industrial economy, but *because of* it. Impoverished black people are not excluded from systems of money, economy, and markets. Instead, they are incorporated into these on highly unfavourable terms: as casual labourers, poorly paid workers, social-grant recipients, and impoverished consumers (Du Toit & Neves, 2007).
- **South Africa's poor are impoverished in a context where others enjoy high levels of wealth:** South Africa suffers from one of the highest levels of income inequality in the world (read the box headed 'Poverty versus inequality', which gives further detail on this issue).

Poverty versus inequality

Despite a large proportion of its population living in poverty, South Africa is not a particularly poor country. It is, by global standards, an upper middle-income country, but it has one of the highest levels of income inequality in the world. **Income inequality** – the size of the gap between the rich and the poor – not only undermines human welfare and the accumulation of human capital (such as health and education), but it also generates additional social problems for everybody.

Income inequality
the size of the gap between the rich and the poor

Highly unequal societies are, therefore, arguably different from societies in which most people are poor (such as those of Mali or Chad) or mostly affluent (like those of most Western European countries or Japan). A high level of income inequality erodes social cohesion between citizens, which typically leads to high levels of violence and crime. Income inequality also tends to feed into political and economic arrangements that perpetuate the interests of **elites** (that is, people who are more affluent), frequently creating a vicious cycle of inequality that increases over time. In this way, income inequality, and its socially deleterious consequences, tends to be reinforced.

Elites
people who are more affluent and socially influential

Migrant labour
workers who travel away from their usual region of residence in order access employment opportunities

Normative assumption
the assumption that a particular widespread phenomenon, practice or arrangement is normal, and even desirable

The dynamics of poverty and the conditions which created it in South Africa have shaped the lives of black families for well over a century. The apartheid system was built on **migrant labour**, with black adults often separated from their families and children. Many of these dynamics have persisted in the post-apartheid period, and many black children continue to be raised by grandmothers, aunts, and sisters.

Migrant labour and domestic work reflect many of the inequalities of South African society. Typically, the black domestic workers who tend the children of middle-class people have their own children looked after by other poor black women, often in distant rural areas or townships. These spatially extended 'care chains' (Hochschild, 2000) are evident in many societies. They reflect a general trend: the demands of caring for the young, the very elderly, and the sick are often 'pushed down' on to the poorest-paid and most vulnerable of female workers.

South African families have not only been shaped by the legacy of poverty and migrant labour, but also by African cultural mores. Understanding of black families is sometimes impeded by the uncritical assumption that they are nuclear in form – in other words, a family unit consisting of two parents, and their biological children (recall that chapter eight mentioned this type of family). This **normative assumption** is pervasive and underpins much social theorising and development psychology in the West. It also contains powerful assumptions concerning the universality – and desirability – of childbearing in marriage, the primacy of maternal care, and residency in household units apart from extended kin or grandparents. All of these assumptions are at odds with the reality of the South African context. Evidence from anthropology and demography has questioned whether black households have ever been (or are even becoming) ordered in nuclear-family units (Russell, 2004). This evidence raises critical questions concerning the applicability, in the African context, of many standard assumptions regarding development.

Poverty and human development

How does poverty impact on human development? This section examines this question, but first a clear understanding of poverty is necessary. A common-sense understanding of poverty is as deprivation: as a lack of income and assets, or other important material dimensions such as adequate food, water, shelter, clothing, or access to health services. When people lack income, assets or basic possessions, it is readily agreed that they are poor. Drawing on income-based and asset-based notions of poverty, the points discussed below can be made about poverty.

Poverty and adverse circumstances often create a downward spiral of destitution

Poverty and the adverse circumstances associated with it often create a downward spiral of destitution and deepening of poverty over time. Poverty is not just the condition of material lack or deprivation; poverty is to be especially vulnerable to 'shocks' (unpredictable adverse events) that undermine the ability to survive or generate a livelihood. These 'shocks' can include illness, deaths in the family, the loss of employment, natural disasters (fires, droughts, floods), and even price shocks (sharp rises in food or fuel price).

Poverty sometimes creates conditions which make escape from it difficult

Poverty tends to create '**poverty traps**', reinforcing circumstances from which escape is difficult (Carter, 2007). For instance, many poor people find themselves in situations in which their poor health, low education, poor nutrition, and shortage of productive assets (for example tools, transport, a phone for communication) limit their ability to access economic opportunity and, therefore, their ability to escape their poverty. People sometimes talk metaphorically of the poor 'pulling themselves up by their own bootstraps', but this is, after all, difficult if a person has no boots!

Poverty trap
circumstance of deep, incapacitating, and self-reinforcing poverty from which escape is particularly difficult

Short-term survival is sometimes prioritised at the cost of escape from long-term poverty

Impoverished people are sometimes forced to prioritise their short-term survival at the cost of escape from long-term poverty. For example, when vulnerable people encounter a livelihood shock, often they respond in ways that jeopardise their long-term well-being, such as taking children out of school, or cutting back on meals or health care. These survival strategies ultimately undermine the prospects of long-term escape from poverty (Wood, 2003). For example, in rural communities it is not uncommon for droughts or floods to result in the distressed sale of valuable assets, such as livestock or ploughs, at giveaway prices, or desperate acts such as eating seed saved for the following season's crop. As impoverished people have fewer resources and options than better-resourced people, they are sometimes compelled to survive by engaging in activities that they know will undermine their well-being, and that of their children.

While income and assets are important, they seldom give a complete picture of poverty

Capabilities approach to poverty and underdevelopment
an approach that understands poverty and underdevelopment as reflecting people's absence of choices and opportunities to attain their full potential

To begin with, income is not very well correlated or matched to other measures of human development and well-being. Even at the level of countries, basic measures of human development such as health (life expectancy, infant mortality), education (literacy), and access to services (such as electricity and water) seldom correspond to national income. For example, the small island nation of Cuba, with a long history of redistributive investment in social services such as education and public health, has human-development indices that are comparable with or better than its much larger, and more affluent, neighbour, the USA. Understanding poverty simply as a lack of income or assets potentially obscures its causes and dynamics. Several people, including Nobel Prize winner Amartya Sen, argue for what has been called the **capabilities approach**. This approach understands poverty and underdevelopment as reflecting people's absence of choices and opportunities to attain their full potential. Conversely, Sen describes development as 'the removal of the various types of unfreedoms that leave people with little choice and little opportunity of exercising their reasoned agency' (1999, p. xiii). In this formulation, development, and the task of responding to poverty, is not simply about addressing the absence of income; it is about the lifting of the constraints (economic, material, social, and, even, psychological) that inhibit humans' attaining their potential. This is an important notion for developmental psychology because it suggests some of the relational aspects of poverty – an important idea that the next section will discuss further.

CHECK YOUR PROGRESS
- Describe the factors and historical legacies that perpetuate poverty in current day South Africa.
- 'Income-focused ways of defining poverty can be limited and reveal only a partial picture of poverty.' Discuss this statement, and describe alternative ways of examining and defining poverty.

Psychology and poverty

Sen's (1999) capabilities approach and his notion of poverty as 'unfreedom' are useful for thinking about poverty because they draw attention to the relational aspects of poverty and allow a consideration of the place of human agency (thinking, feeling, acting) in relation to the broader social, cultural, economic, and political process and structure. Sen examined famines and identified how starvation occurred, despite there being, on average, enough food – poor people simply could not access the food.

Therefore, poverty is often a distributional and, even, relational problem. This attention to context, including the social and political context, underscores the relational dimensions of poverty seldom captured by examination of income alone. These relational dimensions include the marginalisation, social isolation, vulnerability to exploitation, and erosion of personal dignity that often characterise the lives of the poor. The careful linking of the individual lifeworld to context also enables consideration of social and cultural dynamics, new technologies, health threats, social conflicts, and, even, changing dynamics related to the environment and climate.

This issue – the relationship between individual and society, human agency and social structure – is at the core of many of the human sciences, including developmental psychology. The critical challenge remains one of how to understand the way in which people act in the world and the extent to which the world influences the context in which individuals exercise their choices and actions. However, psychology has often struggled to reconcile these two poles. While some schools of thought – such as behaviourism, which chapter two discussed in some detail – have placed great emphasis on the role of the external world, much psychology has a strong bias towards internal-level and individual-level understandings. Consequently, psychological studies examining poverty have often tended to locate the causes of poverty in the characteristics of the poor themselves, in explanations at the individual level. In this, psychology has served to place responsibility for poverty implicitly onto the poor themselves, by, for instance, postulating a 'culture of poverty' (read the box headed 'Is there a culture of poverty?' for further discussion of this point).

Is there a culture of poverty?

One of the early applications of psychological theory in understanding poverty was the **Culture of Poverty theory** in the 1960s. This concept explained the causes of poverty in terms of the social, cultural, and psychological factors on the part of the poor, such as low-self esteem and low aspirations, deviant attitudes and deviant behaviours, and poor or

Culture of Poverty theory

a series of theoretical debates that sought to understand the social, cultural, and psychological determinants of poverty low-quality nurturing or parenting (due to overworked, absent or ill parents). While it is easy to see the roots of poverty in characteristics such as inferior education and health, it is important to remember that these typically flow from social, political, and economic relations and structures (Green, 2006). Much Culture of Poverty theorising tended to ignore these factors and to locate the causes of poverty in the poor themselves, subtly blaming them for their own poverty. In the USA, where much of the Culture of Poverty debate took place, many people noted that the debate ignored the intergenerational creation and transmission of poverty, and the way in which it often results from racial discrimination (Corcoran, 1995). Therefore, a critical error that interventions underpinned by psychological theory risk, when responding to poverty, is to lose sight of the influence of these larger structural determinants.

Although psychology has long been concerned with the affects of adversity on human development and psychological functioning, mainstream psychology has not paid very explicit attention to poverty. Instead, Marxism and the work of postcolonial theorist Franz Fanon offer useful theoretical tools for understanding and responding to the challenge of poverty.

Marxist structural analysis of social and economic relations not only draws attention to the underlying structural determinants of poverty and marginality, but it also suggests the way in which the workings of ideology serve to obscure these underlying structural determinants from view. The concept of **alienation** is useful here. Alienation is a central notion in Marxist analysis and describes both an estrangement from, but also an obscuring of, the material conditions that influence people's lives. These twin notions contained in alienation suggest the way in which the marginalised and vulnerable come to internalise, and even unwittingly perpetuate, their oppression and marginality.

Franz Fanon drew on the Marxist notion of alienation, but located it in relation to the context of the racism and domination associated with colonialism (Fanon, 1986). He explained that in societies with a recent colonial history, this legacy of domination, racism, and deprivation is internalised in individual psychopathology, in a 'colonialism of the mind'. Even in postcolonial contexts, such as South Africa, the sense of alienation, 'unfreedom', and lack of personal agency associated with poverty and marginality are shaped by the racialised legacy of colonialism.

Marxist structural analysis
a form of analysis drawing on the insights of Karl Marx, which argues that the structure of the economy and state function in the interests of ruling elites and capitalists

Alienation
a philosophical concept from Marxism, which refers to the manner in which people are distanced from a full understanding of their place in the world and the economy by capitalism

Psychology and poverty in South Africa

South African psychology has long been accused of paying inadequate attention to poverty, racism, and violence (Duncan, Stevens & Bowman, 2004). Only a relatively small group of progressive psychologists and practitioners have made contributions to addressing South Africa's legacy of poverty and deprivation in a handful of domains. These domains have included the following:

- **Mental health:** In terms of mental health, the following has long been understood: 'Poverty, familial strain, educational deficit and illnesses such as malnutrition all increase the risk of psychological disorder and handicap in children' (Dawes & Donald, 1994, p. 5). Work concerned with mental health has, accordingly, sought to respond to these challenges, often through the provision of appropriate clinical services.

- **Human development:** Psychological knowledge has also been used in an interdisciplinary fashion, to examine an intervention in relation to human development more generally. Examples of this include the longitudinal (that is, across time) 'Birth-to-twenty' research project, which examines health, socio-political, and demographic changes in relation to a group of young South Africans (read the box headed 'Researching poverty and child development', which discusses this project). Work in the human-development mould frequently takes a more interdisciplinary and public-health focus.

- **Social development:** Finally, beyond the contexts of mental health or human development, some psychologists have documented the contribution of psychology to transformative social change, for example the use of participatory methods in social development (Gilbert, 1997; Van Vlaenderen & Neves, 2004; Van der Riet, 2008). In this way a number of tools from psychology offer useful insights into the process of social change and socio-economic development more generally.

Researching poverty and child development

Research methods within the human sciences and psychology are important, and often contentious, because the choice of method often shapes what researchers can possibly find in the course of research. Knowledge of poverty has improved in the last few decades through the use of large-scale quantitative (statistical) surveys:

- **Cross-sectional household surveys** typically collect data from a representative group of households sampled by factors such as geography, race, and income, for example. This method can give a good 'snapshot' image of poverty at a particular time. However, repeated surveys over time are needed to reveal dynamic changes in poverty, for example whether poverty is increasing or decreasing.

- **Panel surveys** collect data (information) from the same households over time (that is, they are longitudinal), enabling a better understanding of the ways in which households get into, stay in, or move out of poverty. This is very useful information for both researchers and government

Cross-sectional household survey
large-scale quantitative (statistical) survey that typically collects data from a representative group of households sampled by various factors

Panel survey
large-scale quantitative (statistical) survey that collects data from the same households over time

policymakers. South Africa also has one large-scale, specifically child-focused longitudinal survey, namely the 'Birth-to-twenty', which has tracked the development of a large group of children since 1990 (see http://www.wits.ac.za/birthto20/ for more details). Many of the children initially surveyed have grown into adulthood, and are themselves having children, enabling South African researchers to start to understand better the intergenerational transitions, tipping points, and impact of antecedent events in human development.

Finally, psychology offers a number of theoretical tools and methods to understand poverty in non-statistical ways, for example understanding the personal experience of poverty, as it links up to larger social and economic structures.

Poverty, children, and human development

Earnings mobility
the relative difference between the average salaries of children, compared to those of their parents, in order to see if children are materially rising above their parents

An important characteristic of poverty is its tendency to be reproduced from generation to generation. Even in advanced industrial economies such as those of the USA and the United Kingdom, **earnings mobility** (the relative difference between the average salaries of children, compared to those of their parents) is comparatively low (Bowles, Gintis & Groves, 2005; Ichino & Moretti, 2011). In other words, rich parents seldom have children who grow up to be poor; while many children of poor parents themselves grow up to be poor. Economic status is therefore 'transmitted' intergenerationally, from parents to their children. This happens because children not only acquire financial assets (such as an inheritance) from their parents or caregivers, but they also receive care and nurturing, and access health care and educational opportunities (Harper, Marcus & Moore, 2003). These factors shape children's physical, psychological, and cognitive development, and their potential economic productivity in later life. For example, children affected by a discrete event – the early 1980s drought in Zimbabwe – collectively lost (that is, they never gained it) an average of more than two centimeters of height, and almost half a grade of schooling, and as a group experienced four months of school delay. Using employment data, economists calculated that these health and educational deficits translated into a loss of approximately seven per cent of each child's entire lifetime earnings (Hoddinott & Kinsey, 2001). It is clear that poverty not only undermines the immediate well-being of children, but it also erodes their future health, their optimal educational accomplishment, and, ultimately, their economic productivity.

The important points discussed on the next page need to be stressed.

Economic mobility is a product of caregivers' individual agency and the larger structural context

The likelihood of a child's 'economic mobility' (that is, an upward rise in income, relative to his or her parents), is not only a product of caregivers' individual agency (their time, resources, attention, and nurturing), but is also a product of the larger structural context, and the kinds of economic opportunities the economy and political structure presents to the child. For example, to grow up black in South Africa was, for most of the twentieth century, to have these opportunities deliberately limited by state policy.

The processes in the larger structural context differ for different kinds of poor and vulnerable children

These processes are differentiated, or vary, for different kinds of poor and vulnerable children. For instance, asset transfers and inheritance are often most favourable for first-born sons, while in many parts of the world the girl children of poor families typically receive less education than their male siblings.

Similarly, children born to young, single, unmarried or rural mothers often face additional adversity. In South Africa, although many children are born to unmarried mothers, they can be at a disadvantage (compared to children who have a father present in the home), not least because households with fathers tend to have higher average incomes than households in which no father is present.

At critical periods during the human life course, negative events have especially damaging effects

There are particular, sensitive periods during the human life course, when negative events have especially damaging effects. Some of these **critical periods** are so sensitive that deficit or damage at these times lead to long-term and often irreversible damage. An example of such a critical period and sensitivity is pregnancy: when the abuse of drugs or alcohol by the pregnant woman can be damaging to the unborn child – fetal alcohol spectrum disorder (FASD), which is the result of alcohol abuse by a pregnant mother, is not only difficult and expensive to treat, but it cannot be reversed. The notion of these critical periods means that adverse conditions do not have the same effects across the life span. For instance, poor nutrition in early childhood is far more serious than it would be in early adolescence. In contrast, the effects of witnessing violence are more severe for children once they are able to understand

Critical period
particular, sensitive period during the human life course, when specific negative events have especially damaging effects

language and causality than they might be for a small infant incapable of such understanding.

Read the box headed 'Children, public policy, and state social grants' for further consideration of the importance of awareness of the notion of critical periods.

Children, public policy and state social grants

The entitlement of children to receive adequate care is a principle enshrined in the South African Constitution. But quite apart from this rights-based argument, there are sound pragmatic reasons for the state to support early childhood health and nutrition with public money. Around the world, from Latin America to Asia, it has been demonstrated that this kind of government expenditure prevents expensive health problems as children age, and it makes them potentially far more productive adults (they are healthier, stronger, and even have higher average IQ scores). Public money effectively targeted at preventing childhood malnutrition typically saves societies several times the amounts of money they would have to spend remedying the problem later on.

This is a key rationale behind the state's provision of free maternal and childhood health services in South Africa, along with the Child Support Grant, a small monthly cash grant (R280 in 2012) paid to the caregivers of impoverished children. More than 11 million children receive the Child Support Grant, and research has clearly demonstrated that these children have lower rates of childhood malnutrition than children who have not received it (Case, Hosegood & Lund, 2005; Delany, Ismail, Graham & Ramkissoon, 2008). Children who receive the grant are statistically taller and heavier, and less likely to suffer the effects of poor nutrition, than other poor children. Very few areas of state social spending in South Africa translate into such clearly evident human-development benefits.

Poverty, inequality, and vulnerability

Resilience

Children, particularly younger children who are dependent on their caregivers, are vulnerable, and they often suffer disproportionately, relative to older individuals, when faced with conditions of adversity and deprivation. Much psychological research has sought to understand this vulnerability, and, conversely, to understand the workings of resilience – the way in which individuals survive and even thrive under adverse conditions. (Recall that chapter eight discussed both vulnerability and resilience.) Although poverty and deprivation are obvious sources of adversity, violence is also especially commonplace in low-income areas. This violence ranges from the political violence (as was associated with apartheid), to enduring criminal violence, and even domestic and sexual violence.

Resilience and human development

Resilience is shaped by the interplay of both individual and societal factors. Children's resilience is shaped by their cultural learning, socialisation and adaptation during times of social stress and transition. The three points discussed below can be made regarding resilience.

All children do not experience adversity and resilience in the same way

Adversity and resilience are not experienced in the same, or a homogenous, way, even by youths undergoing similar adverse experiences. For instance, humanitarian work to demobilise and reintegrate child soldiers in Ethiopia found differences between boys who had undergone initiation ceremonies into manhood and uninitiated boys of the same age. Initiated boys were better able to deal with the violence of war than were uninitiated boys of a similar age. The uninitiated boys struggled to integrate what they had done and their status as 'boys' (Berry & Boyden, 2000). There is a pervasive ideology that all minors – children under 18 years of age – are vulnerable and passive, but this often is not the case. In South Africa, Straker examined the impact of political violence on township youth in the 1980s. Significantly, the township teens displayed highly diverse capacity to deal with the trauma and violence of state repression: discrete groups of 'leaders', 'followers'. and 'casualties' were evident (Straker, 1992). Individual responses to state-organised repression and violence were therefore not simply reducible to the level of violence to which the teenagers were exposed, but also by the teenagers' life experiences, support networks, and, even, their morality, empathy, and resourcefulness. Although the adversity of exposure to violence can potentially effect psychosocial development (behaviour, emotional, social, and academic), this adversity is potentially tempered by coping resources such as spirituality, family support, resilience, and the degree of maternal coping noted (Barbarin, Richter & De Wet, 2001).

Children can sometimes be more adaptable than adults

Despite their vulnerability and dependency, children can sometimes be more adaptable than adults. For instance, migrant or refugee children often integrate better into host communities than their parents can: the children often learn the language, culture, and social practices more easily. They often successfully manipulate their dual identities, by adopting elements of the host culture that are useful, while still clinging to their old identity for emotional security (Berry & Boyden, 2000).

Acts of resilience and coping can themselves be sources of risk

In many parts of the developing world, girls enter the adult world through marriage and childbearing, boys through aligning themselves in armed conflicts. In hostilities ranging from the gang warfare in the Western Cape's townships to conflict in weak or failed states (such as Somalia, the Democratic Republic of Congo, or Afghanistan), young men are at particularly high risk of injury or death. However for many boys, joining armed groups provides food, clothing, companionship, and, even, physical protection. In South Africa, young women confront conditions of enduring poverty, but in a context with a strong commodity culture. It has been documented that some young women engage in intimate relationships with older men for material goods or benefits (for example groceries, taxi fare, tuition, or consumer goods). Although different from the transient encounters of prostitution, this 'transactional sex' under conditions of unequal power predisposes young women to HIV/Aids (Leclerc-Madlala, 2003). In these examples, adaptive acts of resilience and coping can, paradoxically, be sources of risk and vulnerability.

Figure 10.2 Child soliders

Images of 'youth': From the anti-apartheid struggle to the present

The term 'youth' signifies a particular set of social and political meanings in the South African context. By the 1970s, organised opposition to apartheid was suppressed by the South African state, leading to the liberation movements and their leaders being banned. In 1976, a protest march by school children against the use of Afrikaans as a language of instruction in Soweto erupted into a national wave of unrest. From 1976 into the 1980s, many black youths became radicalised and were at the forefront of violent protest against the apartheid racial order. These youths opposed not only the apartheid state's governance of urban townships, but also the middle-class adult black elites, whom the apartheid state sought to co-opt (for example policemen, administrators, and, even, educationalists). Significantly, this also led to a clash of values within families, between youths and their often more conservative and cautious parents (Chikane, 1986). This clash was embodied in the popular slogan 'liberation before education'; schooling was frequently interrupted during this period. Poor-quality and disrupted schooling saw whole cohorts of black school learners aged well into their twenties, which contributed to prolonging popular conceptions of when 'youth' ends. The popular political legacy of the 'youth', and practice of 'youth' status extending almost into middle adulthood, remains evident even in contemporary South Africa. Not only is the governing political party's youth wing (the ANC Youth League) still arguably an organ of some political influence, but eligibility for its membership terminates only at 35 years of age.

CHECK YOUR PROGRESS

- Discuss the kinds of research methods that are used to study poverty.
- Describe the potential contribution that psychology and psychologists can make to understanding and responding to poverty.
- How can resilience be both positive and negative for children facing conditions of adversity?

CASE STUDY

We return to the case study of Simpiwe, which opened the chapter. Simpiwe's sense of drive and determination saw him accepted into a job-training programme to qualify as a mechanic. He also demonstrated resilience in the face of adversity and setbacks associated with his difficult circumstances. Through successive promotions, his salary improved and he was better able to support his mother (who had since retired to the village), his siblings, and his extended family. Conscious of the opportunities he accessed, Simpiwe paid to send successive nephews and nieces to school.

Simpiwe's extended family, particularly the younger members (nephews and nieces) and older members (mother and grandmother), continue to live at their rural homestead. They subsist on the money Simpiwe and a sister send back monthly, along with the state social pension received by the older women, and several child-support grants.

Nearing his fourth decade and with a young family of his own, Simpiwe readily reflects on the trajectory his life has taken, and how it has improved relative to that of his parents. He is, however, simultaneously mindful of how many of his siblings and childhood friends remain chronically unemployed and poor. In his reflective moments, Simpiwe readily describes the wasted human potential and unrealised capacity of many of those around him.

Questions

1   'Rich parents seldom have children who grow up to be poor; while many children of poor parents themselves grow up to be poor.' Reflect on your own socio-economic status – what kind of economic background do you and your family have? List the ways in which your individual and family background has impacted on your progress to the point you have reached (as a student in tertiary education). To reach this point, what advantages and opportunities have you been able to access, and what obstacles have you had to overcome?

2   Reflect on your personal experience of resilience, or that of your family or people in your community. Considering the points contained in this chapter, and your own experience, describe the factors that you feel strengthen a person's ability to respond to adverse or traumatic events? (Example: Consider your family member or your neighbour in relation to X. What would you best inform the family member or neighbour on this matter?)

3   Critics of social grants, particularly the child-support grant, argue that these grants potentially generate undesirable side effects and dependencies. Drawing on your knowledge of the developmental impact of state cash transfers, how would you address these criticisms and make an argument for state social grants for children.

Conclusion

Preventing and responding to childhood poverty and deprivation requires attention to the following:

* **Context:** Addressing childhood poverty requires careful attention to the specific context. In much of the world, child labour and girls dropping out of school early are major obstacles to ending poverty.

However, in present-day South Africa, neither of these particular factors are significant problems: child labour is rare, and females receive comparable levels of schooling to males. Responding to poverty appropriately demands an understanding of its causes and context. In South Africa, these include an underperforming education system and limited labour-market opportunities, particularly for young people.

- **Health and nutrition:** Addressing poverty requires attention to child health and nutrition. Not only are the effects of early childhood malnutrition lifelong and difficult to remediate, but inadequate nutrition and poor health are also frequently transmitted to the next generation, thereby perpetuating the cycle of poverty. Child health requires access to appropriate health services, whereas nutrition requires efforts to promote food security and supplementation.

- **Educational and work opportunities:** Addressing poverty requires the provision of opportunities for education (typically through state investment in schools and teachers), and ensuring that the labour market works in a way that enables young people to enter it, either through employment, or forms of self-employment.

- **Support for caregivers:** Human development needs to be supported by state polices that support the critical role of adults and caregivers in child development. Such support ranges from cash transfers to the caregivers of young children to the provision of early childhood development and childcare facilities.

References

Banerjee, A., Galiani, S., Levinsohn, J. & Woolard, I. (2006). *Why has unemployment risen in the new South Africa? CID Working Paper No. 134*. Boston MA: Centre for International Development, Harvard University.

Barbarin, O.A., Richter, L. & De Wet, T. (2001). Exposure to violence, coping resources and psychological adjustment of South African Children. *American Journal of Orthopsychiatry, 71*, (1), 16–25.

Berry, J. & Boyden, J. (2000). Children in adversity. *Forced Migration Review, 9*, 33–36.

Bhorat, H. & Kanbur, R. (Eds). (2006). *Poverty and policy in post-apartheid South Africa*. Pretoria: HSRC Press.

Bowles, S., Gintis, H. & Groves, M.O. (2005). *Unequal chances: Family background and economic success*. New York and Princeton: Russell Sage Foundation and Princeton University Press.

Carter, M. (2007). Poverty traps and natural disasters in Honduras and Ethiopia. *World Development, 35*, (5), 835–856.

Case, A., Hosegood, V. & Lund, F. (2005). The reach and impact of Child Support Grants: Evidence from KwaZulu-Natal. *Development Southern Africa, 22*, (4), 267–482.

Chikane, Frank (1986). *Growing up in a divided society. The contexts of childhood in South Africa*. Johannesburg: Raven Press.

Corcoran, M. (1995) Rags to riches: Poverty and mobility in the United States. *Annual Review of Sociology, 21*, 237.

Dawes, A. & Donald, D. (1994). Understanding the psychological consequences of adversity. In A. Dawes and D. Donald (Eds). *Childhood and adversity* (p. 1–27). Cape Town: David Philip.

Delany, A., Ismail, Z., Graham, L. & Ramkissoon, Y. (2008). *Review of the child support grant: Uses, implementation and obstacles. Report commissioned for Department of Social Development, South African Social Security Agency and the United Nations Children's Fund.* Johannesburg: Community Agency for Social Enquiry.

Duncan, N., Stevens, G. & Bowman, B. (2004). South African psychology and racism: Historical determinants and future prospects. In D. Hook (Ed.). *Critical psychology* (p. 360–388). Cape Town: UCT Press.

Du Toit, A. & Neves, D. (2007). In search of South Africa's second economy. *Africanus, 37*, (2),145–174.

Fanon, Franz (1986). *Black skin, white masks.* London: Pluto Press.

Gilbert, A. (1997). Small voices against the wind: Local knowledge and social transformation. *Peace and Conflict: Journal of Peace Psychology, 3*, (3), 275–292.

Green, M. (2006). Representing poverty and attacking representations: Perspectives on poverty from social anthropology. *Journal of Development Studies, 42*, (7), 1108–1129.

Harper, C., Marcus, R. & Moore, K. (2003). Enduring poverty and the conditions of childhood: Life course and intergenerational poverty transmissions. *World Development, 31*, (3), 535–555.

Hochschild, A.R. (2000). Global care chains and emotional surplus value. In W. Hutton and A. Giddens (Eds). *On the edge: Living with global capitalism* (p. 130–146). London: Jonathan Cape.

Hoogeveen, J.H. & Özler, B. (1996) Poverty and inequality in post-apartheid South Africa: 1995–2000. In H. Bhorat & R. Kanbur (Eds). *Poverty and policy in post-apartheid South Africa.* Cape Town: HSRC Press.

Hoddinott, J. & Kinsey, B. (2001). Child growth in the time of drought. *Oxford Bulletin of Economics and Statistics, 63*, (4), 409–436.

Ichino, A.K.L. & Moretti, E. (2011). The political economy of intergenerational income mobility. *Economic Inquiry, 49*, (1), 46–69.

Leclerc-Madlala, S. (2003). Transactional sex and the pursuit of modernity. *Social Dynamics, 29*, (2), 213–233.

Philip, K. (2010). Inequality and economic marginalisation: How the structure of the economy impacts on opportunities on the margins. *Law Democracy and Development, 14* [WWW document]. URL www.ldd.org.za/index.php?option=com_zine%view=article&id=282.

Russell, Margo (2004). *Understanding Black households in Southern Africa: The African kinship and Western nuclear family systems.* Working Paper. Centre for Social Science Research: University of Cape Town.

Seekings, J. & Nattrass, N. (2005). *Class, race and inequality in South Africa.* London & New Haven: Yale University Press.

Sen, Amartya. (1999). *Development as freedom.* Oxford: Oxford University Press.

Straker, Gill (1992). *Faces in the revolution: The psychological effect of violence on township youth in South Africa.* Cape Town: David Philip.

Van der Riet, M. (2008). Diagramming as meditational means: Vygotskian theory and participatory research. *South African Journal of Psychology, 38*, (3), 455–465.

Van Vlaenderen, H. & Neves, D. (2004). Activity theory as a framework for psychological research and practice in developing societies. In D. Hook (Ed). *Critical psychology* (p. 425–444). Cape Town: UCT Press.

Wood, G. (2003). Staying secure, staying poor: The 'Faustian Bargain'. *World Development, 31*, (3), 455–471.

CHAPTER ELEVEN

CHILDREN AND VIOLENCE IN SOUTH AFRICA

Crain Soudien and Joanne Hardman

CASE STUDY

Malcolm is 12 years old. He lives with his mother, two sisters, grandmother, and uncle in a two-bedroom apartment in Mitchell's Plain, a large suburb of Cape Town, which has a high incidence of drug use and gangsterism. Of particular concern in this area is the growing use of 'tik', a methamphetamine that leads to behavioural changes in those who take it. 'Tik' addiction is increasingly implicated in a number of violent crimes in the area.

Malcolm's mother works part-time as a beautician and the family struggles to support itself. Malcolm started high school this year. While he used to attend an after-school programme for young soccer players, he no longer does so. He now spends his afternoons with a new group of friends he has made at school. Although he obtained good grades for his final year of primary school, his grades have begun to drop dramatically. Normally a confident and extroverted person, Malcolm has become withdrawn and has been disciplined at school for bullying a smaller boy in his class.

LEARNING OBJECTIVES

At the end of this chapter you should be able to

- Describe violence theoretically
- Understand a child's risk in terms of the socio-cultural conditions in which the child develops
- Become familiar with the South African context of development as influenced by violence.

Introduction: Development in the context of violence

Young people in South Africa are the most prominent victims and per-petrators of violence and crime, with 36% of all non-natural deaths occurring in the 15–29 age group. Those under 26 years of age comprise 36% of the prison population and 53% of those awaiting trial, and 69% of those detained by police are in the 18–35 age group (Soudien, 2005, p. 13).

In the midst of the deluge of press reports and enquiries about the persistent incidence of violence in South Africa (Momberg, 'Violence soars amidst stats row', 2009, p. 1), an important discussion has begun in a number of genres about Africa's **masculinities**, especially those of young black men. While violence affects everyone, as 97,5 per cent of the prison population in South Africa is male, this chapter focuses very specifically on how violence is formative of male identities in South Africa.

Masculinity
having the characteristics of an adult male

The range of the literature about the impact of violence in the formation of male **identities** in South Africa is not large, but it has been taken up in fiction (the work of Mgqolozana (2008) is fictional but draws on his own biography), in monographs (Zevenbergen, 2008), and in the world of visual representation (see the work of Nicholas Hlobo (2009), for example). These discussions explore two issues that have not been well discussed:

Identity
the distinctive characteristics of an individual

*   What makes a man a man in the African context?
*   Is the proper character or nature of manliness that of aggression and violence?

The first issue has received more attention. Journalistic writing and also some of the kind of writing that is referred to above, poses the question, often obliquely, about what is necessary for a man to be a man. A useful illustration of this arises in a recent article by Momberg (2009), which explores the increased incidence of violence. The article features the following comment from Barbara Louw of Inter Trauma Nexus, made in the context of a description of the doubling in recent times of the number of women seeking counselling:

In the past you would be held up and robbed, and only some members of the gang would be armed. Now all are armed, they are taking their time and are more sophisticated. People are suffering. These criminals enter with such force and all the women I have treated have expressed high levels of fear ... (Momberg, 'Violence soars amidst stats row', 2009, p. 1).

Citing Barbara Holtmann of Action for a Safe South Africa, Momberg (2009, p. 1) goes on to report that violence was becoming more overt: 'That level of preparedness *for what it takes* is worrying' (our emphasis).

Outside journalistic explorations of the subject, social commentators such as Steinberg (2005) and Zevenbergen (2008) have begun to ask the question in more reflective ways. Steinberg looks particularly at prison masculinities, where it is clear how deeply the ritual of doing 'what it takes' – showing fearlessness, never mind the consequences – in the perpetration of violence on the body of another is present in contemporary discourses of manliness. Whether a crisis of manhood is evident in these developments is an important issue to consider.

Whether or not, however, a crisis in this regard is unfolding in South Africa, there clearly are critical issues around which both a public debate and scholarly reflection are necessary. In stimulating these, commentators such as Steinberg and Zevenbergen are deeply important. Inherent in both is the interesting question of how young people are being brought up, and a concern with how they are socialised into adulthood. Central, of course, to the discussion of rites of passage is the experience of initiation. While this discussion is interested in the question of **initiation** and draws attention to commentary on it, it does not, however, make it a focus. It refers to it in so far as it is assumed that it has a bearing on young people's capacity for making judgements relating to violence. Illustrating this, Mgqolozana explains:

> *according to the elders, if a boy reached a stage where he was problematic in society, there was only one way to curb this, and that was 'the obvious'. The boy's mischief was considered to be an indication of wanting a rite of passage into manhood. The things that were done at the mountain were held to be so powerful that they could root out any foolish notions from a boy's stubborn head, sending him back with a clear sense of right and wrong (Mgqolozana, 2008, p. 21).*

Mgqolozana's response to this construction of the purpose of initiation is ambiguous. He makes the point that 'as a traditional tool for turning boys into men it can enrich. It is very good. The metaphoric aspect is what we are losing' (Mgqolozana, 2008 , p. 13). Both Mgqolozana and Hlobo, as Gevisser (2009, p. 14) makes clear, talk to the virtue and even necessity of initiation, but neither is uncritical of it. Mgqolazana is critical of it because of the dangers inherent in it: 'I want people to think about a tradition that leads to deaths and amputations. And not only deaths but the psychological trauma that goes with it' (Mgqolozana, 2008).

What these explorations do is raise the question of the proper character of contemporary African manliness. Is this manliness inherently about the capacity to be violent? To what degree is 'what it takes' inherently manly?

Initiation
a ritual, test, ceremony or time of instruction with which a new member is admitted to knowledge, an organisation or a position

Is it about physical prowess? The major issue this chapter seeks to address pivots on the question of 'what it takes to be a modern South African man' – critically, that which the subtext of 'what it takes' implies and draws attention to, and most notably the necessity for learning and exemplifying the qualities of manliness. This chapter follows in the wake of work such as that of Zevenbergen (2008), which asks what it means to be a man today. However, this chapter also seeks, more urgently, to work with the question, as Žižek does somewhat more generally in relation to being human, of whether a person 'can be a man without repudiating violence' (Žižek, 2008, p. 216). Žižek asks: 'How can one wholly repudiate violence when struggle and aggression are part of life?' (2008, p. 216). Is being a man, to claim a masculinity, fundamentally about a man's capacity for violence? Is violence in manliness, in a man's masculinity, unavoidable? Is masculinity about violence and violence about masculinity?

Several difficulties immediately suggest themselves as these questions are posed. How might an answer to such a question even be begun? Is it a **philosophical** question that can only be answered in an abstract way? Or is the question an empirical one? Are men, and specifically South African men, in terms of the data on crime, necessarily associated with violence? This chapter draws on theory as well as evidence to address these questions.

Drawing on the work of Gandhi in relation to modern masculinity and Žižek's critique of modern liberal **ideology**, and particularly modern liberal ideology's encouragement of individuals to achieve independence from each other, the chapter argues that structural factors conspire to reify the contention that men are inherently violent. The chapter draws on a small body of explicit interviews with young men on the subject of violence, to show how much young men are struggling to make meaning for themselves as men. The chapter suggests:

- That the major tropes of South African history – as structuring resources for the sense of the selves men project – make it extremely difficult for men to work with the task of self-reflection
- That the tendency in this male discourse is towards an assimilation and absorption of the dominant history of South Africa. In this dominant history, racism, gendered forms of identity, and their entailments of violence are profoundly difficult to avoid.

The chapter begins with Žižek and shows how deeply violence is instantiated into the everyday. Then the chapter moves to Gandhi, to mount an argument for a counter view of **ontology** embedded in the capacity for reflection. The second part of the chapter draws on an ongoing project that, essentially, has sought to engage young people with high levels of formal education on the nature of violence in contemporary South

Philosophy
investigation of the principles, causes, or nature of reality, values, or knowledge, based on logical reasoning rather than empirical methods

Ideology
the body of ideas reflecting the social needs and aspirations of an individual, group, class, or culture

Ontology
a branch of metaphysics that deals with the nature of reality

Africa to explore how they are thinking about violence (Soudien, 2005). The analytic approach taken to these interviews is essentially to assess the degree to which the young men in the interviews are able to engage with the history of violence in their lives, and the degree to which they are able to resist the lure of their history.

Žižek and the nature of modern violence: 'Stepping back'

Žižek makes the argument that violence has become normalised in the world. The nature of this violence is complex because it is so deeply woven into the fabric of the everyday through the strategies of the modern state and the ways and manners of **capitalism**.

Three kinds of violence: Subjective violence, objective violence, and systemic violence

There are three kinds of violence, Žižek explains. These are subjective violence, objective violence, and systemic violence. The value of Žižek's work is that he shows how preoccupied the modern world is with the obvious, and how it is unable to understand the web of ideology in which it is caught. The point he is seeking to make is how this web has structured pathways for people's thoughts that have made it extremely difficult for people to imagine possibilities outside and away from what they have come to understand as being 'their reality.'

Subjective violence is the most visible form of violence. Its most obvious features are crime, terror, international conflict, and civil unrest (Žižek, 2008, p. 1). Žižek describes this kind of violence as being at the forefront of people's minds, performed as it is by identifiable agents. People see it; people experience it bodily. Wait, however, he urges, because this kind of violence is 'just the most visible portion of a triumvirate that also includes two objective kinds of violence. First there is a "symbolic" violence embodied in language and its forms … Second, there is what I call "systemic" violence …' (Žižek, 2008, p. 2). The latter two parts of the triumvirate together constitute what Žižek calls objective violence and subjective violence.

Important in grasping the substance of Žižek's thesis is the point about the extent to which subjective violence masks, or provides a cover for, the pervasive presence of the objective nature of violence. Žižek argues that subjective violence is understood against what is generally understood to be a 'non-violent zero level'. When this zero-level, or the normal peaceful state of the world, is perturbed, violence is seen to issue forth. 'However,' he argues, 'objective violence is precisely the violence inherent to this "normal" state of things' (Žižek, 2008, p. 2). The effect of approaching

Capitalism
an economy that is largely market-based, consisting of both private and public ownership of the means of production

violence only through an engagement with the egregious is that it 'prevents us from thinking', he argues.

Violence as the life-force that animates the everyday

The central point to emerge from Žižek's argument is that certain features of the contemporary order – such as people's attitudes, and their norms of life – no longer appear as being ideologically marked: 'they appear to be neutral, non-ideological, natural, commonsensical. We designate as ideology that which stands out from this background: extreme religious zeal or dedication to a particular political orientation' (Žižek, 2008, p. 36). It is, however, precisely this neutralisation that marks out ideology at its purest and at its most effective. Violence is everywhere, built into the fabric and the texture of the everyday. Obscured or not, it is the life-force that animates the everyday: 'It is deeply symptomatic that our Western societies, which display such sensitivity to different forms of harassment, are at the same time able to mobilise a multitude of mechanisms destined to render us insensitive to the most brutal forms of violence' (Žižek, 2008, p. 207).

Repudiating violence: 'Learn, learn, learn'

If it is everywhere how can people, asks Žižek, 'repudiate violence when struggle and aggression are part of life?' (Žižek, 2008, p. 63). His response is interesting and is made early in the thesis of his 2008 book *Violence*. It is necessary, he says, paraphrasing Lenin, to 'learn, learn, learn' (Žižek, 2008, p. 8). He argues that people have been seduced by hypocritical moral outrage which says to them that 'a woman is raped every six seconds in this country', or 'in the time it takes you to read this paragraph, ten children will die of hunger', and which has urged upon them a false sense of urgency (Žižek, 2008, p. 6). There is a fundamental anti-theoretical gloss to this urgency. It leads people not to think. And this is what is most critically required right now. People need to be making a critical analysis of their current situation in the world. This requires a level of courage in which each person takes full responsibility. To exercise this responsibility, what is necessary is 'to "learn, learn and learn" what causes this violence' (Žižek, 2008, p. 8). It is necessary to step back, he urges; '(t)he truly difficult thing is to step back, to withdraw' (Žižek, 2008, p. 217). Learning, in this approach, is about studying. Interesting about this approach is the idea of the formation of the consciousness as a deeply cognitive exercise. It is deliberate. Gandhi's approach is no less so, but is arrived at through a different route. Central to that route is essentially learning through self-sacrifice. The next section will discuss Gandhi's ideas in some detail.

ACTIVITY

Teenagers scare the living shit out of me

They're gonna clean up your looks
With all the lies in the books
To make a citizen out of you
Because they sleep with a gun
And keep an eye on you, son
So they can watch all the things you do

Because the drugs never work
They're gonna give you a smirk
'Cause they got methods of keeping you clean
They're gonna rip up your heads
Your aspirations to shreds
Another cog in the murder machine

Chorus:
They said all Teenagers scare
The living shit out of me
They could care less
As long as someone'll bleed
So darken your clothes
Or strike a violent pose
Maybe they'll leave you alone
But not me

The boys and girls in the clique
The awful names that they stick
You're never gonna fit in much, kid
But if you're troubled and hurt
What you got under your shirt
Will make them pay for the things that they did

(http://www.sing365.com/music/lyric.nsf/Teenagers-lyrics-My-Chemical-Romance/ 9659549F61FA2E7A4825720D00296F41)

This song, by My Chemical Romance, points to subtle violence experienced by teenagers as they negotiate their journey into adulthood. Think of Žižek's notion of violence. Can you find any forms of objective violence in the lyrics of this song? What about subjective violence?

Gandhi and the ontologies of violence

A crucial feature of the *Hind Swaraj* (Gandhi, 1938) is Gandhi's discussion of the self. The *Hind Swaraj* is best remembered in South Africa and India as an anticolonial text. However, it is *Swaraj* as a statement of ontology, of being human and particularly of being human in a time of social complexity, that informs this chapter.

The central element of the self in *Swaraj* is captured in the extract below:

> *When we are slaves, we think that the whole universe is enslaved ... As a matter of fact, it is not so ... If we bear in mind the above fact, we can see that if we become free, India is free. And in this thought you have a definition of Swaraj. It is Swaraj when we* learn to rule ourselves *[our emphasis]. It is, therefore, in the palm of our hands. Do not consider this Swaraj to be like a dream. There is no idea of sitting still ... (Gandhi, 1938, p. 47)*

Central in this extract is the idea of 'learn(ing) to rule ourselves'. Many interpretations can be made of Gandhi's statement here, but for the purposes of this chapter it is the idea of identity, self-identity, as a deliberate, conscious, and learnt construct. It is important to highlight here this quality of identity as a 'learnt' value. Available in *Hind Swaraj* is a statement about *learning* to act in and through history. This learning – 'the right state of mind' – 'is not a private cultural or psychological experience, and ... not a secret defiance but a public ethic and a political program' (Connell, 2007, p. 186). Out of this learning emanates a statement about the self as a project.

This project of the self is, as Nandy (2005) says, a project about self-actualisation. He argues that Gandhi offered 'an alternative language of public life and an alternative set of political and social values, and he tried to actualize them as if it was the most natural thing to do' (Nandy, 2005, p. 85). Often underexplored is Gandhi's understanding of the making of subjectivity and the learnt dimensions of humanness. Choice is emphasised in Nandy, for example, but less noticed is the persistent invocation in Gandhi's writing about learning about control and self-restraint. This was evident in *Hind Swaraj* early, where Gandhi explicitly spoke of learning how to conduct oneself. The self presented here is the product not simply of experience, but also of a profoundly **cognising agent**.

Cognising agent
thinking person; someone who is able to reflect on his or her own agency

CHECK YOUR PROGRESS
* What are the core differences between objective violence and subjective violence, according to Žižek?
* What do you understand by Gandhi's notion of the 'self'?

A socio-cultural approach to understanding violence in South Africa

Žižek's theorising about violence provides a basis for understanding violence as both visible and often invisible. Gandhi's work points to the importance of understanding history in understanding how identities are formed. Both theorists – Žižek and Gandhi – provide a useful basis for understanding violence as socio-culturally contingent.

For the purposes of this chapter, it is useful to understand children as developing within certain socio-cultural and historical contexts. Vygotsky's appreciation of the mediated nature of cultural development, discussed in chapter two (Vygotsky, 1978; 1986), suggests that a child growing up in a context in which violence is endemic will develop in certain ways. Vygotsky's conception of the cultural self as mediated by socio-cultural context provides a basis from which to understand how some children become implicated in violence as they grow up, and why others do not. What is it that makes one child join a gang and become a violent hijacker, while another goes on to study at university? The developing child is subjected to factors that can both protect him or her, or put him or her at risk.

While Vygotsky's work provides the basis for understanding risk and resilience as mediated, his view of context is not well developed beyond the notion of mediation. Drawing on Bronfenbrenner's (1979) ecosystemic theory (which was discussed earlier in chapters two and seven) allows a more nuanced understanding of the context surrounding the child as incorporating the following: the individual child; the microsystem; the mesosystem; exosystem; macrosystem; and chronosystem. Look at Figure 11.1, which depicts these graphically.

Table 11.1 outlines how risk and protective factors influencing development in a violent context might be viewed from an ecological point of view.

Table 11.1 helps an understanding of how contextual factors come into play in a child's development. It also points to the importance of understanding context and history in order to understand the impact violence has on development. The next section turns to an investigation of the context in which South African children develop from infants into adults.

Figure 11.1 The context surrounding the child incorporates the individual child; the microsystem; the mesosystem; exosystem; macrosystem and chronosystem (http://schoolworkhelper.net/2010/11/growth-and-development-theory-urie-bron fenbrenner-1917-2005/)

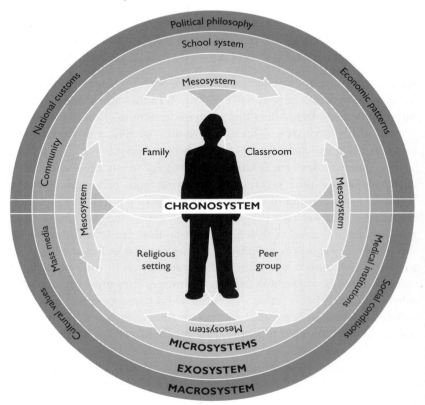

Table 11.1 Risk and protective factors influencing development in a violent context

Ecological level	Risk factors	Protective factors
Individual	• Drug abuse • Negotiating identity construction • Feelings of esteem related to gang membership	• Good health

Table 11.1 *(Continued)*

Ecological level	Risk factors	Protective factors
Microsystem	• Difficult family context (domestic violence; single-parent family; family substance abuse/addiction) • Dropping out of school • Peers who are gangsters	• Access to 'safe' facilities, such as after-school clubs • Membership of a faith-based organisation • Stable, structured school environment • Educated parents • Access to cognitive resources, such as books in the home
Exosystem	• Unsafe neighbourhood • Gangsterism and violence in the neighbourhood • High incidence of drug abuse in neighbourhood • Violent role-models on TV	• Community policing • Many faith-based organisations • Health and social services (such as grants)
Macrosystem	• Poverty • Continuous changing of school curricula	• Employment • Stable education policies

ACTIVITY

Fatal teenage gang fights see pupils pulling out of school

Continuous fights between teenage gangs in Khayelitsha, which residents say resulted in the death of three school children last week, is leading to pupils dropping out of school due to the constant fear of attack ... At least nine pupils have dropped out of Esangweni Secondary school in Kuyasa this year said principal Mvuyisi Mbotshelwa this week.

He said following last week's attacks two of his pupils were currently fighting for their lives at Groote Schuur hospital after being stabbed and beaten with weapons such as axes and pangas last week. A visit to two high schools in Khayelitsha revealed that up to six different gangs can be found in a single school and affiliated pupils are as young as 12 or 13-years-old. In Esangweni High School alone, the Vura (VR6), the Moola Boys, Hard Living (HL), the Vato (VL), the Grabians (RG) and the Pakistan's all mingle on the playing field ('Fatal teenage gang', 2012, p. 3877).

Drawing on Bronfenbrenner's work, suggest what course of action you think the principal and parents at this school should take to protect the student body.

South African male discourses: The context

Leoschut and Burton (2006), on the basis of a nationwide study conducted in 333 areas amongst 5 000 young people between the ages of 12 and 22 (also *Cape Argus*, Tuesday May 16, 2006, p. 12), showed that young people experienced significant rates of victimisation. More than two-fifths (41,4 per cent) had experienced some form of victimisation in the year preceding the administration of the survey that generated these results. These rates were almost double those of adult South Africans (Leoschut & Burton, 2006, p. 45). The nature of this victimisation reflects intense experiences of personal danger, with up to 16,5 per cent of the subjects experiencing assault to their persons; 9,4 percent having been robbed; and 4,2 per cent having been sexually assaulted. Young coloured males were more likely to be assaulted than other young people were: up to 19,6 per cent of young coloured males reported that they had experienced assault. Significant numbers of the respondents reported that they had been victims of crimes twice (the lowest figure being 145 in the Northern Cape, and the highest 33,3 per cent in Limpopo). Up to 11,7 per cent of the respondents in Mpumalanga indicated that they had been through a form of trauma three times (Leoschut & Burton, 2006, p. 48). Four out of five of those who had been victims of crime also reported being exposed to violence in their neighbourhoods. Theft of personal property was the most prominent experience amongst young people, with up to 19,5 per cent claiming to have had something stolen from them in the previous year (2004) (Leoschut & Burton, 2006, p. 50). Significantly, up to 26 per cent of the crimes reported by the young people took place at school. Interestingly, alcohol and drugs played a great role in assaults. Of the victims, 27,1 per cent claimed that their assailants were intoxicated at the time. Equally interestingly, 1 in 10 of the respondents themselves was under the influence of either drugs or alcohol at the time of the assault.

The extent to which young people themselves are perpetrators is another important aspect of emerging figures on crime, as the finding of the Leoschut and Burton study about theft at school being a major problem suggests. Many reports showing the extent of youth involvement in violent and other criminal activity have become available. In 2004, Deon Ruiters, national programme specialist at National Institute for Crime Prevention and Reintegration of Offenders (Nicro), reported that there had been a 5 per cent increase in the number of children convicted of violent crime (Nicro, 2004). The same report stated that of 3 968 children who were in custody at the beginning of 2004, 1 680 were there for violent crimes. Michael Earl-Taylor, a researcher at a crime-prevention centre at Rhodes University, described this behaviour as 'learned behaviour', saying, 'Very often these children have been subject to violence themselves. And they are re-enacting their own trauma on other innocent victims' (Earl-Taylor, 'Rape: Teachers' biggest threat', 2002). It is the case, however, as the work of the Institute for Security Studies shows (Makoba, 'Hordes of children jamming', 2006, p. 6), that almost half the children awaiting trial in secure facilities in the Western Cape and Gauteng are there because adults allegedly enlisted them in crime. The *Annual report* of the National Commissioner of South African Police Service goes on to say that gangs play a large role in this enlistment (National Commissioner of South African Police Service, 2002). Children commented that gangs helped to define their aspirations: 'Growing up in gangster areas, you get involved. You want to be like them. The gang is attractive with its gold and rings. A recent report from the Khayelitsha Magistrate's Court in Cape Town suggests that 'hordes of looting children (are) jamming up court rolls' (Makoba, 'Hordes of children jamming', 2006, p. 6). The chief prosecutor at the court reported that after a major strike of security guards and the absence of security at public places such as shopping malls, the incidence of young people involved in petty crime had escalated dramatically. Of the 30 or 40 cases that were being heard at his court, more than 80 per cent involved children. Another report from Childline, an emergency child-support group in KwaZulu-Natal, suggests that more than three-quarters of sexually abused children who seek help have been hurt by other children (Cullinan, 'Culprits of child abuse', p. 12). Significantly, about 70 per cent of child offenders, said Linda Naidoo, Childline Director in KwaZulu-Natal, had been exposed to domestic violence: 'Sometimes their mother is being abused and they are powerless to protect her. They channel this powerlessness into aggression and wanting control over others in other situations' (Yutar, 'Youth of SA', 2006). Naidoo went on to claim also that other child offenders faced peer pressure to have sex, were unsupervised, and lacked parental moral guidance.

Family structure in the South African situation, however, produces decidedly ambiguous results. In the majority of African households, either mothers are not married to their fathers, or do not have fathers living in the same house as mothers. Mothers carry the burden of raising their children. They struggle, however, to do what they believe is the right thing for their children. A mother in the Nyanga township of Cape Town, participating in a public forum about youth gangs stoning cars on the N2 (a national road), spoke of having found a stash of 'pills and two guns' under her 14-year-old son's bed. After she had taken him to the police station, he was released without having to appear in court. Another mother in the forum reflected the helplessness felt in the meeting: 'What are we expected to do if we live with these problem children' (Yutar, 'Youth of SA', 2006).

The presence of male figures in homes is, interestingly, not an unalloyed good either. A study by Barbarin and Richter (1999) discovered that homes in which the mother had a male partner were very much more likely to produce greater hardship for children. Children were more likely to experience hunger when a male partner was present than when he was absent. Much of this, of course, is directly related to socio-economic class and, it might be suggested, would not be replicated in middle-class families. Nevertheless, as psychologist Megan Beyer remarks (*Tatler*, 2005, p. 16), something of a male crisis exists in South Africa, with 79 per cent of suicides being committed by males, and males making up 97,5 per cent of all prison inmates. The role played by mothers as boys make the transition to adulthood is crucial, Beyer says, in modelling for them a range of emotional dispositions they can take beyond acting in aggressive ways.

Families that themselves showed a predisposition to aggression in solving problems tended to have children who were more likely to be alienated and themselves aggressive (Leoschut & Burton, 2006). Interestingly, the study by Leoschut and Burton (2006) (see *Cape Argus*, May 16, 2006, p. 5) revealed that almost half of 'young South Africans between the ages of 12 and 22 – some 44 per cent – have a family member who is serving, or has served, a term in prison for a committing a violent crime'. The work of Straker (1992) with militant youth bears out this relationship strongly. One in five in the Leoschut and Burton (2006) study had witnessed acts of domestic violence in their homes (see *Cape Argus*, Tuesday May 16, 2006, p. 5). The most aggressive youth in the Straker (1992) study were those who came from families in which violence and aggression were most evident. The study by Leoschut and Burton (2006) for the Centre for Justice and Crime Prevention gave credence to this statement, finding that 20 per cent of their sample of 5 000 young people reported that they had thought of committing a crime while, 10 per cent had actually done so. 'That translates into approximately one million youths who are quite open about acknowledging that they had committed a crime,' said Patrick Burton, the director of the Centre (Leoschut & Burton, 2006, p. 17).

An important aspect of these studies is their emphasis on the social forces responsible for producing the kinds of families in which young people grow up. The Straker (1992) study makes the argument that racism, urbanisation, and modernisation are at the heart of the character of South Africa's youth and their identity. Steinberg, author of *The number*, a study of gang culture, had the following to say about this state of affairs:

> *South Africa had several social factors widely acknowledged to be conducive to causing crime. These were the demographics of an increasingly youthful population, a history going back four of five generations of often violent and coercive relocation of communities and people on the move with a resultant weakening of the social fabric, and the co-existence of political equality and economic inequality (Cape Argus, Tuesday May 16, 2006, p. 5)*

South African male discourses of violence: The pragmatics of restraint

In working with the thinking of young people around violence, it is important to distinguish two connected articulations of their experience and interpretations of these experiences. The first articulation relates to the personal. The second relates a larger context: violence in the public domain. The point at which they come together and need to be interpreted together is at the level of the force of history. This section will discuss each articulation in turn.

The personal

Generally the personal discourse of most of the young men with whom this project (Soudien, 2011) worked articulates high levels of commitment to the idea of self-restraint. In each one of them real ambiguities emerge around personal moral dilemmas: Do you beat a naughty child? Do you beat a disobedient partner? Do you fight back when you are being attacked?

Interestingly in the interviews with the young people, only one subject (F, 11 August, 2009) explicitly declared his support for the necessity of violence. The physical punishment meted out to children by older people – for example '… the child doesn't know (right from wrong) … you have to tell him … you punish him to correct him' – was entirely justifiable as an act of love. More critically, however, F made the argument for the necessity of violence in the context of response: '… you have to defend yourself when someone attacks you … that is what we call self-defence, … as the barber says: eye for an eye, a tooth for a tooth … You use violence for me, I will talk with violence as well, I can do nothing (else) …'

Some of the respondents in the study were able to hold to the ideal in their explanations of their personal behaviour. Respondent A (21 July, 2009), for example, sustains his argument that violence was not justifiable under any circumstances. He says, repeatedly, for example in his interview, 'I don't think it addresses the problem.' Respondent P (23 July, 2009) is similarly resolute in his thinking: 'Under no circumstances (is any kind of violence defensible) ... it is not acceptable ... I don't accept beating people up ... even a male ... it doesn't solve anything, so, if you don't get your way just drop it. It is not worth fighting for.'

The ideal of restraint is ever-present in most young people's view of themselves in relation to those around them. It remains a puzzle, however. Respondent M (15 July, 2009) explains: 'In my own life I don't feel it a lot, I don't feel it playing a role.' When asked under what circumstances he would contemplate 'disciplining' his partner, he argues, 'None at all! I don't think ... that is not even a point that you can bring up ... to try and justify that.' A few minutes later, however, he argues that it is 'totally acceptable (to beat a child) ... that is not violence ... if it is used in the right context I think that it is something that is necessary ...' Later, also, he goes on to argue, '... I don't believe in violence per se ... but I think violence is the last resort ... if I had an argument with you we would start with words and I would try and persuade you ... but obviously our views would differ and after a while when I see that I am not able to persuade you, I will use force ... that is the way the human is.'

Respondent A2 (22 July, 2009) likewise vehemently disagrees with the idea of beating a partner, but like M accepts that beating a child is right: '... I grew up in a Xhosa family where I would be smacked now and then ... and ... it basically showed you to differentiate wrong from right ...' A person's behaviour is, he says, 'automatic. What you do automatically... is you act: react physically.' Respondent J (28 July, 2009) makes the point in relation to violence against both children and women, that 'nothing gives you the authority to raise your hand on somebody else, ... being really hands on violence on somebody is totally wrong ...' But then even Respondent J demurs: 'spanking a child ... maybe ...'

Read the application box headed 'Law to ban spanking in the UK', which further explores the issue of spanking.

The dilemmas are intense for most of the young men. There is an ambiguity around wanting to be restrained in an ideal world and then there is the reality of what it means to operate as a man in South Africa.

Two explanations of this ineluctable reality emerge in the engagements. At one level it is Steinberg's history of the self – the history of four generations of socialisation – which is repeatedly recruited as the young men think their way through these ideals. At another level it is the history of the body – male biology. In terms of the former, many of the young

Law to ban spanking in the UK

The UK will come under increasing pressure to ban all smacking and corporal punishment of children as the European human rights body steps up pressure for a change in the law. The Council of Europe – which monitors compliance with the European convention on human rights – will criticise the UK because it has not banned smacking more than 10 years after a ruling in 1998 that the practice could violate children's rights against inhuman and degrading treatment.

'The campaign to abolish corporal punishment across the Council of Europe is gathering momentum; 20 countries have formally abolished laws allowing it in the past three years' said Maud de Boer-Buquicchio, deputy secretary general of the Council of Europe ... 'We are talking about fundamental human rights,' she said. 'Not only do children have the same human rights as adults, but they are more vulnerable than adults. They need more protection and not less' (Hirsch, 2010).

- Should children be spanked if they are naughty? What do you think? What are the reasons for your response?
- Why is spanking a 'human rights' issue?

people referred to 'living conditions' – the structure of poverty in family life in South Africa. Respondent M3 (4 August, 2009), for example, makes the point that 'in this country a lot of issues surrounding violence have to do with the kind of living conditions ... Um ja, I think generally speaking the poorer people are more prone to reacting to violence or using violence as a means of expression ... generally speaking it is based on the economic conditions and social issues of certain individuals who move on to violence because they have more to fight for so to speak.'

For many, this instinct to react is in the genes. Respondent J (28 July, 2009) argues that 'males are more violent, ... obviously because (they are) ... more physical.' Respondent R goes further (31 July, 2009), '... this is a human being's nature ... Even a thousand years ago we also had violence ... It is because of our gene ... I think girls, they play another style. Not like us.' Respondent M2 (4 August, 2009), who made the argument that it was not acceptable under any circumstances to beat another ('it is not for you to discipline someone who is a human being ... No ..., no hitting!'), says, nonetheless, 'Men are more physical than women ... men are different to women. Men operate differently ...' For respondent M, it is 'a primal emotion, if you want to call it that. It sits with each one of us. You see it in each one of us ... If you can think it you can do it.' Such is the nature of men.

ACTIVITY

In South Africa, 97,5 per cent of the prison population is male. Respondent J in the paragraph preceding this box suggests that 'males are more violent'. Underlying this assertion is a reference to the hormone testosterone, commonly thought to make men more prone to violence. Castration studies have shown that, indeed, testosterone is necessary for violence; however, recent research indicates that while it may be a necessary ingredient for violence, it is not a sufficient cause of violent behaviour. Scientists currently hypothesise that testosterone does indeed lead to aggression, but that it is central not to violence, but to dominance-seeking behaviours. People who are more dominant, it appears, have higher levels of testosterone. Frank McAndrew has observed: 'From what we can tell now, testosterone is generated to prepare the body to respond to competition and/or challenges to one's status. Any stimulus or event which signals either of these things can trigger an increase in testosterone levels' (Mims, 2007, p. 2).

1   Do you agree with respondent J? Give reasons for your answer.
2   How, theoretically, can the high incidence of males in prison be accounted for?

The larger context

Critically, though young people equivocate in relation to personal history, they have even more difficulty in thinking their way through the history of the public moment – the larger history through which they expect to be read and expect to be interpreted. In attempting to understand this larger history and how they see themselves in relation to it, they experience a general difficulty in articulating both a sense of themselves in history and, more critically, their capacity to imagine their way through the compulsions of this history. A number of the subjects indicate an awareness of this history and its compulsions and recognise how these operate as stratagems of objective violence. They see and understand how violence is structured into the everyday as a seductive pull on their identities. Respondent A is profoundly aware of how '… it has happened in many instances that violence is seen as … fighting for human rights … If you look at Khayelitsha today, … there is protest, … you see police shooting at people and people throwing stones at the police … this current democracy, it is attacking the poor, … almost protest against it … all of them have been crushed … by force … the state has done this deliberately … they want to "authorisement" – I don't know the right English – … formalise everything … But I am just disappointed … but it takes character … it is important that people remain calm and non-violent in anything that they do …'

How they are to remain calm and non-violent is an enormous challenge. When respondent A is asked how he would face this challenge, and if he will offer himself up to arrest if necessary, he says, 'Ha, ha … I don't want to think about that.'

When they do think about the options open to them, many young people are deeply conflicted. The nature of this experience is projected as that which is inherently violent against which little else is possible. Respondent A, who above had expressed an understanding of the objective nature of the violence he confronted in society, says that 'if you look at South Africa more black people would be more violent, would be far more violent than white people … I am not saying it is excuse, but you know how people are socialised … The frustration in villages in the Eastern Cape … people not having decent jobs …' that adds to the frustration …' Violence in this context, says A, is necessary. For some respondents, for achieving the goal, 'in extreme cases you have to use force … I would say South Africans need violence.' As J says, 'obviously you are going to have to negotiate with the enemy … sort of find a mutual ground, finding your rights but if that doesn't happen then obviously it is going to go to the next level … using force to fight for your rights … using violence to get your rights is the only way these days …'

In some of the respondents' attempts to come to understand the role of this violence, the racial nature of South Africa is foremost in their thinking. This racial thinking takes poignant form in the attempts by both black young men and white young men to understand the situation in which they find themselves. M3 argues: 'I find that Zulu guys to be more aggressive and I also find that some Afrikaans to be more aggressive more so than English speakers or Sotho or Tswana … I find these two to be the most aggressive the most likely to enter violence …' F says, about places he knows in Cape Town: '… the Northern Suburbs … it is an Afrikaans area. People are really violent. They are looking at your special accent … as black guy. They know that you don't speak Afrikaans but they will speak to you in Afrikaans … It is an act of violence …'

M2, speaking against the backdrop of recent events in South Africa, explains:

I am not a violent person but, my God, if I stay another five years I am going to end up hitting someone, because … it is something that happens inside of you … this continual anger … this moral outrage, this continual moral outrage. An inability to do anything about it. If I felt that I belonged here, if I felt that … you know because I feel that I don't belong here, because I am White and Afrikaans, I am male, I am everything that is bad for…, you don't belong here. If

*I wasn't in that category and I felt that I really belonged then maybe
I would feel that my anger is justified and that somebody should
listen to me, but I don't. That is why I want to leave because I feel
that I kind of ... verbalised ... oh just another whitey, oh disgruntled white people must just leave the country if they are moaning
about crime. You know.*

Important about the attempts of these South African men to think
their way through the puzzle of violence is an awareness, like that of both
Žižek and Gandhi, that as human beings they are called upon to think
their way through the challenge in front of them. They repeatedly invoke
the ideal of rationality. This is often associated with 'character'. But they
succumb, in their explanations of the worlds they live in, to the primal,
the primordial, and even the biological. It is just so: thought defeated
by instinct. That this instinct is the product of time and space is only
partially historicised.

CHECK YOUR PROGRESS

* Read the report in the box headed '*Baby, woman murdered at Delmas
  daycare*'. The report points to the levels of violence in South Africa,
  where even a five-month-old baby can become the target of murder. In
  this chapter M2 states: 'I am not a violent person but, my God, if I stay
  another five years I am going to end up hitting someone, because ... it
  is something that happens inside of you ... this continual anger ... this
  moral outrage, this continual moral outrage.' Given what you have read
  in this section of the chapter, how can you explain, from a theoretical
  perspective, the violence described in the report?
* What do you think about M2's point of view about becoming violent
  because of 'moral outrage'? Can you explain his viewpoint using Bronfenbrenner's model?

It is this challenge that is urgent in South Africa now. What the
interviews suggest is that in the economy of resources available to
individuals, including their own sense of agency, the structuring
forces of history are extremely powerful. These structuring forces –
physically encoded in the world that shapes up visually in front of
them, and then also in the formal ideas they have to make sense of
this visible reality – are so pervasive that the only resistance to them
that they have to offer, their education and its cognitive properties, is
patently insufficient.

Baby, woman murdered at Delmas daycare

Cape Town – A caregiver and a 5-month-old baby boy were found murdered in Delmas, in Mpumalanga, police said on Wednesday. The mother of the murdered baby had phoned Margrietha de Goede, the caregiver, a few times to check on her child who was sick, but there was no answer. The woman and a friend then went to the day mother's house, but became concerned when they heard a child crying. They broke a window to gain entry to the house where they found an 18-month child, and called police when De Goede and the other baby, Wiehan Botes, could not be found. Police arrived and made the grisly discovery of Wiehan's body under a bed, a police spokesperson said. De Goede, in her 60's, was later found dead in a garden shed. Police forensics officials were on the scene until after 18:00 (Du Plessis, 2012).

CASE STUDY

At the beginning of the chapter you read about Malcolm, who is 12 years old. Read the opening case study again and answer the following questions:

1   Can you describe Malcolm's behaviour, using Bronfenbrenner's model?
2   Drawing on socio-cultural theory and Bronfenbrenner's work, what interventions can you suggest to assist Malcolm and his family?

Questions

1   Use this chapter to think through a violent event you have witnessed or heard about. What can you and others do, practically, to address issues of violence in South Africa?

2   Now you have read about the impact violence can have on a child's development, think back to the case study about Malcolm, which started this chapter. Imagine you are faced in your practice with a child who presents with behavioural difficulties. How would you go about working with that child, given what you have learnt in this chapter? Use Bronfenbrenner's model to inform a therapy plan.

Conclusion

This chapter has looked at how violence potentially influences developmental trajectories. The chapter did this by focusing on understanding violence theoretically, using the work of Žižek and Gandhi and situating this work within a psychological paradigm using Vygotsky and

Bronfenbrenner's work. The chapter drew on empirical work, in the form of interviews, to illustrate how young men in South Africa construct their notions of self in a violent context.

References

Barbarin, O. & Richter , L. (1999). Adversity and psycho-social competence of South African children. *American Journal of Orthopsychiatry, 69*, (3), 319–327.

Bronfenbrenner, Urie (1979). *The ecology of human development: Experiments by nature and design.* Cambridge, MA: Harvard University Press.

Cape Argus (2006, May 16), p. 5.

Connell, Raewyn (2007). *Southern theory.* Cambridge: Polity.

Cullinan, K. (2006, June 1). Culprits of child abuse are increasingly children. *Cape Argus*, p. 12.

Du Plessis, W. (2012, May 23). *Baby, woman murdered at Delmas daycare.* [WWW document]. URL http://m.news24.com/news24/SouthAfrica/News/Baby-woman-found-murdered-at-daycare-20120523. 14 June 2012.

Earl-Taylor, M. (2002, January 25). Rape: Teachers' biggest threat. *Daily Dispatch.*

Fatal teenage gang fights see pupils pulling out of school. (2012, April 13). [WWW Document]. http://westcapenews.com/?p=3877. 14 June 2012.

Gandhi, Mohandas K. (1938). *Indian home rule or* Hind Swaraj. Ahmedabad: Navajivan Publishing House.

Gevisser, M. (2009, July 19). *South African rites.* [WWW document]. http://www.nytimes.com/2009/07/19/magazine/19lives-t.html. 14 June 2012.

Hirsch, A. (2010, April 25). *Europe presses UK to introduce total ban on smacking children.* [WWW document]. URL http://www.guardian.co.uk/world/2010/apr/25/law-reform-smacking-europe-uk. 14 June 2012.

Hlobo, Nicholas. (2009). *Nicholas Hlobo. Standard Bank young artist award.* Cape Town: Michael Stevenson, p. 1–108.

Leoschut, L. & Burton, P. (2006). *How rich the rewards? Results of the 2005 National Youth Victimisation Study.* Monograph 1. Cape Town: Centre for Justice and Crime Prevention.

Makoba, N. (2006, May 25). Hordes of children jamming up court rolls. *Cape Argus*, p. 6.

Mims, C. (2007, July 5). *Strange but true: Testosterone alone does not cause violence.* [WWW Document]. http://www.scientificamerican.com/article.cfm?id=strange-but-true-testosterone-alone-doesnt-cause-violence&page=2. 14 June 2012.

Mgqolozana, Thando (2008). *A man who is not a man.* Pietermaritzburg: University of KwaZulu-Natal Press.

Momberg, E. (2009, August 9). Violence soars amidst stats row. *Sunday Independent*, p. 1.

Nandy, Ashis (2005). *Exiled at home.* New Delhi: Oxford University Press.

National Commissioner of South African Police Service (2002). *Annual report: 1 April 2001 to 31 March 2002.* Pretoria: South African Police Service.

Nicro (2004). *Annual report.* [WWW document]. URL http://www.nicro.org.za/wp-content/uploads/2011/06/Nicro_AR_20041.pdf. 14 June 2012.

'Over 1000 SA children die each year from abuse and violence.' (2005, June 23). *Cape Times,* p. 13.

Soudien, C. (2005) The ethics of self-rule: Violence and masculinity in contemporary South Africa. *Public Culture, 23,* (2), 13–26.

Soudien, C. (2011). The ethics of self-rule: Violence and masculinity in contemporary South Africa. *Public Culture, 23*, (2), 275–284.

Steinberg, Jonny. (2005). *The number.* Cape Town: Jonathan Ball.

Straker, J. (1992). *Faces in the revolution.* Cape Town: David Philip.

Tatler (2005, March 17), p. 16.

Vygotsky, Lev S. (1978). *Mind in society: The development of higher psychological processes.* (M. Cole, V. John-Steiner, S. Scribner, & E. Souberman, Trans.). (Eds). Cambridge, MA: Harvard University Press.

Vygotsky, L. S. (1978). *Thought and language.* (E. Hanfmann & G. Vakar, Trans.). (Eds). Cambridge, MA: MIT Press.

Yutar, D. (2006, May 16). Youth of SA caught in a cycle of violence. *Cape Argus.*

Zevenbergen, Aernout (2008). *Spots of a leopard: On being a man.* Laughing Leopard Productions.

Žižek, Slavoj. 2008. *Violence.* New York: Picador.

CHAPTER TWELVE

HEALTH BARRIERS THAT IMPEDE CHILDHOOD DEVELOPMENT

Jenny Jansen and Louise Stroud

CASE STUDY

On the same summer day when 6-year-old Catie Hoch beat her own personal best jumping rope – 100 in a row – the doctors discovered that the pain in her side was from a tumor on her kidney. Her mother describes how her whole life changed in that split second. There was no longer control and even less control as the cancer spread. It was during that time that Gina began to read aloud the first three books about a schoolboy wizard named Harry Potter, who knew something about fighting fierce, deadly enemies. Maybe that's why, when they took the train from their home in upstate New York to New York City for treatment, Catie wore a red cape, a red lightening-shaped scar on her forehead, a wand and big black glasses. She was ready for anything (Gibbs, 2003, p. 41–42).

LEARNING OBJECTIVES

By the end of this chapter you should be able to:

- Describe developmental, cognitive and scholastic barriers that impede progress in the area of scholastic functioning
- Highlight socio-economic and cultural barriers that impede progress – these include poverty, limited aspirations and exacerbated peer pressure in the light of poor socio-economic status, as well as the cultural decline with regard to moral value systems
- Identify health barriers, including Aids and other chronic conditions such as epilepsy, brain injury and cerebral palsy
- Discuss early childhood education in the South African context.

Introduction

In the previous chapters childhood and adolescent development has been comprehensively discussed based on a variety of theories of development. From these chapters, the conclusion can be drawn that children and adolescents move through orderly developmental sequences. However, various intrinsic and extrinsic factors – some of which are culture, environmental conditions and disease – may serve to delay the normal development of both children and adolescents.

Normal development itself may be divided into domains: those of physical and motor, cognitive and social–emotional development. Each of these aspects of development influences and is influenced by others (Sigelman & Rider, 2003). For instance, a problem in one area may affect the functioning of the other domains and consequently affect a child in his or her entirety, causing barriers to healthy development.

Developmental, cognitive and scholastic barriers that impede progress

The first section of this chapter will deal with barriers that are related to school. Most of a child's life is taken up with school-related activities, and failure to succeed in this environment creates barriers in the areas of health, self-esteem and aspirations for the future. Underachievement is not only multi-factorial, but is also often the result of the complicated interactions between these factors. Interestingly, these factors often change as a child progresses from primary school to high school, and yet they remain barriers to normal development. The importance of understanding the impact of these developmental, cognitive and scholastic barriers on the developing child cannot be underestimated. 'We like *Harry Potter* because, even if it tells stories about magic, it talks about real problems like the ones you can have in school,' says 11-year-old Caroline, who lives in Rome (Gibbs, 2003, p. 45).

Barriers or factors relevant to primary-school children

A variety of factors that could impede progress at school can be identified in children who attend primary school. These include, to name but a few:
* Health barriers
* Poor attendance at school
* Specific learning disabilities (SLD)
* Low general cognitive ability
* Attention deficit and hyperactivity disorder (ADHD).

This section will discuss these specific barriers.

Health barriers relevant to primary-school children

Physical barriers

Physical barriers often impede a child's progress at primary school. When motor delay occurs in a child, in isolation from other delays, differential diagnoses could include **spina bifida**, **ataxia**, **spinal muscular atrophy**, and **myopathy**. All these motor deficits require specialist assistance and ongoing care, as they are lifelong conditions. Most of these children need special schooling, support for parents and siblings, and good medical care.

Sensory barriers

Sensory barriers – which include hearing and visual impairments – can influence a child's development and consequential progress at school. Warning signs for possible hearing-related problems include the following:
- Ear problems that recur during early childhood
- Lack of startle when a loud noise is made
- Very loud or soft talking
- Non-responsivity when called.

Depending on the degree, this restriction of sound can result in severe impairments in speech and language. Lags can occur, as most of information dissemination takes place via auditory information. A child's deficit may present as poor memory skills, poor comprehension ability, and,

Spina bifida
developmental condition (existing from or before birth) caused by the incomplete closing of a fetus's embryonic neural tube; a portion of the spinal cord may visibly protrude through unfused and incompletely formed vertebrae bones to the exterior of an infant's body

Ataxia
a nervous system dysfunction that affects the coordination and control of an individual's speech, balance and movement

Spinal muscular atrophy
an incurable disease caused by a genetic defect which affects the proteins necessary for motor neuron survival; this results in the death of neuronal cells, which leads to system-wide muscle atrophy, or wasting

Myopathy
a muscular disease involving non-functioning muscle fibres, which results in muscle weakness

Figure 12.1 Spina bifida

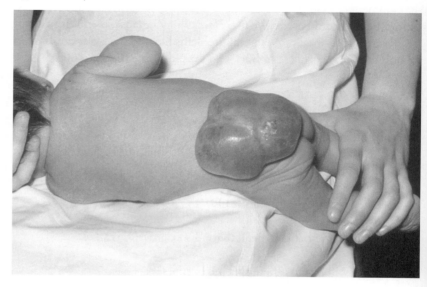

ultimately, behavioral difficulties. Failure to address this barrier could lead to isolation or paranoia, or a child who presents as lonely and withdrawn both at home and at school.

The term '**visual handicap**' is used to identify children with a congenital or acquired defect in the visual system. It includes children with a wide range of vision, from totally blind, to those with enough sight to move around independently (Cleland & Swartz, 1982). The World Health Organisation (1980) provides the following definitions:

- **Visual impairment:** any loss or abnormality of psychological, physiological or anatomical structure or function
- **Visual disability:** any restriction or lack (resulting from impairment) of ability to perform an activity in the manner or within the range considered normal for a human being
- **Visual handicap:** a disadvantage for an individual or a disability that limits or prevents the fulfilment of a role that is normal (depending on age, sex, and social and cultural factors).

Low-vision and blind children and adolescents have a huge impact on a family. Ordinarily, a family provides for the protection, nurturance, and socialisation of its members, but having a child who has a disability makes this task difficult. Establishing values and setting goals usually become more difficult for such families as physical, financial, and emotional resources become strained. Such strain could lead to a divorce.

The birth of a low-vision or blind child alters family patterns, which leads to new and differing family roles. This child may be the firstborn, but as a result of his or her problem, the child becomes the so-called 'baby' who receives constant attention. Parental anxiety can lead to overprotection of the child who has the disability and underattention to other family members. Limited concentration on personal needs often also occurs, which can later lead to resentment and rejection of the disabled child (Shapiro, 1983).

Cross-ethnic comparisons have shown that stress differs amongst the cultures: black parents experience more stress in the area of family problems, coloured parents experience stress in the area of parental problems, while white parents experience stress relating to problems regarding the child's future (Jansen, 1991).

Visual impairment
any loss or abnormality of psychological, physiological or anatomical structure or function

Visual disability
any restriction or lack (resulting from impairment) of ability to perform an activity in the manner or within the range considered normal for a human being

Visual handicap
a disadvantage for an individual or a disability that limits or prevents the fulfilment of a role that is normal (depending on age, sex, and social and cultural factors)

Full Service schools
institutions that directly address the problems that create barriers to learning through adopting a holistic approach to education, integrating academics; family-support, health and social services; and community-development programmes to support their learners needs

Additional barriers to the development and functionality of low-vision and blind children

Low-vision learners need to be accommodated at **Full Service schools**, which are schools that are currently being piloted in some areas in South Africa. These schools, selected by the national Department of Education, cater for learners with medium needs and learners with mild disabilities. To a large degree, they are mainstream schools that are specially equipped to address a full range of barriers to learning. Currently, these schools are not well resourced due to financial constraints. At present, Full Service schools do not have the physical or human resources to assist such learners, resulting in their placement at schools for the blind. There are limited schooling and tertiary opportunities for such children. Schools for the blind are usually located in urban areas, in some provinces. The financial constraints of hostel placement and school fees for these children place a huge financial burden on the parents, or, often, prevent the children from attending school. Many of these schools designated for blind children do not cater for low-vision children, and although there are many devices to assist low-vision children, these devices are too expensive for the government or parents and caregivers to purchase. It is important to remember that the needs of low-vision children are different to those of blind learners; these children need different assistive devices to meet the inclusive demands of society. Schools for the blind do not exist in all provinces, and there is a lack of policies that transcend provincial borders by the education departments in some provinces. This lack prevents children from attending school in other provinces. Further, many tertiary institutions are not ready to accommodate these types of learner, and at present the academic future for such children looks bleak.

Poor attendance at school

Poor attendance at school is an astounding frequent occurrence in the lives of many primary-school children. There are numerous reasons for this:
* Many families' inability to enrol their children at the school of their choice because the school is full
* Many families' lack of means to fund transport to the next-nearest school if their children cannot be enrolled in the school of their choice
* Truancy as a result of poor achievement and resultant lack of motivation
* The need of many parents to relocate frequently in order to find employment, resulting in their children either being out of school for long periods of time or being regularly exposed to different schools.

These are school-related barriers that directly impact on children's physical and mental health. Further, lack of motivation, strikes, intimidation, and absenteeism negatively impact on educators' regular attendance at school. The lack of attractive physical amenities, limited teaching material, and huge classes make for an environment that is not conducive to learning. Some teachers may be totally insensitive to the child's needs, may have inappropriate expectations, may not be trained to teach the subject allocated to them, and may employ poor methods of teaching. All of these factors influence the degree to which children master the skills required of them.

Specific learning disabilities

Specific learning disabilities (SLDs), or learning disabilities, is a general term that refers to a heterogeneous group of disorders manifested by significant difficulties in the acquisition and use of abilities in listening, speaking, reading, writing, reasoning or mathematics. The disorders are intrinsic to an individual, and are presumed to be due to central nervous system dysfunction. They may occur across the lifespan. Problems in self-regulatory behaviours, social perception, and social interaction may exist within the learning disabilities, but do not constitute a learning disability per se. Although a learning disability may occur concomitantly with other handicapping conditions (for example sensory impairment and serious emotional disturbance) or with extrinsic influences (such as cultural differences or insufficient or inappropriate instruction), they are not the result of those conditions (NJCLD, 1988, p. 1.)

Specific learning disabilities
a general term that refers to a heterogeneous group of disorders manifested by significant difficulties in the acquisition and use of abilities in listening, speaking, reading, writing, reasoning or mathematics

Figure 12.2 Children with specific learning disabilities may require extra help with learning

Learning disabilities do not occur in a vacuum, but, rather, within the family system. Fortier and Wanlass (1984) note that disability in a child results in a crisis that affects the health of the family as a whole. These crises can be, for example, behavioural (which includes the care of the child), or emotional (involving working through grief, guilt, isolation, and helplessness), or require the family, including the disabled child, to work through stigmatisation.

Low general cognitive ability

Many children with low general cognitive ability, or global developmental delay as represented by intellectual-assessment scores that reflect the below-average to borderline range with regard to both the verbal and non-verbal scores, are able to progress through primary school, where most of the content is predominately concrete and factual in nature. (However, at high school, the workload increases and tasks become more abstract. Then these learners cannot cope and they need to be referred for appropriate alternative placement. Parental expectation also has to be dealt with.)

Attention deficit and hyperactivity disorder

According to Venter (1988), the clinical diagnosis for attention deficit and hyperactivity disorder (ADHD) rests in three domains, two of which are usually present:
- Inappropriate restlessness
- Severe difficulty in paying attention
- Impulsive cognitive and behavioural lifestyle.

Children with ADHD often have learning disabilities, perceptual deficits, and poor self-esteem. Special schooling with a transdisciplinary staff is needed to assist with the multitude of social, psychological, and cognitive barriers that accompany this condition.

(The condition of ADHD tends to worsen in high school, where it is accompanied by a variety of psychological conditions, such as oppositional–defiant disorder, drug abuse, obsessive–compulsive disorder, and boredom with tasks that do not immediately gratify needs.)

ACTIVITY

Select *one* of the barriers or influencing factors on development discussed above and develop an action plan that both identifies and addresses the potential needs of the primary-school children affected by it. Your action plan should be written as an essay of no less than 500 words.

Barriers or factors relevant to high-school children

A further variety of factors can impede children's progress at high school. These include, to name but a few:

- Factors that were present at primary school, but had limited impact in that context
- Limited motivation and excessive free time
- Drugs, clubs, gangs, and peer pressure
- Emotional disorders of adolescence, especially depression and anxiety
- A low level of language acquisition and an emphasis on auditory processes
- Other deficits.

This section will discuss these specific barriers.

Factors that were present at primary school, but had limited impact in that context

Factors which were present before, but which had limited impact on a child's functioning in primary school, may affect his or her functioning at high school. Teachers' inability to diagnose low general cognitive ability, possible ADHD, SLDs, and other conditions could have left gaps in learning, which now cannot be closed. Organisational strategies and poor habits of learning, which were adequate in the lower grades, are inappropriate to the workload and expectations of high school.

Limited motivation and excessive free time

Motivation to attend an institution such as school, with its discipline and rules, can become limited when an adolescent is struggling academically on a daily basis.

Adolescents' classes change for each area of study, so little bonding takes place with educators. Many schools – especially those in poorer socio-economic areas – do not offer sport and extramural activities, and consequently many adolescents finds themselves with excessive free time.

Drugs, clubs, gangs, and peer pressure

The adult world of drugs, clubs, and gangs starts to become the order of the day. Adolescents, with all the pressures of change, are particularly vulnerable to the attractions of chemical substance abuse. Between the ages of 13 and 19, the transition from childhood to adulthood takes place, and with this transition goes societal vulnerability. This includes sexual awkwardness, physical awkwardness, and the need to prove that one is not a sissy. Unfortunately adolescents' peers do not always see 'proof of coolness' in being a good academic or sportsman, but instead, see it in an ability to participate in general risk-taking behaviours involving drinking, drug taking, and smoking. These activities are often popular with adolescents who need to prove that they are not 'chicken' in order to be accepted by their peers. They are also a manner to disguise poor school performance. They can even replace boredom and act as an escape from domestic violence.

Emotional disorders of adolescence, especially depression and anxiety

According to Venter (1988), depression and anxiety are the most debilitating emotional disorders of adolescence. They may be primary in nature, as part of the emotional upheaval of puberty, but they can also be secondary, due to poor self-esteem, drug abuse, a sense of failure and peer rejection. Furthermore, co-morbid psychological conditions can occur if a child with ADHD is not able to develop an **internal locus of control** before reaching adolescence. These co-morbid behaviours – such as immediate gratification and impulsivity – can cause behaviours that could get adolescents into constant trouble with any perceived authoritarian body, such as the school, the family, or the law.

Internal locus of control
the belief that events are derived from an individual's own actions and that each person has control over how life events influence them; individuals operating under an *external* locus of control, in contrast, believe that they have little or no influence over their environments and life events

A low level of language acquisition and an emphasis on auditory processes

In South Africa, children are exposed to a variety of languages. This often adds to a low level of language acquisition, which is recognised only in high school. In the technologically advanced society of today, visual-information input has taken the place of auditory processes. However, most teaching and dissemination of information to learners is auditory, placing a greater emphasis on the auditory processes, which include vocabulary, auditory memory, and conceptual thought processes. Language assists with the development of higher-order cognitive abilities, which are necessary for successful learning in high school. The deficits associated with a low level of language acquisition become prominent in high school, causing poor performance.

Further deficits

Further deficits also become stumbling blocks in high school. These include organisational deficits (usually as a result of ADHD), memory impairments, and poor fine-motor co-ordination.

These deficits and others mentioned in this section all have an effect on health and cognitive, social, and emotional development, and become psychological barriers when the child's developmental needs are not met. In this context, this quotation from Lucretius, from the first century BC, is apt:

> *If things could come from nothing, time would not be of the essence, for their growth, their ripening to full maturity. Babies would be young men in the blink of an eye, and full-grown forests would come leaping out from the ground. Ridiculous! We know that all things grow, little by little, as indeed they must, from their essential nature (in Honoré, 2008, p. 37).*

CHECK YOUR PROGRESS

- Explain the differences between a visual impairment, a visual disability and a visual handicap.
- If a primary-school child is experiencing difficulty in acquiring and using listening, speaking, reading, writing, reasoning or mathematics abilities, then which disability might that child have?
- List and discuss three potential factors that could negatively affect a high-school learner's ability to motivate or apply him- or herself academically.

Health barriers caused by cultural and contextual factors

Child and adolescent development occurs in various domains, for example:
- Social–emotional (changes in social relationships)
- Biological (changes in physical being)
- Cognitive (changes in thoughts, intelligence, and language).

Recently the concept of child development has been broadened to include transactions between the child and his or her environment, with developmentalists focusing on different areas of emphasis. Some theorists focus on genetic and biological antecedents. Others, such as Craig (1996), state that development cannot be boxed, because it involves an interaction between environmental and biological elements, which impact on child development to a greater or lesser extent. Against this background, this section will discuss barriers that impact on social development within the South African context. These include:
- Rural–urban relocation
- Environments that reduce children's safety and freedom to interact and play socially without the fear

- Socio-economic status
- The civil status of women
- Employment issues with regard to women
- Malnutrition
- Fetal alcohol spectrum disorder.

Rural–urban relocation

After the 1994 democratic elections in South Africa and the abolition of the pass laws, a huge rural-to-urban migration occurred (Lynch, 2005). However, this transition did not bring about change in the social growth or growth in economic activity. According to a statistical survey in 2004, this migration resulted in massive housing shortages, poor-quality housing and safety hazards that children in the rural areas had not experienced before (Statistics South Africa, 2004). This situation had severe implications for the socio-economic conditions of poorly educated people, who were, and still are, confronted with low levels of literacy, limited job creation, and transport problems, and now have to focus on the lowest needs in **Maslow's hierarchy**. Children's immediate environment has implications not only for their health and hygiene, but also for their overall development. Rural–urban relocation is a contextual barrier for those children who are currently living below the poverty line as a result of this occurrence.

Maslow's hierarchy
a theory in psychology, as proposed by Abraham Maslow, which describes the stages of human motivation leading to growth and development, starting at having most basic physiological needs met, progressing to the meeting of 'higher order' needs

Environments that reduce children's safety and freedom to interact and play socially without fear

South Africa has one of the highest rates of crime in the world (*African Economic Outlook*, 2006). South African children live in a country that can be classified as a 'war zone'. This environment reduces children's freedom to interact and play socially without the fear of being abused, hurt, and unprotected. Play is a physical activity and not only stimulates the physical development of a child, but also promotes social development, encourages language, and, consequently, improves cognitive development. Play stimulates imaginative thinking, and in this way assists children in dealing with the dangers of the real world. The type of environments prevalent in South Africa impact on cognitive, psychological, and physical health.

Socio-economic status

Most rural and informal settlements are inhabited by the lower economic strata of the South African population. These informal settlements feature poor infrastructure (such as street lighting), poor public transport and a lack of proper town planning. All these elements elicit questions around safety.

Figure 12.3 Socio-economic status is a major barrier to child and adolescent development

A further challenge is that of limited sanitation and access to quality water within households. Families living in such conditions live in survival mode, with no energy left to develop the skills as their counterparts whose living conditions do not present such challenges. Thus socio-economic status is a major barrier to child and adolescent development.

The civil status of women

Attitudes to the civil status of women affect the level of social support available to mothers, and indirectly to their children. Although South Africa has undergone societal changes with regard to women in the higher echelons of society, the civil status of women of a lower economic status is still impacted upon by the ramifications of emasculation during colonialism. This legacy of ongoing oppression of women in the family system, especially in groups of lower socio-economic status, represents a resistance to changes in these behaviours.

Violence against women is supported in subtle ways by previous cultural and traditional behaviours. Mothers may thus develop a low sense of self-esteem, which negatively impacts upon their mothering skills. Adolescents, especially male adolescents, find it difficult to obey rules and discipline such mothers attempt to implement. These mothers' feelings of self-worth contribute to the moral and social norms of the household: if a mother is perceived as having limited status, this view will be transferred to the children.

Employment issues with regard to women

There is currently a high rate of unemployment amongst women in South Africa, and a 'glass ceiling' is often present when it comes to promotion of women in higher-paying work positions. According to *African Economic Outlook* (2006), there is an elevated rate of unemployment for single mothers who would, if they were employed, be obligated to leave their children in the care of significant others from a very young age. A study by Van der Kolk (1987) indicates that neglected children have a brain mass of 30 per cent less than children who have had regular maternal input.

Private, community, and domestic services comprise the largest employment sector in South Africa, particularly for black women. Much of the employment in this sector is informal and done mainly by women. Furthermore, the income generated by this type of employment is low, obligating women to work longer hours (May, 1988).

A mother's work burden can have an adverse effect on her child's development. According to UNICEF (2006), 20 per cent of South African children do not live with their mothers, and this phenomenon tends to increase these children's chances for both abuse and neglect. UNICEF estimated that 500 000 female children are sexually victimised annually. According to Van der Kolk (1987), abused children are twice as likely to have abnormal activity in the fontal and temporal regions of the brain as children who do not experience abuse. Van der Kolk's studies showed that victims of childhood abuse experience changes in the brain that can lead to learning problems.

Malnutrition

Malnutrition is probably the most critical environmental factor influencing normal biological development in South Africa. According to statistics South Africa (2004), a household survey done in 1999 revealed that 2,4 million households in South Africa reported that children younger than seven years old go hungry every day. Nutritional factors affect growth and overall developmental potential, and also weaken the body's resistance to infection (Jareg & Jareg, 1994).

Poverty and its ramifications are serious barriers to normal development of children and adolescents. Poverty is the basic cause of malnutrition. According to UNICEF (2006), 61 per cent of children in

South Africa live in poverty. According to the same source, three million children in South Africa are in need of a child-support grant due to financial constrains, but only 1 per cent of this total currently receive child-support grants. Medical investigations by UNICEF indicate that children in South Africa display marginal Vitamin A status, 20 per cent are anaemic and 10 per cent are iron deficient. Many of these children do not have the nutritional stamina to develop biologically, interact socially, and meet the psychological demands made upon them by the home and school environments.

Fetal alcohol spectrum disorder

As a result of the excessive and regular alcohol intake by certain pregnant mothers in South Africa, some children are born with fetal alcohol spectrum disorder (FASD), and consequently have intellectual disability. This condition leads to high numbers of illiterate and innumerate children who cannot be accommodated in special schools, because there are limited facilities of this sort. These children spend their days in the street.

ACTIVITY

Play stimulates imaginative thinking, and in this way assists children in dealing with the dangers of the real world. Children growing up in violent societies have less opportunity than others freely to explore, play and develop creative coping strategies to help them navigate life challenges well.

Imagine that you are a psychologist working with parents, teachers and other professionals in a local township. How might you assist this group of people in developing strategies to support and stimulate children's imaginative thinking/coping strategies to deal best with the violent society in which they live?

CHECK YOUR PROGRESS

- Why would children from poor socio-economic backgrounds (who typically receive inferior educations, resulting in low levels of literacy, and who face limited job opportunities) not be able to focus on the higher-order needs of esteem and self-actualisation, as proposed by Maslow's hierarchy of needs?
- Which is the most critical environmental factor influencing normal biological development in South Africa? Why is this so?

Health barriers such as Aids and other chronic conditions

J.K. Rowling, the author of the books featuring Harry Potter, has stated that she admires bravery above almost every characteristic in children (Gibbs, 2003). She has said that bravery is a very glamorous virtue – bravery in all sorts of places. It is, as Rowling attests in the first chapter of her first book featuring Harry Potter, the virtue that cannot be faked. She says you either walk in the woods full of giant spiders, or you don't; stand up to bullies, or hide from them; hang on to hope, or surrender to fear. She addresses children as though they know as much as, or more than, she does about the things that matter. Rowling mixes real-life struggles with the imaginary. Children like the characters she has made – Harry above all, not because he is fantastic but because he is familiar (Gibbs, 2003, p. 42–45). And so it is that books like those featuring Harry Potter inspire children who are experiencing health barriers – for example HIV and Aids, brain injury, epilepsy, and cerebral palsy – to find the hero within.

HIV and Aids

Retrovirus
a virus containing RNA that can convert its genetic material into DNA by means of the enzyme reverse transcriptase; this allows the virus to become integrated into the DNA of the cells of its host

HIV is a **retrovirus** found within the tissue fluids of the body. It impairs the body's natural defence system through the destruction and/or functional impairment of the CD4 cells that are pivotal to the immune reaction. Thus immunity declines and the body becomes more vulnerable to attack, resulting in the proliferation of more and more opportunistic infections and malignancies, until immune suppression and Aids results.

Presently there is no cure for this disease. Infants and young children infected with Aids acquire the disease from their mothers pre- or postnatally. According to Whiteside and Sunter (2000), there is a 30 per cent possibility of infected mothers transmitting the disease to their unborn infants. HIV may cause a wide spectrum of disease, as infants' immune systems continue to develop in the first year of life, and they are particularly vulnerable to the effect of HIV early on. This health barrier can cause abnormalities from birth, or children may take some time to present with developmental compromise. Because the central nervous system is involved, children fail to attain developmental milestones. These milestones can be divided into two areas: cognitive delays and motor delays. Daily living skills of children are also impacted. Such dysfunction may manifest in the deterioration of play, loss of acquired language, and loss of socially adapted skills (Belman, 1992).

The effects of the pandemic in the South African context are vast. At a macro level, this impact surfaces more slowly than at the micro level, but it is inevitable, as the cumulative weight of death and illness under-lie long-term social and economic consequences that will become more evident as time passes. As the number of Aids-related deaths increases, the effects on the macro level of society become evident in family systems, and ultimately in a transformation of the structure of society. There is an increase in the prevalence of the extended family system and the child-headed family system, as well as in the number of orphans. Young adolescents often need to earn a living at a young age and are denied the opportunity of living a normal life. This leads to these children living impoverished lives and to their being unable to develop skills beyond those of daily survival. The situation that these children find themselves in leads to a decline in the quality of their socialisation, due to factors such as unstable backgrounds, reduced supervision, and the need for children to take on the roles of parents.

Children with HIV experience frequent separations from their primary caregivers (Chase et al., 1995). Such separation may occur for a variety of reasons, but it is often due either to multiple demands within the family to care for others, or to illness of either child or caregiver. This separation can have a severe impact on the development of the child, and may interfere with the attachment process between child and caregiver. Attachment is vital to the development of emotional maturity and is particularly evident in a child's sense of security (Sigelman & Rider, 2003). Such children may receive less attention and stimulation than others, which can result in a deficit in social skills. It may also lead to their having a limited knowledge base as a result of lack of cognitive stimulation. These factors impact on normal development and readiness to learn.

According to Belman (1992), it has been found that HIV-positive children generally show developmental abnormalities, cognitive impairment and motor impairment. Although these children are able to acquire new skills, they usually develop at a slower rate, due to emotional factors such as those as mentioned above, or as a result neurological impairment. This suggests that HIV may compromise the usual developmental pattern; it may be deduced that children who are HIV positive require greater assistance in their developmental skills.

HIV causes a general decrease in numbers of students in formal education, due to the dual pressure on some children to both provide and care for sick individuals, particularly in child-headed families. Lack of education increases these children's problems in formal education, and possibly results in an increase in individual vulnerability. A child's further education can also be compromised by the loss of educators to HIV-related diseases. The impact is both moral and economic, as these barriers can produce a sector of the population that is illiterate and unskilled.

ACTIVITY

1   Think of a time in your own childhood where you, like the characters in the series of Harry Potter books, had to 'find the hero within' you. What, do you feel, helped you to do this? What might have helped you more?
2   Think of a few strategies that you could use with HIV-positive children to help them find their own inner heroes to overcome the barriers (developmental abnormalities, cognitive impairment and motor impairment) that they experience because of this developmental barrier.

Brain injury

Health barriers can also be caused by brain injury. This phenomenon is increasing in the South African context due to such factors as:
*   Children being injured in motor-vehicle accidents, which can cause epilepsy, physical disabilities (for example cerebral palsy), and impaired cognitive functioning
*   Decreasing availability of medical care, especially in rural areas
*   Increasing numbers of pregnancies amongst teenagers
*   Neurological problems resulting from problems within medical provision in South Africa.

Epilepsy

Epilepsy is an illness characterised by seizures. When there is a damaged area in the brain tissue, the neurons in that area are prone to short bursts of abnormal and electrical discharge. The brain malfunctions, and the normal balance is replaced by a state of electrical chaos.

There are two main groups of seizures:
*   **Partial seizure:** This affects a specific part on one side of the brain. For example, when the area that controls the left arm is affected, seizures manifest as a jerking of the left arm. This is known as a simple partial seizure.
*   **Generalised seizure:** This affects a larger area of the brain, and includes both tonic-clonic and absence seizures. A tonic-clonic seizure is referred to as a grand mal seizure and there is evidence of **convulsions**. In this category are also absence seizures formerly called petit mal. This type of seizure is not easy to detect as there is a brief period of absence with no convulsions.

Convulsions
involuntary contraction of the muscles, producing contortions of the body and limbs

For school-going children, support by both educators and parents is critical, in order to make sure that a child with epilepsy is prepared for the ridicule he or she may encounter. Such a condition is permanent, except for febrile convulsions caused by a high fever. Children who experience febrile convulsions usually outgrow this particular type of epilepsy.

There is a misconception that epileptic children are less intelligent than children who do not have epilepsy. This is not the case, and most of these children attend a normal school. However, they can present with specific learning difficulties. Other complications include the side effects of medication, and poor control of medication, which can lead to toxic levels of medication in the bloodstream. Blood levels need to be checked regularly to control the side effects of toxic levels of anticonvulsant medication.

Absence seizures in children can cause them to lose out on the information given during lessons, causing possible learning difficulties. Other complications include injury as a result of falls, and breathing in food or saliva during a seizure, which can cause aspiration pneumonia.

Absence seizures
absence spells when a person loses consciousness briefly

Cerebral palsy

Cerebral palsy is characterised by varying degrees of disturbance of voluntary movements, including paralysis, weakness, and lack of coordination, which is caused by injury to the brain. In most cases, cerebral palsy is congenital, that is, damage is caused to the brain during pregnancy or at birth. However, infections, disease, or severe head injury can cause this condition at any time of life.

It has already been mentioned that medical care is becoming increasingly difficult to access; this condition can also be caused by

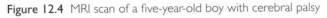

Figure 12.4 MRI scan of a five-year-old boy with cerebral palsy

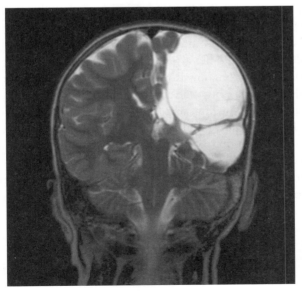

Rubella
a mild highly contagious viral infection, mainly of childhood, causing enlargement of lymph nodes in the neck and a widespread pink rash (also known as German measles)

Rhesus incompatibility
an incompatibility that may develop when an Rh-positive man impregnates a woman who has an Rh-negative blood type and an Rh-positive fetus is conceived

Enuresis
involuntary passing of urine

medical conditions which are not treated. Prenatal conditions include **rubella**, which occurs in the first trimester, **rhesus incompatibility**, natural anoxia, use of drugs, and metabolic disorders such as maternal diabetes. Perinatal causes include prolonged labour, breech delivery, anoxia, and prematurity. High fever and other related factors can also cause this condition if the brain is compromised in any way. Postnatal factors include direct trauma to the brain and infection. Physical abuse and motor-vehicle accidents can also result in injury to the brain and can also cause this health barrier.

The main types of cerebral palsy include the following:

- **Spasticity:** This type occurs when injury is on the brain surface or when the injury involves the nerves leading from the surface through the brain substance to the spinal cord. This type is characterised by the loss of voluntary motor control.
- **Athetosis:** This type is caused by injury to the brain motor switchboard, resulting in involuntary jerky movements, especially in the fingers and wrists. There are two types, namely tension and non-tension. In the tension type the muscles are always tense, and this limits the movement of the limbs. A child with non-tension athetoid cerebral palsy has contorted movements without spasticity.
- **Ataxia:** This type occurs when the injury occurs in the cerebellum, and it is characterised by a lack of coordination and sense of balance.

Intellectual abilities of these children with cerebral palsy range from being superior to cognitively challenged. Other co-morbid problems include epilepsy, visual and hearing problems, and specific learning deficits, behavioural and socialisation deficits, and **enuresis**.

Recall the situation of Catie in the case study that started this chapter. Gibbs (2003) concludes her article by indicating Catie's death on the 18 May 2000. She describes how Rowling wrote to Catie's parents three days after her death, stating how she considered herself privileged to have had contact with Catie. Rowling, who had got to know Catie well during her period of fighting a chronic illness, said that she 'had left footprints on her heart' (Gibbs, 2003, p. 47). Catie's parents went on to establish the Catie Hoch Foundation to help young patients with cancer.

William Blake (in Honoré, 2008, p. 12) throws light on the importance of investing in the lives of children:

> To see a world in a grain of sand,
> And a heaven in a wildflower
> Hold infinity in the palm of your hand,
> And eternity in an hour.

CHECK YOUR PROGRESS

- Explain the differences between the three main forms of cerebral palsy and suggest ways in which each type might specifically interfere with a child's overall emotional, cognitive, social or scholastic development.
- List three deteriorations or dysfunctions that may manifest in children with HIV/Aids.

Early childhood education in the South African context

I like a teacher who gives you something to take home to think about besides home work (Lily Tomlin, in Honoré, 2008, p. 145).

Early childhood education in the South African context deserves consideration in this chapter. Although the plurality of educational programmes for preschool and foundation-phase children may exist in most developing countries (Spodeck & Sarcho, 2006), sadly, the same cannot be said for this group of children in South Africa. The result is that there is a danger of producing another lost generation of learners, should educational research not rise to the occasion and guide the process of learning and teaching.

At present South African children may enter the formal schooling system from five years and six months of age, if they are able to cope with the needs of formal schooling. Schooling is compulsory in the year in which the child turns seven years of age. Many parents who work tend to enrol their children at school at a very young age so that they can go to work; by making this decision, the parents avoid paying day-care centre fees or preschool fees because many of the schools that these children attend are 'no fee paying' schools.

Research has indicated that child characteristics, family characteristics, and quality of child care (as measured by, for example, caregiver–child ratio, level of education and training of caregivers, degree of healthiness and safety of the environment, and degree of positiveness, sensitivity and responsiveness in caregiving) have an effect on children's intellectual and social development (Spodeck & Sarcho, 2006). At present, many South African children attend day-care facilities where the caregiver–child ratios exceed the efficacy levels, and where caregivers often do not have adequate training.

The lack of preschools and the difficulty of access to these schools have forced the South African government to plan to attach preschools to all primary schools by 2014. However, there are challenges to be overcome. As a result of present lack of funds for educational activities, there is limited training for these teachers, and there will be consequential gaps with regard to childhood theory and concomitant skill development. Therefore, these teachers will not be allowed to practise as preschool teachers, but rather as Early Childhood Development (ECD) practitioners, and they will be paid a stipend for their services. Again, learning barriers will be created, as the skills needed for successful mainstream learning may not be part of the programme offered. The skills needed for successful learning must include locomotor skills, language skills, fine motor abilities, practical reasoning, and memory abilities, as well as socialisation and life skills. Without the consolidation of these skills, children will not be able to cope with formal school.

It is important to understand the education policy pertaining to learners experiencing barriers in South Africa. Some of these children attend mainstream schools, yet if their barriers are too high to enable them to cope with the demands of such schools, they can be referred to special schools, pending availability. As a result of the costs of specialised schooling, the government developed the concept of **inclusive education**. This refers to the placement of learners with disabilities in general educational classrooms alongside learners of the same age who do not have disabilities. The underlying premise of inclusion is that all children can learn and belong in mainstream and community life (Reynolds & Fletcher-Janzen, 2001).

Inclusive education
the placement of learners with disabilities in general educational classrooms alongside learners of the same age who do not have disabilities

The new focus for inclusion is no longer on the learner who needs to fit the system, but on the responsibility of the system to modify itself to fit the individual. The South African government is currently piloting Full Service schools in certain areas. These schools, selected by the national Department of Education, cater for medium-levels-of-needs learners with different disabilities. To a large degree, Full Service schools the are mainstream schools that are specially equipped to address a full range of barriers to learning. The effectiveness of these schools has not been researched, and at present there is argument for and against inclusion practice. Some of the arguments include the fact that the full inclusion of a special-needs learner can cause disruptions for other learners (McCarty, 2006).

However, specialised education is still of importance in South Africa and involves education of a specialised nature to address the high needs of learners who have not been able to benefit from support in the mainstream: these needs include:
- Psychological treatment
- Dental treatment
- Therapeutic treatment
- Artificial medical aids and apparatus
- Transport.

Exam concessions are available to all learners with special needs at both special and mainstream schools. This type of alternative examination procedure can be defined as a purposeful intervention in order to prevent or overcome the obstacles that might keep learners with disabilities from learning and full participation in school and society.

Part of the specialised-education approach involves the use of resource centers. A **resource centre** is a specialised environment that provides a range of support services to ordinary public schools and includes all special schools with their expertise.

In order for a child to be placed in a specialised educational setting, information needs to be obtained through continuous assessment and collaborative work by a team of professionals based at an ordinary mainstream school. These professionals are what are called the Institution Level Based Support Team. Each school must have such a team, and their main focus is to assist classroom teachers to develop individualised programmes for learners experiencing learning difficulties.

In order to assist children with special health barriers and co-morbid learning barriers, it is essential for practitioners to have a good medical and social understanding of child development and what it involves. According to the national Department of Education, inclusive education is here to stay. Unfortunately there is a lack of resources, educators and finance to make it a viable option at this stage. Despite these challenges, the words of Albert Einstein ring ever true: 'Education is what remains after one has forgotten everything he learned at school' (Honoré, 2008, p. 113).

Resource centre
a specialised environment that provides a range of support services to ordinary public schools and includes all special schools with their expertise

CASE STUDY

Lulama and Maggie were best friends. They attended the same primary school and were in the same Grade 5 class. Lulama lived in the township close to the school, while Maggie lived in the suburbs. Lulama and Maggie loved spending as much time together as they could, both at school and after school. They climbed trees, rode their bicycles, swam, played hopscotch, and enjoyed watching DVDs together. They even did their homework together.

One day while they were out riding their bicycles, Maggie was knocked over by a car. She was taken to the hospital and admitted to the Intensive Care Unit. Maggie was unconscious and had sustained a mild traumatic brain injury. For the next two weeks Lulama spent as much time as she could at the hospital, visiting Maggie. She would talk to her and hold her hand, and tell her that she was missing her. She drew her pictures and read stories to her. Eventually Maggie regained consciousness and was discharged from the hospital once the medical team was happy with her progress. Maggie couldn't wait to go home. When she arrived home, Lulama was waiting for her in the driveway, all smiles, with a welcome-home helium balloon in her hand, which said 'BFF — Best Friends Forever'!

John O'Farrell, in *May Contain Nuts*, says, 'I wanted to do everything for my children: clear every obstacle from their path, fight every battle, and take every blow' (in Honoré, 2008). Honoré confirms the given message that 'childhood is too precious to be left to children, and that children are too precious to be left alone' (2008, p. 4.). However, Honoré warns that the overzealous meddling by adults could lead to a new kind of childhood being forged. Now, more than ever before, children have become targets of adult anxiety and intervention. It is not always possible for adults to prevent unfortunate barriers impacting upon children's health, yet it is possible for children to be brave as they face very real developmental challenges brought to bear upon them.

Questions

1 Did you experience any form of barrier to development in your own childhood? What strategies did you, your parents, your teachers and others implement to cope with these developmental barriers and influencers? Were they successful? What would you do differently now, knowing what you do today?

2 Which of the developmental barriers described and explored in this chapter stirs your sense of advocacy (the desire to address an issue proactively) or piques your interest the most? How might you be able to assist children proactively in the future better to reach and navigate developmental milestones as they face this developmental barrier head on?

Conclusion

South Africa may present a picture of a middle-income developing country, but the lifting of the veil of apartheid reveals a darker picture of endemic poverty. Moreover, South African children differ in cultural heritage and degree of acculturation, language, urban/rural location, socio-economic background, education level of parents, health preparation for schooling, and many other influences and illnesses that shape human development (Lloyd & Payne, 2002; SARPN, 2006; Statistics South Africa, 2004). Health, cognitive, location, and general living standards can, as a result of this diverse social situation, be seen as insurmountable barriers for those children who experience life in the transitioning country that is South Africa. In the words of Gabriela Mistral, Nobel Prize-winning poet from Chile:

> ... *we are guilty of many errors and faults, but our worst crime is abandoning the children, neglecting the fountain of life. Many of the things we need can wait. The child cannot. Right now is the time his bones are being formed and his senses being developed. To him we cannot answer 'Tomorrow', his name is 'Today'* (Mistral, n.d.).

References

African Economic Outlook (2006). *South Africa.* [WWW document]. URL http://www.oecd.org/dev/publications/africanoutlook. 14 December 2011.

Belman, A.L. (1992) Acquired immunodeficiency syndrome and the child's central nervous system. *Paediatric Neurology, 39,* (4), 619–713.

Chase, C., Vibbert, M., Pelton, S., Coulter, D.L. & Cabral, H. (1995). Early neurodevelopmental growth in children with vertically transmitted human immunodeficiency virus infection. *Archive Pediatric Adolescent,* 850–855.

Cleland, C.C. & Swartz, J.D. (1982). *Exceptionalities through the lifespan.* New York: Macmillan.

Craig, Grace J. (1996). *Human development* (7th ed.). Upper Saddle River, NJ: Prentice Hall.

Fortier, L.M. & Wanlass, R.L. (1984). Family crisis following the diagnosis of a handicapped child. *Family Relations, 33,* 13–24.

Gibbs, N. (2003, June 23). The real Harry Potter. *Time,* 41–42.

Honoré, Carl (2008). *Under pressure: Rescuing our children from the culture of hyper-parenting.* New York: HarperCollins Publishers.

Jansen, Jennifer M. (1991). Stress and coping in families with physically handicapped children. Unpublished thesis, University of Port Elizabeth.

Jareg, E. & Jareg, P. (1994). *Reaching children through dialogue.* China: The Macmillan Press.

Lezak, M.D., Howieson, D.B., Loring, D.W., Hannay, H.J. & Fischer, J.S. (2004). *Neuropsychological assessment* (4th ed.). New York: Oxford University Press.

Lloyd, C. & Payne, J. (2002). In search of the high skills society: Some reflections on current visions. ESRC Research Centre on Skills, Knowledge and Organisational Performance (SKOPE) research paper: University of Warwick, United Kingdom.

Lynch, Kenny (2005). *Rural–urban interaction in the developing world.* Abingdon: Routledge.

May, J. (1998). *Poverty and inequality in South Africa: Summary report. Report prepared for the Office of the Executive Deputy President and the Inter-Ministerial Committee for Poverty and Inequality.* [WWW document] URL http//www.policy.org.za/html/govdocs/reports/poverty.html?rebookmark=1. 11 September 2009.

McCarty, Kristine (2006) *Full inclusion: Benefits and disadvantages of inclusive schooling: An overview.* Retrieved from the ERIC database. (ED 496074), p. 1.

Mistral, Gabriela. 'His name is Today'. In [WWW document] URL www.bernardvanleer.org/files/chetna/Child_rights_booklet-4.pdf. 20 July 2012

National Joint Committee on Learning Disabilities (NJCLD) (1998). [Letter to NJCD members] Full inclusion: Benefits and disadvantages of inclusive schooling: An overview from ERIC database (ED496074), p. 1.

Reynolds, C.R. & Fletcher-Janzen, E. (2001). *Concise encyclopedia of special education: A reference for the education of the handicapped and other exceptional children and adults* (2nd ed.). Hoboken, NJ: Wiley & Sons.

South African Regional Poverty Network (SARPN) (2006). *Fact Sheet: Poverty in South Africa.* Human Sciences Research Council. [WWW document] URL http://www.sarpn.org.za. 11 December 2011.

Shapiro, Johanna (1983). Family reactions and coping strategies in response to the physically ill or handicapped child: A review. *Social Science Medical Journal, 17,* 14, 913–931.

Sigelman, C.K. & Rider, E.A. (2003). *Life-span human development* (4th ed.). Belmont, CA: Wadsworth/Thomson.

Spodeck, B. & Sarcho, O.N. (2006). *Handbook of research on the education of young children* (2nd ed.). New Jersey: Lawrence Erlbaum Associates, Inc.

Statistics South Africa (2004). *Perceived health and other health indicators in South Africa*. [WWW document]. URL www.statssa.gov.za. 1 January 2011.

UNICEF (2006). *Global database on undernutrition* [WWW document]. URL http://www.unicef.org/southafrica/overview.html. 14 November 2011.

Van der Kolk, Besse A. (1987). *Psychological trauma*. Washington, DC: American Psychiatric Association.

Venter, A. (1995). Learning problems in adolescents. *Continuing Medical Education Journal, November*, 1319–1325.

Whiteside, A.W. and Sunter, C. (2000). *AIDS: The challenge for South Africa*. Cape Town: Human & Rousseau.

World Health Organisation (1980). *International classification of impairments, disabilities and handicaps*. Geneva: WHO.

Glossary

A

A, not B, error: The tendency of infants to search for a hidden object in the location they last found it (A) rather than in a new place to which they saw it being moved (B)

Absence seizures: Absence spells when a person loses consciousness briefly

Accommodation: Adjusting thinking as a result of new knowledge

Adolescent growth spurt: The rapid increase in physical growth that occurs during adolescence

Aetiology: Refers to the cause of an illness; the root of the symptom

Alienation: A complex philosophical concept from Marxism, and one which essentially refers to the manner in which people are estranged (or distanced) from a full understanding their place in the world (and crucially) the economy by capitalism

Assimilation: Incorporating new information into existing knowledge; understanding novel situations in terms of one's existing cognitive structures

Ataxia: A nervous system dysfunction that affects the coordination and control of an individual's speech, balance and movement

Autonomy: The ability to function independently as a separate, self-governing individual; in Western societies, achieving autonomy is an important developmental task of adolescence

Avolition: An inability to pursue goals or act on decisions, a lack of drive or motivation

B

Basic avenues of learning: The avenues/channels through which children collect and assimilate environmental stimuli to make sense of their worlds cognitively and to develop mentally; these basic avenues are a child's eyes, hands, speech ability and hearing

Behavioural states: Recognisable and well-defined associations of variables, which are stable over time and with clear transitions between each

Body mass index: A measure of a person's proportion of body fat; it is calculated by dividing a person's weight in kilograms by the square of their height in metres

Bullying: Repeated, intentional and organised acts of aggression that are directed towards particular peers (victims)

C

Capabilities approach to poverty and underdevelopment: An approach that focuses on what individuals are capable of; it understands poverty and underdevelopment as capacity-deprivation, the absence of choices and opportunities for individuals to attain their full potential

Capitalism: An economy that is largely market-based, consisting of both private and public ownership of the means of production

Cephalocaudal trend: Development proceeds in a 'head-to-tail' direction, from the top of the body downward

Chemosensation: Fetal responses to smell and taste

Child: An individual young person, between birth and the age of 18 years

Child-directed speech: Language used by adults speaking with infants; it is spoken in a higher, more sing-song voice than normal, with simple words and sentences and much repetition

Childhood: The structural site occupied by children as a collectivity; a developmental stage of the life course common to all children

Childhood career development: The development of occupational awareness and occupational aspirations during childhood

Childhood indicators: Indicators that assess children's standard of living, welfare support, marginalisation, and well-being and that measure distributive justice between age groups and between children of various ethnic and social groups; indicators track trends along these dimensions, making them effective tools for evaluating policy implementation

Children: Young people, between birth and the age of 18 years

Class inclusion: The awareness that lower categories (known as subordinate classes) are included in larger, higher categories (known as superordinate classes)

Cliques: Small groups of peers comprising 2 to 12 members, usually same sex and age

Cognising agent: Thinking person; someone who is able to reflect on his or her own agency

Conditioned response: Response that has been learned in relation to a previously neutral stimulus

Conservation: A child's ability to recognise that some properties of an object can remain constant even across physical transformations; the realisation that certain characteristics of objects such as quantity, volume and weight stay the same when the outward appearance of the object is changed

Convulsions: Involuntary contraction of the muscles, producing contortions of the body and limbs

Coregulation: Maccoby's term for the process in which control of the child's behaviour during middle childhood relies on cooperation and a sharing of responsibility between parents and children

Co-sleeping: The practice of infants sleeping in the same bed as their mothers

Critical period: Particular, sensitive periods during the human life course when negative events can have especially damaging effects, or alternatively if crucial competencies are not mastered the process of catching up is very difficult

Cross-sectional household survey: Often large-scale quantitative (statistical) survey that typically collects data from a representative group of households sampled by various factors at one point in time

Crowds: Larger groups defined by reputation and stereotypes, and having social status in, for example, a school or community

Culture of Poverty theory: A series of theoretical debates that sought to understood the social, cultural, and psychological determinants of poverty

Culture: Understood in this text to be a person's knowledge, beliefs, and behaviours shaped through symbolic interaction with members of their group through social means

D

Decentration: The ability to focus on two or more aspects of an object or situation at the same time

Deductive: Deductive reasoning refers to drawing inferences about specific things from a general law; so for example: all swans are white; this is a swan; therefore it is white

Deferred imitation: A child's ability to remember and copy the actions he or she has previously observed another person perform, but has not practised

Dependent variable: The variable that changes due to the manipulation of the independent variable

Developmental norm: The average age at which half of infants have mastered a particular skill

Dose-dependent effect: The greater the exposure, the greater the effect on the fetus

Dualism: Derived from the Latin word 'duo' (meaning two), this refers to something in two parts; in this text, the debate about development is situated either in a nature or in a nurture framework

E

Earnings mobility: The relative difference between the average salaries of children, compared to those of their parents, in order to see if children are materially rising above their parents; earnings mobility is a measure of the opportunities for the improvement of welfare from one generation to the next

Egocentric thinking: The difficulty that young children have in recognising a point of view other than their own

Elaboration: A memory strategy that involves creating meaningful links between the items to be remembered by adding either words or images

Elites: People who are more affluent

Embryo: An organism in the early stages of growth and differentiation, from fertilisation to the beginning of the third month of pregnancy (in humans); after that point in time, an embryo is called a fetus

Embryonic period: The second stage of the prenatal period, beginning during the middle of the second week and concluding at the end of the eighth week

Empathy: The intellectual identification with or vicarious experiencing of the feelings, thoughts, or attitudes of another; the attribution of one's own feelings to an object

Empirical: Information collected using the senses

Enuresis: Involuntary passing of urine

Epigenetic principle: Each stage of the life cycle is characterised by events or crises that must be satisfactorily resolved in order for development to proceed smoothly

Equilibration: A biological imperative to maintain balance cognitively

Ethical: A term that derives from philosophy, where ethics is concerned with understanding and systematising notions of right and wrong; an ethical study is one in which the researcher aims to do no harm to the participants or to distort the participants' reality in any way

Evolution: Gradual changes in the physical structure of an organism over generations

Evolutionary developmental psychology: A field of study that focuses on the interaction between genes and the environment in a child's development

Expanding: Restating, in a grammatically complete form, what a child has said – a strategy that adults use to enhance the child's language

Experience sampling method: A research technique that asks participants to stop at certain times and make notes of their experience or behaviour

F

Fantasy corner: An area in a preschool classroom that is set aside for children to engage in imaginative play; the area is structured and has spaces for 'make-believe' activities, dress-up areas, and various toys and/or materials that can be used in imaginative play

Fetal alcohol effects: Learning and behavioural problems an individual manifests due to lower doses of alcohol in pregnancy than the doses that result in FASD

Fetal origins hypothesis: Hypothesis that argues that postnatal health may be influenced by prenatal factors – the environment experienced during an individual's prenatal life 'programs' the functional capacity of the individual's organs, and this has a subsequent effect on the individual's health

Fetal period: The third stage of the prenatal period, following from the end of the embryonic period, beginning at nine weeks, and ending with the onset of labour and birth of the baby

Fetal tobacco syndrome: A syndrome evident in children born to mothers who smoke five or more cigarettes a day during pregnancy, which causes retarded growth in babies and may later negatively affect the cognitive performance in children

Fetus: An unborn offspring, from the embryo stage (the end of the eighth week after conception, when the major structures have formed) until birth

Fine motor development: Control over smaller movements, such as reaching and grasping, and later eating with a spoon, tying shoe laces and writing

Foreclosure: An identity status characterising individuals who have committed themselves to an identity, but without much thought – they are becoming what others want them to become

Formative education: One that attempts to shape, form or mould a person according to (hopefully) positive and healthy outcomes

Friendship: A voluntary relationship involving an affectionate bond

Full Service schools: Institutions that directly address the problems that create barriers to learning through adopting a holistic approach to education, integrating academics; family-support, health and social services; and community-development programs to support their learners' needs

G

General genetic law: Foundation of Vygotskian thought; law that states that higher cognitive functions – thinking, reasoning and problem-solving – begin as real relations between people, interpsychologically, before being internalised intrapsychologically

Generalisability: The ability of findings to talk to the larger population

Germinal period: The first stage of the prenatal period, beginning with the fertilisation of the egg by the sperm and concluding with the establishment of the pregnancy, approximately two weeks later

Gross motor development: Control over large muscle movements that help infants get around in the environment, such as crawling, standing and walking

H

Habituation: Learning not to respond to a stimulus that is repeated over and over – or in other words, learning to be bored by the familiar; waning of response to stimuli

Helpless orientation: A tendency to avoid challenges and to give up in the face of obstacles or failure

Human capital: A concept that refers to the aggregate capacity (including ability, knowledge, skill, and motivation) possessed by an individual, or a group of individuals, within a specific context; at its most basic level, the human capital an individual possesses is highly reliant on both sound health and education

Hysteria: Hysteria was used to describe neurotic behaviour; in the nineteenth and early twentieth centuries, it was used almost exclusively to describe neuroses in women; hence the word 'hysteria', which relates to the womb

I

Identity: A person's clear and consistent sense of who he or she is, what he or she believes and values, what he or she is going to do with his or her life, and where he or she fits into society; the distinctive characteristics of an individual

Identity achievement: An identity status characterising individuals who have seriously considered identity issues, resolved them, and made a commitment to particular goals and values

Identity diffusion: An identity status characterising individuals who have not given much thought to who they are, and have not committed themselves to particular goals or values

Ideology: The body of ideas reflecting the social needs and aspirations of an individual, group, class, or culture

Inclusive education: The placement of learners with disabilities in general educational classrooms alongside learners of the same age who do not have disabilities

Income inequality: The extent to which the total income is equally (or unequally) distributed across individuals or households in an economy; measures of income inequality therefore refer to the extent and prevalence of the gap between the wealth of the rich and the poor; South Africa has comparatively high levels of income inequality – it has many very poor people and significant numbers of affluent people

Independent variable: The variable that the researcher thinks will cause the effect

Infantile amnesia: The inability of adults and older children to remember events that occurred before the age of about two or three years

Information-processing approach: An approach to cognitive development in which the human mind is studied by comparing it to the workings of a computer

Informed consent: Relates to giving participants sufficient information about research for them to make a decision about whether they want to participate or not in the study; this is an ethical principle that requires that researchers are transparent in their approach to studying people

Initiation: A ritual, test, ceremony or time of instruction with which a new member is admitted to knowledge, an organisation or a position

Internal locus of control: A phenomenon from personality psychology, which indicates the extent to which an individual believes that he or she can control events that affect him or her – internal locus of control indicates that people believe they are able to control their life by taking certain actions; in contrast, people with an external locus of control believe that their decisions and life are controlled by environmental factors over which they no influence

Interpsychologically: The process of cultural development that refers to learning as happening first between people

Intra-individual influences: Personal factors within individuals (such as their age, gender, and personality) that could impact on their career development

Intrapsychologically: The process of cultural development that refers to the internalisation of knowledge learnt interpsychologically

K

Knowledge base: The term given to how much a person knows about the content area to be learned

L

Labelling: Identifying the names of objects – a strategy that adults use to enhance the child's language

Language acquision device (LAD): An inborn biological system that prepares a child to detect and learn the sounds and grammatical rules of language; predisposition that enables a child to acquire language

Lifespan lifespace theory: A theory developed by Donald Super to conceptualise career development in terms of sequential life stages and different life roles over the lifespan

M

Marxist structural analysis: A form of analysis, drawing on the insights of Karl Marx, which argues that the structure of the economy and state function in the interests of ruling elites and those that control the economy ('capitalists' in Marxist terminology)

Masculinity: Having the characteristics of an adult male

Maslow's hierarchy: A theory in psychology, as proposed by Abraham Maslow, which describes the stages of human motivation leading to growth and development; Maslow proposed that humans develop according to successful need acquisition, starting at having their most basic physiological needs (for food, water, sex etc.) met, progressing to the meeting of 'higher order' needs such as the need for self-actualisation; children whose basic needs are neglected would therefore struggle to reach, achieve and have their 'higher order' needs met

Mastery orientation: A tendency to seek challenges and to persist in the face of failure

Maturation: The biological processes underlying development

Mediation: In Vygotskian theory, the active guidance of a more expert peer or teacher, which moves a child from a state of not knowing to a state of knowing

Menarche: A girl's first menstrual period

Metacognition: A person's ability to think about his or her own thought processes; the ability to think about thinking

Metamemory: A person's knowledge of memory and memory processes

Migrant labour: Workers who travel away from their usual region of residence in order to access employment opportunities; the term is more readily applied to semi-skilled and unskilled workers, rather than high-skilled and waged workers

Migration: Movement of progenitor cells from where they are formed in the wall of the neural tube during the cellular development of the brain

Moral reasoning: The process in which an individual tries to determine the difference between what is right and what is wrong in a personal situation by using logic

Moratorium: An identity status characterising individuals who are actively exploring identity issues or experiencing an identity crisis, but who have not yet committed themselves to an identity

Motor development: The sequence of changes in coordination of the muscles that are required for movements or physical activities

Myelin: Fatty coating that insulates neurons and increases the speed at which they can send messages (in the form of electrical impulses) to other neurons

Myelination: Process of forming a fatty coating around neurons; myelination increases the speed at which neurons can send messages to other neurons

Myopathy: A muscular disease involving non-functioning muscle fibres, which results in muscle weakness

N

Nativist: Used here to refer to the nature side of the nature versus nurture debate indicating that thinking is innate

Natural selection: The evolutionary process whereby organisms better adapted to their environment tend to survive and produce more off-spring

Nature versus nurture debate: Debate about which of nature or nurture impacts primarily on a developing child; about whether a child may be thought of as a blank slate on which the environment writes (nurture), or is born with the mental structures needed to engage with the world (nature)

Neglect: Failure to provide basic needs

Neural tube defects: A group of birth defects that affect the backbone and sometimes the spinal cord

Normative assumption: The assumption that a particular widespread phenomenon, practice or arrangement is normal, and even desirable

O

Obesity: The condition of having excessive body fat. A person is described as being obese if their body mass index is greater than 30kg/m^2

Object permanence: The realisation that things continue to exist even when these things are not being perceived – that is, when they cannot be seen, heard or touched

Ontogenesis: The development of an individual organism or anatomical or behavioral feature from the earliest stage to maturity

Ontogenetic adaptations: A fetus's adaptations to its life in the womb

Ontology: A branch of metaphysics that deals with the nature of reality

Operant conditioning: A method of learning that occurs through rewarding specific behaviours that a person wants to see repeated; operant conditioning sets up an association between a behaviour and the consequence of that behaviour

Operation: Piaget's term for the mental activity that a person carries out 'inside his or her head' or in his or her imagination to reach a logical conclusion

Organisation: A memory strategy that involves sorting the items into meaningful groups or chunks when trying to learn or remember

Overextension: The young child's tendency to apply a word to objects that are not related to, or are inappropriate for, the word's meaning (for example using the word 'dog' to refer to all four-legged animals)

P

Panel survey: Large-scale quantitative (statistical) survey that collects data from the same households over time (longitudinal)

Peer: A person who is of similar age and developmental level as the self; a social equal

Person permanence: A special form of object permanence – the understanding that a person exists even when he or she can't be perceived

Philosophy: Investigation of the principles, causes, or nature of reality, values, or knowledge, based on logical reasoning rather than empirical methods

Plasticity: Capacity of the brain to change in response to positive and negative influences from the environment

Poverty trap: A set of self-reinforcing circumstances which cause poverty to persist, making escape from it difficult

Poverty: A theoretically complex concept usually taken to refer to a state of having insufficient resources to meet basic human needs, such as the lack of food, water, clothes or housing; however, many accounts of poverty expand on the notion of material deprivation, and stress both the relational aspects of poverty, including the absence of choice and opportunities which frequently characterise it

Prenatal period: The period beginning at conception and ending at birth

Proband: In genetics, the first affected individual in a family who brings a genetic disorder to the attention of the medical community

Proliferation: The production of nerve cells during the cellular development of the brain

Proximodistal trend: Development proceeds from 'near to far', from the centre of the body outward

Puberty: The period of human development in which a person becomes sexually mature and capable of producing a child

R

Randomly: Using chance procedures, for example to assign someone to either a control or an experimental group; the reasoning here is that there is as good a chance of being in the control as in the experimental group – the researcher might flip a coin, for example, to assign participants to either group

Rationalist: Refers here to a philosophical position that states that people do not learn empirically, but that they come to knowledge because they are born with an innate capacity to think

Recursive interaction: In the context of chapter nine, how children influence and are influenced by the socio-cultural and environmental contexts in which they develop

Reflexes: Involuntary movements elicited in response to stimulation

Rehearsal: A memory strategy that involves repeating items one is trying to learn and remember

Relational aggression: Behaviour that is intended to harm someone by damaging their friendships or reputation or deliberately excluding them from the group

Repression: The psychological process involved in keeping unacceptable impulses hidden to protect the conscious mind

Resilience: A process whereby people bounce back from adversity and go on with their lives

Resource centre: A specialised environment that provides a range of support services to ordinary public schools and includes all special schools with their expertise

Retrovirus: A virus containing RNA that can convert its genetic material into DNA by means of the enzyme reverse transcriptase; this allows the virus to become integrated into the DNA of the cells of its host

Reversibility: In Piaget's theory, the ability to reverse an action by mentally performing the opposite action.

Rhesus incompatibility: An incompatibility that may develop when an Rh-positive man impregnates a woman who has an Rh-negative blood type and an Rh-positive fetus is conceived

Risk factors: Determinants that increase the possibility of negative effects on children

Rubella: A mild highly contagious viral infection, mainly of childhood, causing enlargement of lymph nodes in the neck and a widespread pink rash (also known as German measles)

S

Scaffolding: Jerome Bruner's term for a form of teaching in which the level of support offered is adjusted to fit the learner's current level of performance

Scientific: Differing from common sense, because data is rigorously collected using agreed-upon, tested methods

Self-esteem: A person's overall evaluation of his or her worth

Self-regulation: The ability to attend selectively to specific aspects of a situation; to start something that one might not want to, and to stop an activity that one is enjoying

Semenarche: A boy's first ejaculation or discharge of semen

Semiotic function: A child's developing ability to make something represent something that is not present

Separation anxiety: The distress that infants experience when they are separated from a primary caregiver or attachment figure

Sibling: A brother or sister

Social comparison: The process of judging the appearance, abilities, and behaviour of the self in relation to those of others

Socially embedded: Firmly set or located in a social context, and therefore influenced by it

Sociometric techniques: Methods for studying peer group acceptance (who is liked or disliked in a group)

Specific learning disabilities: A general term that refers to a heterogeneous group of disorders manifested by significant difficulties in the acquisition and use of abilities in listening, speaking, reading, writing, reasoning or mathematics

Spina bifida: A developmental condition (existing from or before birth) caused by the incomplete closing of a fetus's embryonic neural tube; a portion of the spinal cord may visibly protrude through unfused and incompletely formed vertebrae bones to the exterior of an infant's body

Spinal muscular atrophy: An incurable disease caused by a genetic defect which affects the proteins necessary for motor neuron survival; this results in the death of neuronal cells, which leads to system-wide muscle atrophy, or wasting

Stranger anxiety: The fear or discomfort that infants experience in the presence of new or unfamiliar people

Strange-situation test: Test assessing the quality of an infant's attachment to a parent

Symbolic functioning: The use of mental symbols, words, or pictures which one uses to represent something which is not physically present

Synapses: Tiny gaps between neurons, which are bridged with the help of chemicals called neurotransmitters

Synaptic exuberance: The period during infancy in which connections between brain cells known as neurons develop rapidly

Synaptogenesis: The process by which nerve cells communicate with each other or with end organs, during the cellular development of the brain

System theory: A theory that views different levels and groups of people as interactive systems, where the functioning of the whole is dependent on the interaction between all parts

Systematically: In a considered way; for example, assigning people to experimental and control groups in a way that is informed by particular theory or variables that the researcher wants to highlight

T

Tabula rasa: A blank slate

Telegraphic speech: A simplified form of speech in which only the most important words are used to express ideas

Temperament: An individual's genetically based behavioural style and characteristic way of emotionally responding to events

Teratogens: Substances that exert an adverse influence on development

Teratology: The study of adverse consequences of exposure to environmental agents

Theory of circumscription and compromise: A theory, developed by Gottfredson, that describes how children eliminate occupational aspirations on the basis of gender and social status as they grow older, leading them to choose from a range of acceptable occupations

U

Unconscious: This part of the mind is not available to a person's conscious mind, yet it affects behaviour

Underextension: The young child's tendency to apply a word too narrowly; it occurs when children fail to use a word to name a relevant event or object (for example using 'dog' to refer only to the family pet)

Upper middle-income country: A country classified by the World Bank, on the basis of several economic indicators, as ranking towards the top end of the middle-income countries; upper middle-income countries generally have average per person incomes of US$4 000 to US$12 000 per annum; upper middle-income countries currently include China, Chile, Russia, Brazil, Malaysia, Turkey, Thailand, Iran, Peru, Argentina, and South Africa

V

Variable: An element, feature, fact or quantity that can vary, and therefore can be manipulated during experiments to see whether relationships exist between the two or more things manipulated

Victims: In the context of bullying, children who are selectively and actively harmed, psychologically and physically, by bullies

Violation-of-expectations research: A method in which researchers show infants a possible event (one that follows physical laws) and an impossible event (a variation of the first event that conflicts with normal expectations or the laws of physics)

Visual disability: Any restriction or lack (resulting from impairment) of ability to perform an activity in the manner or within the range considered normal for a human being

Visual handicap: A disadvantage for an individual or a disability that limits or prevents the fulfilment of a role that is normal (depending on age, sex, and social and cultural factors)

Visual impairment: Any loss or abnormality of psychological, physiological or anatomical structure or function

Vocabulary spurt: The rapid increase in learning new words that begins at approximately 18 months of age

Index

Please note: Page numbers in *italics* refer to Figures; those in **bold** refer to Case studies and boxes.